SOCIETY AND THE VICTORIANS

HISTORY OF THE ELEMENTARY SCHOOL
CONTEST IN ENGLAND

THE STRUGGLE FOR NATIONAL EDUCATION

SOCIETY & THE VICTORIANS
General Editors: John Spiers and Cecil Ballantine

The Harvester Press series 'Society & the Victorians' makes
available again important works by and about the Victorians.
Each of the titles chosen has been either out of print and difficult
to find, or exceedingly rare for many years. A few titles, although
available in the secondhand market, are needed in modern critical
editions and the series attempts to meet this demand.

Scholars of established reputation provide substantial
introductions, and the majority of titles have textual notes and a
full bibliography. Texts are reprinted from the best editions.

History of the Elementary School Contest in England

FRANCIS ADAMS

TOGETHER WITH

The Struggle for National Education

JOHN MORLEY

Edited with an introduction by
ASA BRIGGS
Vice-Chancellor and Professor of History
University of Sussex

THE HARVESTER PRESS 1972

THE HARVESTER PRESS LIMITED
Publishers

50 Grand Parade
Brighton Sussex
BN2 2QA
England

'History of the Elementary School Contest in England' first
published in 1882 by Chapman and Hall

'The Struggle for National Education' first published in 1873 by
Chapman and Hall

This edition first published in 1972 by
The Harvester Press Limited Brighton

Introduction © Asa Briggs 1972

'Society & The Victorians' No. 6
LC Card No. 72-124049
ISBN 0 901759 21 X

Printed in England by
Redwood Press Limited, Trowbridge, Wiltshire

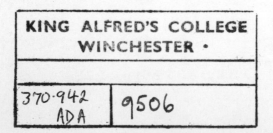

Contents

Introduction

Buried away in the Birmingham Reference Library are two massive folios containing letters, papers, reports and bulletins of the National Education League which was founded in Birmingham in 1869.[1] There is nothing private in either of the two folios. There *was* a private history of the League, a history of personal ambition and rivalry, but it was not recorded in that place. Yet all the essential materials for the public record are present there, and it was largely from these materials that Francis Adams wrote his interesting and informative *History of the Elementary School Contest* in 1882, five years after the League was dissolved. It remains the most useful single monograph on the subject, one which no historian of English education in the nineteenth century can afford to neglect.

Adams's use of the Birmingham materials may be compared with the use William Lovett, the Chartist leader, made of a similar bundle of Chartist papers which are also assembled in bulky folios in the Lovett Collection in the same Birmingham Library. Lovett, too, wanted to get the record of 'struggle' straight: the word 'struggle' came naturally to him, as it did to Adams. He, too, was always interested in history in the making. Yet he was also interested in the social significance of his own autobiography and in the external forces which had helped to make him what he was, and he called the autobiographical volume which he published in 1876 *The Life and Struggles of William Lovett*. Lovett was a self-made working man, proud of his own self-education. Adams, a solicitor by occupation, was far more self-effacing. He almost writes himself out of the story. We know very little about him except that he was a solicitor, that his office was in Temple Street in the heart of the city and that he lived in Bristol Road, that soon after the formation of the League in 1869 he became its secretary (which also had an honorary secretary far better known than himself) and that after two changes of residence first to Yardley and then to West Croydon in Sussex he died in 1891 at the early age of fifty.[2]

His *History of the Elementary School Contest* has very little to say about the personalities who gave the League its particular

ix

'Brummagem' flavour and who determined the tactics, sometimes devious, ultimately unsuccessful, which it pursued—the most remarkable personality, Joseph Chamberlain, perhaps significantly, never springs to life—but it directs attention to all the relevant educational and political issues, local and national, and seeks to place them in historical perspective. It can be supplemented by a number of other works by Adams, including a sketch of Brougham, one of the early-nineteenth-century pioneers of education, and a lively public lecture on education delivered at Huntingdon in 1870.[3] In this lecture Adams stated something of his own philosophy:

> Let me say that the members of the League were not anxious to make this question one of political warfare. It would have been a pleasure to them if for once in the history of this country a great work, having for its object the benefit of the multitude, had been suffered to proceed on its way undisturbed by the bitterness of party conflicts. But, sir, this has not been permitted. Our old enemies—the enemies of free-trade, of religious liberty, and popular government—the old obstructive party—ever on the watch for an opportunity to impede—has risen up against us to prevent, if possible, the accomplishment of our object. Though we did not seek it—though we would gladly have avoided it—we accept the situation which has been forced upon us, if not without regret, at any rate without despair... We are charged with seeking to revolutionise the country. We hope so. There is nothing we desire more than to effect a revolution; but it will be a bloodless one—one which will put into the hands of the people no weapons but those of peace and industry, one which will break down no barriers except those which impede the way to a higher civilisation.[4]

Adams anticipated the idea of 'the silent social revolution' associated with long-term educational advance,[5] but like so many of the Birmingham 'crusaders' of the 1870s he was anxious to carry his message into the heart of the enemy's camp. The honorary secretary of the League, Jesse Collings, shared the same philosophy: he was always more active in the countryside than he was in Birmingham itself.

The *History of the Elementary School Contest* is concerned almost as much with the perennial battle between 'the progressives' and 'the old obstructive party' as it is with education itself. Not surprisingly the study goes back to early beginnings, and Adams starts with the middle ages. The Dissenters, whose cause he propounded, always looked back through time, particularly to the seventeenth century, which they saw as the critical century in the battle for civil freedom. As a recent historian has remarked, 'the real corpus of thought uniting the middle class, or the Liberal section of it, was not a Benthamite, utilitarian, or natural-law view of the world, not American or economical principles, but something of a different order: a view or recollection of English history.'[6] Within that view of history persecution (trial by ordeal) played an important, even crucial, part: 'These persecutions tested the vitality and strengthened the determination of English nonconformity, and became powerful stimulants to the growth of the civil and religious freedom they were designed to crush.'[7] So, too, did the sense of progress with the great material advances of the recent past deriving from earlier victories:

> The foundation of all that has been achieved since then [the 1770s]—the social progress, the material comforts, the diffusion of wealth, the advancement of science and mechanics, the development of industry, the improvement in morals, and the stride in religious and political freedom was strengthened and firmly established in this early period [before the 1770s]; and in the struggle between the democratic and aristocratic principle, the former took definite form and asserted itself with all the consciousness and confidence of ultimate triumph.[8]

In the nineteenth century the battle against Church rates had been the militant culmination of many old battles. It ended significantly enough on the eve of the articulation of the Education issue in 1868, when Gladstone, despite his zealous Churchmanship, consented to take charge of a Compulsory Church Rates Abolition Bill.[9] Adams considered all questions of education in broad evolutionary terms: 'The history of education is a part of this wider history of the progress of society, and in its completeness is only to be found in connection with the general advance which has taken place during the last two centuries.'[10] Turning back to the seventeenth century he stated categorically that 'it was during this period that the great struggle for intellectual, political and religious freedoms was proceeding, the triumph of which could alone render a state system of education tolerable or desirable.'[11]

This approach explains the at-first-sight curious balance of his book. Four chapters out of nine deal with the period before the League was formed. They outline the reasons why England, unlike several far less economically developed countries in Europe, failed to develop an effective 'national system' of education.[12] They also describe the activities both of voluntary societies, on which English educational provision long depended, and of pressure groups which demanded reform. Adams had little use for 'voluntaryist' arguments which had for long captivated large numbers of nonconformists: 'It was evident the Voluntaryists did not rely upon the law of supply and demand, but on sectarian and party rivalry and zeal which is quite a different thing.'[13] Anglican 'realists' might have argued that the voluntary provision of education was 'the only scheme that could have been introduced into our free, tolerant, dissentient and jealous country' and have extolled 'the most gigantic effort ever made by private charity to perform a public duty', but Adams was quite unimpressed: 'The voluntary movement was beaten by the irresistible logic of facts, which no easy improvisation of first principles, no versatility in the arrangement of statistics, and indeed no generosity of purse and service should successfully encounter.'[14]

Adams believed that only the State could act effectively and continuously in matters of education, but before it would be prepared to act it was necessary for public opinion to be mobilised: he emphasised 'the necessity of combined action out of Parliament to secure that pressure of public opinion which is the only guarantee of useful legislation.'[15] It is not surprising, therefore, that one of his heroes was Richard Cobden, who had devoted his energies after the repeal of the corn laws to a number of other causes amongst which education figured prominently. He presents a useful account of the activities of the National Public School Association which had its origins, like the Anti-Corn Law League, in the city of Manchester.[16] It was this Association, guided by Cobden, which according to Adams propounded 'the first comprehensive and elaborate scheme put forward for securing national education; based on the principle that the cost should be thrown on property, that the management should be confided to local representatives, and that the people should be taught to regard education, not as a bone of contention between churches and sects, but as the right of free citizens.'[17]

Unlike most Birmingham men, Adams was unusually appreciative of initiatives coming out of Manchester. Indeed when he came to the founding of the League in 1869, he pointed out that George Dixon, member of parliament for Birmingham and mayor of the city in 1866-7, approached people in Manchester to take a lead. He quotes Dixon as saying: 'Had my suggestions been favourably received by the gentlemen to whom they were made, Birmingham would not have originated the League, but would have followed Manchester, which in my opinion ought to have headed, and was entitled to lead a national movement.'[18] It is doubtful if Chamberlain would ever have assented to this proposition. Yet the Manchester Education Aid Society, founded in 1864 was the model for the Birmingham Education Aid Society founded three years later,[19] and it is interesting that after the League had been formed its critics chose Manchester as the centre of the rival National Education Union.[20]

While Adams insisted upon 'agitation' as a necessary element in educational advance, he was aware also that over long periods of time change often took place quietly behind the scenes. He noted, for example, that the increase in educational finance in the 1850s owed little either to debate in Parliament or to pressure from outside it: 'The capitation grant was a conspicuous feature in the new plans of the Government [in 1853], and the way in which it was adopted is a curious illustration of the manner in which the power of the Education Department was capable of extension, almost without the exercise of parliamentary authority and supervision.'[21] He obviously recognised what recent historians of nineteenth-century administration have identified as 'cumulative pressures' from within the system making for change without the stimulus of political agitation.[22] He was unimpressed, however, by James Kay-Shuttleworth, whose indefatigable activities, often well out of public view, have been praised by many subsequent historians of education:[23] for the secretary of the League the compromises which had been forced upon Kay-Shuttleworth seemed far too much like those propounded by Forster in 1870.[24] By comparison he was exceptionally kind to Robert Lowe, the author of the revised code, whose attitudes towards education have been criticised even more sharply during the twentieth-century than they were at the time. Adams called Lowe 'the most able Minister who has yet held the post of Vice-President', and praised his stolid unwillingness to be 'taken in' by the 'propaganda' of the voluntary societies, his relentless scepticism about 'proprietary rights' in school ownership and management, and his genuine concern for the quality of education. We should not be surprised at his verdict, for there was a direct link between Lowe's proposals and the main proposals of Forster's Education Act which the League itself supported.[25] Adams went on to compare Forster unfavourably with Lowe.[26]

When he reached the critical point in time when education became a major issue in English politics, the late 1860s, Adams had relatively little to offer by way of analysis of the reasons for the 'crisis' and the 'advance'. Like Bagehot before him—and many other commentators—he referred to the death of Lord Palmerston in 1865 (Bagehot went further and spoke of a change of generation[27]), and he mentioned, albeit briefly, some of the statistical enquiries in the provinces which brought to light the extent of the educational problem, particularly in the great cities, and the inadequacy of the voluntary agencies to cope with it.[28] He also made reference to the comparative position in England and in other countries.[29] Yet he did not draw a direct causal connection between the passing of the Reform Act of 1867, which granted the vote to large sections of the urban working classes, and the introduction and passing of an education act.

Much has subsequently been written about these two measures as cause and effect, with certain key passages serving as texts in the argument, notably Lowe's 'I believe it will be absolutely necessary to compel our future masters to learn their letters.'[30] In fact, Lowe was convinced of the need for public-provided elementary education *before* 1867 as were all Liberals of a 'progressive' cast of mind, including many who were to be bitterly opposed to the activities of the League. Adams was right to emphasise the continuities; indeed, he anticipated the sensible verdict of a recent historian that 'the impulse to action on popular education and the impulse towards parliamentary reform seem to have had common roots.'[31] This was certainly true of Birmingham where Dixon, for example, had 'long taken a great interest in the subject' of education.[32] The Society of 1867 preceded the passing of the Reform Act, and Chamberlain was writing to the United States for information about the American school system before Birmingham working men were enfranchised.[33]

It is interesting also to note that Adams makes nothing of economic arguments in accounting for the timing of the new agitation. All his emphasis is on the momentum of popular Liberalism. In his Huntingdon lecture he referred to 'the position of England in industrial competition', but he did not develop the point. He stressed rather as the leading question 'how and where shall the children of the masses be trained in streets, gutters, kennels, and hovels, encompassed by misery, vice, dirt, poverty and crime... or in properly appointed and conducted schools, and subject to the influence of law, order, self-restraint, cleanliness and knowledge'.[34] There is ample evidence from Adams's book that he believed that education was necessary for the simplest of reasons, well put by one of the first working-men members of parliament, Thomas Burt, 'We say educate a man, not simply because he has got political power, and simply to make him a good workman; but educate him because he is a man.'[35] This view, rooted in a tradition which went back to the eighteenth century, may well have been more widespread during the late 1860s than some historians of education have implied.

Certainly the element of 'economic necessity' behind the 1870
Act has often been exaggerated. Trade was good and competition
was less evident than it had been at the time of the Paris Universal
Exhibition of 1867 and was to be later in the 1870s. Moreover,
many of the supporters of educational advance believed (for
political and social reasons) that it was even more urgently
necessary to introduce public provided education in the
agricultural areas than in the large industrial cities. This was the
view of Henry Fawcett, member of parliament and economist, for
example, who was briefly to be associated, as a radical, with the
activities of the League. Fawcett has been described
(misleadingly) as 'an educationalist pure and simple': the vital
question for him was 'universal compulsion'.[36]

Unsophisticated 'functionalist' approaches to nineteenth
century educational history which relate provision to 'social need'
do not help us much with problems of the timing either of
agitation or of legislation. Nor do they help us to explain the
differences in chronology and patterns of provision between
England and other countries. They are at once too comprehensive
and too vague. It is more profitable, perhaps, to examine the
dynamics of agitation and the conflicts and compromises
embedded in legislation. There was a time when the conflicts
seemed archaic and dull and when the compromises were passed
over complacently as expressions of a distinctive English genius
for institutional adaptation. Now in the aftermath of the
celebrations of the centenary of the Education Act, when there is
no shortage of educational topics for current debate, perspectives
have shifted. It is for this reason alone that Adams's account of the
activities of the League has acquired a new kind of interest. The
present position contrasts sharply with that in 1932 when J. L.
Garvin, Chamberlain's biographer, wrote with feeling, 'No
Ezekiel's wind can make dry bones live in some valleys. Nothing
seems more dead and gone today than the educational battles of
the early seventies in the Victorian age.'[37] Now the way the
battles were fought is arousing almost as much interest as the
battle cries of the antagonists. Because Adams was personally
involved in all the affairs of the League he is a witness as well as a
historian, an actor, indeed, as well as an observer. Yet given his
self-effacing temperament, which has already been noted, he
never places himself in the centre of the picture. Nor did he ever
resort to 'sensationalism'. As has been noted, he devotes four of
his nine chapters to the period before the advent of the League
and three to the period of excitement after the passing of
Forster's Act.

He begins his account of the League with the briefest

reference to an historic conversation between Dixon and Collings. Yet he does not quote what Collings is reputed to have said to Dixon: 'if we could have an Education Society on the right lines, the very stones in the street would rise and join us.'[38] The exact date of this conversation is not known, and Adams does not give us the date of the first meeting held at Dixon's house, The Dales, on 7 January 1869, when many of the leading figures in the later history of the League were already present. Already before the League was founded there were some differences of approach. Some of them were temperamental. Dixon had an established position in Birmingham. Born in 1820, he had arrived in Birmingham in 1838 and had first joined the Town Council in 1863: he was Mayor in 1866, and in 1869 was said to be 'probably the most popular man' in the city.[39] Yet he was a less strong personality than he appeared to be: in 1843 Charlotte Brontë, who met him in Brussels, had described him unkindly as 'a pretty-looking and pretty-behaved young man, apparently constructed without a backbone'.[40]

No one could ever have described Chamberlain in these terms. He had arrived in Birmingham sixteen years after Dixon, when he was eighteen years old, and from the start he was intensely ambitious. As a friend wrote of him long afterwards, 'He far surpassed in ability any previous local leaders. . . I remember him appearing at a meeting in a seal-skin top-coat. This made people gasp. A man daring enough to dress thus must be a Caesar or a Napoleon.'[41] He was to clash swords with Dixon in 1876 when he replaced Dixon as member of parliament for the city,[42] and he was to engage in even more bitter argument with him in 1878 when Dixon, who had always been uneasy about the power of the Liberal caucus, stated in public that it was nonsense to argue that 'Chamberlain is Birmingham or Birmingham Chamberlain'.[43] The rift was healed and Dixon followed Chamberlain in opposition to Irish home rule in 1886,[44] but there was an obvious contrast of spirit, purpose and ability. Dixon was an Anglican, deeply interested in education for its own sake and was to serve continuously on the Birmingham School Board from 1870 to the time of his death in 1898, the year when he was made Freeman of the City.[45] Chamberlain, chairman of the League's Executive Committee, was undoubtedly interested in education, but he was also interested in militant nonconformist campaigning of the political kind expounded by the Liberation Society, launched in 1853 on the foundations of the earlier (1844) British Anti-State Church Association. He was already a master of political calculation, and in a letter to Dixon after Forster introduced his Education Bill he expressed attitudes which Dixon never shared:

I wish our side would fight like the Conservatives—the Bill would then have been doomed long ago. The Tories are never afraid of being factious and it is a great advantage to them. . . It [the bill] is not National Education at all—it is a trick to strengthen the Church of England against the Liberation Society. . . I would rather see a Tory Ministry in power than a Liberal Government truckling to Tory prejudices.[46]

This letter should be compared with Dixon's comments at the opening of the third annual meeting of the League over which he presided in October 1871:

Some of our opponents consider the League a discredited and defeated party. But what are the facts? Every one of the six means by which we have proposed to secure the education of the children of this country were vehemently denounced by our opponents. . . Yet when I again read them to you, you will be unable to resist the conclusion that all the measures we proposed have either been carried, or that we have secured in the Education Act of 1870 a lever, by the wise use of which their adoption has become merely a question of time.[47]

Before turning to the 'six means' and to the 'objects' of the League which were set out in their first public circular reprinted by Adams,[48] a little more should be said of the mix of personalities. Collings was a Chamberlain man through and through, a *confidant* and a henchman rather than an independent political personality in his own right. William Harris, the chairman of the Parliamentary Committee, was a very different kind of person. Far from borrowing his ideas from Chamberlain there is considerable evidence that he implanted his own ideas in the mind of the budding politician.[49] He had been the organiser of the Liberal victory at the general election of 1868, and long after the controversial idea of the 'caucus' had been perfected Chamberlain wrote that 'the whole credit of having initiated and carried out this new machinery belongs to my friend, Mr. Harris'.[50] J. T. Bunce, the chairman of the Publications Committee, was editor of the influential *Birmingham Daily Post* for which Wright wrote articles. He was an enterprising and hard-working journalist with whom Chamberlain remained in regular contact throughout his life: he was also a lively historian of the city which he believed had 'a living personality' peculiar to itself.[51] R. F. Martineau, chairman of the Branches Committee, belonged to one of the small group of local families which constituted something of a ruling class in Birmingham.[52] George Dawson, a member of the Executive, was 'the prophet' of the 'civic gospel' for which Birmingham became famous.[53] The other great Birmingham nonconformist, Dr. R. W. Dale, minister of Carrs Lane Chapel, at first, however, stood aloof. 'It was painful for him,' his biographer writes, 'to stand apart from Mr. Dixon, Mr. Chamberlain, Mr. Collings and other friends with whom he had worked for public ends; but he could not accept the fundamental principle of the League that the schools aided by local rates should be free.'[54] Nonetheless, he joined the League later in 1869 and thereafter 'took his share of the fighting'.[55]

In such company Adams was doubtless a servant rather than a maker of policy, and he was never listed in the impressive catalogues of subscribers to the League, some of whom gave it large sums of money.[56] Yet he was close to Dixon, and through his editorship of the *Monthly Paper* of the League, first published in December 1869, he was in regular communication with Bunce. He was also active in places outside Birmingham—forty-three branches of the League had been created (Including one in Oxford University with Kenelm Digby as secretary) by the time of the first issue of the *Monthly Paper*—and in all contacts with working-class associations to which the League attached the utmost importance from the start. Robert Applegarth, the trade-union leader, was a member of the Executive Committee of the League,[57] W. R. Cramer was a stirring campaigner, and George Howell was one of Adams's regular correspondents, suggesting a number of interesting organisational features, including a membership card which would give status to the small subscribers.[58] Many of the trade unionists came into the League straight from the Reform League which had just been dissolved. Yet it was the aggressive middle-class leadership of the League rather than the working-class presence which was most sharply criticised by contemporaries. The efficiency of the apparatus frightened many people, including Liberals outside Birmingham and provoked more opposition inside Birmingham itself than Adams implied in his History. It needed an aristocrat to try to put Birmingham in its place. 'There is nothing that *riles* mankind so much,' Lord Houghton (formerly Richard Monckton Milnes) wrote to Forster in 1869, 'as seeing the objects they desire accomplished by other means than their own. Thus the Radicals are as indignant at popular education being brought about with Conservative assistance as Mazzini and Garibaldi at the unity of Italy being brought about by Victor Emmanuel. But the Mialls of England and Italy must submit to their lot. *Sic vos non vobis* is the law of the world.'[59] Edward Miall, one of the most uncompromising of the militant dissenters, was Forster's colleague as member of Parliament for Bradford, and they had already found it difficult to work easily together. Yet it was to Birmingham rather than to Bradford that 'the Mialls of England' looked in 1869 and 1870, and Forster's biographer rightly heads his chapter on education in 1870 'The Struggle with the Birmingham League.'[60]

It is a mistake, however, to believe that in 1869 and 1870 the advancement of the cause of education depended solely on the League and on people who shared its philosophy. The real issue was much more complicated. Education had been mentioned in the Queen's speech of 1868, and there were many Tories who were anxious for national legislation. Nor could the Leaguers themselves avoid the intricacies and complications of educational policy. Whereas the Anti-Corn Law League earlier in the century had been able to carry out its crusades on the basis of a simple formula—and that a negative one—the repeal of the corn laws, the League, when it tried to take the initiative, was forced to draft an outline of a comprehensive educational scheme, not all parts of which would appeal even to its own adherents. Thus, Fawcett was very unhappy as a doctrinaire political economist about the idea of *free* education, and many nonconformists, even those who had abandoned any lingering belief in voluntaryism, were never happy about the term *secular* education. Whatever compromises Forster was forced to make from inside government, the League also had to pick its way warily with the public, particularly at the beginning. Adams does not quote the first draft plan of the League which is to be found in the Birmingham Collection, placed immediately after Dixon's invitation to the first Provisional Committee meeting.[61] Interestingly enough, this draft does not use the adjective 'unsectarian' which was incorporated in the first published circular of the League which Adams prints (not quite in full). Instead of clause four of the circular it employs the words—'in all schools aided by local rates and under the management of local authorities, theology peculiar to any religious denomination shall form no part of the school teaching.' This might have been a better formula than that eventually adopted. What is most significant, however, was the refusal of the League at the start to use the word 'secular' in its propaganda, even though Dixon himself had used it in inviting the little group of people to his home to found the League. In his own words nearly two years later, 'it was decided' at the first meeting 'that the word "secular" did not represent the views we entertained, and "unsectarian" was inserted in the programme without a single dissentient voice.'[62]

Earlier in the century Cobden had recognised the political difficulties in using the adjective 'secular' even if it was made clear that it carried with it no anti-religious bias.[63] The use of the word 'unsectarian', however, caused at least as many political difficulties for the League. What exactly did it mean? Adams says nothing of the origins of this problem in his book, but he, as much as his colleagues, had to deal with its ramifications in his letters and speeches.[64] Inside the League there was always a strong group which would have preferred the term 'secular'. It was particularly strong in London and included most of the working-class leaders whom both Dixon and Chamberlain were anxious to attract. Miall was at one with them on this issue:

> There can be no doubt that the desire of its [the League's] members is compulsory secular education. Then why not say so? Only on the ground that education is secular can compulsion be justified. Even the reading of the Bible without comment, or the employment of the Lord's prayer would be an injustice. . . necessitating for its relief that clumsy and invidious device 'a conscience clause'.[65]

The Times was to note later that at the conferences of the League it was 'the secular party' which got most cheers.[66] Yet in their effort to move cautiously on this issue the leaders of the League settled for an uneasy compromise. After Fawcett had stated at the first national conference of the League in October 1869 that Bible reading might be permissible in public elementary schools, Dixon and Collings replied that the League had no intention of interfering in religion but wished to leave it to local educational authorities to decide whether to keep the Bible in such schools provided that in all circumstances it would be read 'without note or comment'.[67] Adams himself questioned the soundness of this decision:

> As events proved, it might have been wiser to have gone at first for the absolute separation on all points, of religious and secular teaching. Bible reading was satisfactory to no considerable party; and the permissive use of the Bible did not prevent the members of the League from being denounced on Church and Tory platforms as the enemies of religion, of Government and of morals.[68]

That this compromise did not impress some members of the League even in Birmingham itself was clear by January 1870 when a group of working men asked that it should be set aside. They were only too well aware that it did not impress the League's opponents in Birmingham. A satirical verse published by a leading local Tory, Sebastian Evans, depicted the new public elementary school as a bleak, godless place. In a nightmare of the future he caught a glimpse of:

A dismal house which I knew was a school . . .
The one word 'League' grim lettered in black.
'Twas the dismalest house the world ever saw
Where to pray to God was to break the law.[69]

In London and in the countryside there was even more criticism, not always set out so politely in conventional verse.

There was another compromise—or rather evasion—which complicated the approach of the League in 1869. It urged the building of rate-aided schools, but it left vague its attitude to the finance of the existing voluntary schools. It talked of 'supplementing' such schools, but it often seemed to be arguing that they should be superseded. The evasion was irritating to many members of the League, particularly in Wales, where feeling against the Church was extremely strong,[70] and a matter for challenge from the opponents of the League in whatever part of the country they were. Indeed, it was on this point above all others that the rival organisation, the National Education Union, brought into existence in November 1869, chose to fight. After George Dawson had told the first general meeting of the League in October that if its plans were adopted 'the existing system must go by a slow, sure, and, I hope, painless extinction,' his words were eagerly seized upon as a declaration of the true intent of the League. Dixon himself, though he accepted the existence of Church schools, argued that in time they would be superseded by (not supplemented by) rate-aided schools because rate-aided schools would offer better teaching. Similar points were made by Adams in his Huntingdon speech where he cited Lowe in support of his view that the voluntary schools provided inferior teaching.[71]

There was a third problem which checked the momentum of the League as the year 1869 drew to a close—the problem of time-tabling. At its general meeting in October a drafting committee had been appointed to prepare a bill. Adams says little about it, though the motion proposing it was introduced by Fawcett and seconded by Thorold Rogers, the radical Oxford don, who in later life was to edit the speeches of Bright. The reason why he does not discuss it is not simply that the committee got swallowed up in bigger problems after Forster had introduced his official bill in Parliament in February 1870 but that the committee very quickly ran into difficulties inside itself, with feelings sometimes running high. Amendments to the first draft of the League's bill, prepared in November, were invited from members of the Executive committee, with the correspondence being kept secret, and although the headings of the bill were published later in December, some of the controversial details were left out.[72] It became clear during the following month that many of them were not acceptable to some of the leading members of the League. Before Forster fully realised the perils of an Education bill, the League itself knew how difficult it was to relate principle to practice. In its case, it relied more and more on militant nonconformity—with a continuing drive for labour support—and in January 1870, before Forster introduced his bill it summoned separately a meeting of working-men and a conference of nonconformist ministers.[73] In this respect it was following in the footsteps of the Anti-Corn Law League,[74] but it was also inaugurating a burst of pressure-group politics which was to destroy not 'the obstructive party' but Gladstone's Liberal government.

It is important to examine side by side the chronology of League activities in the autumn and early winter of 1869-70 and the chronology of official government initiative in relation to an Education bill, for at a critical point in the story the League instead of pressing for legislation began to demand its post-ponement. The first reference to an Education bill in Forster's diary was on October 10th 1869,[75] but Forster had been anxious to proceed even earlier[76]—there was also a pre-history Cabinet interest—and Gladstone had written to Lord de Grey (afterwards the Marquis of Ripon), President of the Council, eight days before Forster's reference stating that 'it would be very desirable that we should avail ourselves of some early occasion on our gathering in London to lay the foundation stone of our Education measure for England.'[77] Forster was not a member of the Cabinet and during the next few weeks he had to take soundings about the prospects for immediate progress at a time when the general political situation was not entirely propitious. He wanted to move quickly and decisively, and his main moves were being prepared when the League held its first general meeting one day later in October and started to plan, as Adams says, in terms of an agitation which might last ten years.[78]

Forster's important Memorandum of 21 October took a completely different approach from the outset to that of the League. The object of the League, as stated in its first circular, was 'the establishment of a system which shall secure the education of every child in England and Wales.'[79] Forster stated as his object—'to supplement the present voluntary system—that is to fill up its gaps at least cost of public money, with least loss of voluntary cooperation, and with most aid from the parents.'[80] He explicitly condemned the League:

> The complete logical machinery of the Birmingham League would quickly undermine the existing schools, would relieve

the parents of all payment, would entail upon the country an enormous expense and—a far more dangerous loss than that of money—would drive out of the field most of those who care for education, and oblige the Government to make use solely of official or municipal agency.[81]

Whether all the leaders of the League would have approved of the accuracy of the assessment—the word 'solely' was a far more explicit statement than any of them chose to make—there was evidently the widest of gulfs between Forster and the League.

Yet it would be a mistake to believe that Forster was doing anything more than state the position as accurately as he saw it. When he wrote, there was no rival body to the League in the country, although a few days later the National Education Union held its inaugural meeting in Manchester on 3 and 4 November. The object of the Union—that of 'judiciously supplementing the present system of denominational education'[82]—seemed to be nearer to Forster's object than that of the League. Forster, nonetheless, had not been strongly influenced by the kind of thinking (or feeling) subsequently represented in the Union, and according to A. J. Mundella, the radical member of Parliament for Sheffield, who was seeing a lot of Forster around this time, Forster 'ridiculed' the Union when it came into existence.[83] He went ahead with his own planning, consulting Mundella, who had attended the first meeting of the League and had accepted membership of it with marked reservations,[84] and even Applegarth with whom he had been in correspondence earlier.[85] Mundella, who disliked the 'secularists' and what they stood for, had himself been associated earlier with Applegarth and the trade unionists on labour questions, and he was delighted to be of any assistance he could to Forster. He was told by Forster on 5 December that he hoped the education question would 'be settled this year', that is to say, within the current parliamentary session. The cabinet had accepted Forster's memorandum as the basis for legislation on 24 November.[86]

When Forster told Mundella of his hope, rumours were circulating in London that the government was not going to rush the measure. These rumours were reported in the newspapers at the end of November and during the first few days of December, along with commentary on the likely reasons for delay—not cabinet procrastination on an urgent social question but the preference of some members of the cabinet for a comprehensive measure on League lines:

The Chancellor of the Exchequer [Lowe] and those who concur with him in the view that immediate legislation is not expedient are understood to be, on the whole, favourable to the scheme of the National Education League, and we are informed that one of the considerations by which they are influenced is the probability that if further time is allowed for discussion it will be made evident that the preponderance of public opinion is in the direction of the Birmingham plan.[87]

Forster was worried by the rumours and wrote to the Liberal whip, George Grenfell Glyn, for an assurance that his bill would be introduced as quickly as possible: 'we shall gain nothing, but lose much, by departing from the true ground, that the conditions of the education problem are different in Ireland [a source of cabinet dissension] and England.'[88] He also corrected the substance of the rumours: 'There was one specially ridiculous *canard* that Lowe urges delay, whereas he, as well as Bruce, have with me the strongest possible opinion that we ought to make up our minds to prepare a bill and carry it.'[89] Glyn refused to give a 'specific engagement'. At the same time, he pointed out that '*two big questions* can't go on at the *same time* in the House, and that land [the Irish land bill] is No.1.'[90] Bright was one of the members of the cabinet who favoured delay, and he was the member most in direct touch with the League: in a public speech a few weeks later (just before illness removed him at a critical time, as it so often did in his career, from the public scene) he put the matter more vividly than Glyn, 'You cannot easily drive six omnibuses abreast through Temple Bar.'[91]

Bright was not speaking just for himself. A new voice in English politics—that of Chamberlain—was also heard. If the Government bill was to be a compromise, he told a Birmingham breakfast meeting in January 1870, it should be held over. In the meantime, the League would mobilise opinion for a more comprehensive measure.[92] He was backed by nonconformist journals and was obviously speaking for the League Executive. Adams says little of this development, nor does he deal with Forster's public *riposte*—a speech at Bradford on January 17th. Referring directly to Bright's metaphor, Forster expressed the hope that when the Irish land omnibus had passed through Temple Bar Lord de Grey and he would be allowed to drive the education bus through. The religious difficulty, he added, in another transport metaphor, which he was never to be allowed to forget, would be 'cantered over': 'Almost everybody in the country sees the importance of the end we are aiming at and almost all are convinced that the end must be attained at once.'[93] On 4 February Forster was given the green light. 'The bill is through—compulsion and all,' de Grey wrote to him, 'to be brought in as at present advised on Thursday the 17th. This is first-rate.'[94] On the 8th he gave notice of the bill, and on the 17th, as planned, he introduced it.

Instead of dealing with this sequence of events—not all of which, of course, was known to him—Adams dwelt on the struggle in the provinces between the League and the Union. He was on familiar ground. This was not the first time in nineteenth-century political history when two rival organisations, each professing the need for change, had been pitted against each other: 'The contest between the rival societies was conducted with much animation, and before the assembling of Parliament there was not a town of any importance in England where meetings or conferences had not been held.'[95]

Only a few years earlier the Reform League, many of whose members, as we have seen, joined the National Education League,[96] and the Reform Union had both been engaged (with different composition and outlook) in the fight for the extension of the franchise. Their activities had had a complementary as well as a competitive element. There was no novelty in 1869 and 1870, therefore, in the League and the Union vying with each other in holding of mass meetings, presenting star speakers and circulating propagandist literature. Yet there was a fundamental difference in the situation. The League was genuinely reformist: it went out on the offensive as the Anti-Corn Law League before it. It could not afford to do otherwise. The Union, however, was socially respectable and, for the most part, politically conservative. Its reform ideas were limited and strongly tinged with paternalism as well as with residual voluntaryism: it considered the 'education of the poor' within a traditionalist context. It did not need to attack. This is not to say that its leaders believed that education was an issue which was lacking in urgency. They thought the time was ripe for action and that reform should not be postponed. Two years earlier T. H. Huxley had rightly identified among the 'classes of men' who favoured an expansion of education sections of the clergy 'seeking to stem infidelity'.[97] The Union included many Anglicans interested in education for broader reasons than this: it also included those nonconformists, led by Edward Baines, the Leeds newspaper proprietor, who was opposed to the abolition or erosion of denominational education.

It was perhaps an exaggeration for Adams to argue at Huntingdon in language he never employed in his book:

> The Union would have slumbered for ever in the womb of obscurity, had not the League been founded. It was then that the supporters of the Union hastened to the walls to array themselves once more, as the party of which they are

composed has so often done before, against the just demands of the people! Their object is the supremacy of class interests, the perpetuation of priestly interference in national concerns, and the conservation of the spirit of priestly interference in national concerns, and the conservation of the spirit of servility and dependence.[98]

Yet the remarks bring out the obvious social difference between the Union and the League which Adams insisted upon even when he was recollecting in comparative tranquillity: 'Their lists were wholly uncontaminated by any agitation with popular institutions, or their representatives.'[99] The Union had two archbishops, five dukes, one marquess, eighteen earls, twenty-one bishops and twenty-one barons among its sponsors. It also won the support from the sidelines of the venerable Lord Shaftesbury. It might follow the League in seeking the glamour of mass meetings, but more important in its calculations was the knowledge that it could rely on the steady backing of established power in every constituency. It had no need to emulate the League's policy of centralising business from a head office in Birmingham in the same way as the Anti-Corn Law League had centralised business from its headquarters in Manchester.[100] In the last resort if operations in the constituencies proved inadequate, it looked not to Manchester but to Canterbury, York, Oxford, Cambridge and Westminster. Not surprisingly, it did not need to try to draft an Education bill of its own: it concentrated on other people's Education bills which it did not like.

Not surprisingly, too, the Leaguers were afraid of its influence, not least on a Liberal government which included a substantial majority of Anglicans and a sizeable number of Whigs.[101] 'We do *not* assume that Forster will bring in a rotten bill,' Dixon had written at the end of October 1869 to George Melly, the Liberal member of Parliament for Stoke, 'but what I do assume is this, that exactly in proportion to Forster's estimate of the strength of the League, will be the liberal colouring of the Bill. He will be afraid of the Churches until we convince him that we are stronger. He is not yet so convinced. He thinks that the Manchester Union will grow faster than the Birmingham League.'[102] It is doubtful whether Forster ever thought in these terms, but the letter tells us a great deal about Dixon and the League. Once Forster had produced his proposals in February 1870 all the pent-up fears were unleashed.[103] Thereafter the Leaguers depicted Forster as a weak man who could easily be knocked off his balance by social as well as by political pressure. It was sometimes suggested, indeed, that he preferred Conservatives to Liberals. In Adams's view 'From the beginning of the parliamentary discussion he was adopted as the *protégé* and instrument of the Tories and the clergy, a position which ought not to have been a comfortable one for a strong Liberal statesman.'[104] The fact that many Liberals were put off by language of this kind never stopped it from being uttered. Indeed, Chamberlain eventually extended his indictment to many other Liberals besides Forster.[105]

There was, however, a brief calm before the storm. When Forster first introduced his Bill he was received with great respect in the House. As an experienced parliamentary reporter put it: 'So interesting was the subject, so clearly did Mr. Forster unfold his scheme, that whilst he was speaking we took no note of time, not even to mark its flight; nor did any one else that we observed, for the attention of the House during all that long space was close and unbroken.'[106] Although in the light of what happened later it may be significant that the same reporter quoted an old Conservative member as saying 'I like to listen to Forster because there is no nonsense about him',[107] even the Leaguers in Parliament were sufficiently impressed not to challenge him at once. 'Until the next day, when the cold print of the speech was under the eyes of Chamberlain and the other Nonconformist leaders, they did not at all seize what it meant.'[108]

To put Forster's speech into perspective—and Adams does not do justice to it—it is important to bear in mind first that it undermined all the Union's favourite arguments by concentrating even in the title of the bill, on 'national education' and not on 'the education of the poor'; second, that it paid a tribute to the pressure of public opinion; third, that Dixon as well as Mundella was praised; fourth, that the issue was deliberately raised above party politics; fifth that it was explicitly stated that 'the Government has not brought forward this measure with any notion of a compromise.' The 'sanguine' views of Forster's Conservative predecessor, Lord Robert Montagu, were dismissed, and there were many telling phrases, like the terse summary of the situation as Forster saw it—'much imperfect education and much absolute ignorance.' The relationship between the extension of the franchise and education was put in its proper context: 'I am one of those who would not wait until the people were educated before I would trust them with political power. If we had thus waited we might have waited long for education; but now that we have given them political power we must not wait any longer to give them education.' Even the international dimension was introduced: 'Civilised communities throughout the world are massing themselves together, each mass being measured by its force; and if we are to hold our position among men of our own race or among the nations of the world we must make up the smallness of our numbers by increasing the intellectual force of the individual.' The speech was a speech with broad horizons in view. It asked for confidence: 'We think it will be supported by both those who wish to protect the present system of education and those who wish to change it.'[109]

There was, in fact, immediate praise from all sides. Melly wished the bill 'God speed as it went down into the country, as one of the noblest messages of peace and goodwill to all classes';[110] Sir John Pakington said that he had never listened to a speech 'with more heartfelt satisfaction' than to the speech Forster had just delivered;[111] Cowper-Temple, Anglican chairman of the Union, who is remembered in history for an amendment which he was subsequently to propose, said how gratified he had been with the spirit in which the plan had been introduced. 'The spirit was one of tolerance and comprehensiveness.'[112] Only the last speaker, G. H. Whalley, member of parliament for Peterborough struck a discordant note, and he was not a Leaguer but an opponent of education, who believed, he said, that the experience 'of conferring education upon children irrespective of their parents had not been satisfactory.' 'The result was not the diminution of crime or pauperism; there did not follow any of the effects which we desired to achieve by a national system of education.'[113]

The atmosphere of 'tolerance and comprehensiveness' was dissipated by the time the bill was read a second time. What went down well at Westminster did not go down well in Birmingham. Adams briefly mentions the deputation which went to see Gladstone on 9 March. In the context of the later personal and political relationship between Gladstone and Chamberlain the interview has a special interest of its own. Mundella was not happy about what happened.[114] But Chamberlain revealed some of the political qualities which were to ensure his subsequent, if always controversial, political success. One admirer present at the meeting noted how he was able to secure 'the earnest and rapt attention of Mr. Gladstone while purposely ruffling the temper of Mr. Forster.'[115] We know now that Gladstone had many reservations, some of them fundamental, about Forster's bill and the fact that he had been willing to find a place for it in a crowded session was more perhaps on account of his 'especial commitment to the strenuous prosecution of government business' than 'because he was keenly interested in teaching children to write or read.'[116] He would have preferred a simpler solution to that of Forster—with school boards being given a 'free discretion with regard to denominational education'. As a

Churchman, he may also have believed that there was a better chance for the continuation of Church-sponsored education in 1870 than there was likely to be later, and it may well be that, for this reason—as well as for reasons of pressure on him of business relating to other issues—he raised no objections to what de Grey and Forster were proposing. Yet he did not share the objection, which he thought Forster 'entertained', 'to a law which should permit a strict limitation of the State-aided as well as of the rate-aided teaching to secular instruction'.[117] His responsibility in 1870, he wrote later, was one of concurrence rather than of authorship.[118] But there was a touch of ruthlessness in his summing up: 'Forster undoubtedly... became in some sense the scapegoat of the Government. I do not know that I personally can relieve him from much of his responsibility.'[119] We miss in this statement the kind of human concern for education which characterised Forster—even the human concern for politicians.[120] Forster made his own position quite clear on 1 April 1870 to Charles Kingsley, who had been a member of the League and had wrongly had his name quoted as being present on the deputation: 'I still fully believe that I shall get my bill through this year, but I wish parsons, Church and *other*, would all remember as much as you do that children are growing into savages while they are trying to prevent one another from helping them.'[121] He had an acute sense that his bill dealt only with the rudiments of education and that in order to get the rudiments provided there would have to be, if not compromise, friendly give-and-take. He would have agreed with G. M. Young that education was 'the great Victorian omission'.[122]

It was after the deputation to Gladstone that the League took the decision to oppose the second reading of the bill, an unusual step, which was scheduled for 14 March. By then a Central Nonconformist Committee had been set up in Birmingham on 3 March with Dale and the Rev. H. W. Crosskey, minister of the Unitarian Church of the Messiah, Birmingham, as honorary secretaries.[123] Adams's opposite number as operating secretary was Francis Schnadhorst, 'the spectacled, sallow, sombre' Birmingham draper, who within a short period of time was to establish himself as one of the most brilliant organisers in the country.[124] Mundella had been right when he wrote to Leader after Gladstone had received the League's deputation that 'the secularists in the League are pushing the Nonconformists into antagonism about the religious question'.[125] The antagonism was to persist and grow between 1870 and 1873, and Chamberlain was already clear in March 1870 that there was the possibility of pressing for 'the disestablishment of the English Church'.[126]

Indeed, once thought of in these terms the ruinous question was to influence the whole shape of national—as distinct from educational—politics. Meanwhile, with Forster's bill on its agenda, the League set aside its own. It gained a new momentum in the provinces where it now had 113 branches. It had prepared a special publication, one of nineteen publications in all on its list, which dealt with 'regulations' for forming branches and conducting business.[127]

The amendment on the second reading of the bill was proposed by Dixon and seconded by Alfred Illingworth, member of parliament for Knaresborough who lived in Forster's own constituency. The debate on the amendment is described by Adams.[128] Dixon's could not be said to have been a good speech, but it sounded warnings about future agitation and directed the attention of parliament to what was happening out-of-doors:

> Already the tocsin had been sounded and the forces were mustering; and it would be found that the Churches were on one side, and the Nonconformist bodies on the other. Which would be likely to prevail? If they consulted history they would not be left in much doubt; and behind these armies there stood an enfranchised people, and the people had always given their votes in favour of equality.[129]

In reply Forster made it clear that he had already received notice of a number of other amendments which would be put later and carefully considered, but he did not succeed this time in winning the same kind of support he had received less than a month earlier. Mundella and Lowe both backed him from the Liberal benches, but Henry Winterbotham, member of parliament for Stroud, who because of early death soon disappeared from the political scene, urged postponement just because more time was needed in order to rouse a popular agitation: 'A year is not a long time in a nation's life. It is long enough in the present circumstances for public opinion to be formed; and the nation which has tarried so long might well have ensured another year's beneficent delay.'[130] He quoted a comment of Brougham in 1825 that 'the people themselves must be the great agents in accomplishing the work of their own instruction'.[131] Miall was, as always, intransigent:

> Everyone knew that when they got into Committee, questions of principle were usually frittered away, and they thought, therefore, it was better for them to state fully, fairly, and impressively before the House the fault they found in the Bill, and that they could not do, unless they raised the question on the second reading.[132]

It was only after Gladstone, who said that it had been 'a most animated and interesting debate', had promised that there should be further examination by the government of some of the issues raised, that Dixon withdrew his amendment.[133]

During the course of the debate Vernon Harcourt, member of parliament for Oxford, who supported Dixon's amendment, coined the term 'the Irreconcilables' to refer to the Nonconformist opponents of the Bill. Yet he and those like him who vociferously objected to Conservatives supporting Forster were given short shrift by the prime minister:

> We surely do not think it necessary. . . to regard Gentlemen opposite as our natural enemies. . . We are here, no doubt, for the purpose of arguing manfully and stoutly our own particular principles; but, if without compromising those principles, we find occasions arise when, whatever the circumstances, we are in harmony with Gentlemen who sit on the opposite side of the House, and there is an approximation to oneness of mind, that I think is no subject for regret, but a matter for satisfaction.[134]

Adams passes over this observation and turns to the debate on the different clauses of the bill as amended by the government which were laid on the table on 26 May. It is not necessary to add to his account of what happened in Birmingham and the provinces during the intervening weeks when 'public feeling' was deliberately whipped up as much as possible. The most important single event was the second deputation to see Gladstone, this time a deputation from the Central Nonconformist Committee, on 11 April. Meanwhile Bradford Leaguers were putting the maximum amount of local pressure on Forster. For reasons set out by Adams the changes proposed by the government were thought to be 'imperfect'[135] and the League went on to mobilise additional funds, to hold mass meetings and to summon its Council on 16 June.[136] Gladstone was at last beginning to be fully aware of the wide range of problems associated with educational legislation. In one of the very few references to education in his correspondence with his colleague and friend Lord Granville we find him writing in a letter of 30 May asking him to read a paper: 'I am loath to trouble you with a quarter of an hour's reading but the subject of Education is so important & so arduous in regard to the "religious difficulty" that I am perhaps justified in attempting this infliction.'[137] Granville replied very diplomatically, 'I like your plan, always subject of course to its being acceptable to your house.'[138]

The House went into committee on 16 June several months after it had first been planned to do so, and by then a formidable battery of amendments had been assembled. 'The natural interest, warming into eagerness, which the House and the country feel with reference to the measure,' the prime minister began his introduction to the debate, 'has caused the Notice Paper to be charged and loaded with a number of motions, all of which express alternative and different methods of proceeding with regard to questions bearing upon religion, but all of which it is not possible, according to the forms of the House, to bring under consideration upon equal terms.'[139] 'Nothing except a general disposition to make sacrifices of cherished principles,' he went on, 'for the purpose of arriving at a common result, can enable us to go through a work so difficult as that before us.'[140] Immediately, however, he fired the flames of the nonconformist revolt by accepting on behalf of the government an amendment from Cowper-Temple, a Whig back bencher and an Evangelical Churchman, who proposed first that no catechism or other distinctive religious formulary should be taught in a Board School, *and* second that voluntary schools should receive no assistance from the rates. In accepting this amendment Gladstone on his own initiative (not mentioned by Adams) pledged an increase in annual government aid to the denominational schools from one-third to one-half of the total cost. He also proposed to discontinue the building grant to these schools after a period of grace to which the nonconformists had already objected. Yet such discontinuation was not based on principle but on pragmatism: 'The building of schools is the easiest of all the efforts made by the promoters. Their great difficulty is the maintenance of the schools; and when we give liberal assistance to the maintenance, I think we may fairly leave to the locality the cost of the building.'[141]

One of the best speeches in the subsequent debate was that of Disraeli who described Gladstone's speech as introducing 'an entirely new bill', a subject with which he was familiar enough in the light of his own experiences in 1867.[142] Thereafter Disraeli could enjoy the spectacle of Liberal dissension reasonably uninterrupted. He saw the issue as it faced Gladstone in straight political terms; he had written earlier: 'Gladstone, I apprehend, is prepared to secularise, if he were only convinced he could keep his majority together by that process. But the elements of the calculation are various and discordant, and every possible result, therefore doubtful.'[143]

During the debates on the various amendments the elements of the calculation were always doubtful, and there was as much strange cross-voting as there had been in 1867.[144] Yet the fact that the Conservatives either supported Forster or abstained (except on the question on the use of the ballot in school board elections) and that there was a solid group of Liberals always prepared to support the government ensured that there would always be a government majority. It also ensured, of course, that the Leaguers and their friends would be in a perpetual minority, and it was for this reason that Miall complained in a famous passage in the concluding debate on the third reading that he and his supporters had been made to pass through the Valley of Humiliation.[145] His remark was prompted by a comment of Cowper-Temple that the Nonconformists had failed to secure any of their main objectives. 'They laughed who won,' said Miall bitterly. 'All the desires of the Church had been met, at least all the desires which it was thought could be conveniently put forward by the Church.' As a 'fair moiety of the party now in power', the Nonconformists had not been dealt with 'considerately': 'once bit, twice shy'.[146] It was this colloquialism rather than Miall's oblique reference to the Old Testament which roused Gladstone to reply in an equally famous passage:

> I hope my hon. Friend will not continue that support to the Government one moment longer than he deems it consistent with his sense of duty and right. . . So long as my hon. Friend thinks fit to give us his support we will cooperate with my hon. Friend for every purpose we have in common; but when we think his opinions and demands exacting, when we think he looks too much to that section of the community he adorns, and too little to the interests of the people at large, we must then recollect that we are the Government of the Queen.[147]

Gladstone was saying no more on this occasion than he had said at the beginning of the long debates, debates which are well worth reading in full for the light they throw not only on nineteenth-century attitudes to politics and the role of government but on attitudes to religion in a period of transition. He also went back in his last speech to a defence of the continuation of voluntary schools which must have been anathema to the League:

> It was with us an absolute necessity—a necessity of honour and a necessity of policy—to respect and to favour the educational establishments and machinery we found existing in the country. It was impossible for us to join in the language or to adopt the tone which was so conscientiously and consistently taken by some Members of the House who look upon these voluntary schools, having generally a denominational character, as admirable passing expedients. . .[148]

There was clearly as big a gulf between the League and Gladstone--not to speak of Forster—at the end of the debates as there had been at the beginning, and it was natural that Dixon should open his own brief speech by giving notice that during the next session he would move for leave to bring in a bill to amend the Elementary Education Act of 1870.[149] To measure the gulf we should place alongside Gladstone's declaration of faith the statement of principle enunciated by Henry Richard, the Liberal member for Merthyr:

> If he knew anything of the principles of Nonconformity, one of the most fundamental and universally acknowledged of them was this—that it was not right to take money received from the general taxation of the country, and apply it to purposes of religious instruction and worship. . . For if they claimed the right to compel one man to pay for the support of another man's religion, and to enforce that by law, they passed at once into the region of religious persecution.[150]

Once more we are back in the seventeenth century.

One man who at the end of the debates had both feet planted firmly in the nineteenth century was Melly. He had some witty things to say, as usual, though he chose to say them outside Parliament: 'This bill contained immense probabilities of good and great possibilities of evil. The Liberals accepted it because of its probable good and the Tories because of its possible evil.'[151] Inside Parliament he appealed for conciliation even between Gladstone and Miall. While confessing his mixed feelings he joined hands with Sir John Pakington in urging 'bygones to be bygones'. 'He would rather look forward than backward,' he said, 'in relation to this great measure of popular education. He valued the object above the means of attaining' and the education of their children 'above "a religious difficulty" or party ties.'[152] Thereafter Melly did his best to make the Act work.[153]

We can see after a century that the act was a great landmark in educational history, although we have rightly been warned against studying that branch of history 'as a series of legislative enactments, with its students jumping from one Act of Parliament to another, like mountain goats from peak to peak'.[154] Few people came straight down from the mountain in the summer of 1870. The Act received the royal assent on 29 August, but as Adams says the irritation remained and grew. Leaguer feeling was reinforced by strong expressions of dissatisfaction with the bill on the part of intellectual leaders. Adams quotes John Stuart Mill.[155] A different kind of political philosopher, T. H. Green, shared the same sentiments. He objected to the voluntary schools being given a 'needless term of grace' and pressed for compulsory attendance, a subject on which Mundella had always felt strongly and which he went so far as to suggest should have been the sole plank in the League platform like the repeal of the corn laws between 1839 and 1846.[156]

Yet very soon after the Act had become a *fait accompli* it began to be put into operation with Leaguers working hard to make the most of it while continuing to demand amendment in the future.[157] School Boards were quickly set up in the League strongholds—Birmingham and Leeds founded their Boards on the same day—and even outside the big towns it was the districts with a large proportion of nonconformists which were the most zealous in creating Boards.[158] Adams gives a good account both of this educational activity and of the continuing political pressure which the League was seeking further to increase. He describes the nonconformist conference in Birmingham held at Dale's chapel on 19 October and the second annual meeting of the League held six days later at the Queen's Hotel.[159] At the first of these meetings the Central Nonconformist Committee decided to ask for all grants of money for denominational education to be withdrawn: Dale had already been preaching this programme, which had the full support of Chamberlain and he followed up the Birmingham meeting by visiting Manchester towards the end of November when the audience in a packed Free Trade Hall heard him speak on 'The Politics of Nonconformity'.[160] If the government did not concede nonconformist demands, he thundered, 'let the Liberal party be broken in pieces and forever destroyed'.[161] At the third annual conference of the League held a year later equally strong language could still be heard. Dilke, for example, argued that

> every gathering of Liberals in the kingdom is a meeting for the denunciation of the Liberal ministry... If the Liberal party breaks up, it will be from the want of ecclesiastical Liberalism on the part of the Government. The only means by which that can be prevented is by such Parliamentary action as will enable us to out-number and beat the Government, and will enable us, if strong enough, to know who are our friends and who are our foes.[162]

From speeches of this kind we can conclude that the emotional temperature of the League rose sharply after Forster's 1870 Act had passed. 'Let a few hundreds throughout the country refuse to pay the new education rates,' Joseph Cowen of Newcastle told the Conference, 'and the obstinacy of the Vice-President of the Education Department would have to give way. He would find behind him a force he could not control... Their battle should be short, sharp and decisive; and the sooner they

went into the strife, the sooner it would be over.'[163] By then the
League had 315 branches.[164]

Six points should be made about the period of fierce agitation
which was further intensified in 1872. First, the League
deliberately took up a more extreme position in January 1872
than it ever had done before, demanding universal School Boards
to control all existing schools and to provide secular instruction,
with denominations being left to service religious instruction in
out-of-school hours.[165] The decisions of the Executive
Committee on these points, which were almost unanimous, were
ratified by the third annual general meeting in November. At last,
therefore, the Bible-reading compromise was cast aside, with
Chamberlain proposing the change.[166] Second, the League began
to make preparations for intervention at elections. Chamberlain
collected notes on the political situation in different constituencies, and along with other League speakers invaded the
strongholds of those Liberals who were unwilling to accept the
League programme in its entirety. In March 1872, for example,
he went to Stroud, and attacked Winterbotham, who had joined
Gladstone's ministry: he refused to listen to any appeals for
Liberal unity: 'What matters it to education—what matters it to
the welfare and prosperity of the nation—whether a Tory
government sits on the Cabinet benches or a Liberal Government
passing Tory measures?'[167] In another speech later in the year he
described himself as 'one of that little knot of fanatics, one of
those much abused beings, a political dissenter,' adding that he
'gloried in it'.[168] The climax of this irreconcilable policy was the
Bath by-election of June 1873 described by Adams.[169]

Third, there were enough 'fanatics' in different parts of the
country to go further and seek martyrdom by refusing to pay the
education rates. One of the noisiest centres of this extreme
movement was Sheffield, where the peak of the agitation was not
reached until late 1872 and early 1873,[170] and it was Sheffield
which Chamberlain was to contest at the general election of
1874. He was to stand then on an extreme anti-Church
programme, about which the radical Mundella, one of the sitting
members, had grave reservations, and he even went so far as to
argue that 'education should be made free by the simple
expedient of utilising the revenue of the established church', a
proposition which alienated even some Liberals who accepted the
League programme.[171]

Fourth, even where there was not quite so much party
political drama, the life of the new School Boards, as Adams
shows, was often characterised by fierce political and religious
strife. Birmingham itself, where the 'denominationalists' won a

surprising majority on the first School Board through the operation of the controversial cumulative vote, was one of the great storm centres. 'The fortnightly meetings of the Board were looked forward to with the greatest interest and zest, partly because of the principles at stake, though no doubt also because of the intellectual enjoyment they afforded.'[172] With considerable skill the Liberal town council kept the Board in check and prevented its anti-League majority putting into effect the provisions of clause 25 of the Act. Adams is particularly bitter about the financial support given by Forster to those Boards which accepted his policies and his resistance to those Boards where League influence was strong.[173] In fairness to Forster, however, it should be noted that government policy was to press places which, like Chester, were dilatory and obstructive in providing public education, to move faster, and that the means available to central government to discriminate in such circumstances were restricted. Straight educational (as distinct from political) propaganda was still necessary in the course of education, particularly in the rural areas, if there was to be education advance for there were farmers, in the words of one inspector, who were often 'anxious to avoid a rate for the furtherance of an object to which they have as yet contributed little besides hostility.'[174] Conservative politicians were most afraid of 'mischievous' League influence in places of this kind.[175]

Fifth, though the problems of the Boards and the debates inside them ranged widely over a broad span of problems, including the control of property and the quality of education, the ideological conflict with which the League was preoccupied (if never exclusively) centred on clause 25 of the Act which empowered Boards in those cases where the parents' poverty could be proved to pay fees at any public elementary school whether the school was a Board school or not. This clause had been allowed to pass the Commons without any amendment and without a division,[176] and a few Boards began to pay fees to denominational schools before building schools of their own. Manchester was one of them. 'This injustice—so palpable, so unforeseen,' writes Dale's biographer, 'roused the indignation of Nonconformists, even if they had been lukewarm before.'[177] Any Board which paid such fees, Adams concluded sharply, was 'in fact merely a relief agency for the denominational managers'. The sums of money paid out by Boards under this heading were remarkably small, but, as Disraeli recognised, they had a quite disproportionate symbolic significance. Adams put it briefly: 'the 25th clause was merely the key of a position, chosen upon which to fight the issue, whether the country was prepared to accept in perpetuity the system of sectarian schools supported by public rates.'[178] Just because of the echoes of the Church rates contest, this particular question was never to lose its punch.

Yet the militant Nonconformists were always in danger of over-playing their hand in 1872 and 1873. Sixth—and it is much the most important point of all—however much they or their local and national leaders campaigned against the 25th clause and other sections of the Act, they were demonstrating as a minority rather than communicating politically with the majority, even the majority within their own party. The political effect of their strident campaign was essentially destructive, for, as the *Economist* had put it during the year 1870 itself, 'a broad and symmetrical plan with a revolutionary tendency' never appealed to 'any large mass of English electors'.[179] The Leaguers made a great deal of noise, which was fully reported in the Press and they intervened, often causing great local bitterness, in a number of by-elections, but, as H. J. Hanham has written, they made comparatively little impression on the ordinary Liberal voter 'unless he were already thinking of voting Conservative or abstaining', in which cases League activities confirmed him in his intention.[180] Hanham argues that the nonconformist organisations in 1873 and 1874 were more like the Lord's Day Observance Society than the Anti-Corn Law League on which they modelled themselves, and it is clear from contemporary evidence and from recent historical scholarship that they were linked closely in mood and to some extent in tactics with the United Kingdom Alliance, the temperance organisation which lived within a Victorian world of its own.[181] There was one obvious difference between the League and the Anti-Corn Law League, of which Chamberlain became fully aware[182]—the fact that, as Hanham puts it, since the former was concerned in the last resort with the stomach and the latter with the mind and the character, the appeal of the latter was less direct and compelling to large numbers of people. It might attract minorities with a traditional strand of militancy and active consciences, but at most by-elections the actual League vote was negligible, and even in those localities where 'big' local names were associated with League propaganda there was seldom solid mass support. 'The ordinary nonconformist (even), and particularly the ordinary Wesleyan, had no wish to be an agitator except perhaps for better living conditions.'[183]

This kind of hard evaluation is missing from Adams's account.[184] Nor, of course, was Adams in a position to know (from unpublished private sources) how, at least from the beginning of 1872, Chamberlain and a number of other prominent Leaguers, like Dilke, had become convinced that the education question by itself was of limited interest to the electorate. Indeed, they may well have been aware of this from the start. Certainly by January 1872 Bright, who throughout his life was afraid of splits in the Liberal party, told Dale that the working classes, who in his view and that of many other politicians, played a strategic role in post-Reform Act politics, had 'little real interest' in a dispute between 'Church Parsons and Dissenting Parsons'.[185] His own reaction to this line of argument was the opposite of Chamberlain's. Although he stated in public that the 1870 Act was 'the worst Act passed by a Liberal Government since 1832,'[186] he re-joined Gladstone's weakening government in August 1873 after Gladstone had tempted him by pointing to other and in his opinion more popular issues than education, like the repeal of the income tax.[187] Harcourt, one of the fiercest critics of the Act, also joined the government in the autumn of 1873. Chamberlain, by contrast, wished not to make peace but to broaden the front of Liberal opposition to the government by raising other issues than education—among them 'Free Land' and 'Free Labour'—outside the House of Commons. He was quite prepared to face the consequence that the Liberal government, in relation to which he was a young, provincial outsider, might lose the next general election. In particular, he believed that working-class support for a full, radical programme depended on what he called 'an extension of the argument'. Though there were to be many criticisms later that the Education Act of 1870 was designed to keep the working classes in order,[188] Chamberlain was anxious at the time to keep them in movement. He expressed his views with characteristic frankness in a letter to John Morley months before the dissolution of Parliament: 'I have long felt that there is not force in the Education question to make it the sole fighting issue for our friends. From the commencement it has failed to evoke any great popular enthusiasm... The assistance of the working classes is not to be looked for without much extension of the argument.'[189]

In the curious political circumstances of 1873, when the Liberal government, continuing what Adams called its 'creeping process of disintegration',[190] faced as many challenges from outside Westminster as from the Conservatives in the House, education was no longer, for all the virulence of the League, the issue with the most popular potential. The failure of the League—and ultimately its abolition—was clinched by Gladstone's timing of the general election. Disraeli had made it clear during the course of 1873 that he was utterly uninterested in profiting

from persistent Liberal divisions to throw the government out
and form a minority Conservative government. He had his eye on
winning full power at a general election after Liberal disintegration had crept even further. Yet when Gladstone in
January 1874 announced a general election a month later he
could not have chosen a worse time. Thinking of everything
except education and particularly of abolishing the income tax,
the issue with which he had baited Bright, he took all his
supporters by surprise. The League in particular was unprepared.
For all the attention it had devoted in 1872 to electoral
organisation and its efficient financing, it found it difficult to
discuss such matters publicly in the autumn of 1873 because of
'uncertainty respecting ministerial intentions'.[191] For the first
time in its brief history, therefore, its annual meeting in 1873 was
'of a formal character'.[192] When Gladstone's announcement
came, 'members and candidates were scattered abroad; constituencies were unprepared; plans were not matured, and
differences were unreconciled.'[193] Adams claims that out of 425
Liberal candidates 300 were pledged to the repeal of the 25th
section,[194] but there is little evidence that this issue swayed the
electorate. 'The prominent members of the League had various
fortunes.'[195] The Liberals as a whole suffered a disastrous defeat.
In England the Conservatives won sixty-five seats, in Scotland
twelve and even in Wales three. There was evidence of substantial
nonconformist abstentions from the polling, though, as the
Webbs wrote later, 'it will be a question for the historian of
British politics whether the unexpected rout of the Liberal
party. . . was not due more to the active hostility of the Trade
Unionists than to the sullen abstention of the Nonconformists.'[196] The rout was far less unexpected than the timing of
the election, and the most recent political historian of the period
concludes that leaving issues on one side there was 'widespread
relief' in 1874 that 'politics would become less exciting'.[197] In
other words, the whole tactics of the League had been wrong.

After the defeat it was by no means certain, however, that the
League would be dissolved. It would have been possible to argue
in 1874 that with a Conservative government in power it would
and should begin a new lease of life. Adams himself talked of the
defeat not being 'an unmixed evil' since it 'prepared the way for
the reunion of the party on a more liberal basis'.[198] In fact, the
League was doomed for two reasons. First, the return of a
Conservative government did not check educational advance.
Lord Sandon's educational code of 1875 came to Adams as 'a
surprise' and though he was shocked by the spectacle of Whitehall
being 'crowded by clerical wirepullers and friars of all colours'[199]

(probably the most colourful passage in the whole of his book), he could not deny that with compulsion in 1876 (free education was not to follow until 1891) 'the object for which the League was established was now guaranteed by legislation'.[200] Second, however, the leaders of the League—or at least the most politically ambitious of them—were beginning to think of the League as redundant. They were moving away from a conception of pressure politics towards a novel conception of party politics, eventually to be expressed in the foundation in 1877 of the National Liberal Federation. Education was merely to be one item, and a not very prominent item, in the new 'popular' Liberal agenda.

Adams does not tell us how he viewed this shift of attitudes which he may well have known about only after the main moves had been made. What is clear, however, from the last pages of his book is that, whatever may have been the motives or actions of the League's leaders before and after it was dissolved, he himself remained passionately devoted to the cause of education. He was one of the small minority of Englishmen devoted consistently and continuously to education whether or not (and it usually is not) in the forefront of national politics. He paid a warm tribute to the work of the School Boards:

> They have brought a new energy and capacity into the field of education, they are sustained by the inspiriting influence of public representation, and they have enlisted a class of workers who pursue education for its own sake, and who had little sympathy with the narrow and antiquated methods of the voluntary schools... They have raised the ideal of national education.[201]

This passage should be taken into account by historians of the 1902 Act. Yet Adams realised that far more remained to be accomplished than had been achieved. He had little use for 'the amiable philosophy of optimism' which prevailed after the dissolution of the League.[202] 'The region which remains unreclaimed' still needed exploration.[203] England still lagged behind the United States,[204] but in the United States, for all the progress, people were healthily 'not satisfied with the results they have obtained'.[205] 'It is manifest indeed that [in England] whatever temporary modifications and adaptations the system may undergo, the battle of National Education will have to be fought over again before a durable basis is found.'[206] In general he remained convinced that continued mobilisation of opinion was essential to further progress, and ended by quoting Cobden's 'wise words' that 'England cannot afford to have a little National Education'.[207]

Even Adams did not realise just how many obstacles stood in
the way of educational advance after 1870. What would he have
made of Gladstone's advice to Mundella when he became Vice-
President of the Council (Forster's old job) in the new Gladstone
ministry of 1880?

One thing I will venture to say. The charge for education is
enormous. When the object in view is of such value, it is apt
to be assumed, taken for granted, that the money is all
necessary and well laid out. I hope that you will think that it
is the duty of the official man representing the department to
make vigilant inquiry, not only into augmentation, but into
wasteful charges which may have crept in. . .[208]

The Education, Art and Science Grant from central government
then amounted to the vast sum of £4 million.[209] Mundella was
to be subject to perpetual vigilance from the Treasury[210], and he
by then knew from the inside, as Forster had done, how
complicated both the economics and the politics of education
could be. Yet Chamberlain to his credit remained interested in
the popular politics of education at this critical period in the
history of the Liberal party. 'We shall sweep the country with
free education and allotments,' he wrote to Mundella in October
1885, 'and the Tories will be smashed and the Whigs
extinguished.'[211] Even after the Tories had smashed the Liberals
in 1886 and he had joined up with the Whigs, he tried to
emphasise the need for continuing educational advance.[212] Yet
he remained through all the vicissitudes of his life a politician
above all else, and so it had been in the 1870s when he wrote to
Morley months before the general election of 1874 that while it
was 'not feasible to alter the name or objects of the Education
League. . . I look forward to the possibility of organisation on a
wider basis. If we get any compromise from the government
which we can possibly accept, it will probably be well to dissolve
the League, leaving its still unaccomplished work to be taken up
as part of the larger question.'[213] Already the writing was on the
wall.

The League was not formally dissolved until March 1877—the
National Liberal Federation was founded in June—and the
compromises necessary for the dissolution of the League were to
come paradoxically from a Conservative rather than from a
Liberal government. Yet the main issue of whether to concentrate
on education had been settled long before. Chamberlain was
thinking not of an organisation committed to one single political
issue, like the Anti-Corn Law League earlier in the century, but a
new kind of political party. Insofar as he had a historical model in
mind, it was not the Anti-Corn Law League but the Birmingham

Political Union which had campaigned during the Reform Bill struggles of 1830-32.[214] Yet although the Union had encouraged the formation of other Unions in different parts of the country and the word 'union' (rather than 'League') figured prominently in the first propaganda of the new Federation, the Federation represented a fundamentally new approach to political organisation and through its activities triggered off a new kind of debate about 'the caucus'.[215] Already questions of foreign policy were stirring Liberals far more than questions of domestic reform, and the League made its appeal not to sectarian extremists but to broad masses of opinion:

> The Federation is designed to assist the formation of Liberal Associations, on a popular representative basis, throughout the country; to bring such organisations into union, so that by this means the opinions of Liberals, on measures to be supported or resisted, may be readily and authoritatively be ascertained; and to aid in concentrating upon the promotion of reforms found to be generally desired the whole force, strength, and resources of the Liberal party. [216]

Chamberlain himself was soon to claim that 'the Federation is thoroughly representative of the party, and not of any clique within it';[217] Gladstone, having emerged from his brief retirement after the 1874 election, was to address a great meeting in Birmingham prior to its formation;[218] and Forster, not surprisingly was to find himself struggling hard from the start against 'caucus' philosophy in Bradford.[219]

II

To understand more profoundly the political dynamics of all this and the reasons why education ceased to be the major issue of the day it is valuable to turn from Adams to John Morley, whose lengthy pamphlet, *The Struggle for National Education,* was published in 1873. If Adam's book is the most useful single monograph to reprint, Morley's is the single indispensable polemic. Large parts of it first appeared earlier in 1873 in the *Fortnightly Review* which he edited, and many other articles in this periodical are essential reading for an understanding of the politics of the 1870s.[220] In 1873, for example, Chamberlain was writing (at Morley's invitation) that

> it is a mistake to suppose that the revolt of the Irreconcilables will be confined to agitation against the 25th clause of the Education Act... Mr. Forster's persistent determination to sectarianise education may be the first cause of active

opposition, but when disorganisation has once set in the
various elements of dissatisfaction will have full play, and the
party will not again be reunited till a new programme has
been elaborated which shall satisfy the just expectations of
labour as well as conciliate the Nonconformists who have
been driven into rebellion.[221]

The *Fortnightly Review* had been founded in 1865 and Morley
was its second editor, appointed to the post in 1867, the year of
the Second Reform Act.[222] He had been born in Blackburn in
Lancashire in 1838, and although still a very young man in 1867
he was already being commended by John Stuart Mill as 'one of
our best and most rising periodical writers on serious subjects—
moral, social and philosophical, still more than political.'[223] He
did not meet Chamberlain until 1873 (at a League meeting[224])
when his interests had already become more directly political,
and from the start their relationship was 'complementary'.[225]
Morley was immensely impressed by Chamberlain's grasp of
practical politics just as Chamberlain was impressed by the range
and power of Morley's mind, and although their ways were
eventually to diverge—and to diverge sharply—in 1873, when
Morley's book was published, they could not have felt a stronger
sense of affinity. It was in that year that Morley turned down an
invitation to stand for Parliament telling Chamberlain, who was
desperately anxious himself, as we have seen, to find a place
there, that he would be 'happiest of all to remain the mere
penman of the Education cause'.[226]

Morley, however, was far more than a 'mere penman'. He was
an intellectual in politics, a man influenced by both English and
foreign ideas. In the background of his personal experience was
Oxford, not Birmingham, though he had a strong and intuitive
understanding of the flavour of the provinces and of the power of
nonconformity as a force to be reckoned with there. 'He was not
a Nonconformist,' he told a nonconformist audience, 'or rather
he was a Nonconformist and something more', while Hamer has
said that he was as much a Nonconformist minus Christianity as
the positivists were Roman Catholics minus Christianity.[227]
While he conceived of the struggle for national education, as
Adams did, as part of a bigger and longer struggle, his
perspectives and philosophies were different. He believed that the
country, like other European countries, was passing through a
critical period of transition in which ideas and institutions were
being tested. In the aftermath of the Reform Act of 1867 which
had opened the way to a 'new ruling class'[228] what was most
needed was the unifying vision of a 'national cause' which would
transcend interest and class and mobilise large-scale moral as well

as political support. Education was such an issue, 'the most serious of national concerns',[229] as the repeal of the corn laws, which he was to deal with so fully in his *Life of Cobden* (1881) had been during the 1840s. 'It is above all things desirable to remove the task of national instruction as far as possible from the region of philanthropy into the drier climate of business and public duty.'[230] Yet before it could be so removed there would have to be the heat of argument. He did not mind opposition. 'Every reform,' he had written in 1865, 'has been carried out in spite of hostile public opinion.'[231] He saw himself as a leading opinion-maker, the *Fortnightly Review* as the major organ of communication with 'the respectable middle classes',[232] and education as an issue raising a cluster of related national themes of urgent importance—the improvement of the working classes, the abolition of privilege and the extension of local self-government, all subjects which had long interested him. 'True statesmanship,' he maintained, 'lies in the right discernment of the progressive forces of a given society, in strenuous development of them, and in courageous reliance upon them.'[233]

There were positivist undertones in such a statement. Yet in his sensitive probing of Morley's mind and motives Hamer has illuminated his attitudes more clearly. Morley had moved away from positivism before he met Chamberlain and had already found in the idea of a 'collective national impulse', generating the articulation and mobilisation of a 'national cause', a substitute for a belief in 'systems'. He had come to consider it to be the duty of opinion-makers and politicians working together to present great issues to the electorate, taking each question singly in order to avoid confusion and to maximise involvement. Hamer, borrowing one of Morley's own words from a different context, calls this process 'focalising'.[234]

Hamer's analysis is particularly interesting for the historian of English educational politics for two reasons. First, we cannot understand what has happened in terms of 'system'. There never has been a 'system' of education in England as there was in Prussia, and in order to sort out problems both of substance and of chronology it is essential to trace policy as 'the resultant of many diverse forces'.[235] Second, there has been no built-in pressure in England as there has been in the United States (or parts of it) to expand educational opportunities. When Roebuck raised the educational issue in 1833 he apologised for taking up the time of the House of Commons on such an uninteresting topic, and in 1891 half way through the debate on the first reading of the government's proposals to provide free education the House was counted out to make sure that forty members were present.[236] Against this background the 'focalising' periods in the history of English education stand out dramatically, posing fundamental questions about conflict and consensus in society and the capacity to change.[237] The issues develop or change as do modes of expression but the relations between contending interests and parties maintain certain common patterns.

The late 1860s and 1870s were one of those periods, and Morley, whose tastes and purposes were more than polemical, gives a more convincing explanation of why it was than Adams does. Indeed, he takes up eloquently, if superficially, the main economic and political 'reasons' for educational advance which have been set out in the context of the recent discussions centred on the centenary of the 1870 Act while also underlining religious reasons (on the part of the Church) which have been neglected recently or overlooked.[238] His central question is familiar enough. 'Will rude vigour, undisciplined by intellectual training, undirected by intellectual skill, uninformed by knowledge, suffice for England in the conditions of modern society?' he asks.[239] Unfortunately this question is crudely functionalist, and Morley himself was the first to admit that primary education by itself could not be expected to achieve more than limited results. 'Skill in reading and counting will not protect its possessor against the mischief that is wrought by overcrowding, by exhausting labour in childhood and youth, by unbounded temptations to get drunk, by inveterate traditions and class habits of self-indulgence.'[240] Morley had no clear view of the relationship between primary education and later stages of education as a continuing process. Indeed, he did not believe that the state should supply higher education free. 'The ground of state interference in education is the expediency, not of having citizens who know Latin and history and drawing, but of making sure that every child shall have a chance of acquiring mastery over the essential instruments of knowledge.'[241] Dr. Rigg's conclusion that, given 1870, eventually there would follow logically 'national provision of elementary schools, and grammar schools, and high schools'[242] he dismissed as 'this bubble of an argument' which 'barely needs puncturing'. In an address which he gave in 1876 and which he chose to reprint he argued the interesting thesis that it was of 'questionable expediency to invite the cleverest members of any class to leave it—instead of making their abilities available in it, and so raising the whole class along with, and by means of their own rise.'[243]

In the light of the next 'focalising' period in educational history—the late 1890s and early 1900s—Morley's perspectives in 1873 seemed confined and outmoded and his book a document with little abiding interest. Yet his concept of 'focalising' applied as much to this new period as to the old and the arguments, some of them going back to 1870, some pointing to the future,[244] were just as bitter. Educational policy continued to rouse differences when the debate passed from primary to secondary and then to higher education, with the social argument intertwined with the educational and the political, and even though in retrospect later 'focalising' periods during the First and Second World Wars seemed to involve consensus rather than conflict, the fear of controversy remained strong.[245] When R. A. Butler opened the question of educational reform in 1941 he was told by Churchill that 'it would be the greatest mistake to raise the 1902 controversy during the War... Your main task at present is to get the schools working as well as possible under all the difficulties. . .'[246]

'Focalising' periods have been followed, of course, by longer periods of administrative implementation, and during these periods there has usually been a lull in public opinion along with a quiet consolidation of resistance to change on the part of existing interests. Relatively little has been written about this process. Why does the earlier excitement evaporate? Is there a pattern here? Morley, thinking of his own experiences during the 1870s, would have explained the evaporation in political rather than in social terms. After Chamberlain had ceased to believe that the education issue should be pressed on its own, Morley stuck to his belief in politicians raising one issue and one only at a time. 'Shall we not fight with most effect,' he asked Chamberlain in August 1873, 'by stirring the Nonconformists and leaving other people alone?'[247] He never became converted to Chamberlain's views on 'party' and 'programmes' even after the formation of the National Liberal Federation in 1877.[248] Nonetheless he dropped the issue of education himself in 1874 and in 1875 in favour of the bigger issue, as he had then come to see it, of Disestablishment of the Church of England, and later he dropped that too. Curiously, it was Forster who influenced him most in dropping the latter issue by warning him that the outcome of pressing it might be the opposite of that which he intended.[249] Moreover, Morley had come to recognise himself through experience that the enthusiasts for Disestablishment were people 'who live in exclusively dissenting circles, or have no opportunity for surveying our society widely in its varied strata.'[250] This was a very different kind of conclusion from that which a reader of *The Struggle for National Education* might have expected. 'Dissent,' Morley wrote then, 'offers little that touches the fastidious and sentimental love, which is so much in fashion in our times, for the picturesque, the gorgeous, the romantic, the sweetly reasonable.' And yet 'it possesses a heroic political record. It has little in the way of splendour and state, but it has a consistent legend of civil enlightenment. It may lack majesty, but it has always shown honest instincts.'[251]

Matthew Arnold, Forster's nephew, had written *Culture and Anarchy* four years earlier, drawing attention to the place of nonconformity in English life. Morley, having made his generalisations, was at pains to emphasise that 'the present aspect of the question of national education in England' was not 'only a new version of the old quarrel between conventicle and steeple-house'.[252] He followed Adams in praising 'the intrepid spirits' of the Puritan past,[253] yet he concentrated, as Adams did not, on international currents of anti-clericalism in the present. 'While the statesmen of every other country in Europe from Austria downwards are fully aware that the priests had too much power,' he wrote, 'it was left for Liberal leaders in England to find out that priests had too little power and straightway to hasten to make it greater.'[254] This was a remarkable anti-clerical statement for a future biographer of Gladstone to make. Yet Morley, like a continental liberal, believed that 'the state church stands for a decaying order of ideas and for ideas that grow narrower and more intense in proportion as they fall out of harmony with the intellectual life of the time.'[255]

At various places in his book Morley was more willing to deal in personalities than Adams, and in this connection also it is fascinating to read a future biographer of Gladstone comparing unfavourably the prime minister's attitudes at the time of the passing of the Education Act of 1870 with the attitudes of Disraeli at the time of the passing of the Reform Act of 1867:

> Mr. Disraeli had the satisfaction of dishing the Whigs who were his enemies. Mr. Gladstone, on the other hand, dished the dissenters who were his friends. Unfortunately he omitted one element of prime importance in these rather naive transactions. He forgot to educate his party. The result of this one slight oversight has been a serious disaster.[256]

The judgement confirms Morley's considerable admiration for Disraeli's 'realism'.[257] Morley also compared Gladstone unfavourably with Bright whom he was later to accuse of 'an unlimited self-confidence which amounted to a corruption of the soul':[258] 'As a body the nonconformists are staunch and active in their hostility to the measure which a sounder and an older Liberal than Mr. Gladstone has described as the worst measure passed by any Liberal government since 1832.'[259]

It was memorable passages like this in the first few pages of Morley's pamphlet which were seized upon at the time, and there was one equally memorable passage of a different kind towards the end. After saying that he could not admit that the owners of the sectarian schools had the shadow of a vested interest, Morley plunged on boldly in a direction which would have shocked Gladstone even more than his personal remarks about him:

> It is simply monstrous to urge that these volunteers are for ever to stop the way to the formation of a national force. The owners of the schools only provided half the original cost of the buildings, and they have always provided a great deal less than half of the cost of the maintenance of the school. On what principle does this constitute an eternal right to the everlasting control of our educational system, and an inexpugnable claim to exclude all other schools from their parishes?[260]

And in his very last sentence he was in the front line with Chamberlain:

> if we are to impose a heavier burden on the country for the sake of providing gratuitous instruction, people may begin to look around them and ask, whether after all the whole of the endowments of the National Church are at present put to the most wise, just and useful purposes that the electors can think of.[261]

It is Morley the politician and commentator, not Morley the educationist, who lives through this pamphlet, despite the fact that he devoted so much space to talking about the quality of education.[262] And the final questions which he leaves in our mind are ones well put by Adams. Would there have been a better education act than that Forster introduced in 1870 if the education issue had been 'focalised' more in public before a national act was introduced? Was it better, rather, to get an act as soon as possible as Forster wished? Adams had no doubt:

> Looking back on half a century of procrastination and trifling, it may seem paradoxical to hold that the Act of 1870 was introduced prematurely, yet there are grounds for the belief that a stronger and more liberal measure, and one which, in an educational sense would have been economy of time, could have been passed if legislation had been delayed for another year.[263]

Looking back after a century of massive if uneven educational change probably few historians today would argue that it was unwise to make a start in 1870, a very belated start. They are more concerned with the effects of education on class groupings and opportunities, the subject which Morley and Chamberlain broached as outsiders to the working class, than they are with the battle between nonconformists and Church of England which neither side was able to win. In dealing with the developing educational system after 1870, therefore, they will have a different agenda from either Adams or Morley. They will wish to trace the association between education, work and poor law, to assess the effects of compulsion, to trace the effects educationally of the continuing routine operation of the Revised Code before and after 1870, and to explore in detail (as some of the local case studies have already begun to explore for particular places) the role of schools in their neighbourhoods, the attitudes not only of children but of parents, and the recruitment and education of the teaching profession.

NOTES

[1] A Collection of Circulars, Leaflets etc. relating to the National Education League, 1869–1875 *(Birmingham Collection, 68340)*.

[2] *Morris's Commercial Directory and Gazetteer of Warwickshire and Birmingham,* (1866), p.46; *Croydon Advertiser* 17 January 1891, which has the briefest of obituaries.

[3] F. Adams, *Lord Brougham* (London and Birmingham, 1869); *Lecture on Education delivered at Huntingdon on Thursday 17 February 1870* (Cambridge, 1870). See also his *The Free School System of the United States* (1875), a factual account which was widely praised both for its accuracy and for its shunning of rhetoric.

[4] loc.cit., p.20.

[5] See G.A.N. Lowndes, *The Silent Social Revolution* (1st ed., 1937).

[6] J. Vincent, *The Formation of the Liberal Party, 1857–1868* (1966), pp. xxviii–xxix.

[7] See below, p.25.

[8] See below, pp. 42–3.

[9] S. Maccoby, *English Radicalism, 1853–1886* (1938), p.103. The issue is put into its social and religious context in J. T. Mills, *John Bright and the Quakers,* Vol.II (1935), pp. 81ff., which in the same chapter deals with Bright's views on education.

[10] See below, p.43.

[11] See below, p.28. For a twentieth-century view of the chronological relationship between the different pressures as part of the same story, see T. H. Marshall, *Citizenship and Social Class* (1950).

[12] See below, p.99.

[13] See below p.129

[14] See the interesting article in the *Quarterly Review,* Vol.110 (1861), 'The Education of the Poor', p.486: see also below, p.138.

[15] See below, p.155.

16There is no reference to the campaigns for education in the interesting collection of articles *Popular Movements, c.1830–1850* (ed. J. T. Ward, 1970).

17See below, p.152.

18See below p.195. For the rivalry between Manchester and Birmingham, see A. Briggs, *Victorian Cities* (1963), pp.187ff.

19See below, p.193 for the way in which the Aid Society in Manchester developed into an Education Bill Committee. The object of the Committee was to secure that where 'voluntary agency has failed' localities should be permitted to 'invoke the help of the municipal organisation'. (A. Redford, *The History of Local Government in Manchester*, Vol.III (1940), pp.149–50). See also the useful book by S. E. Maltby, *Manchester and the Movement for National Elementary Education* (1918)

20There was a second body in Manchester in 1869 and 1870, the Manchester Education Bill Committee. It was opposed to both the League and the Union, but its members played an important part in the parliamentary debates on Forster's bill.

21See below, pp.164–5.

22For the beginnings of the new approach to the dynamics of nineteenth-century administration, see O. MacDonagh, 'The Nineteenth-Century Revolution in Government' in the *Historical Journal*, Vol.II (1958). There are many subsequent contributions to the discussion, particularly in *Victorian Studies*.

23For Kay-Shuttleworth's approach to the history of the subject, see *Four Periods of Public Education* (1862). His account should be compared with that of Adams. See also F. Smith, *The Life of Sir James Kay-Shuttleworth (1923)*.

24Kay-Shuttleworth wrote to Forster in 1870 telling him to remain calm: 'You will have to do what I have done over and over again in this cause—you will have to disappoint some of your friends in order that the education of the people may not be indefinitely postponed.' (Quoted in T. Wemyss Reid, *Life of the Rt. Hon. William Edward Forster*, Vol.I (1888), p.495).

25Lowe wrote *Primary and Secondary Education* in 1867. In an important memorandum of 21 October 1869 (printed in Reid, op.cit., pp.463–70) Forster compared Lowe's plans with those of Bruce, who had introduced bills on the subject, the National Education Union and the Birmingham League. He called Lowe's the best.

26See below, p.189. For his part, Forster, like his well-known relative, Matthew Arnold, strongly criticised Lowe's Revised Code. (Reid, op.cit., p.441; M. Arnold, 'The Twice-Revised Code' in *Fraser's Magazine*, March 1862).

27W. Bagehot, Introduction to the second edition of *The English Constitution* (1872). 'If there had been no Reform Act at all there would, nevertheless, have been a great change in English politics. There has been a change of the sort which, above all, generates other changes—a change of generation.'

28For the statistical enquiries, see M. Sturt, *The Education of the People* (1967), pp.296ff.; below, p.169. Forster sent his most experienced inspectors to report on facts relating to Birmingham, Leeds, Liverpool and Manchester before he drafted his bill. See also W. P. McCann, 'Elementary Education in England and Wales on the Eve of the 1870 Education Act' in the *Journal of Educational Administration and History*, Vol.II (1969).

29See below, p.175.

30A. P. Martin, *Life and Letters of the Rt. Hon. Robert Lowe, Vol.II (1893), p.323.*

[31]G. Sutherland, *Elementary Education in the Nineteenth Century* (The Historical Association, 1971), p.27.

[32]J. L. Garvin, *The Life of Joseph Chamberlain,* Vol.I (1932), p.90. In 1868 Collings published *An Outline of the American School System.* For a 'grass roots' opinion, see an interesting prize essay of 1868 in the Birmingham Collection. Its author A. B. Greenwood stated that 'national education is not only desirable, but it is a necessity. That question has passed beyond the region of controversy . . . some legislative measure must before long be at least proposed. The problem is, what kind of measure will be best in our present circumstances.' Bruce introduced two Education bills in 1867 and 1868.

[33]The point was, nonetheless, developed and exploited in Birmingham itself. In January 1868 the Chamber of Commerce sponsored a meeting in Birmingham at which A. J. Mundella was one of the speakers. Technical education was also given an impetus by the Universal Exhibition in Paris in 1867 which was followed by the setting up of the short-lived Society of Artisans. See J. A. Langford, *Modern Birmingham and Its Institutions,* Vol.II (1877), pp.402—6.

[34]F. Adams, loc.cit., p.13 (where he quoted Dr. Lyon Playfair, who had been pushing the economic argument for decades) and p.4.

[35]A. Watson, *A Great Labour Leader* (1908), p.104. R. H. Tawney at a later date was the leading academic voice propounding this philosophy: in demanding educational change he referred trenchantly to 'the vulgar irrelevancies of class and income'.

[36]H. Paul, *A History of Modern England,* Vol.III (1905), p.213; L. Stephen, *Life of Henry Fawcett* (1886), p.253. Government could do little to help the 'neglected' agricultural labourers in his opinion except through the extension of education.

[37]Garvin, op.cit., p.102.

[38]Quoted in ibid. p.89.

[39]G. Kenrick, *Nine Famous Birmingham Men* (1900), p.53.

[40]W. Gerin, *Charlotte Brontë, The Evolution of Genius*(1967 edn.), p.220.

[41]R. S. Kirk, 'Recollections of Chamberlain and His Times' in the *Searchlight,* 13 November 1913.

[42]Garvin, op.cit., pp.225—6, where the incident is passed over lightly. Chamberlain at the crucial moment wrote to Collings that 'everything must have an end, even his [Dixon's] indecision' (letter of 26 May 1876 in the Chamberlain Papers). W. T. Bunce appears to have forced Dixon's decision to retire by announcing it in the *Birmingham Daily Post,* which he edited. Chamberlain was then mayor of Birmingham. It says much for Dixon's generosity that he congratulated Chamberlain with warmth and wished him luck in relation to the parliamentary debates on a new Education bill.

[43]Garvin, op.cit., p.225. He does not quote a letter of 9 May 1878 from Chamberlain to Collings (Chamberlain Papers) saying that Dixon was 'a man who has done all the mischief of which his weakness is capable'.

[44]Dixon wrote to Chamberlain on 30 April 1880 (Chamberlain Papers) stating that 'the estrangement has been one of the most painful episodes of my life'. He was returned to Parliament for Edgbaston in 1885 and after the Liberal split of 1886 became treasurer of Chamberlain's new National Radical Union. See A. Briggs, *History of Birmingham* (1952), pp.182—3.

[45]See ibid, esp.pp.331—2. The resolution conferring the freedom said that Dixon had been honoured 'in grateful acknowledgement of his eminent public services and in recognition of his untiring energy and devotion in the interests of Elementary Education'. See also *The Victoria History of the County of Warwick,* Vol.VII (1964), pp.492ff. Dixon had a

Higher Grade School named after him in 1898; Chamberlain, however, was made a Freeman in 1888, the first on the roll.

[46]Quoted in Garvin, op.cit., p.118. The letter was written on 16 July 1870.

[47]*Report of the Third Annual Meeting of the Members of the National Education League Held in Birmingham on Tuesday and Wednesday, 17th and 18th October 1871* (1871), p.9.

[48]See below, p.197.

[49]Garvin, op.cit., pp.147—8.

[50]*Ibid*, p.261. See also F. H. Herrick, 'The Origins of the National Liberal Federation' in the *Journal of Modern History* Vol.XVII (1945).

[51]See his *History of the Corporation of Birmingham,* Vols.I and II (1885). For his views on Birmingham's place in national life, see his speech on being made a Freeman in 1899 (Briggs, op.cit., p.328). 'Through the columns of the most powerful newspaper in the Midland Counties,' wrote Dr. Dale, 'the new ideas about municipal life and duty were pressed on the whole community,' (N. M. Marris, *The Rt. Hon. Joseph Chamberlain* (1900), p.101). See also for a later period M. Hurst, *Joseph Chamberlain and West Midland Politics* (Dugdale Society Occasional Papers, 1962).

[52]See Briggs, op.cit. pp.2—3.

[53]Marris, op.cit., p.101.

[54]A. W. W. Dale, *The Life of R. W. Dale of Birmingham—by His Son* (1899), p.273.

[55]Ibid, p.274. One of Dale's most influential Congregationalist colleagues, Samuel Morley, refused consistently to have anything to do with the League and Dale had to spend a considerable amount of time 'fighting' inside his own denomination. Morley supported Forster and refused to condemn schools organised by religious bodies, whether Anglican or nonconformist. 'If it had not been for religious men,' he declared in a parliamentary speech in June 1870, 'he would like to know where the education of England would be. Let them drive forth religion in all its forms from the schools, and where would religion or education be fifty years hence?' (Quoted in E. Hodder, *Life of Samuel Morley* (1889), p.254).

[56]Of the original funds of the League Chamberlain (along with sixteen others) gave £1,000. Annual subscribers paying £100 in 1870 included Dixon, Sir Charles Dilke, Archibald Kenrick, G. B. Lloyd, the mayor of Birmingham, and R. L. Chance. Of the eighteen subscribers paying this sum, twelve lived in Birmingham. The other six included Sir Titus Salt of Bradford and Thomas Thomasson of Bolton.

[57]For Applegarth's career—he also belonged to the First International and was well-known to Marx—see A. Briggs, *Victorian People* (1954), chapter 7. By October 1870 twenty unions were backing the League (The Beehive, 29 October 1870) and at the first general meeting Chamberlain boasted that 'directly or indirectly, from 800,000 to 1,000,000 working men have, at their meetings in Birmingham, given their support to the platform of the League' (Quoted in Simon, op.cit., pp.363—4).

[58]Howell to Dixon (October 1869) in a letter in the Howell Papers. In writing to Dixon Howell signed himself 'your obedient servant'. Howell explained to Dixon (letter of October 1869) that he could not afford to pay the expenses of attending Executive Committee meetings regularly. (Cf. a letter to Collings, 8 December 1869). Yet he wrote to Dixon on 1 November 1869, 'I shall be at liberty, if the Executive think proper, to go into the country for the EL. I will arrange with Mr. Applegarth as to the towns most suited to begin with'. He mentioned Leeds and Bradford where the trade-union element was powerful.

[59]T. Wemyss Reid, *Life of the Rt. Hon. William Edward Forster,* Vol.I (1888), p.522.

[60]See ibid, pp.44—55 and Chapter XIII, *passim.*

[61]See below, p.197.

[62]Letter to the *Birmingham Daily Post,* 29 November 1870.

[63]J. Morley, *Life of Cobden* (1903 edn.), p.548. 'If you propose to leave out religion,' he told his friend George Combe, 'they denounce you as an atheist, and then reason and argument might as well be addressed to the clouds.' (Quoted in D. Read, *Cobden and Bright, A Victorian Political Partnership* (1967), pp.180—1).

[64]See, for example, Howell to Dixon in a letter of 11 August 1869 (Howell Collection); 'I am anxious to know from you as to whether the word "Unsectarian" in Article Four of your Means ... will cover "Undenominational" the latter, no doubt, referring to management, the former to subject matter ... If you desire it your reply shall be quite private.'

[65]*The Daily News,* 7 October 1870.

[66]*The Times,* 15 October 1870.

[67]*Report of the First General Meeting of Members of the National Education League held at Birmingham ... on October 12th and 13th 1869* (1869), p.194.

[68]See below, p.202. In his Huntingdon speech Adams said openly, 'There has been considerable difference of opinion on this subject. Many of the members of the League think that the Bible ought to be excluded altogether, and, speaking as an individual member of the League, I strongly adhere to that view—but that is not the accepted programme of the League'. Such a statement from its secretary could hardly have disarmed its opponents. And similar opinions were expressed publicly by some of its most influential backers, for example, Sir Charles Dilke. (See *The Times,* 4 January 1870).

[69]S. Evans, *A League Scholar* (1870). The poem was originally published in the Christmas number of the *Birmingham Gazette* which argued the opposite case to that presented in the *Birmingham Daily Post.* It retained its consistency, and as late as 1875 (12 July) was lampooning Earl (formerly Lord John) Russell's scheme of free education whereby 'working-men now getting £3 or £4 a week are to have their children taught for nothing'. 'Why,' it asked, 'does not Lord Russell propose universal and free bakers' shops?' This, of course, was not an original remark.

[70]The Welsh situation is particularly interesting. Between 1852 and 1868 there had been no Welsh nonconformist member of Parliament. The Reform Act changed the picture, and after 1868 nonconformity and nationalism became openly interlinked. Henry Richard, G. O. Morgan, Morgan Lloyd, Watkin Williams and J. Roberts, all returned to Parliament in 1868, would never have followed a lead from Birmingham without exercising independent judgement. See J. V. Morgan, *Welsh Political and Educational Leaders in the Victorian Era* (1908). A separate Alliance was set up in Wales with a more radical programme than that of the League.

[71]He also pooh-poohed the idea that 'the due influence' of religion should rest on control of the very young. 'We do not believe that the due influence of religion is to be secured with the incongruous mixture of its most solemn truths with the childish rudiments of letters.' (loc.cit., p.18). 'Bear in mind,' he added, 'that it is not necessary that all children should be sent to the League schools. We do not interfere with the right of parents to educate their children at home, or to send them to denominational schools if they prefer them.' (Ibid. p.16).

72 *Birmingham Daily Post,* 22 December 1869.

73 Report of a Conference, *18 January 1870.*

74 See R. G. Cowherd, *The Politics of English Dissent* (1956), Ch.10; N. McCord, *The Anti-Corn Law League* (1958). One of the crucial differences between the 1840s and the 1870s, however, was the rise of *organised* labour (see below, p.206), and the League recognised the role of the trade unions. Although it was essentially a middle-class organisation in its composition and its leadership, its style was less specifically middle-class. The Mayor of Birmingham might invite delegates to the first general conference to a *soirée* with evening dress (the invitation card can be seen in the Birmingham Collection), but it would not have been quite so easy for Chamberlain to echo Cobden's words, 'we have carried it [our agitation] on by those means by which the middle class usually carries on its movements. We have had our meeting of Dissenting ministers; we have obtained the cooperation of the ladies; we have resorted to parties. . .' (Morley, *Life of Cobden,* Vol.I (1881), p.249).

75 Reid, op.cit., p.463.

76 Ibid, p.442. He had been a member of Sir John Pakington's Committee on Education in 1864. Pakington was the chief Tory advocate of a scheme for national education. For their divisions during the government of 1866—8, see P. Smith, *Disraelian Conservatism and Social Reform* (1967), pp. 72—95, 104—112.

77 Letter of Gladstone to de Grey, 2 October 1869 (Ripon Papers).

78 See below, p.203.

79 See below, p.320.

80 Reid, op.cit., p.464. In an earlier speech, parts of which are quoted in ibid, p.461, he had stated in the spring of 1869 that he was anxious 'not to destroy anything in the existing system which was good, if they could avoid it'.

81 Ibid, pp.465—6.

82 *Report of the National Education Union Congress, 3 and 4 November 1969.*

83 Letter from Mundella to R. Leader, the Sheffield journalist, 7 November 1869 (Leader Collection).

84 See W. H. G. Armytage, *A. J. Mundella* (1951), p.74. It is interesting how many of the liveliest members of the League had, to use a favourite Victorian word, 'reservations'. (See, for example, Dale, op.cit., p.273). While joining, they reserved their individual freedom.

85 Armytage, op.cit., pp.75—6. Reid, op.cit., pp.454—5 quotes a friendly letter from Applegarth to Forster written earlier in 1869 after Forster's election as member of Parliament for Bradford had been confirmed after an official enquiry.

86 Reid, op.cit., p.472.

87 *The Times,* 1 December 1869, quoting the *Manchester Guardian* correspondent whose views were expressed in the *Guardian* a day earlier.

88 Quoted in Reid, op.cit., p.474.

89 Ibid. Forster was referring to articles in the *Observer,* the well-established Sunday newspaper.

90 Ibid, p.476. Glyn said tersely of the *Observer,* it 'has no inspiration now, and is doing no good.'

91 *The Times,* 12 January 1870; R. A. J. Walling (ed.), *The Diaries of John Bright* (1930), p.339.

92 *The Times,* 13 January 1870; *The Birmingham Daily Post,* 13 January 1870. He stated that 'half measures' would delay a proper solution 'perhaps for another decade, and until it would be too late for this country to overtake the progress which more enlightened nations would make in

the meantime'. Bright, who was present was immensely impressed with this speech. (Morris, op.cit., pp.82—3).

[93]The Times, 18 January 1870; The Bradford Observer, 13 January 1870.

[94]Quoted in Reid, op.cit., p.477.

[95]See below, p.208.

[96]See Maccoby, op.cit., Ch.VI; F. B. Smith, The Making of the Second Reform Bill (1966); M. Cowling, 1867, Disraeli, Gladstone and Revolution (1967).

[97]Quoted in J. W. Adamson, English Education, 1789—1902 (1965), p.317.

[98]Adams, loc.cit., pp.7—8.

[99]See below, p.207.

[100]For Cobden's frankness about Manchester, see a letter quoted in Reid, op.cit., p.43: 'My hopes of agitation are anchored upon Manchester. We can do more there with a sovereign than a united committee in London with two . . . . . Let all our funds and our energies be expended in working the question from Manchester as a centre.' The Monthly Paper of the League shows even in the provincial reports just how much initiative came from Birmingham. The point was recognised in Punch, always a friend to national education, when it firmly fixed the Birmingham label on the League:

    Let us hope with new meaning annexed,
    The Brummagem title to see
    Worn by those who solve questions long vexed
    And make things that have but seemed, to be.

(Quoted, with interesting and better written additional verses, in Marris, op.cit., p.79).

[101]See D. Southgate, The Passing of the Whigs (1962), pp.337ff.

[102]Letter from Dixon to Melly, 30 October 1869 (Melly Papers). Melly was the author of The Children of Liverpool and the Rival Schemes of National Education (1869). 'The objection to the scheme of the National Union,' he wrote tersely, 'is simple. Firstly, it does not go far enough, and when it moves at all, it moves in the wrong direction.'

[103]Forster had given some foretaste of his proposals in an interview in December 1869. (See The Times, 12 December 1869). The Liberal Daily News commented (12 December 1869) that 'the probability is that the Government measure may be a compromise'. Talk of postponement grew louder after this.

[104]See below, p.215. For a quite different verdict, see J. F. Bright, History of England, 1837—1880, Growth of Democracy (1893), p.466: 'Mr Forster exhibited in his management of the Bill an unwearied assiduity, an ability, and an earnestness, which excited universal admiration.'

[105]See his scathing article in the Fortnightly Review, Vol.XIV (1873), 'The Liberal Party and Its Leaders': 'many Liberals act as if the possession of political power were in itself the end, instead of the means by which it is to be secured.'

[106]W. White, The Inner Life of the House of Commons Vol.II (1897), p.165.

[107]Ibid, p.167.

[108]Garvin, op.cit., pp.107—8. Even then, according to Reid, op.cit., p.480, 'the press hailed the scheme with a chorus of approbation, and everybody seemed disposed to congratulate its author upon the manner in which he had solved a great problem'. Chamberlain had chosen that day to have inserted in The Times a full-page advertisement giving the names of subscribers to the League's funds. This was at that time 'an uncommon

stroke of publicity'. (Garvin, op.cit., p.113). He wrote to Dixon telling him frankly that 'strong exception was taken to the first paragraph in your speech . . . in which you are alleged to have said that the country would receive the bill with satisfaction'. (Letter in the Chamberlain Papers quoted by D. Fraser, *Joseph Chamberlain* (1966), p.8).

[109]*Hansard,* Third Series, Vol.CXCIX (187□), cols. 438—66.

[110]Ibid, col.478.

[111]Ibid, col.483.

[112]Ibid, col.480.

[113]Ibid, col.498. For the predominance of the 'social control' argument in relation to earlier educational history, see R. Johnson, 'Educational Policy and Social Control in Early Victorian England' in *Past and Present,* (1970).

[114]Armytage, op.cit. p.78 quotes an important letter from Mundella to Leader criticising the League the day after the deputation.

[115]Garvin, op.cit., p.113.

[116]See his article 'Mr Forster and Ireland' in *The Nineteenth Century,* Vol.XXIV (1888).

[117]Vincent, op.cit., p.224.

[118]Gladstone, loc.cit., p.453.

[119]Ibid.

[120]Gladstone was far kinder to Forster at the time of the debate on the third reading. See *Hansard,* Vol.CCIII, col. 746.

[121]Quoted in Reid, op.cit., pp.490—1. It was in reply to a friendly letter from Kingsley.

[122]G. M. Young, *Daylight and Champaign* (1937), pp.154—5.

[123]Dale, op.cit., p.276. See also R. A. Armstrong, *Henry William Crosskey* (1895).

[124]See A. Briggs, *History of Birmingham,* p.168.

[125]Armytage, op.cit., p.78.

[126]Letter to Dixon, 3 March 1870, quoted in Frazer, op.cit., p.8.

[127]Monthly Paper, March 1870.

[128]See below, p.217ff.

[129]*Hansard,* Vol.CXCIX, col.1925.

[130]Ibid, col. 1966.

[131]Ibid, col. 1955.

[132]Ibid, cols. 2027—8.

[133]*Hansard,* Vol.CC, col. 303.

[134]Ibid, col. 293.

[135]See below, p.223.

[136]Dale, op.cit., pp.276—9, gives a more graphic account than Adams. Dale thought that none of the government's amendments 'touch those provisions which provoked the strongest hostility'.

[137]A. Ramm (ed.), *The Political Correspondence of Mr. Gladstone and Lord Granville,* Vol.I (1952), p.99.

[138]Letter of 31 May in ibid, p.100.

[139]*Hansard,* Vol.CCII, col. 266.

[140]Ibid, col. 267.

[141]Ibid, col. 281. Gladstone had refused to accept an alternative radical amendment proposed by Harcourt.

[142]Later in the session a member was to complain that there had been three bills. 'They had had the original bill, the Easter edition and the Whitsuntide edition.' *(Hansard,* Vol.CCIII, col. 750).

[143]Letter of 14 May to Sir Stafford Northcote, quoted in W. P. Monypenny and G. E. Buckle, *The Life of Benjamin Disraeli,* Vol.II (1929), p.463.

[144]For the pattern in 1867, see A. Briggs, *Victorian People* (1954), Ch.10. On one motion in 1867 132 Liberals voted on one side and 121 on the other side, backed by 132 Conservatives. 133 Liberals and 132 Conservatives abstained.

[145]*Hansard,* Vol.CCIII, col.742.

[146]Ibid, col. 743.

[147]Ibid, col. 745.

[148]Ibid, col. 746.

[149]Ibid, col. 737.

[150]*Hansard,* Vol.CCII, cols. 498—9.

[151]Quoted by Joseph Chamberlain. See C. W. Boyd (ed.), *Mr. Chamberlain's Speeches,* Vol.I (1914), p.7.

[152]*Hansard,* Vol.CCIII, col. 756.

[153]See below, p.236.

[154]E. Midwinter, *Nineteenth Century Education* (1970), p.3.

[155]See below, p.235—6.

[156]Green was an active member of the Oxford Branch of the League. For a useful analysis of his views, see M. Richter, *The Politics of Conscience* (1964), pp.350ff. For Mundella on compulsion, see Armytage, op.cit., p.78.

[157]See below, p.236.

[158]Sturt, op.cit., p.307.

[159]See below, p.259. A 'secularist' amendment was defeated at this conference.

[160]Dale, op.cit., p.286. The lecture was subsequently published.

[161]Ibid.

[162]*Report of the Third Annual Meeting of the National Education League held in Birmingham on 17 and 18 October 1871 (1871),* p.29.

[163]Ibid, p.46.

[164]*Monthly Paper,* October 1871. See below, p.266.

[165]See below, p.277.

[166]See below, p.279. For the organised opposition stimulated by the change in tactics, see below, p.285.

[167]Quoted in Garvin, op.cit., p.132.

[168]*Ibid.*

[169]See below, p.291ff.

[170]See the interesting book by W. S. Fowler, *A Study in Radicalism and Dissent, The Life and Times of H. J. Wilson* (1961). There is a history of the Sheffield School Board by J. H. Bingham. *The Period of the Sheffield School Board, 1870—1903* (Sheffield, 1949). For the views of another militant, J. C. Cox of Belper, see Adams's quotation of one of his speeches, below, p.273.

[171]Armytage, op.cit., p.139. The election was complicated by the fact that Allott, a local nonconformist, had been rejected as candidate in favour of Chamberlain. Chamberlain did not come out of the election very well. He confessed that he did not like being beaten (Letter to W. H. Duignan 7 February 1874, in the Chamberlain Papers) and he urged Wilson to reply to *The Times* which had stated that his defeat was 'proof of the unpopularity of my Educational principles'. (Letter of 18 February 1874, printed in Fowler, op.cit., p.124).

[172]See below, p.255.

[173]See below, p.258.

[174]Quoted in Sturt, op.cit., p.310. The best source for the early history of the Boards, some of which have been the subject of theses and articles, is the *School Board Chronicle* which proclaimed itself 'the Hansard to the great educational Parliament of the United Kingdom'. The League itself

was forced to recognise the need for drawing a distinction between its polemical and educational work in the autumn of 1873. See below, p.298.

[175]See Sutherland, op.cit., p.35 for a remarkable 1875 memorandum by Sandon warning against rural Boards facilitating 'training in political organisation which the politicians of the Birmingham League desire and which will be mischievous to the state'.

[176]Clause 22 of the original bill which allowed School Boards to subsidise denominational schools had been dropped by Gladstone before the Committee stage. Perhaps this led nonconformists to overlook clause 25 which at that point was numbered clause 24.

[177]Dale, op.cit., p.282.

[178]See below, pp.256—7.

[179]The Economist, 12 March 1870.

[180]H. J. Hanham, Elections and Party Management: Politics in the Time of Gladstone and Disraeli (1959), p.119.

[181]B. Harrison, Drink and the Victorians (1971), p.290.

[182]'Education for the Ignorant cannot have the same meaning that belonged to Bread for the Starving.' (Quoted in Fraser, op.cit., p.12).

[183]Hanham, op.cit., p.120.

[184]Yet he does make the telling admission en passant that 'the agitation against the Act proceeded from citizens rather than from the parents of scholars'. (See below, p.281). For the resistance of working-class families to education see H. Pelling, Popular Politics and Society in Late-Victorian Britain (1968), pp.1—19.

[185]Quoted in Fraser, op.cit., p.12. The letter was dated 1 January 1872.

[186]The remark was made in a speech at a protest meeting held by the League and the Nonconformist Committee in the Westminster Palace Hotel on 1 July 1873.

[187]J. Bright, Diaries, p.359. For the reactions of Adams, see below, p.296.

[188]H. G. Wells thought of the Act as 'an act to educate the lower classes for employment on lower class lines and with specially trained inferior teachers' (Experiment in Autobiography (1943), p.93) while R. H. Tawney stated that 'the elementary schools of 1870 were intended in the main to produce an orderly, civil, obedient population with sufficient education to understand a command' (Education, the Socialist Policy (1924), p.22). Lovett believed that after the passing of the Act 'the Working Classes should bestir themselves, and resolve to have vote and voice in determining how their children should be educated'. (op.cit., pp.397—8).

[189]Quoted in Garvin, op.cit., p.146.

[190]See below, p.287.

[191]See below, p.298.

[192]See below, ibid.

[193]See below, p.299.

[194]See below, p.300.

[195]See below, ibid.

[196]S. and B. Webb, The History of Trade Unionism (1902), p.270. Some nonconformists, like Spurgeon, thought that the continuing attack on Forster was uncharitable. See Freeman, 5 March 1875.

[197]T. Lloyd, The General Election of 1880 (1968), p.6.

[198]See below, p.301. A League leaflet published after the election recalled the election of 1841. If the Anti-Corn Law League did not despair and the Reform League did not despair, why should we?' See also the Monthly Paper, March 1874: 'we have now the advantage of being able to contend for truly liberal principles without being accused of weakening and dividing the Liberal Party'.

[199]See below, p.312. The Monthly Paper, April 1875, was genuinely

impressed. 'The Education Department has astonished the country by framing a code in the interests of education . . . a step more bold and decisive than any which the Department under Mr. Forster ventured to take.'

200See below, p.327. For evidence of a surviving undertow of 'unfashionable' conservative opposition to educational advance, see the *Guardian,* 16 June 1875.

201See below, p.340. Chamberlain himself made an excellent speech on 'Six Years of Educational Work in Birmingham' on 2 November 1896 which was reported in the local newspapers.

202See below, p.329.

203See below, p.329.

204See below, pp.332—3.

205See below, ibid.

206See below, p.337.

207See below, p.341. For the continuing denominational conflict, see M. Cruickshank, *Church and State in English Education from 1870 to the Present Day* (1963).

208Quoted in Armytage, op.cit., p.199.

209It had stood at £1.62 million in 1870. See B. R. Mitchell, *Abstract of British Historical Statistics* (1962), p.397. In 1880 expenditure on the Army amounted to £15 million and on the Navy to £10.2 million. Total gross expenditure was £81.5 million.

210See, for example, Armytage, op.cit. p.235.

211Ibid, p.229. Mundella had written on 21 January 1885 (ibid, p.226). 'While Chamberlain is urging me to go in for free schools, the Treasury is demanding a reduction of my estimates.'

212He keenly supported the new Education Code of 1890. He was also strongly in favour of free education. Yet he supported aid to voluntary schools in 1896. (See Marris, op.cit., pp.288—90). See also an interesting letter to Dale on 1 May 1891, quoted in Fraser, op.cit., pp.144—5.

213Letter of 23 August 1873 quoted in ibid, p.191. He had become Mayor of Birmingham in 1873 and was largely concerned during the next few years with the implementation of the 'civic gospel'. His first speech in the House of Commons was on Lord Sandon's Education Bill. (See Marris, op.cit., pp.143—4.)

214See F. H. Herrick, 'The Origins of the National Liberal Federation' in the *Journal of Modern History,* Vol.XVII (1945); Hanham, op.cit., esp. Ch.7; Briggs, *History of Birmingham,* esp.Ch.6.

215See Hanham, op.cit.; H. Pelling, *America and the British Left* (1956), Ch.3.

216*Proceedings Attending the Formation of the National Federation of Liberal Associations* (1877), p.7. The chief officers had all been associated with the League, though Dixon was noticeably conspicuous by his absence. Chamberlain was President, Harris Chairman of the General Committee, Collings Honorary Secretary and J. S. Wright Treasurer. The other noticeable change was that Schnadhorst and not Adams was the Secretary.

217Quoted in Hanham, op.cit., p.141.

218It is interesting to read the comments on Gladstone's visit in *The Life of William Ewart Gladstone* (1899) written by Forster's biographer Sir Wemyss Reid, pp.622—3. Gladstone made two speeches in Birmingham— one on Bulgarian atrocities and the other on Federation. Gladstone defended the new form of organisation 'on the ground that it carried out the Liberal principle that each member of the Liberal party should feel himself to possess a personal share in directing the policy of the party'.

219See T. Wemyss Reid, *Life of Forster* (1895 edn.), pp.246ff. The

story is well told day by day in the pages of the Liberal *Bradford Observer*.
[220]*The Fortnightly Review,* Vol.XIV (1873), pp.143–62, 303–325, 411–433.
[221]J. Chamberlain, 'The Liberal Party and its Leaders' in ibid, p.293.
[222]See E. M. Everett, *The Party of Humanity: The Fortnightly Review and its Contributors* (1939).
[223]H. S. R. Elliot (ed.), *The Letters of John Stuart Mill,* Vol.II (1910), p.95.
[224]J. Morley, *Recollections* (1917), Vol.I, p.148.
[225]See the excellent chapter in D. A. Hamer, *John Morley, Liberal Intellectual in Politics* (1968), 'Morley and Chamberlain', pp.112–129.
[226]Letter to Chamberlain, 6 August 1873 in ibid, p.116.
[227]Ibid, p.96.
[228]See below, p.108.
[229]Letter to Chamberlain, quoted in Hamer, op.cit., p.105.
[230]See below, pp.127–8.
[231]J. Morley, *Modern Characteristics,* (1865), p.204.
[232]J. Morley, 'The Political Prelude' in the *Fortnightly Review,* Vol.IV, New Series (1868), pp.103–114.
[233]See below, p.71.
[234]Hamer, op.cit., p.90.
[235]See the excellent article on 'Education' by Sir Joshua Fitch in the Tenth Edition of the *Encyclopaedia Britannica,* Vol.XXVII (1902), pp.655–77.
[236]See Sturt, op.cit., p.67, p.380.
[237]See J. Rex, *Key Problems of Sociological Theory* (1961), pp.122ff.
[238]See below, p.104.ff.
[239]See below, p.104.
[240]See below, p.113.
[241]See below, p.148.
[242]See below, p.147.
[243]J. Morley, *Miscellanies,* Vol.III (1886), p.27.
[244]See O. Banks, *Parity and Prestige in English Secondary Education* (1955) and E. Eaglesham, *From School Board to Local Authority* (1956).
[245]For educational policy during the Wars see A. Marwick, *Britain in the Century of Total War* (1968), pp.65–6, 317–19.
[246]R. A. Butler, *The Art of the Possible* (1971), p.100.
[247]Quoted in Hamer, op.cit., p.94. He wrote to his friend Harrison a week later that 'Englishmen are not touched by big programmes . . . They like to go step by step' (ibid, p.94).
[248]J. Morley, *On Compromise,* pp.97–8: Letter to Chamberlain on the 'caucus', 20 October 1878, quoted in Hamer, op.cit., p.100.
[249]Quoted in ibid, p.111.
[250]Letter to Chamberlain, 12 November 1875 in ibid, p.111.
[251]See below, p.7.
[252]See below, p.1.
[253]J. Morley, *On Compromise,* (1874) p.113.
[254]See below, p.63.
[255]See below, p.66.
[256]See below, p.15.
[257]See J. H. Morgan, *John, Viscount Morley* (1924), p.88.
[258]Ibid, p.94. Cf. J. Morley, *Life of Gladstone* (1903), Book 6, Ch.3.
[259]See below, p.2.
[260]See below, p.156.
[261]See below, pp.165–6.
[262]See below, pp.34ff.
[263]See below, p.323.

HISTORY OF
THE ELEMENTARY SCHOOL
CONTEST IN ENGLAND.

BY

FRANCIS ADAMS,

AUTHOR OF

"THE FREE SCHOOL SYSTEM OF THE UNITED STATES."

LONDON :

CHAPMAN AND HALL, LIMITED,

11, HENRIETTA STREET, COVENT GARDEN, W.C.

—

1882.

INTRODUCTION.

A preliminary word as to the scope of this book may save misconception. It does not profess to be a history of education in any comprehensive sense. With the philosophy of education it has nothing to do. The most that has been attempted is to present an outline of the struggle, as far as it has gone, to obtain a legal recognition of the duty of the State to give elementary instruction to its children.

Such a sketch necessarily fails to do justice to many who have taken part in the labour. From the nature of the materials to work upon, the Parliamentary contest occupies the most prominent place in the record. Yet the fight has not been always the thickest or hardest in Parliament. The work of creating and leading opinion in the country has been of even greater importance, but it has generally been performed by men of comparatively obscure position, the account of whose efforts is often inaccessible, or has perished. There is another class to whom it may seem scant justice is done—those, who following the duty lying nearest to them, have spent their energies and their means in the practical extension of education around them. When the complete history of education is written it may be expected to comprise some account of their noble efforts, but that is not within the design of these pages.

The Scotch and Irish systems, and such ancillary measures as the Factory and Workshop Laws, Reformatory, Industrial, and Vagrant Schools, are touched only incidentally, and as they bear on the main lines of the story.

It is proper I should also add, that although the views expressed may be presumed to be in general harmony with those of the members of the League, no one but myself is responsible for any statement, whether of fact or opinion, contained in the book.

FRANCIS ADAMS.

YARDLEY, BIRMINGHAM,
January, 1882.

CONTENTS.

CHAPTER I.

PERIOD.—PREVIOUS TO 1800.

CHAPTER II.

CHAPTER III.

CHAPTER IV.

CHAPTER V.

CHAPTER VI.

PERIOD.—FROM THE PASSING OF THE EDUCATION ACT, 1870,
TO THE ADOPTION BY THE LEAGUE OF THE SECULAR
PLATFORM, 1872.

CHAPTER IX.

CONCLUSION.

xii.

APPENDIX.

CHAPTER I.

PERIOD.—PREVIOUS TO 1800.

BEFORE attempting any description of the struggle for National Education, which has been confined almost wholly within the present century, it will be well to state what previous efforts were made by Society or by the Government to provide instruction for the children of the poor, or to give them legislative protection.

In examining the education controversies of the last eighty years, frequent references will be found to ancient systems existing in England, but even with the aid of an extensive knowledge of English History, one may be at a loss to know what is meant.

When Mr. Froude writes of the "Old English" education, he is careful to explain that he means the apprentice system, but others have not taken the same pains to make themselves intelligible. Mrs. Trimmer, who, towards the end of the last and in the beginning of the present century, wrote numberless educational pamphlets, essays, and lesson books for children, was enthusiastic for the ancient system founded by "our pious forefathers," and it is only by much diligence that the reader finds she referred to the Act of Uniformity, and the Canons of the Church. Sir James Kay Shuttleworth, who has been regarded as a conclusive authority on the subject, speaks of "the School" as having been "transferred by the Reformation from the Priesthood to the Congregation;" ([1]) which leads to the supposition that there was at that period something approaching to a system, and capable of being transferred. This, however, is true only in a limited sense.

[1] Preface to "Public Education."

1

Of the apprentice system, as it existed in the time of Henry VIII., Mr. Froude speaks with high approval, and he appears to look with some regret on its decay. ([1]) The best that can be said is, that it was better than nothing ; and how well-soever it may have answered the wants of an earlier period, it gradually became unsuited to the growing necessities of the country. It neither was nor pretended to be a system of education, as we use the expression in these days ; and even as a system of industrial training, it was, outside London, where the apprentices very soon became organised and powerful, cruel in its application, irregular and barbarous in its method, and strongly partook of the character of slavery, which was hardly extinct when the early apprenticeship laws were made.

Industrial education was of very early date, beginning in the tenth century in the time of Dunstan, Archbishop of Canterbury, who directed the priests to instruct youth in trades. ([2]) The chief Apprentice Acts however date from the time of Henry VIII. Acts dealing with the system had been framed previously, some of which encouraged it, while others placed it under restrictions.

Very early in history there were guilds of traders, members of religious orders, having powers which gradually increased, for the regulation of industry, and after the conquest these guilds became very powerful. Apprenticeship was one of their regulations, and the condition of admittance to trade. ([3])

With great cunning Edward III. had, about 1337, enticed a large number of Dutch apprentices to England, and scattered them about the country to teach the people the manufacture of cloth. ([4]) This led to the extension and

---

[1] English History, 1, 44-76, and Short Studies, 263.
[2] Hook's Lives of Archbishops, 1, 419.
[3] Spencer's Descriptive Sociology, 4.   [4] Fuller's Church History, 2, 185.

general adoption of the system, and was also the beginning of the cloth manufacture in England.

It was not, however, until the period of the Reformation that laws were passed making apprenticeship necessary. The injunctions of Henry VIII. to the clergy, commanded them to exhort the people to bring up all children to some trade or way of living. (¹) The pulpit, however, does not seem to have been effectual for the purpose, and therefore at a later period, justices of the peace, constables, and other authorities, were empowered to take up children between the ages of five and thirteen, who were found begging or idle, and appoint them to masters of husbandry or other crafts. (²)

The Act was aimed at the prevailing vices of the times : idleness and vagabondage, evils which had been very prevalent before the dissolution of the monasteries, but which were suddenly and largely increased by that event. Some idea of the state of the country in this " merry " age may be gathered from the fact that in Henry VIII.'s reign 72,000 people were executed for robbery and theft. (³) The policy was continued and extended by Edward VI. Children " idly wandering about " might be taken by any person before a justice of the peace and straightway apprenticed, and they might even be removed from their parents. A child who ran away from his master might be recaptured and punished in chains, and " used in all points as a slave," and masters were empowered to sell and bequeath the services of such " slave children." (⁴) In certain cases they became slaves for life. It was thus that the Ministers of Edward VI. undertook to give effect to his pious wish, that children when they came to man's estate might not " loiter " and " neglect," but " think their travail sweet and honest." (⁵) These

¹ Burnet's History of the Reformation, 1, part 1, 410. ² 27 Henry VIII., c. 5.
³ Nicholls' History of the Poor Law, 1, 130.
⁴ 1 Edward VI., chapter 3. ⁵ Burnet's Reformation, 2, part 2, 104.

enactments more than justify Mr. Senior's opinion that the earlier poor laws were " an attempt substantially to restore the expiring system of slavery." (¹)

By two statutes of Elizabeth the system was further rivetted upon the country. Churchwardens and overseers had authority, with the assent of justices, to bind all children, whose parents were not able to maintain them, " where they should see convenient."

Persons were compelled by law to receive apprentices, and various Statutes of Labourers restricted the exercise of any manual labour to persons who had been apprenticed for seven years. (²) This latter provision, notwithstanding the attacks of Adam Smith and other political economists, continued in force down to 1814; and the compulsory reception of apprentices was not finally abolished until the reign of the present Queen. Whatsoever individual benefit may have been derived from the apprentice laws, which, under favourable conditions, must have been great, there is every reason to believe that they were generally made the instruments of rapacity and cruelty. There was no obligation upon the masters to give any instruction in letters to their apprentices, and though they formally undertook to teach them their business, they gave generally only as much technical training as enabled them to get from them the fullest amount of labour. The original object and principle of the system was industrial education, but its chief and practical effect soon became the restriction of labour.

It was not until the present century that the health and education of children were taken in any degree under the care of the Government. About 1802, the first Sir Robert Peel, father of the Prime Minister, passed a bill restricting the hours of labour for apprentices in cotton and woollen

¹ *Edinburgh Review*, No. 149, p. 2.
² 5 Elizabeth, cap. 4. 39 Elizabeth and 43 Elizabeth, cap. 2.

mills, and providing that during the first four years of service, instruction in reading, writing, and arithmetic should be given at the expense of the master, in some part of each working day. ([1]) The act, however, was easily evaded. The letter could be fulfilled by nominal performance, while in practice it was altogether powerless and ineffective. Some small measure of protection was subsequently given to young children by an Act passed in 1819, prohibiting their employment in factories under nine years of age. ([2])

In 1833, the exertions of Lord Ashley, the present Earl of Shaftesbury, secured a further reform, and the daily labour of children under thirteen was restricted to eight hours, and that of older children to twelve hours per day. ([3]) These concessions were regarded, and in the then existing circumstances, actually were of great importance and value. ([4])

The debates on the early factory bills of this century will satisfy any one how urgently a strong legislative and administrative control was needed. The growth of all branches of manufacturing industry had created a great demand for cheap labour, and as children's labour was the cheapest to be had, it was eagerly sought after. Almost as soon as they could walk, the little children were swept into cotton manufactories. Waggon loads of children were taken from the London streets and apprenticed to manufacturers in Lancashire. In defiance or in evasion of the law, they often began to work at the age of five or six, and the ordinary hours of labour were twelve hours per day, often protracted to fifteen. Such laws as existed failed to guard their health, to provide for their education, to preserve their morals, or to protect their persons from abominable cruelties. Sir Samuel Romilly wrote of them, "the poor children have not a human being in the world to whom they can look up for redress." Their

[1] Duke of Newcastle's Commission, Report, 202. [2] Ibid, 202. [3] 3 and 4, Wm. IV. c. 103. [4] Walpole's History of England, 3, 208.

sufferings were often unendurable. For girls, apprenticeship was the beginning of a life of shame, and for boys, one of misery and vice. ([1]) Such is the history in outline of the apprentice system. Various circumstances combined to break it down altogether. The Act of Geo. III. repealing the restrictions on labour ([2]) hastened its destruction; and the introduction of machinery, and the revolution in many departments of industry, completed the work.

That the system had been deeply rooted in a past society is proved by the fact, that charities of the value of £50,000 per annum had been left for providing apprentice premiums, ranging in amount generally from £5 to £25. ([3]) The charities were of themselves an evil, and the cause of much fraud and malversation. All that was good in the system of apprenticeship is still capable of preservation under a judicious scheme of technical education, and this it seems would be the most legitimate purpose to which the funds, which are still available, could be applied.

We owe to the Roman Catholic Church the first planting of Education in England, as well as in Scotland, ([4]) and that intimate connection of the subject with religion, which preserved in dark ages the desire for knowledge. But while this alliance has sometimes advanced education, it has often proved one of the most effective agencies for preventing its spread amongst the masses; and is wholly responsible for the acrimonious controversies of modern times. Theodore, Archbishop of Canterbury in 680, laid the foundation, by turning St. Augustine's monastery into a school of learning. Dean Hook tells us that Theodore "found the English people eager to be instructed and appetent of knowledge" and that he converted all the larger and better monasteries into schools,

---

[1] Walpole's History, 1, 187; 3, 200.   [2] 54, Geo. III., c. 94.
[3] Report of Newcastle Commission, p. 531.
[4] Lecky's Eighteenth Century, 2, 42.

in which the laity as well as the clergy imbibed a respect, and sometimes a love for literature. (¹) In them ancient manuscripts were transcribed, and the foundation of libraries was laid. The oldest grammar school now extant—that of Carlisle, dates from about the period referred to. The present foundation was erected by William Rufus towards the close of the eleventh century, but tradition says that it was built on the ruins of an earlier school, established by St. Cuthbert in 686, but destroyed in 800. (²)

The first English tax was a tax for education, and was raised in the eighth century to support a Saxon school at Rome. (³)

The vicissitudes of education in those early days were great. There was the same tendency in the monasteries, then as in later years, to relapse into idleness and dissipation. The monks had also frequently to fight for existence, and all traces of gentle culture were lost in the necessity for military training. Two centuries after the time of Theodore, when Alfred was king, and Plegmund was Archbishop of Canterbury, the country had fallen into a condition of great ignorance. There was, however, another revival. Alfred was anxious that all English youth of position should be put to learning until they could read English writing, (⁴) and he even attempted to found something like a system, by passing a law that all freeholders who possessed two hides of land should give their sons a liberal education. (⁵) These were schools for the nobility. During the same period we learn of a famous school at York. (⁶)

A century later the work was carried on by Dunstan. The monks again were the teachers of the people, in manual

---

¹ Hook's Lives of Archbishops, 1, 163.
² Schools Enquiry Commission, 37 app.
³ Spencer's Descriptive Sociology, table 2.
⁴ Hook's Lives, 1, 337.   ⁵ Carlisle's Grammar Schools, 1, xiii.
⁶ Spencer's Descriptive Sociology, table 2.

arts as well as in learning, and the Canons of Dunstan ordered all priests diligently to instruct youth, and dispose them to trades, that they might have a support to the Church. ([1])

The ecclesiastics were skilful workers in metals. Every priest was a handicraftsman. Attached to every monastery were carpenters, smiths, shoe makers, millers, bakers, and farm servants, and they provided the industrial education of the period. ([2])

From the monasteries sprang the humanising and civilising influences of the age. In the Anglo-Norman era they were the popular institutions of the country, as well as the schools in which ecclesiastics and statesmen were trained. At this period the school room was open to all who chose to profit by it, though these were probably few in number. ([3])

After the Conquest, Cathedral schools were established where "fair and beautiful writing" was taught, and many persons of rank and fortune were educated. ([4]) Of those which remain Hereford is the oldest. It was probably founded soon after the Conquest. ([5]) Many Jewish schools were also set up, which were open to Christian children.

In the time of Roger Bacon, and after the granting of the great Charter, we are told that schools were erected in every city, town, burgh, and castle. ([6]) So that historians have concluded that the ignorance of the laity was owing to taste rather than to the want of opportunity.

Mr. Herbert Spencer holds the opinion that in the 11th and 12th centuries, besides monastic schools, there were village elementary schools, and some city schools and academies for higher culture. In 1179 the Council of Lateran decreed a school in every cathedral, with head

---

[1] Hook's Lives, 1, 419.

[2] Spencer's Descriptive Sociology, table 2.   [3] Hook's Lives, 2, 21.

[4] Carlisle's Grammar School, 1, 19.   [5] Schools Enquiry Commission, 37, App.

[6] Carlisle's Grammar Schools, xxi.

masters having authority over all subordinate teachers in the house. About the same period lay teachers were first heard of. The Universities of Oxford and Cambridge were founded about 1200. The only literature of the common people, at this time, were the unwritten songs. (¹) Of the pre-reformation schools, William of Wykeham's foundation, at Winchester, is one of the most famous. This was established about the year 1373 or 1387, and from this time, Dean Hook tells us, the public mind became habituated to the idea of the ultimate confiscation of monastic property for the purpose of establishing schools and colleges. (²)

The respect and devotion of the people for the monasteries began to decline as early as the 12th century. The opportunities they offered for instruction were little used, and the 15th century found the people in the grossest possible ignorance. Parishes were neglected, the Universities were deserted, and no rewards were held out to learning. (³) This period, however, contemporaneous with the introduction of the printing press, the reformation of the Universities, and the revival of learning throughout Europe, was the dawn of a new era in education, and within thirty years before the Reformation, more Grammar schools were erected and endowed in England than had been established in the three hundred years preceding. (⁴)

There is no complete record of the provision for Education prior to the Reformation. Much that passes for history, has no other basis than tradition. There are authorities which go to show that there were schools connected with every monastery and convent. In his life of Bishop Ken, Mr. Bowles says that before the Reformation, there was a school in every church over the porch. (⁵) As some estimates

¹ Spencer's Descriptive Sociology, table 3.
² Hook's Lives, N.S., 2, 3.   ³ Hook's Lives, 5, 291.
⁴ Tanner's Notitia Monastica, xx, iv.   ⁵ Bowles' Life of Ken, 2, 98.

place the number of churches as high as 50,000 ([1]) this would account for an ample provision for the whole population. These estimates may however be dismissed as unreliable and unsustained by proof. Doubtless many foundations were lost in the wreck and waste of the Reformation. Only thirty-five Grammar schools, established prior to the time of Henry VIII. have been inherited by this generation. ([2]) Of existing endowments for primary schools, only three or four are known to have been founded before the Reformation, though there are about two hundred, of the foundation of which the dates are unknown, and which are doubtless the relics of a long past age. There are also several hundreds ([3]) of small unattached educational charities of unknown origin, some of which probably, protected by their insignificance, escaped from the fingers of Henry and his courtiers, and so have come down to our own day; but the conclusion of the Schools Enquiry Commission, that it was not till after the Reformation that numerous endowments were left for primary education alone, is probably the correct one. ([4]) The general conclusion derived from the authorities is, that the schools connected with the monasteries were intended chiefly as seminaries for the clergy. "They bred their novices to letters, and to this end every great monastery had a peculiar college in each of the universities," and even to the time of their demolition "they maintained a great number of children at school, for the service of the Church." ([5]) Their primary purpose was to recruit the ranks of the clergy. It was the presumption in law and fact that if a man could read he was an ecclesiastic, and was entitled to his "benefit of clergy." In the reign of Henry VII.

---

[1] Dodd's Church History, 1, 420.

[2] Schools Enquiry Commission Report, 37 App.

[3] See Analytical Digest of Charity Commissioners Report, 1842.

[4] Schools Enquiry Commission Report, 119.

[5] Dodd's Church History, 1, 278.

the law regulating benefit of clergy was amended, and from that time recognised a distinction between offences rather than persons, and admitted the title of some laymen to its advantages. But reading as a qualification for its benefits was not abolished till 1706. ([1])

This provision of the law which at one period entitled a criminal to be tried in an ecclesiastical court, and which down to the present century secured a mitigated penalty, had at one time given an impulse to learning. ([2]) In later times it became a mere fiction and was retained only to lighten the severity of a terrible criminal code. In its origin it was intended for the protection of the clergy alone, and is conclusive as to the main object and use of the monastic schools. It may, however, be readily granted that many of the laity were taught in the monasteries, and that numbers of children received instruction there who would otherwise have gone without it altogether. In the darkest period of our history, the monasteries were the nurseries of education. Many of their highest dignitaries were its chief promoters and protectors, and were the founders of libraries. It was in the Abbey at Westminster that Caxton on his return to England first used his printing press, ([3]) and he received his earliest encouragement from priests of the Roman Church. This is the view taken by Roman Catholics, ([4]) and it is in the main supported by impartial examination. ([5])

When we come to test the results of this net-work of educational establishments, they are found to be greatly disappointing, and we wonder how such vast means were employed to so little good purpose. At the period of the Reformation, the rank and file of the country clergy who had received their education at the monasteries could do

<hr />

[1] Spencer's Descriptive Sociology, Table 6, p. 9. [2] Hook's Lives, 3, 39.
[3] Tanner's Notitia Monastica, xxvi. [4] Dodd's Church History, 1, 276.
[5] Strype's Memorials, 1, 532.

little more than read. (^{1}) Herein lay one of the difficulties of the Reformation. The ignorance of many of the clergy was so great that they could not read the new offices. In the performance of their duties they reverted to memory, and preferred to say the old prayers which they knew by heart. (^{2}) The poorer classes, except those destined for minor clerical offices, had never caught the infection of knowledge, or even got within the outer circle of its influence. In a disputation at Westminster during Elizabeth's reign, " whether it was against the Word of God to use a tongue unknown to the people," the Dean of St. Paul's, who argued on behalf of a section of the Bishops, said, " The people of England do not understand their own tongue better than Eunuchus did the Hebrew." (^{3}) The people knew nothing of religion beyond its outward forms and pageantry. (^{4}) Even the richer classes were almost wholly without elementary instruction. Henry VII. was illiterate. At the time of Henry VIII.'s accession, if Princes could read and write, more was not expected of them. (^{5}) Latimer's sermons are sufficient to satisfy us how little the teaching of the monasteries had touched the higher classes, who were unfitted for any offices of state; (^{6}) while the poor had been lost sight of altogether. In the latter days of the monasteries they had almost given up the pretence of teaching. Burnet affirms that while they had in their hands the chief encouragements of learning, they did nothing for it, but decried and disparaged it, saying it would bring in heresy and a great deal of mischief. (^{7}) Mr. Froude agrees that the people were taught only what they could teach themselves. (^{8}) Nothing is more manifest, than that the desire for knowledge and the impetus given to learning for which the sixteenth

1 Burnet's Reformation, 2, part 1, 375.   2 Hook's Lives, N.S. 4, 125.
3 Burnet's Reformation, 2, part 2, 471.   4 Ibid. 2, part 1.
5 Ibid. 1, part 1, 17.   6 The Ploughers, 28.
7 Burnet's Reformation, 1, part 1, 39.   8 History of England, 1, 58.

century was remarkable, proceeded not from the teaching of the monasteries, but from the group of English scholars who derived their inspiration from the Greek teachers who had found in Florence a refuge from the persecutions of Constantinople. Amongst them the most remarkable were Colet, Dean of St. Paul's and founder of St. Paul's School, Lilly, the author of the grammar, Warham, Archbishop of Canterbury, Latimer, Sir Thomas More, Grocyn, the first English teacher of Greek, and Erasmus. ([1])

Before Henry's rule had become a settled law of tyranny and spoliation, the beginning of the Reformation was full of promise for the spread of knowledge. Sir Thomas More had dreamed of an ideal state in which all in their childhood were instructed in learning.([2]) Erasmus yearned for the time when all should be able to read the Scriptures for themselves. " I long for the day," he said, " when the husbandman shall sing portions of them to himself as he follows the plough, when the weaver shall hum them to the tune of his shuttle, when the traveller shall while away with their stories the weariness of his journey." ([3]) Henry VIII. was himself a fair scholar, and took the new learning under his own especial patronage. Cranmer had projected liberal designs for ecclesiastical and civil education. ([4]) Latimer was never weary of preaching the duty of teaching the young. " They that do somewhat for the furtherance of learning, for maintaining of schools and scholars, they sanctify God's holy name." ([5])

[1] Green's Short History, 297, and Hook's Lives, 1, N.S. 267.

[2] Utopia, Arber's reprint, 2, 86, and Green, 312.

[3] Green's History, p. 308.

[4] Dean Hook discredits the intentions assigned to Cranmer (Lives of Archbishops, N.S., 2, 30), but Strype, Burnet, and older writers are unanimous on the other side, and his speeches prove that he was in favour of educating the children of the poor. That he shared in the spoils of the monasteries is true. That was the gross temptation and spirit of his time.

[5] Latimer's Sermons, Parker Society, 1, 349.

The means were at hand for the establishment of a vast and comprehensive system in its various grades. A comparatively small portion of the wealth of the dispossessed monasteries would have sufficed for the purpose, and the mind of the nation had been prepared for such an application of the funds. The clergy were docile and obedient and anxious to save what they could, while such a disposition would have preserved for their support, no inconsiderable share of the spoils. Even as it was, no obstinate opposition was offered to the changes introduced by Henry. In little more than twenty years, says Burnet, there were four great changes made in religion, and in all these the mainbody of the nation turned with the stream." [1]

The people, except when driven by want, and goaded by oppression, were law abiding and peaceable. Nor was there such a jealousy between the clergy and laity as to prevent co-operation in the work of education. Colet committed his great foundation at St. Paul's to the management of a lay corporation, having found "many laymen as conscientious as clergymen in discharging their trust in this kind." [2] Cranmer, in discussing with Henry the re-establishment of Christ Church at Canterbury, had advocated the separation of the lectureships upon divinity and humanity. [3] Sir James Kay Shuttleworth goes the length of affirming that the schools at the Reformation "were not confided to the clergy, or subjected to the visitation of the bishop." [4] This, however, as will be seen is a mistake. There was no such transference of the control of education from the priesthood to the congregation as he contends for, either in theory or in practice;

---

[1] Burnet's Reformation, 2, part 1, preface xx.
[2] Fuller's Church History, 3, 19.   [3] Burnet's Reformation, 3, part 3, 209.
    [4] Public Education, 13, 242. It is a mere refinement to say that the power of visitation was not given by Statute or by common law. The accuracy of this statement may be doubted, but, at any rate, the schools were by the *de facto* law, placed under the control of the clergy.

but considering the spirit of the time, a great opportunity was lost of laying a broad foundation for schools, in which clergy and laity might have worked together to promote instruction, and carry out the principles of the Reformation.

There is little doubt that it was comprehended within the first design of the Reformation, to make substantial provision for education. It was one of the serious charges against the monasteries that their duties in this respect had been neglected, and the instructions for the first visitation, provided that enquiries should be made under this head. ([1]) The same reasons for their suppression was given after-wards when experience had proved it to be a mere pretence. The preamble to the bill for the dissolution of the greater monasteries alleged as its object, "that these houses might be converted to better uses; God's word set forth, children brought up in learning" ([2]) and so forth. The King assured the people that there should be no detriment to piety or learning. ([3]) Out of this second conversion of church property, it was proposed to found eighteen bishoprics, and with them Cranmer designed to connect ecclesiastical and civil colleges, and grammar schools. ([4])

He had hoped further to found Grammar schools in every shire in England "where children might have been brought up to learning freely, without great cost to their friends and kinsfolk." ([5]) But the scheme had to run the gauntlet of many perils, and it ended in the creation of six bishoprics, in which the educational features held a very subordinate place. Burnet says the popish party turned the King's foundation another way. ([6]) The more reasonable explanation is that

---

[1] Burnet's Reformation, 1, part 2, 212.
[2] Burnet's Reformation, 1, part 1, 475.   [3] Dodd's Church History, 1, 287.
[4] Shuttleworth's Public Education, 32.
[5] Cranmer's Works, Parker Society, 2, 16.
[6] Burnet's Reformation, 2, part 1, 546.

the designs, if they were ever serious on the King's part, were frustrated by the greed, and rapacious spirit of the time. All was scramble, wreck, and confusion. The cry of those in possession was *sauve qui peut*—the aim of others, to get all they could. The Commissioners enriched themselves, and the ancestors of more than one of the rich families of later times, laid the foundation of their fortunes in this reign. They gave promises to the clergy, and bribes to Cromwell and the country gentry to conceal their depredations. ([1]) The liberality of the King's nature, especially in dealing with the goods of others, was not consistent with any well-ordered scheme of re-construction, civil or ecclesiastical. "Small merits of courtiers met with a prodigious recompense for their services ; not only the cooks, but the meanest turn-broach in the King's kitchen did lick his fingers," ([2]) and such gifts as were made for education, often shrank in their passage through the hands of a covetous steward. ([3]) The Universities were robbed of exhibitions and pensions, ([4]) and every ecclesiastical foundation was impoverished. The seizure of first the lesser, then the greater monasteries, and lastly the collegiate churches, hospitals, and chauntries, has been described as the three great mouthfuls made by Henry. He did not however live to swallow them all. He reduced into possession only the lesser and greater monasteries. Out of the spoils of these, this munificent patron of letters and learning, as he loved to be considered, founded six cathedrals and ten grammar schools, ([5]) during a reign which extended over thirty-five years ; which began with an immense treasure bequeathed by his father, and which was undisturbed by foreign wars or domestic broils. There were also during his

[1] Burnet's Reformation, 1, part 1, 39.
[2] Fuller's Church History, 3, 438.   [3] Ibid 3, 444.
[4] Carlisle's Grammar Schools, xxv.
[5] Schools Enquiry Commission, 39 App.

reign some fifty other grammar schools endowed by private individuals. Of the foundations for primary education, the dates of which are fixed, not more than six are known to be the fruit of this period, though it is fair to assume that some of those of which the origin is lost in obscurity, may have had their beginning in this reign.

The short and quiet reign of Edward VI. was more honorably distinguished. In six years fifty grammar schools were established, of which the King founded twenty-seven. Roman Catholic historians comment, with bitter irony on the fact, that they were all that survived the spoliation of so many chauntries and collegiate churches. Between two and three thousand of these institutions fell to the hands of Edward's Ministers. The bill, which authorised their seizure and settlement on the Crown, declared that they should be employed for good and godly uses, the maintenance of grammar schools, the augmentation of the universities, the provision of additional curates, and the assistance of the poor and needy. ([1]) Only a small portion of this great wealth escaped through the hands of the Commissioners, and while many schools were destroyed and shut up, as Fuller says, " only for a smack of Popery," ([2]) very few were erected in their places. The bulk of the Church property was squandered amongst the parasites of the Court. ([3]) Even Burnet who is usually very tender of the reputation of the Reformers, cannot forbear to complain of the gross and insatiable scrambling after the goods of the Church, ([4]) which was the marked feature of the age, and was encouraged by the King's youth and weakness. Occasionally a bold preacher such as Lever, the master of St. John's, Cambridge, spoke openly to the King of the robbery of the schools " to the most miserable drowning of youth

---

[1] 1 Edward VI., c. 14.   [2] Fuller's History, 3, 475.
[3] Dodd's Church History, 2, 14.   [4] Burnet's Reformation, 3, 215.

in ignorance, and sore decay of the universities" ([1]) or a wise adviser like Martin Bucer urged on him the duty of making education the care of the State. ([2]) To such men we probably owe even the small provision that was made.

In Mary's troubled reign of five years, she established of her own bounty, a grammar school for each year, and some fifteen schools were also established by private citizens. ([3])

Elizabeth reigned forty-five years and founded twenty-five grammar schools. But the importance of knowledge was now beginning to make itself felt through society, and we owe a large number of foundations to the private benefactions of the time. Altogether there were founded in Elizabeth's reign 137 grammar schools, so that out of about 700 foundations for secondary education, 250 owe their origin distinctly to the period of the Reformation, ([4]) that is, to the almost complete century which elapsed between the death of Henry VII. and the accession of James I. Between forty and fifty non-classical schools, and about twenty unattached endowments for educational purposes had their rise in the same time, and probably some others, the origin of which has not been traced. But of the 4,300 charities for primary education reported on by the Commissioners between 1818 and 1842, by far the greater number were established long after the Reformation, and most of them after the Revolution and Restoration. It would not be just, however, to measure the educational work of the Reformation era by the narrow standard of the mere provisions of means. Amongst the leaders of the Reformation were men who held much more comprehensive views on the subject of popular education, than any who preceded or followed them in high office, until the present century was well advanced. Cranmer eloquently advocated the rights of the poor to a place on the

---

[1] Dodd's Church History, 2, 14. [2] Burnet's Reformation, 2, part 1, 289.
[3] Schools Enquiry Commission Report, App. 49. [4] Ibid, Report, 39, 57. App.

foundations of the time, ([1]) and it is only by a technical definition of terms, and a narrow interpretation of founders' intentions, that the grammar schools have been confined to middle class education; and partly also because these schools, as schools for the poor, were in advance of the times, and of the desires of the people. Latimer made the instruction of the poor one of the chief burthens of his discourses, and bitterly complained of those who "withdraw the goods wherewith schools should be maintained and take it to themselves." ([2]) Ridley encouraged Edward VI. in his educational designs, ([3]) and even Bonner was induced by some paramount influence to issue injunctions to his clergy to teach the children of his parishioners to read English. ([4])

The long interval of three centuries had elapsed before we again find men of influence in the Councils of the State— such men as Brougham, Russell, and Melbourne, urging the duty and policy of universal education. Though Henry VIII. did not give much himself towards education he was urgent upon others, and especially on the clergy, to provide for it; and he was the instrument by which a desire for instruction was awakened in the popular mind. Before the translation of the Scriptures into the vulgar tongue, popular education, connected as it was with a religious institution, and dependent on religious enthusiasm for its support, had but narrow ground to stand upon. Henry's warrant allowing all his subjects to read the Bible in their own language, and imposing penalties on those who hindered them, ([5]) was the charter of popular education. It is of comparatively small importance what his motives were, or whether he was actuated by spite against the clergy or otherwise. An impulse was given to

[1] Cranmer's Works, Parker Society, 2, 398.   [2] Latimer's Works, Parker Society, 1, 349.   [3] Ridley's Works, Parker Society, xiii, note.
[4] Burnet's Reformation, 2, part 1, 571, and 1 part 2, 382.
[5] Burnet's Reformation, 1 part 1, 410, 452.

the desire for knowledge which it had never received before, and which has never since been wholly spent. Many persons put their children to school that they might take them to St. Paul's to hear them read the Scriptures. ([1]) Even aged persons, eager to avail themselves of a new privilege, took lessons in the art of reading. ([2]) Henry, Edward, and Elizabeth, taxed the clergy to make provision for instruction, and compelled them to provide exhibitions at the Universities and Grammar Schools. Whoever among the clergy had an income of £100 a year was compelled to maintain a poor scholar at Oxford or Cambridge, ([3]) and Carlisle says that in Elizabeth's reign there was a tax of one-thirtieth on ecclesiastical benefices for maintaining schools. ([4])

As Church property was considered to be the proper provision for education, so the education of the age was committed entirely to the direction of the clergy. Education was not a civil but an ecclesiastical matter, and its aim was religious, not political. The teachers were commanded to make the catechism the beginning and foundation of instruction in their schools, ([5]) and all having cure of souls, and also chantry priests, were ordered to teach children to read English, "taking moderately of their parents that be able to pay, which shall so put them to learning." ([6])

So early as the seventh year of his reign Henry commanded the Bishops to make yearly visitation of all schools in their Dioceses. ([7]) At the beginning of Edward VI.'s reign, education was still further confined to a Church mould by the Act of Uniformity ([8])—the first of those exclusive acts, and the earliest statutory manifestation of the exclusive spirit which have done so much to hinder progress.

---

[1] Burnet's Reformation, 2, part 1, 549. [2] Hook's Lives, N.S., 2, part 141.
[3] Hook's Lives, N.S., 2, 239. [4] Carlisle's Grammar Schools, xxxix.
[5] Burnet's Reformation, 3, part 2, 269. [6] Ibid, 3, part 2, 193.
[7] Ibid, p. 269. [8] 2. and 3. Edward VI., c. 1.

By this act it was ordained that the Book of Common Prayer, and none other, should be used ; and all curates were ordered to call on their parishioners every six weeks to teach their children the Catechism. ([1]) But there was a step in advance in this reign, as the priests were now ordered to teach writing as well as reading. ([2]) When Mary came to the throne similar injunctions were given to the clergy to take charge of education, ([3]) and the Bishops were required to examine the schoolmasters to see that they exercised their offices without corrupt teaching, and, if necessary, to remove them. ([4]) And strict orders were given them to examine whether the common schools were well kept, and the schoolmasters diligent in teaching. ([5])

The prospects of education at the commencement of Elizabeth's reign appeared somewhat brighter. It was expected that great care would be taken of the Universities and public schools, " that the next generation might be betimes seasoned with the love of knowledge and religion." ([6]) Such expectations, however, were disappointed. Beyond the grammar schools which she founded, Elizabeth did little to promote the spread of knowledge, and the impetus it had gained at an earlier time slackened rather than increased. More care was given to Ireland than to England. An Act was passed for erecting free schools in every diocese in Ireland. ([7]) In England the Queen's chief care was to preserve teaching on the right ground, as soon as she could determine in her mind what that ground was. When she had declared for the Protestant side, and was firmly seated on the throne, she took vigorous measures for rooting out heresy from Church and School. The Act of Uniformity,

[1] Burnet's Reformation, 2, part 2, 288.   [2] Dodd's Church History, 2, xlvi.
[3] Hook's Lives, N.S., 3, 429.
[4] Cardwell's Annals of Church, 1, 112, 114.   [5] Ibid, 174.
[6] Burnet's Reformation, 2, part 1, 679.   [7] Hallam's History, 3, 371.

which had been repealed by Mary, was again restored, and all schoolmasters were required to have a license from the ordinary. ([1]) This license was strict in its conditions, was held during the pleasure of the Bishop, was available only in the particular diocese for which it was granted, and was dependent on good behaviour. ([2])

In a letter from the Council to Archbishop Grindal, directions were given that all schoolmasters should be examined by the Bishop, and that if any were found to be corrupt or unworthy they should be displaced. This matter was declared to be " of no small moment, and chiefly to be looked into by every Bishop of his diocese." ([3]) A return was required of the names of all schoolmasters, whether they taught publicly or privately, and whether any were suspected.

Churchwardens were directed to report whether any schoolmasters taught without a license, and the Act of Uniformity was ordered to be strictly enforced in regard to them. ([4]) The use of one grammar, as well as one prayer-book, was enforced. Lilly's celebrated grammar was the one authorised. A Bishop finding some scholars ignorant of its rules exclaimed, " what ! are there Puritans also in grammar ?" ([5]) The memorable Convocation of 1562, from which the Church derived the thirty-nine articles, and the second book of Homilies, supplied also Dean Nowell's catechism, the use of which was now vigorously enforced. Parents and masters having children, servants, or apprentices, upwards of eight years old, who could not say the catechism, were fined ten shillings in respect of each child. ([6])

[1] Cardwell's Annals, 1, 195.
[2] For form of License see Strype's Life of Whitgift, 1, 468.
[3] Cardwell's Annals, 1, 394.
[4] Cardwell's Annals, 1, 402.   [5] Fuller's Church History, 3, 21.
[6] Cardwell's Synodalia, 2, 510.

These enactments were aimed, in the first place, principally against those who clung to the ancient faith, but they were equally convenient as a weapon against the Puritans when they came to be troublesome. The Roman Catholics were the first to feel their weight. At first the Queen had no great reason to dread a Roman Catholic opposition. Out of 9,400 beneficed men only 189 left their benefices on account of the change in religion at this time. ([1]) But it by no means followed, because the clergy ostensibly accepted the changes imposed by Elizabeth, that they were disposed to give them implicit assent, or even obedience. Many of them looked forward to the time when a Roman Catholic Sovereign might succeed Elizabeth, as Mary had succeeded Edward VI. Also large numbers of the gentry remained Catholic at heart. The destruction of the monasteries deprived them of all means of education for their children, as they were not allowed to have private tutors. These circumstances gave rise to a new order of instructors for Roman Catholic children—the Seminary Priests. Colleges were founded at Douay, Lisbon, Rouen, Bruges, St. Omer, Brussels, and other places. The teachers these colleges sent forth were amongst the most celebrated the world has ever known. Many of them belonged to the Order of Jesuits, whose success in the education of youth is thus described by Macaulay:—" The liberal education of youth passed almost entirely into their hands, and was conducted by them with conspicuous ability. They appear to have discovered the precise point to which intellectual culture can be carried without risk of intellectual emancipation. Enmity itself was compelled to own that in the art of managing and forming the tender mind they had no equals." ([2]) These were the teachers into whose arms the policy of Elizabeth drove large numbers of the youth of England. Catholic colleges and seminaries were filled with

[1] Burnet's Reformation, 2, part 1, 720.　　[2] Macaulay's History, 1, 344.

English children belonging to the higher classes, and soon Catholic priests were found pursuing their calling under every form of disguise. The aims of these teachers were not in the first instance civil or political, nor was it their chief object to supply English Roman Catholics with the means for the cultivation of letters. It was their business to educate for the Roman Catholic priesthood, and, incidentally, to keep all secular education under their direction. It is said of them that while great attention was given to pupils destined for the Church, the abilities of such as were to be employed in secular affairs were neglected. ([1]) They had secondary political designs upon the throne of England, and, as it is alleged, upon the life of the Queen. ([2])

Whether Elizabeth was ever in personal danger, or whether such allegations were only a cover for the savage measures she took, will always be in dispute. She was equal to the emergency, whether a reality or a pretence. A severe law was passed against all who did not observe the regulations of the Church of England in their most minute detail, ([3]) and a proclamation was issued commanding all persons whose children, wards or relations were receiving their education abroad to recall them within four months. ([4]) It was forbidden to worship God in the Roman Catholic manner in public and private. Seminary priests who came to England were hunted down. The prisons were filled with delinquents, and large sums of money were extorted from them. Roman Catholics were not allowed to have their children educated at the Universities unless they would conform. To send them abroad was held to be criminal. ([5])

---

[1] Buckle's History of Civilisation, 2, 336. [2] Hook's Lives, N.S., 4, 456.
[3] Hook's Lives, N.S., 5, 144. [4] Dodd's Church History, 3, 15.
[5] Ibid, 69.

Five or six acts were passed in this reign against Catholic schoolmasters and teachers. Seminary Priests taken in England were executed. Two hundred of them perished in this way, and a larger number died of diseases contracted in the horrible prisons to which they were consigned. ([1]) Preaching and reading in private houses was forbidden. The Queen's power of wardship was used to compel the education of catholic youth in protestant tenets. ([2]) The Court of Star Chamber exercised a rigorous censorship over the press. ([3]) In the latter years of Elizabeth a savage act was passed against the Puritans. All who refused to conform were required to abjure the kingdom under pain of death, and for some degrees of non-conformity they were adjudged to die. ([4]) The Court of High Commission assumed control over every expression of thought, and every religious office. Two hundred of the best ministers were driven from their parsonages. The conventicles were closed, and the congregations were compelled to seek refuge in Amsterdam. At a later time they became the colonists of New England. These persecutions tested the vitality and strengthened the conscience and determination of English non-conformity, and became powerful stimulants to the growth of the civil and religious freedom they were designed to crush.

There are very scanty materials upon which to form any precise judgment of the actual progress of education amongst the poorer classes during the hundred years of the Reformation struggle. The histories of that period are not histories of the poor, except as it is found in Poor Law Acts and in the wars of the times ; but of Kings and Queens, and courts —of the struggles between the crown and the nobles— between ecclesiastics and laymen, for power—of the slow and

---

[1] Green's History, 402. [2] Ibid, 607. [3] Ibid, 460.
[4] Burnet's Own Times, 2, 495, and Statute 35 Elizabeth, chap. 1.

4

painful development of institutions which have been made native by adoption; and in a measure of the middle class, which with the growth of trade and commerce was then pushing itself into a commanding position—all of which forms a part of the education of the nation, but is withal an incomplete record of the efforts of the commonalty for existence and improvement. In the higher classes the first effect of the Reformation was to discourage learning. When Edward VI. came to the throne the Grammar Schools had become disused, "parents choosing any other calling for their children rather than bring them up to letters." ([1]) With the destruction of the monasteries, the opportunities for study and leisure, and the rewards which they offered had disappeared, and those who had formerly followed literary callings now betook themselves to mechanical pursuits, or other illiberal employments. In a letter, dated 1550, Roger Ascham lamented the ruin of the Grammar Schools, throughout the country; and that the Universities and the public schools were neglected alike by professors and pupils. ([2]) Burnet says no care was taken for the education of youth except those who were bred for learning, and the commons saw the gentry were likely to reduce them to a very low condition. ([3]) The clergy were the only instructors of the lower classes. They were, especially in the country, grossly ignorant. ([4]) They were reluctant teachers, and often so poor that they had to follow some manual occupation for their living. ([5]) If they had at any time carried out the injunctions of Henry and Edward to teach the children, the habit soon fell into entire disuse, and even the catechising was neglected.

During the long reign of Elizabeth there was a partial

[1] Strype's Cranmer, 234.
[2] Spencer's Descriptive Soceology, 25. [3] Burnet's Reformation, 2 part 1, 211.
[4] Pepys' Diary, 4, 263. [5] Burnet's Reformation, 2, part 1, 375.

revival of knowledge amongst the upper and middle classes. The grammar schools and Universities took up the work of the monasteries, and a new knowledge and mental energy were diffused amongst the middle classses and country gentry. ([1]) The burst of noble literature for which Elizabeth's reign is famous was an educating influence of the most lofty kind. Authorship, under court protection, began to be a regular profession. The clericy or learned body, as such, was disappearing, and literature was addressed to a wider circle of readers. " The abundance, indeed, of printers and printed books at the close of the Queen's reign, shows that the world of readers and writers had widened far beyond the small circle of scholars and courtiers with which it began." ([2]) The Reformation moreover had given to the people a book which had the most intense charm and interest for them— the Bible—and had supplied them with what before was wanting—a literature which they could comprehend. It was out of the study of this book that Puritanism rose and grew into a force, giving a new moral and religious impulse to society, and the conception of social equality which in time was to be productive of such great results. But towards the end of Elizabeth's reign all freedom of thought, spiritual and intellectual, had fallen under the despotism of the Ecclesiastical Commission, which even had powers to amend the statutes of colleges and schools. ([3]) A beginning however had been made, and the desire for knowledge was so far enkindled that neither the neglect nor tyranny of Governments or of dynasties could extinguish it.

The two hundred years following the death of Elizabeth are bare of records of Government attempts to extend instruction amongst the people. The Restoration and Revolution, and accession of the Brunswicks, occasioned no effort to raise the structure of political power on the

[1] Green's History, 399.   [2] Ibid, 393.   [3] Ibid, 457.

education of the people. ([1]) Yet it was during this period that the great struggle for intellectual, political, and religious freedom was proceeding, the triumph of which could alone render a state system of education tolerable or desirable. In order to understand the claims to the control of education put forward in our own day it is necessary to review briefly these events so far as they bear on the subject. It is not the object of this work to consider them in their wider relations to the great subject of civil and religious freedom.

One of the marked features in the reign of James I., is, that the foundation of grammar schools, (which was almost suspended as an object of the crown and court) proceeded at an increased ratio, at the cost of private individuals. The King in his reign founded four schools, whilst the private foundations were over eighty. During all the subsequent troubles, the foundation of grammar schools by private individuals went on steadily. Between the beginning of the reign of James I., and the flight of James II., 288 schools were established, but of these only seven owe their foundation to the rulers of the nation. ([2])

It was also during the same era that private foundations for distinctly primary education had their beginning. Before the year 1600 benefactions for this purpose, the origin of which have been traced, were exceedingly rare ; but during the century following there were nearly seven hundred endowments left for this purpose, of which about two thirds followed the Restoration, ([3]) the period from which Mr. Green dates the forces of modern England. ([4]) Their distribution however extends over the whole century, and marks the impulse which had been given by the Reformation to the extension of knowledge. In the

[1] Shuttleworth's Public Education, 33.
[2] Schools Enquiry Commission Report, App.
[3] Analytical Digest of Charity Commissioners Report, 1842.
[4] Green's History, 603.

time of James I., the "licensed" schoolmasters had grown into a class of sufficient number and wealth, to be included in the exaction of benevolences. ([1]) But all education was confined in the one inflexible church groove. The Roman Catholics were disappointed in their hopes of toleration. One of the first acts of James was to renew the proclamation, ordering all Jesuits and seminary priests to depart the realm, and a Canon of the Church ordered ministers to present recusants and schismatics. ([2]) A stricter conformity to the rubric was required, and three hundred Puritan clergy were driven from their parsonages. ([3]) The doctrine of the divine right of Bishops was added to that of the divine right of Kings. The Canons of 1604 renewed the requirements that the schoolmaster should be licensed by the ordinary, and should embrace the articles of religion. They added also a special proviso that curates should be licensed before others.([4]) The catechising of children on Sundays and holy days, and their instruction in the commandments, the Lord's prayer and the articles of religion, was made compulsory on the clergy, and attendance at church was required on pain of excommunication. Students of the universities were ordered to attend, to be thoroughly instructed in points of religion. The duties of schoolmasters were declared.

It is noteworthy that the earlier injunctions of Edward and Elizabeth to teach the poor to read and write were now forgotten, and schoolmasters were enjoined only to teach the catechism, to train their scholars with sentences of Holy Scripture, and to bring them to church. ([5])

In later contests between the Education department and the National society, the question has been raised as to how far these Canons, not having the sanction of Parliament, were

[1] Cardwell's Annals of Church, 2, 144.
[2] Dodd's Church History, 4, 57, and Canon 110.
[3] Green's History, 470.   [4] Cardwell's Synodalia, 291.
[5] Canons, 77, 78, 79.

binding on the laity. The effect of the decisions of the courts is, that they are binding only so far as they declare the ancient law, and custom of the Church and realm. ([1]) But the point is of small significance since the subjection of the schoolmaster to the clergy was expressly declared by statutes 23 Elizabeth, cap. 1, and 1 James I., cap. 4, ([2]) which regulated the granting of licenses by the ordinary.

The practice of catechising never seems to have been general, not so much on account of any resistance by the people, as from disinclination of the clergy. Within thirty years after the passing of the law, the Bishop of Norwich reported to Laud that he had " brought" his diocese into perfect order by requiring the practice of catechising. ([3]) At the same period Dean Hook says that the Puritan preachers regarded the order of catechising as beneath the dignity of their preachers, ([4]) and this was at a time when the mass of the clergy were steady Puritans.

There can be no doubt that the practice of catechising was found difficult to enforce, since after the Restoration the Attorney-General was desired to prepare a bill requiring the clergy to carry out the injunctions. ([5])

Charles I. had found in Laud a willing instrument to give effect to his hostility against the Puritans. The doctrine of passive obedience was added to the principles they were required to instil. They were compelled to take an oath of their approval of the doctrine, discipline, and government of the Church. Hundreds of clergymen were suspended or deprived. The lectureships which had been established in towns were suppressed. Church-wardens were ordered to present on oath the names of all schoolmasters, and to prosecute at the assizes

---

[1] Hook's Lives, N.S., 5, 219, and Lathbury's History of Convocation.
[2] Cardwell's Annals, 2, 274. [3] Ibid, 206. [4] Hook's Lives, N.S., 6, 190.
[5] Cardwell's Annals, 2, 287.

those who had not submitted. (^{1}) Thousands of the best classes of the nation were driven to America. (^{2}) Neither did the Common-wealth bring any recognition of the principles of intellectual or of religious freedom. The Government asserted and enforced the right to provide forms of worship and of faith, and to compel all to come within its creed. The recognised religion was changed. The assembly at Westminster provided a new confession of faith, and directory of public worship. Conformity to Presbyterianism was required on all sides. Episcopalian clergy were driven out in their turn, and forbidden to act as ministers or as schoolmasters. The Barebones Parliament was charged with indifference to progress, and with enmity to knowledge. To deny the doctrine of the Trinity, the divinity of Christ, or that the Bible was the word of God was made punishable by death. A Court of Triers and a rigorous censorship of the press, provided an efficient means, by which an outward conformity to the opinions and regulations of the Government was secured. (^{3})

Great hopes of some relaxation in the harshness and tyranny of the laws were entertained on the Restoration. Charles II. in the famous declaration of Breda had declared " on the word of a King," a " liberty to tender consciences." These hopes were soon extinguished by the Corporation Act, the Act of Uniformity, and other measures which followed each other in rapid succession, the object of which was to root out the last semblance of religious freedom. If Charles was not the chief promoter of this policy, he was one of the most active conspirators. In 1681 both Houses of Parliament had passed a bill repealing the cruel Act of Elizabeth against Non-conform-ists and the King refused to give it his assent. (^{4}) The

---

[1] Cardwell's Synodalia, 1, 403. [2] Green's History, 495, 510.
[3] Green's History, 520, 570. [4] Burnet's Own Times, 2, 495.

object of this persecution and of the Corporation Act and other Acts by which it was enforced, was to drive the Puritants out of the towns, which were their strongholds, and to disperse them and annihilate their influence.

The Act of Uniformity, framed in 1662, on the strength of which the clergy of this century have based their right to the control of education, had a similar aim. It recites the Act of Uniformity of Elizabeth's reign, and that numbers "following their own sensuality, and living without knowledge and due fear of God, did wilfully and schismatically abstain and refuse to come to their parish churches," and required the use of the Book of Common Prayer, the observance of the rights and ceremonies of the established church, and unfeigned assent and consent to its doctrines and ordinances. For the first time school masters were required in express terms to subscribe a declaration of conformity to the Liturgy of the Church; and teaching without the license of the ordinary subjected them to imprisonment. ([1]) The House of Lords remonstrated against the clause, and vainly endeavoured to secure more lenient provisions on behalf of school masters. The Bishops were required particularly to certify the names of all school masters, and whether they were licensed and attended church. ([2])

The Act of Uniformity was followed by the Conventicle Act in 1664—the Five Mile Act in 1665, and another Conventicle Act in 1670. The object of all these measures was the suppressing of unconforming ministers and school masters. The Test Act passed in 1673, requiring from all in the civil and military employment of the State, the oaths of allegiance and supremacy, a declaration against transubstantiation and the reception of the sacrament according to the rites of the Church, was a blow at the Roman Catholics,

---

[1] 13 and 14 Charles II., c. 4.   [2] Cardwell's Annals, 2, 273-4.

when the King was secretly negociating with them; and it was acquiesced in and supported by the Dissenters.

The first effect of the Act of Uniformity, and other persecuting Acts was cruel in the extreme upon a large section of the clergy. Two thousand Church ministers—the best and most learned of their order—the leaders of the London clergy and the heads of the Universities — were driven from their homes. ([1]) Their sufferings were extreme. They were hunted from the towns, prosecuted and imprisoned, and driven to seek shelter under humiliating disguises. The Acts were enforced with such unrelenting severity that upon the declaration of indulgence, twelve years later, 12,000 Quakers were released from gaol. ([2])

The political and social bearings of these Acts in modern times have been unlimited for good. In the expulsion of one-fifth of the English clergy, and that the section most distinguished for high character and learning, a foundation for freedom of opinion was laid, which made religious toleration a question only of time. In the Church itself the immediate effect was to deaden all desire for change, and to stifle all effort for reform, or for social improvement. ([3])

As the severities against the Roman Catholics under Elizabeth led to the establishment of Roman Catholic seminaries, so the persecution of the Puritans under Charles gave rise to another class of Nonconformist schools, some of which attained to considerable celebrity. These were the academies for the education of Dissenting ministers. In their original design they were purely theological seminaries, but in practice they became something more than this; and many sons of the gentry, and some of the nobility, were educated in them for civil employments. ([4]) They afforded the early generations of Dissenters of the middle class, better

---

[1] Green, 610.   [2] Ibid, 613.   [3] Green, 610.
[4] Bogue and Bennett's Dissenters, 2, 75.

means for education than they enjoyed until in recent years the Universities were thrown open to them; and this, notwithstanding that the masters came under the penalty of the law, and were hunted by spies and informers, dragged before justices, and harassed in spiritual courts.

For nearly thirty years this persecution continued, and while it lasted it was safer to be a malefactor than a Dissenter.

The Toleration Act has been described as the Magna Charter of Dissenters; but as Unitarians and Roman Catholics were exempted from its provisions, it was far from conceding the right of complete freedom of opinion and worship. Neither did it repeal by express terms the provisions against schoolmasters. Dr. Calamy says that the clause inserted in the draft act in favour of Dissenting schools was clandestinely blotted out on two occasions. ([1]) It is certain that the Act did not prevent proceedings against Dissenting teachers, as Dr. Doddridge was persecuted for keeping a school in 1700, ([2]) and these prosecutions were not discontinued until King William intimated that he was not pleased with them. ([3]) The middle-class Dissenting schools then sprang into prominence. In the Tory reaction in the first year of Queen Anne's reign, the Lower House of Convocation passed a resolution in strong condemnation of them, as pusuring the place of the Universities, and praying for measures for their suppression. ([4]) Samuel Wesley, father of the revivalist, violently attacked the academies. ([5]) The Archbishop of York said in the House of Lords that he apprehended great danger from their increase, ([6]) and they were freely described by the High Church party as nurseries of sedition.

[1] Calamy's Life, 2, 13. [2] Bogue and Bennett, 3, 313. [3] Ibid, 2, 45.
[4] Cardwell's Synodalia, 2, 713-18. [5] Bogue and Bennett, 2, 90.
[6] Buckle's History, 1, 420.

In 1711, when the Tory reaction was at its height, the Act against occasional conformity was passed, which prevented Dissenters from qualifying for municipal office. ([1]) This was followed in 1714 by the Schism Act, which was intended to crush their seminaries, and did indeed compel them to suspend operations. ([2]) The Act provided that no one might act as tutor or usher without the sanction of the Bishop, and without conforming to the Anglican liturgy. It was, however, aimed at higher rather than lower education, and permitted Dissenters to employ mistresses. It did not extend to the teaching of reading, writing, and arithmetic. ([3]) If the Tory ascendency had been prolonged there was danger that the Toleration Act would have been repealed. The Occasional Conformity Act and the Schism Act were of short duration, being repealed in 1718. ([4]) From this date the period of real toleration begins, though the battle for religious liberty was far from being won.

During the administration of Walpole, the enforcement of the Test and Corporation Acts was gradually relaxed, and they became at last the mere shadow of law. For a hundred years, between 1727 and 1828 they remained upon the Statute Book unenforced, and it was the practice to pass annually a bill of indemnity in favour of those who had violated their provisions. ([5]) Many efforts were made in 1718, 36 and 39 for the alteration of these laws. In 1789 Lord Stanhope made an ineffectual attempt to repeal the Acts imposing penalties on those who absented themselves from church. In 1792, Fox tried in vain to repeal the Penal Statute against Unitarians. ([6]) The Five Mile Act and the Conventicle Act were continued

---

[1] Lecky's History of Eighteenth Century, 1, 95.
[2] Lecky's History of Eighteenth Century, 1, 95, and Bogue and Bennett, 2,24.
[3] Lecky's History of Eighteenth Century, 1, 96.　[4] Lecky's History of Eighteenth Century, 1, 258.
[5] Lecky's Eighteenth Century, 1, 260.　[6] Bogue and Bennett, 4, 187-8.

until 1812, ([1]) and it was left to Lord John Russell to repeal the Test and Corporation Acts in 1828. Catholic emancipation followed in 1829.

The exclusion of the Unitarians from the benefits of the Toleration Acts was occasioned by the alarm which sprang from the rapid spread and increase of Socinianism in 1698— led by Thomas Firmin, who had made himself famous by his efforts to found hospitals, schools, and charities of all descriptions. ([2]) The provisions against the Unitarians were not repealed till 1813. ([3]) During the whole of the eighteenth century the Catholics also remained under severe restrictive and penal laws; and up to 1847 were even denied a share in the education grants of the Government. During the reign of James II. they had enjoyed a short sunshine of prosperity, during which the Jesuits openly set up their schools in London, in defiance of laws which remained unrepealed. ([4]) But this was only a glimpse of freedom. They were refused a share in the toleration of William III., and laws still more severe were enacted against them. By an Act passed in 1699 perpetual imprisonment was decreed against Catholics engaged in education ([5]) and this was followed by other Statutes of William III., and George I., the whole tendency and object of which were to prevent any open teaching of Catholic opinions.

But notwithstanding the neglect of the clergy, and the stagnation within the Church, and the penal laws which kept other sects in subjection, and made self-preservation the paramount law of their existence, the necessity of education for the poor was gaining a gradual though certain recognition. Between the Restoration and the death of Anne, nearly five hundred foundations were established, exclusively for the

[1] Spencer's Descriptive Sociology, 24, English Division.
[2] Burnet's Own Times, 4, 377.   [3] Haydn's Dictionary of Dates, 759.
[4] Green's History, 652.   [5] Lecky's 18th century, 1, 275.

education of the poor. Early in the Eighteenth Century they increased rapidly in number and in the value of their endowments; and in 1750 the charities for primary education reached two thousand in number. (^{1}) They were often small in amount, and they have been in the main very pernicious in their influence on the progress and success of a system of education.

They nevertheless were the most effectual protest of the time against the vice and ignorance which took a delight in flaunting itself before the public eye. It is noteworthy that the greatest activity in the foundation of charity schools prevailed at a time when painted boards invited the poor to get drunk for a penny and dead drunk for twopence, with a promise of clean straw for nothing. (^{2}) The bequests were frequently left in connection with the Church, or some religious establishment, and in many instances were coupled with the condition of exclusive religious teaching; but of 4,000 endowments for primary education fully one-fourth were left for the purposes of secular instruction, wholly unconnected with any religious body and unfettered by conditions. The Schools Enquiry Commission reported that the majority of endowed schools were not for exclusive education, and were under all descriptions of management. (^{3}) In the early part of the Eighteenth Century many schools were founded by subscription, which proves the existence of a collective opinion and the partial recognition of a duty on the part of society.

Mr. Bowles claims for Bishop Ken, as early as 1680-90, that he was the first and most earnest promoter of parochial schools, which he set up in all the parishes of his diocese,

---

1 Analytical Digest of Charity Commissions, 1842.
2 Bogue and Bennett's History of Dissenters, 4, 38.
3 Schools Enquiry Commission Report, 111.

and that he was the originater, or the most active instrument
in the establishment of village and Sunday schools. ([1])

In Atterbury's Charge to the Clergy of Rochester, in
1716, he refers with approval to the late encouragement
of charity schools. ([2]) It was during the same period that
Shenstone wrote his familiar description of village schools :—

> " In every village, marked with little spire,
>   Embowered in trees, and hardly known to fame,
>   There dwells in lowly shed and mean attire,
>   A matron old, whom we schoolmistress name."

It is clear from one of the following couplets that the
dame of that early period, like the one of our own day,
usually combined other occupation with her teaching :—

> " Where sits the dame, disguised in look profound,
>   And eyes her fairy throng, and turns her wheel around."

The marked increase in the number of these schools
provoked Mandeville's Essay on Charity Schools, which,
with the Fable of the Bees was presented at the Middlesex
Sessions. He refers to the distraction the nation had
laboured under for some time, and the " enthusiastic passion
for charity schools." ([3]) The movement was most marked in
the metropolis at this time, and, impressed by what was
nearest to him, Dr. Mandeville over-estimated its energy
and extent. It drew from him a vigorous protest, supported
by much ingenious argument, which was thought worthy
of a serious answer by Bishop Berkeley, and which was
presented by the grand jury of Middlesex as mischievous
and immoral.

There is no doubt that the true reason for the
presentation was, not that it was an attack on education,
but on the doctrine of the Trinity. In regard to the
former he defended amply and forcibly and with a wealth
of reasoning which might have been devoted to a better

---

[1] Life of Ken, by Bowles, 2, 98.   [2] Atterbury's Correspondence, 2, 259.
[3] Mandeville's Charity Schools.

purpose, the terrible doctrine of the governing classes of the time, affirming the necessary subjection and ignorance of the lower classes.

It has been customary to ascribe the origin of the educational movement of the Eighteenth Century to the religious revival led by Wesley and Whitfield; while some authorities have represented that agitation as altogether hostile to the spread of knowledge. Neither of these views is correct in a broad sense. Mere reference to the dates of the charitable foundations will show, that the greatest energy in the foundation of charity schools preceded rather than followed the Methodist revival. Wesley did not return from Georgia until 1737, ([1]) and years passed away before his labours wrought any perceptible influence on the currents of opinion. The educational movement in its religious and philanthropic aspect began much earlier. The Society for Promoting Christian Knowledge was established in 1699. ([2]) As its name implies, it was a religious rather than an educational association. Its object was to promote Christian knowledge, and to erect catechetical schools and to diffuse the Scriptures and the Liturgy. Its progress was slow, and after sixty years of labour it had only enrolled six hundred members. It was a strictly orthodox society. Its rules were approved by the Archbishops and Bishops. Its standing orders provided that devotions should be held before proceeding to work, and that an anniversary meeting should be held to enable the committees to dine together. Its officers were required to be members of the Church of England, and its work was prosecuted on Church and State principles. We hear, also, in 1750, of the establishment of another Society for the Promotion of Christian Knowledge amongst the Poor. This had its

[1] Wesley's Journal, 1, 13.　　[2] Spencer's Descriptive Sociology.

origin in the serious alarm caused by two shocks of earthquake. ([1]) Its object was the distribution of the Scriptures and books of piety amongst the poor. Its founders were evangelical Dissenters, Presbyterians, and Independents, but it soon recommended itself to Christians of all denominations. ([2])

The catechising of children by the dissenting preachers, which had fallen altogether into disuse amongst the clergy, ([3]) now became a regular practice. ([4]) In the labours of this society, the religious work of the Methodists came in as a powerful aid. Whatever foundation there may be for the charge that Methodism has been hostile to research and to the higher forms of knowledge, there is ample proof that Wesley himself was deeply touched by the popular ignorance, and that he devoted a great portion of his life to remove it. One of the objects of the Society which he founded at Oxford, was to have the poor taught to read, ([5]) and amongst his many books there are educational works designed to encourage and facilitate the spread of knowledge.

One direct and immediate result of the religious movement was the foundation of numerous schools in Wales. ([6]) The establishment of Sunday schools became a powerful lever in the same direction. The first Sunday school appears to have been established by the Rev. T. Lindsey, at Catterick, in 1763. ([7]) Another is heard of at Little Lever, near Bolton, in 1775, under the charge of James Hays; but the movement gathered no force until 1781, when it was taken in hand by Mr. Raikes, and the Rev. Thomas Stock of Gloucester. From this time it exercised a most potent influence on the spread of elementary knowledge, though its means were necessarily limited, and its methods imperfect.

[1] Bogue and Bennett's History, 3, 403.   [2] Ibid, 40.
[3] Baxter's Church History, 671.   [4] Bogue and Bennett, 3, 327.
[5] Wesley's Journal, 1, 10.
[6] Lecky's Eighteenth Century, 2, 604.   [7] Buckle's Civilisation, 1, 430.

The Church clergy, as a body, with some notable exceptions, stood aloof from this movement at its origin. In the discussions of the last decade the Dean of Carlisle lays the irreligion of many to the injudicious character of the religious instruction given in the Sunday schools. Bishop Fraser, as a school Inspector, failed to find any which did not leave on his mind an impression of weariness and deadness, Sunday being made often the heaviest day of the seven to the children. ([1]) Making, however, all deductions, the Sunday schools have done a great work for education. Previous to the struggles for reform in 1832, they had produced many working men of sufficient talent and knowledge to become readers, writers, and speakers in the village meetings, ([2]) and had supplied to numbers the beginning of a process of self-education admirable in its results. During the same period we first hear of the establishment of county and foreign school societies, of orphan asylums, of literary and scientific societies, and of boarding schools for higher education, all attesting the gradual advance of opinion throughout society. ([3])

The movement in its entirety and comprehensive character was neither wholly religious nor philanthropic. It was social, industrial, and political, and was in fact the forecoming of the great wave of advancement which later times have witnessed. It was stimulated by many and various influences and forces, which had been slowly, but for a long time, gathering strength, and which acted and re-acted on each other. One of the most influential of these was the growing power of the press. Upon the Restoration a statute had been passed for the regulation of newspapers. This expired in 1679, and with it the hopes of the ruling powers of suppressing free discussion in England. ([4]) In 1695 the

[1] Newcastle Commission, 53. [2] Bamford's Passages in Life of a Radical, 29.
[3] Spencer's Descriptive Sociology. [4] Green's History, 647.

6

Commons refused to pass a bill for the re-establishment of the censorship of the press. This refusal was followed by the issue of a crowd of public prints, ([1]) which now began to appeal to a widening circle of readers. Learning and literature were addressed no longer to a group of scholars, but to the public, and letters were recognised as an honourable and independent profession. Also there arose an increasing boldness in religious discussion, a higher love for independent research, a disregard of mere dictative authority, and in the discussion of principles of government and matters of spiritual belief, the subjection of them to the test of reason. ([2])

In 1709 the first daily paper was established. Pamphlets increased in number, and periodicals and magazines became common. Circulating libraries were established. Printing was extended to country towns. Debating and reading clubs were founded for the trading and working classes. The people also obtained a fresh means of influencing and controlling Parliament, for in 1768-70 we first hear of public meetings being held ([3]) for instruction in political rights, and at the end of the century the right of publishing Parliamentary debates was confirmed.

Some severe laws were passed prohibiting the holding of public meetings and the lending of books, but they were powerless to check the current. The period was also distinguished for great mechanical inventions, which necessarily exercised a stimulating and educating influence on the popular mind.

The foundation of all that has been achieved since—the social progress, the material comforts, the diffusion of wealth, the advancement of science and mechanics, the development

---

[1] Green's History, 683.
[2] Ibid, 603, and Spencer's Descriptive Sociology, Table 5.
Spencer's Descriptive Sociology.

of industry, the improvement in morals, and the stride in religious and political freedom was strengthened and firmly established in this early period ; and in the struggle between the democratic and aristocratic principle, the former took definite form and asserted itself with all the consciousness and confidence of ultimate triumph.

The declaration of Hobbes that the origin of power is in the people, and the end of the power is the good of the people, was about to be supplemented by Bentham's better-known formula, that the true end of government is " the greatest happiness of the greatest number." The history of education is a part of this wider history of the progress of society, and in its completeness is only to be found in connection with the general advance which has taken place during the last two centuries.

CHAPTER II.

PERIOD.—FROM THE BEGINNING OF THE NINETEENTH
CENTURY TO THE EDUCATION GRANTS OF 1834-8.

IT will be seen from the preceding chapter that the modern
movement for popular education sprang from the people,
and that in this, as in other great reforms, " society was the
instigator." The work of the Statesmen of the Reformation
era was not carried out by their successors. The clergy
neglected to follow up even the partial efforts which had
been made by the friars. At a later period they took credit
for resisting the attempts of philosophical and political
theorists, ([1]) and they have never as a class adopted
education as a political and social force, apart from the
religious aspect. They were often illiterate themselves, and,
according to Macaulay, their own children followed the
plough, or went out to service. At the beginning of the
eighteenth century they had recovered their social position,
and on occasion could command a great deal of political
enthusiasm, but as a class they were still greatly impoverished,
and were ignorant and coarse. ([2]) Indeed in all the changes
of the last eighty years there is none greater than that
which has been effected in the character and conduct of the
parochial clergy. Even so late as fifty or sixty years ago,
a decent and regular performance of divine service on
Sunday was all that the most exacting person expected
from a clergyman. He might be non-resident, ignorant of
books, careless of his parish and people, and be thought
none the worse of. He was generally the keenest sportsman

---

[1] Life of Blomfield, 191.   [2] Lecky's Eighteenth Century, 76—79.

in his neighbourhood, the hardest rider, the best shot, and the most expert fisherman. Crabbe's picture of the country clergyman is well known :—

> "A sportsman keen, he shoots throughout the day,
> And skilled at whist, devotes the night to play."

He was often devoted to worse practices, and it is related that when Bishop Blomfield rebuked one of his clergy for drunkenness, he naively pleaded that he had never been drunk on duty. ([1]) The duty of a parish priest to the poor was fulfilled when he preached to them, baptised them, and buried them. ([2]) " Nothing interfered with his sport except an occasional funeral ; and he left the field or the covert, and read the funeral service with his white surplice barely concealing his shooting or hunting dress." ([3]) From this neglect and lethargy the clergy were sharply aroused by the religious revival, the establishment of Sunday schools, and an increasing popular power amongst the Dissenters. The peasantry of the kingdom, wrote Clero Mastix, had been so neglected by the regular clergy, who had the control over all the charities, " as to render the interposition of lay preachers absolutely necessary to snatch the souls of men from ignorance and vice." ([4])

It was a necessary but a rude awakening. They resisted at first, and held back from the new movement. The Bishops denounced Methodists, Dissenters, Sunday-school teachers, and village preachers, as Jacobins in disguise and wolves in sheep's clothing, going about under the specious pretence of instructing youth. ([5]) It was not long, however, before the clergy saw both their duty and their advantage in obtaining the lead and control of the agitation ; and they have been so far successful as to delude some historians, including Mr. Froude, into the belief, that

---

[1] Bishop Blomfield's Life, 78.   [2] Knight's Biography, 1, 200.
[3] Walpole's History of England, 176.   [4] Bogue and Bennett's Dissent, 4, 216.
[5] Bogue and Bennett, 4, 217.

when the cry for the schoolmaster arose, as the only cure for the evils of the time, they were the first to look for the remedy. (¹)

The Government recognised no duty to educate the poor, although it was the accepted opinion that Ministers ought to encourage the development of literary talent by the appointment to places, and the bestowal of pensions. In this way intellectual eminence was often made the instrument of degrading party purposes, as the history of the men of letters of Queen Anne's reign proves. But in regard to the poor, other maxims were in the ascendant, and their government was based on two fundamental principles. These were the application of force and the perpetuation of ignorance. (²) Every positive and negative means was taken to secure these ends, from coercion laws to taxes on knowledge—and even such a detail as the refusal of the Lord Chamberlain's licence to plays which too much favoured the doctrine of popular liberty. (³) Public opinion was always an antagonist, never an ally.

The words of Mandeville will sound brutal to modern ears, but they truly express the axioms of Government which Statesmen were not ashamed to avow a century after they were written. "In a free nation, where slaves are not allowed of, the surest wealth consists in a multitude of laborious poor; for, besides that they are the never-failing nursery of fleets and armies, without them there could be no enjoyment, and no product of any country could be valuable. To make the society happy and people easy under the meanest circumstances, it is requisite that great numbers of them should be ignorant as well as poor. Knowledge both enlarges and multiplies our desires, and the fewer things a man wishes for, the more easily his necessities may be

---

¹ Froude's Short Studies, 264.
² Buckle, 1, 500. ³ Bell's Life of Canning, 76.

supplied." (¹) A century later it did not enter into the
conception of Government policy, that the people had
anything to do with the making of laws. In 1795 Bishop
Horsley said in the House of Lords, that "he did not know
what the mass of the people in any country had to do with
the laws but to obey them." During the reform struggles in
1832, Lady Harrowby asked Mr. Greville, "What did it
signify what the people thought, or what they expressed,
if the army was to be depended on ?" (²) Laws for the
prevention of crime were outside the object of Government
as it was then understood. Dr. Bell, who occupied a famous
place in the early educational controversy, wrote :—" Our
code of laws is solely directed to the punishment of the
offender ; and it has not come within their contemplation to
prevent the offence." (³) The punishment of crime was
indiscriminate and brutal. Hanging was awarded for murder,
cutting and maiming, shooting at, rape, forgery, uttering
bank notes, coining, arson, burglary, larceny in houses,
horse and sheep stealing, and highway robbery. In 1805
sixty-eight persons were executed for such offences. In
the same year the State had actual charge of 200,000
children of paupers, for whose education no provision was
made, and who were subject to influences which were a
training for crime and indolence, and which made it a moral
certainty that they would become a perpetual charge to
the nation in gaols or workhouses.

As examples were not wanting of popular educational
systems, it must be assumed that this pernicious neglect
was the deliberate choice of English statesmen. In 1696
the Estates of Scotland had passed an Act ordaining
that every parish should provide a schoolhouse, and pay
a schoolmaster. The Pilgrim Fathers had organised in

¹ Mandeville, 1, 215.　² Greville's Memoirs, 1, 37.
³ Bell's Analysis of Experiment, 88.

New England common schools which were bearing fruit, and in more than one Continental State, systems of compulsory and universal education had been planted. All these experiments appealed in vain to idle understandings amongst English rulers. Probably the French Revolution, whether regarded as a warning or an example, did more than any other incident to arouse the desire for popular instruction. Thenceforward the diffusion of knowledge became a distinct and avowed article of political faith amongst large classes in this country. ([1])

The doctrine laid down by Adam Smith that the State should facilitate, should encourage, and even impose upon the body of the people the duty of acquiring the essentials of instruction, began to find acceptance at the beginning of the century. This great political economist was prepared for a small measure of compulsion, and would have made municipal privileges and trade rights dependent on examination. Later, his views were sustained by Bentham and Malthus. Even Blackstone, whose tendencies were more conservative, lamented the defects of the law, which left education wholly unprovided for.

Joseph Lancaster and Andrew Bell were the founders of our modern voluntary system of education. They were very unlike in character and disposition and of widely different fortunes. Pursuing at first a common aim, they became bitter personal rivals and enemies, and the leaders, nominally at least of two schools of educationists.

It is not the purpose of this history to enter into the long forgotten controversy which divided and excited their followers seventy years ago ; but as they were the originators respectively of the British and Foreign

[1] Bogue and Bennett, 4, 191.

School Society, and the National Society, and as such, were placed in the forefront of the agitation, no history of education would be complete without some sketch of their work, which however, only became effectual when it fell under stronger direction. Indeed without detracting from the merits of either of them, it may well be questioned whether the methods they introduced have not impeded the advance of education as well as diminished its efficiency. The existence of voluntary schools has often prevented united efforts for the introduction of a general system, in the same manner that educational charities, wretchedly insufficient in amount, and inefficient in their administration, have obstructed a more complete provision. Lancaster and Bell both over-estimated the capabilities of the voluntary societies. The former believed that he could make provision for educating all the children of the nation, while the followers of the latter expressed their intention to alter the character of society, to christianise India, and to prevent revolutions in France. The only country Bell despaired of as irreclaimably depraved, and alike incapable and unworthy of improvement, was the United States of America. Both of them had extravagant ideas of the worth of their machinery, and they succeeded in infecting wiser heads with a confidence in its universal applicability, and its simplicity, economy, and efficiency. It was on the question as to which was the author of the machinery, variously called the Monitorial System, the Madras System, and the Lancastrian System, that their personal rivalries and disputes turned, in the heat of which the direct object was frequently lost sight of. The principle underlying the system was tuition by the scholars themselves. Nearly the same method was followed in the schools of both. In the lack of proper teachers, it was, perhaps,

7

the only available means, but it introduced that vice of spurious economy, which has always attended efforts to improve and extend education. A few millions more or less spent on a foreign war, or in reducing a rebellious colony, or on chastising some wretched horde of savages, are never taken gravely into account in our method of government, but every penny required for raising the condition of the people has always been voted with reluctance.

The Monitorial system was condemned before the dispute as to its authorship had died away. It only concealed the defects of our school provision. It was rejected by Brougham's Select Committee in 1816. ([1]) Sir James Kay Shuttleworth said it had "not only utterly failed, but for the time ruined the confidence of the poor in elementary schools, exhausted the charity of the middle classes, and dragged into the mire of its own dishonour, the public estimate of what was practicable and desirable in the education of the poor." ([2])

"The religious formularies, and the Bible itself, suffered a painful desecration, as the horn-book of ignorant scholars, in charge of almost as ignorant teachers, who were, for the most part, under twelve or thirteen years of age." ([3]) This was vigorous censure, but it has been justified whenever the system has been tested by results.

The Rev. F. D. Maurice wrote "We have been worshipping our own nets, and burning incense to our own drag." ([4]) The Duke of Newcastle's Commission, which included men of wide experience and of all shades of opinion, reported that the first result of inspection had proved the inadequacy of the Monitorial system, the

[1] See Report, 388. [2] Shuttleworth's Public Education, 57. [3] Ibid, 58.
[4] *British and Foreign Review*, January, 1840, 50.

inefficiency of the teachers, and the deplorable condition of the schools. (¹)

It is self-evident that the system is based on the false assumption that the refined work of training the young intellect can be performed without preparation or methodical knowledge on the part of the·teacher. Hence arose the deplorable result that any one was thought good enough for a schoolmaster, and was encouraged to undertake the pursuit, when all else had failed. Not the least mischievous effect of the dispute as to the authorship of the plan was, that it became invested with a sacredness which made all attempts at improvement appear in the light of sacrilege, and thus added another to the many forms of obstruction which were already arrayed against the spread of education.

The true honour which attaches to Lancaster's name is not the doubtful one of inventing the Monitorial system, but that he conceived and tried to realise the idea that all children should be taught the elements of knowledge. The British and Foreign School Society was formed to continue his work, and indirectly he called the National Society into existence, as a rival institution. He has also the high title to permanent respect, that he pursued education as a civil policy, and without bigoted aim, although he unwittingly provoked the sectarian jealousy which has so constantly retarded progress. He was himself an enthusiastic and original teacher. He belonged to a Quaker family living in London, and first began teaching in a shed on his father's premises in 1796 or 1798. Many children were instructed free of expense, and subscriptions were raised for others. His success encouraged him, in 1800, to publish an account of his work, called "Improvements in Education." He upheld that education

¹ Report of Newcastle Commission, 99.

ought to be a national concern, and that this had so long been the public opinion that it would have become so "had not a mere Pharisaical sect-making spirit intervened to prevent it, and that in every party." The state of the existing schools was pitiable. They were mostly taught by dames, and were so bad that only those children who were fit for nothing else were sent to them. Sometimes schools were under the charge of masters, who were generally the refuse of superior schools, and often of society. Their drunkenness was proverbial. This was the condition of affairs against which Lancaster began war, "as a citizen of the world and a friend of mankind, actuated by no sectarian motives." He proposed to found a society for supplying schools, providing teachers, and raising their condition and prospects. He objected to a compulsive law, which however, he admits that intelligent men were even then advocating. The object of the projected society was to be "the promotion of good morals, and the instruction of youth in useful learning." In regard to religion he wrote, "the grand basis of Christianity is broad enough for the whole of mankind to stand upon." He was not without misgivings as to success. The dread of sectarianism and intolerance already kept many persons aloof from educational work. One passage of his pamphlet was a history and a forecast of the struggle :— "It has been generally conceived that if any particular sect obtained the principal care in any national system of education, that party would be likely to possess the greatest power and influence in the State. Fear that the clergy should aggrandise themselves too much has produced opposition from the Dissenters to any proposal of the kind. On the other hand the clergy have opposed anything of this kind which might originate with Dissenters, locally or generally, fearing an increasing interest in the dissenting interest might prove likely to prejudice the interests of the

Establishment." (¹) But whatever apprehensions Lancaster had he went manfully to work to test what could be done, and his energy in applying his system and ·in seeking for support was inexhaustible. In looking for help he discovered Dr. Bell, who had returned from Madras and had published an account of his work there, from which Lancaster had derived some useful hints. (²) At first there seemed a probability that the two might work together in the common cause. Lancaster frankly acknowledged his obligation to Bell, and the latter in his early correspondence admitted Lancaster's "admirable temper, ingenuity, and ability." (³) They were, however, soon separated by the bitterness of the sectarian quarrel, and all the efforts of Whitbread and others to reconcile them failed.

Lancaster's schools prospered exceedingly. He soon had a thousand children under his care. George III. sent for and patronized him, as he had previously sent for Mr. Raikes. (⁴) His Majesty was a friend of education, and was tolerant of Dissenters so long as they were not Roman Catholics. He subscribed £100 towards the schools, and made the Queen and the Royal Princes contribute. New schools were built by the Duke of Bedford and Lord Somerville, and they were visited by Princes, Ambassadors, Peers, and Bishops. (⁵) He was encouraged by the leading Liberals of the day, including Brougham, Romilly, Whitbread, and for a time, Wilberforce. Subscriptions poured in upon him rapidly. His fame extended to America, and teachers were sent for to put his plan into operation.

The Royal patronage of Lancaster, and the prospect of the establishment of a popular school system unconnected with the Church, raised an alarm amongst the

¹ Improvements in Education. ² Ibid, 63. ³ Southey's Life of Bell, 2, 148.
⁴ Life of George III., by Jesse, 10. ⁵ Life of William Allen, 54.

Tories and the clergy. They saw in his operations nothing but an attack on their supremacy, and while he was flattered on the one hand, he was met on the other by unmeasured denunciation as an atheist, an impostor, and the fraudulent appropriator of another man's design. He was, however, his own worst enemy. He had been unaccustomed to the use of money, and was the very opposite of a man of business. He was enthusiastic, imaginative, benevolent, and extravagant. He lavished his whole means upon his schools. Everything he could earn or beg went for their support, and he often provided food as well as instruction for the scholars, running into debt when he had no money. As early as 1804, the school doors were thrown open to all children, free of payment. (¹) Utterly incapable of administration, he was soon involved in ruinous difficulties. Friends came to his rescue time and again, but nothing could save him from eventual bankruptcy. There was a little group of men who were working for the abolition of slavery, for prison reform, and other Liberal measures, and who were nicknamed "The Saints." On one occasion Lancaster went to one of these, Joseph Fox, the surgeon. He owed £4,000. Fox instantly raised £2,000 to relieve the school from immediate embarassment, and he and William Carston became responsible for £4,000 more. A committee was formed in 1808, consisting of Thomas Sturge, William Carston, Joseph Fox, William Allen, John Jackson, and Joseph Forster, to whom were afterwards added, Romilly, Brougham, Whitbread, and others. This was known as the Committee of the Royal British or Lancastrian System of Education, and an attempt was made to put the schools on a business footing. Lancaster was

¹ Porter's Progress of the Nation, 690.

grateful for assistance, although apprehensive of undue interference from the committee. (¹) But his imprudence and thoughtlessness arising from his impulsive and visionary temperament, excited by the notice he had attracted, soon involved the committee in many troubles. It became necessary, therefore, to draw a strict line between his private enterprises and the public work. He was greatly exasperated with his friends and established a separate school at Tooting. Here again he was soon overwhelmed with difficulties and had to make another appeal for relief. The Dukes of Kent, Sussex, and Bedford, with Whitbread and Joseph Hume, came to his assistance; but it was decided to separate the association wholly from his interference and management. In 1814 the committee assumed the title of the British and Foreign School Society, which it has ever since borne. From this time there was a complete severance between Lancaster and his former supporters, and he complained bitterly of their neglect and severity. He went to Scotland and afterwards to America. His life was a series of vicissitudes until in 1838 he was killed by a frightened horse, in New York. Before his death he had admitted the unbounded kindness and important services he had received from Fox, Allen, Carston, and others. Notwithstanding his errors and misfortunes, he will always be held in honour as the first of modern philanthropists, who made a practical effort to secure universal education for the poor. Whatever has been gained since, is owing to the strong public opinion which he created by his energy and devotion.

The British and Foreign School Society soon became a powerful instrument in the field of voluntary education. It continued to receive the Royal patronage, and the

¹ Life of William Allen, 57.

Dukes of Kent and Sussex took an active share in its proceedings. The former, especially, was a zealous advocate of unrestricted education. Many famous men have been connected with it, and it has formed the rallying-ground of a large section of politicians, including those who have had the most influence on the development of national education. It has not escaped the charge of narrowness and sectarianism, but that, unfortunately, is a distinction to which no party can lay claim.

Dr. Andrew Bell, the other central figure of the movement, in personal characteristics stands out in strong contrast to Lancaster. He was a Scotchman, born at St. Andrews, where his father was a barber. In early life he went to America, where he was engaged as a tutor, and occupied his leisure in speculating in tobacco. He returned to Scotland towards the close of the eighteenth century, and took degrees in divinity and medicine. He then went to India, where he obtained several chaplaincies; and also became the director of a Government undertaking establishment. Throughout his life he was a most fortunate pluralist and sinecurist. He had a talent for making safe and profitable investments, for the wise administration of pecuniary affairs, and for pushing his own interests; which however, he always made identical with the spread of education. He died about 1839, at an advanced age, was buried in Westminster Abbey, of which he was Prebendary, and received the posthumous honour of a biography at the hands of Mr. Southey. In India he had honorary charge of the Asylum for Children, at Madras, a position in which he made the important discovery that children can teach each other. In one of his letters home he speaks of the " pleasing sight of a youth of eleven years of age, with his little assistants under him, teaching upwards of fifty boys." (¹) In this school

¹ Southey's Life of Bell.

arrangement, nearly every boy was a master. "He teaches one boy, while another boy teaches him."

On his return to England Dr. Bell published an account of his experiences. On his own showing, his aims, as an educationist, were not extensive. "It is not proposed" he wrote "that the children of the poor should be educated in an expensive manner, or even taught to write and cipher." "It may suffice to teach the generality on an economical plan, to read their Bible and understand the doctrines of our holy religion." To this curriculum he added manual labour and the useful arts. The schools he proposed to found were to be schools of industry. He had been appointed on coming home to the rectory of Swanage, where he opened schools on his own model, and it was here that he was visited by Lancaster. His pamphlet on education attracted little attention until it was made known by Lancaster's more widely circulated writings. Mrs. Trimmer, the editor of the *School Guardian*, also took pains to bring Dr. Bell prominently before the public. This was a lady of great and orthodox piety, who, as a Churchwoman, was very much alarmed at the growing influence and pretensions of Lancaster. She had compiled many books "dear to mothers and aunts" for the Christian Knowledge Society, and had earned from the *Edinburgh Review* the title of the "voluminous female." Sydney Smith had described her as "a lady of respectable opinions, and very moderate talents, defending what is right without judgment, and believing what is holy without charity." ([1]) In her eyes Lancaster was the "Goliath of Schismatics," and she was anxious that he should have a check. She had already published a reply to his pamphlet, in which she declaimed against

[1] Edinburgh Review, 1806.

8

societies of "nominal Christians" and "Sectarists," and referred those who asked for a national system, to the Act of Uniformity. "The standard of Christian education was erected by our pious forefathers at the Reformation, and we have every one of us been enrolled as members of the National Church, and are solemnly engaged to support it ourselves, and to bring up our children according to its holy ordinances." Mrs. Trimmer found a useful ally in Dr. Bell, and it was chiefly by her persuasion that he was induced to come from his retirement and take an active part in the struggle. In 1805 he suggested "a scheme of Education patronised by Church and State, originating in the Government, and superintended by a member of the Establishment." ([1]) In 1806 he addressed a circular to the ministry offering his gratuitous services for establishing schools on his own model, under Government auspices. In the same year he opened schools in Whitechapel, and later, Diocesan Societies were formed for the same purpose. From this time Bell devoted his life to spreading the system, until, in Southey's words, it became "a perpetual torment to him." ([2]) Nevertheless he had his consolation under the patronage of the Church Clergy. His success in founding schools was rapid, and he was gratified by the attention bestowed on him. He became the friend and correspondent of eminent men, and his battles against Lancaster were fought by Coleridge and Southey with a surprising fervour. Coleridge, wrote De Quincey, found "celestial marvels both in the scheme and in the man," ([3]) and in his letters he told him that he was a great man. His discovery was raised to a level with that of printing. ([4]) Southey

[1] Life of Bell, 1, 150. [2] Life of Southey, by his son, 6, 179.
[3] De Quincey's Works, 11, 92. [4] Bell's Life, 2, 479.

called him the greatest benefactor since Luther. Miss Edgeworth introduced him as a character in one of her novels, and mothers amongst the higher classes sought him, in order that they might learn how to get rid of the trouble of their children, and the expense of their education.

The Lancaster and Bell controversy at this remote distance, is not edifying. Notwithstanding that there were quick wits on both sides, it is dull reading. On the one hand Dr. Bell is described "as a foolish old gentleman, seized on eagerly by the Church of England to defraud Lancaster of his discovery." (¹) On the other Lancaster was called liar, quack, and charlatan. (²)

Much ingenuity was exercised to explain away Bell's limitation of his proposed system to industrial arts and the teaching of religion. Dr. Marsh, afterwards Bishop of Peterborough, wrote, "It is indeed lamentable that Dr. Bell was ever induced to insert the paragraph." (³) It became known as "the unfortunate paragraph." Its author set to work to provide "interpretations." There can be no doubt, however, that he meant what he had written. The schools established at Whitechapel were schools of industry for teaching shoemaking and printing. In discussing the matter with Whitbread he proposed to found schools of industry, and, referring to members of the House of Commons, he wrote, "I conceived that there were three for industry to one for education." (⁴)

It is clear, however, that the question of real interest, underlying the surface of this controversy, was not who originated a particular form of mechanical teaching, but which party should have the control of education. The exaltation of Bell against Lancaster, was a mere device

¹ Sydney Smith's Works, 2, 99. ² Bell's Life, 2, 283. ³ Ibid, 329.
⁴ Ibid, 203.

to divert a current of opinion from one channel into another, and to show that the Church had plans of her own, and need not stoop to borrow methods from Dissent. Thenceforward Churchmen were exhorted to support their own schools. The artifice was successful, and many who had taken an interest in Lancastrian schools, including Wilberforce, deserted to the other camp. Southey explains what was in the minds of Churchmen. "They," meaning the children, "must be instructed according to the established religion—fed with the milk of sound doctrine—for States are secure in proportion as the great body of the people are attached to the institutions of their country." "Give us the great boon of parochial education, so connected with the Church as to form a part of the Establishment, and we shall find it a bulwark to the State as well as the Church." ([1]) Mr. John Bowles, one of the founders of the National Society, wrote that Lancaster's system "was incompatible with the safety of the Established Church, and subversive of Christianity itself." ([2]) "The strength and consequently the safety of every establishment must depend upon the numbers that are, upon principle, attached to it." ([3]) "If the youth of the country be not brought up in the Church, it cannot be expected that they will ever find their way into it." ([4]) The same writer lamented the evils of the Toleration Act, which compelled magistrates to license teachers and preachers—the effect being the creation of itinerants and rhapsodists, whose "fanatical rant" drew numbers from the Church.

In these controversies the Church party took credit for much amiability and forbearance in admitting into their schools the children of Dissenters to be taught the doctrines of the Church. The Church of England, wrote Mr. Bowles "breathes a most mild and pure spirit of universal toleration," and in

---

[1] Southey's Life, 4, 385. [2] Letter to Mr. Whitbread, 1.
[3] Ibid, 6. [4] Ibid 25.

proof they threw open their schools to Dissenters, on condition that they were brought up as members of the Church. Mrs. Trimmer wrote "neither would I wish to have poor children, whatever might be the religious persuasion of their parents, excluded from our Church schools. They should be received in them with proper recommendation, on one condition, namely, that they must be taught with the rest."(¹)

The familiar cries of "the Church in danger" and "religion in danger" were raised, and aroused all the dormant energies of bigotry. It was admitted that Lancaster allowed in his schools the use of the Apostles Creed, the Lord's Prayer, and the Commandments; yet it was declared that his system favoured Unitarianism, which was stigmatised as outside the law. The Church had not been alive to a suspicion that religion was in danger, when children were absolutely without instruction, either moral, religious or intellectual; but on a Dissenter coming forward with a plan from which he did not exclude the admitted basis of nearly all sects, it was stigmatised as an attack on the authority of the Church; and its author was denounced in sermons and charges as a deist and infidel.

Dr. Bell has been generally regarded as one of the founders of the National Society, but that honour has been claimed exclusively for Archdeacon Churton, Mr. John Bowles, the Rev. A. H. Norris, and Mr. Joshua Watson. (²) Several years before the society was established, Bell had been organising schools, and assisting in the formation of Diocesan committees; and there can be no doubt that his work led up to its formation. It was at first intended to connect his name with the society, (³) but this design was abandoned. The original prospectus in which his name was mentioned, was altered so as to take "a more distinctly

---

¹ Comparative View by Mrs. Trimmer, 150.
² Churton's Life of Joshua Watson, 56.   ³ Bell's Life, 2, 344.

national ground, and to make Dr. Bell's system appear in its true place, as only the best means of working out the objects of the society." (¹) For some reason, perhaps because of what Southey calls his restless vanity and self-importance, Bell was not recognised as an acceptable colleague by the originators of the Society. In the first instance he was not on the Committee. This exclusion elicited some severe remonstrances from his more intimate friends, and after some protracted and delicate negotiations he was asked to act as superintendent of the society's schools, but his "proper position" was not recognised. (²) In 1813 he was elected an honorary member of the Committee, a position which he held during the remainder of his life. At his death he left £120,000 for founding "Madras" Schools at Edinburgh, Glasgow, Aberdeen, St. Andrew's, and other places. (³)

The National Society takes a conspicuous place in the history of elementary education. It started under the most favourable conditions, having the support of the Archbishops, Bishops, the Lord Chancellor, the Speaker and the members of the Government. The Royal Patronage given to Lancaster had always been a grave trouble to the clergy, and the Radicals and Edinburgh reviewers had known how to make the best use of it. So greatly was the Church party dismayed and irritated by it, that some back stairs influence was employed to convey a caution to the King, and to prevent the establishment of Lancastrian schools at Windsor. (⁴) They saw, however, the advantage of starting their own Society under such auspices, and there was much delicate manœuvering to get the support of the "first gentleman of Europe," who was acting as Regent. His approval was finally signified, and the prospectus of the

---

¹ Life of Watson, 59.   ² Bell's Life, 2, 396.   ³ Life of Southey, 6.
⁴ Bell's Life, by Southey, 2, 159.

Society was issued. Its success, from the first, was assured. Four years after its establishment the Committee were able to report that "their resources were inexhaustible." ([1])

The Society was incorporated by Royal Charter in 1817. Six years later a Royal letter was issued sanctioning parochial collections on its behalf. This custom became triennial, and was equivalent to a guarantee of subscriptions amounting to £10,000 per annum. The title adopted by the society was that of "The National Society for Promoting the Education of the Poor in the Principles of the Established Church." By the original terms of union, all children attending the Society's schools were required to learn the Liturgy and catechism, and to attend Church on Sunday." ([2]) From its earliest days the society has exercised great ascendancy over all topics relating to elementary schools. Not only has it consolidated that system of parish schools which was considered by its supporters to be the best outwork of the Church, but by means of its diocesan and parochial organisation, it has had the power of controlling and swaying public opinion to an extraordinary extent. So great has been the assurance of its members of the influence they could exercise, that frequently in the course of the debates and disputes to be described, they have assumed the authority to dictate the terms upon which the nation should be permitted to possess an elementary school system.

For many years the two great voluntary societies mentioned occupied alone the field of education, and were the centres towards which all the educational forces of society turned. There was hardly a man, eminent as a statesman, politician, or writer, who did not take a side in the controversy between them. The contest has not always been

[1] Bell's Life, by Southey, 3, 28.
[2] Ibid, 2, 408.

dignified, and too frequently the object towards which the nation was moving, has been lost sight of in the jealousies, rivalries, and contentions of the opposite schools of dogmatic belief. It is also too probable that the struggle for supremacy diverted the public mind from the main object, and postponed for many years the establishment of an adequate system. At the same time it would be unjust to undervalue the vast amount of educational work which has been done by both societies. The superior resources of the National Society have enabled it to take and to maintain the lead in the provision of schools ; but in the development and application of a state system of education, it has sustained a series of damaging defeats. Its pretentions to control and determine the character of education have been repeatedly negatived by Parliament, and it has only maintained its influence and position by recognising the advance of public opinion, and by accepting that instruction in circumstances which is one of the conditions of continued social and political existence. This explains why the National Society still administers a vast network of parochial schools, while at the same time the state regulations have been gradually approaching the standard set up by the British and Foreign School Society.

Happily for education, a force more powerful than that wielded by the voluntary societies was coming into existence, and had begun to make itself felt even before their formation. It has been seen that there were writers, and statesmen, who not only disbelieved in the adequacy of voluntary means, but who maintained the political doctrine, that it was the duty of the State to provide elementary education for the poor. The case was one of urgency. Sydney Smith said that " there was no Protestant country in the world, where the education of the poor had been so grossly and infamously neglected as in England." Malthus declared that it was " a great

national disgrace that the education of the lower classes
of the people should be left merely to a few Sunday
schools."

In the session of 1807, Mr. Whitbread, the member
for Bedford, introduced into the House of Commons a
Parochial Schools Bill, which was intended as part of a
larger scheme of poor law reform. The Duke of Portland's
Government had succeeded the Ministry of " all the talents."
Mr. Perceval was Chancellor of the Exchequer, and leader
of the Lower House. Mr. Canning was Foreign Secretary,
and Lord Eldon held the Great Seal. Mr. Whitbread was
a member of the Whig Opposition and was conspicuous
for his ability and influence in his party. The object of
his bill was to enable overseers, with the consent of the
vestry, to raise a sum for the support of education.

For the first time the question was raised in Parliament " whether it was proper that education should be
diffused amongst the lower classes," ([1]) a proposition by
no means of general acceptance, and which, in the ensuing
debate, was opposed by Mr. Windham, the most cultivated
man of his day. The machinery of the bill was simple,
and merely gave to magistrates the power to provide schools
and schoolmasters where they were required. Mr. Whitbread anticipated the usual objections made against
education, that it would teach the poor to despise their
lot, enable them to read seditious books, and make them
insolent and refractory. He showed conclusively that there
must be education of some sort, either of the schools, or
of the street and gutter. Sir Samuel Romilly spoke a
few words in favour of the bill, but with no hope that it
would pass—He notes in his diary " the bill will be lost.
Many persons think the subject requires more consideration ;
but a much greater portion of the House think it expedient

[1] Hansard, F.S., 9, 802.

9

that the people should be kept in a state of ignorance." ([1])
Mr. Perceval, on the part of the Government, assented to
the bill going into Committee for fairness of consideration,
though he feared it might destroy voluntary efforts, and
he was in favour of a previous enquiry into charitable
endowments. His speech is an illustration of the harm
those charities were doing. For years afterwards attempts
to introduce State aid were met by the answer, that there
were abundant endowments for the purpose if only they
were properly administered. Mr. Windham opposed the
bill, because the mutineers at the Nore had read the
newspapers. One orator exclaimed "What produced the
French Revolution? Books." ([2]) There was a general
alarm, noted by Romilly, founded on the supposition, that
if discussion were left free, error would be likely to prevail
over truth. The bill however passed the House of
Commons with some modifications, but preserving the main
principle, that vestries should be able to establish schools
under proper teaching and direction. Still the hopes of
its supporters were not high. It had to run the gauntlet
of Lord Eldon's stern antagonism. He had returned to
the woolsack, to oppose all the weight of his years, his
official position, his abilities and character against what he
considered "the rash delusions of his time," ([3]) and
this was one of them. It was enough that the bill
departed "from the great principle of instruction in this
country, by taking it out of the superintendence and
control of the clergy." ([4]) He avowed that he never
would consent that such a matter should be left to the
majority of the inhabitants. The Archbishop of Canterbury
also appealed to the House "to guard against innovations

[1] Romilly's Diary, 2, 207. [2] Bell's Life of Canning, 218.
[3] Life of Eldon. Twiss. [4] Hansard, F.S., 9, 1176.

which might shake the foundations of their religion." (¹)
The bill was of course rejected. Romilly wrote that it
had been suffered to pass the Commons because it was
known that it would be thrown out by the Lords. (²)
Something, however, had been gained. The representative
House had affirmed the principle, that the State ought
to be responsible for the education of the people, under
local administration. The subject did not come before
Parliament again for nine years, but these essential
requisites of an education system became fixed in the
public mind. The throwing out of bills does not alter or
stay the march of opinion, but acts rather as a powerful
incentive to the progress of ideas.

Upon the death of Mr. Whitbread, in 1815, the
parliamentary guardianship of the question fell into the
stronger hands of Brougham. The history of the subject
between 1816, when he moved for the first Select Committee,
up to 1839, when the Committee of Council was appointed,
is mainly a record of efforts, in which he took a prominent
and distinguished part. During this period he did more
than any other man to keep the flame alive, and to prepare
the basis upon which a system might be built. One of the
class, for the elevation of which he was struggling, who
wrote with discrimination and judgment, and who suffered
for his opinions, said " Our educators are, after all, the
best reformers, and are doing the best for their country,
whether they intend so or not. In this respect Lord
Brougham is the greatest man we have." (³) The light shed
by his efforts for popular intelligence "will illumine his tomb
when his errors and imperfections are forgotten."

In his last days Brougham himself found pleasure in
thinking that what he had done in this department would

¹ Hansard, F.S. 9, 1177. ² Romilly's Diary, 2, 217.
³ Bamford's passages in the Life of a Radical, 12, 29.

be his "most appropriate monument." ([1]) Yet he was unsuccessful in trying to find a safe and practical basis for state elementary schools, and was obliged to confess sadly, in Bacon's phrase, that "propositions have wings, but operation and execution have leaden feet."

The advantages, resulting from the enquiries he caused to be made, were obvious and great, but it is probable that his extra-parliamentary work was his best. It is impossible to over estimate the stimulus which his energy, his industry, his enthusiasm, and his splendid talents gave to the public agitation of the question. In Parliament he was often alone. In the Lords no man was more solitary; but in the country he was sure of an enthusiastic and appreciative following. Often during his career, when defeated by the forces of obstruction and prejudice, he appealed from the decisions of the Legislature directly to the people, and found his reward in their generous confidence and approval. As an instance his celebrated letter to Sir Samuel Romilly "on the Abuse of Charities" may be mentioned, when his Bill for the appointment of a Commission had been mutilated by the Ministry, and its execution entrusted to his enemies. This pamphlet ran through ten large editions, and produced an immense impression in the country. ([2]) This popularity had its disadvantages, and re-acted prejudicially on his parliamentary career. The people formed extravagant expectations of his capabilities to serve them—the higher classes regarded him as a Greek, whose gifts they feared to accept. While his friends were hoping for too much, his enemies were dreading some drastic remedy from him; and when he brought forward the expected bill, it too often satisfied nobody, whatsoever subject it might relate to.

[1] Autobiography, 3, 3.   [2] Harwood's Memoir, 130.

In regard to education he was particularly unfortunate in Parliament; and he has been accused, not without some warrant, of a trick which has been resorted to in more modern times; that of pressing forward his bills by making concessions of principle to his opponents. But it is not necessary to adopt this explanation, to account for his somewhat erratic course in regard to education. Above all things he was an "Educationist," and he was willing to make concessions and sacrifices to existing and opposing circumstances, and even to prejudice and intolerance, in order to obtain education. It was this pre-dominant feeling which animated his letter to the Duke of Bedford. "Let the people be taught say I. I care little in comparison who is to teach them. Let the grand machine of national education be framed and set to work; and I should even view without alarm the tendency of its first movements towards giving help to the power of the clergy." It was this desire which led him to propose the Bill of 1820, which gave such great and just offence to Dissenters. It may also be admitted, with all due respect to his memory, that amongst the causes of his failure was a want of judgment and prudence, which his closest friends and warmest admirers were obliged to acknowledge. Meanwhile they maintained that it was impossible to over-rate his services to the extension of knowledge. ([1])

In the session of 1816 Brougham moved for a Select Committee to enquire into the education of the lower orders in the metropolis. The enquiry was intended to provide a measure for government education in London, which, if successful, might be extended to other towns. He promised that his scheme should admit nothing offensive to any religious opinion, while the "just prejudices" of the Establishment would be respected. He also suggested the

[1] Life of Romilly, 3, 237.

propriety of establishing a school for the training of schoolmasters. ([1])

The report of the Committee was brought up in June, when he gave notice that he should bring the matter before the House in the following session. The abuses which had been discovered in the administration of endowments, together with their great value, had led him to the conclusion, that if they were properly applied, no grants for education would be required from Parliament. Grants should be made in the first instance only for building schools, care being taken to steer clear of religious differences which he said were "daily subsiding." The Government gave its approval to the object, and Canning said that he should contribute his utmost towards it, "being satisfied that the foundation of good order in society was good morals, and that the foundation of good morals was education." ([2]) This concurrence of opinion, and these happy anticipations were only the prelude to a storm of angry contention which agitated society for many years. In the following session Brougham briefly hinted at the enormous abuses attending the management and application of charitable funds. The Committee did not propose legislation, but advised a further enquiry. The powers of the Committee were renewed; the "vested interests" not yet having taken alarm, and Parliament being conciliated by the confident assertions of Brougham that "a very small part of the expense would ultimately rest with the public." ([3]) Sir S. Romilly, Sir J. Mackintosh, Mr. Wilberforce, and Sir F. Burdett were amongst others on the Committee which reported. It was now recommended that a Parliamentary Commission should be appointed to enquire into the application of charitable funds for education in England and Wales, with the object of reforming their administration and extending their advantages to the whole

[1] Hansard, F. S., 34, 631. [2] Ibid, 1235. [3] Ibid, 37, 817.

country. The difficulties did not appear to be insurmountable to the members of the Committee. The financial objection was partly removed by the amount of the charities which were available. In the large towns the voluntary societies were making rapid progress. They wished to avoid the danger of drying up the sources of private charity, and they advised that Parliamentary assistance should be confined to building grants. They did not anticipate opposition on account of religious differences from the large towns where there could be separate schools for Church and Dissent. In the country it was different, and "the progress of education had been materially checked by an unbending adherence to the system of the National Society." (¹) In country districts Brougham supported the application of the parish school system which had worked successfully in Scotland. On May 20, 1818, the Bill passed the House of Commons, Brougham promising that as soon as the report of the Commission was received he would found a bill upon it. At this period he was so deeply interested in the question that he offered to resign his seat in the House if necessary, in order that he might act as a Commissioner. (²) In the House of Lords a strenuous opposition was made to the Bill by the Lord Chancellor, and the contest was the most exciting of the session. "The Chancellor," writes Mr. Twiss, "who regarded it as being, in the shape it then bore, a vexatious measure, likely to deter men of honour and character from taking the responsibility of charitable trusts, took much pains to mitigate and amend it." (³)

It is quite conceivable that Lord Eldon took a personal satisfaction in "amending" a bill of Mr. Brougham's, whose attacks on the Court of Chancery had begun to engage public attention. Brougham declared that the bill was defaced and mutilated, and would deprive the Com-

¹ Hansard, F. S, 38, 589. ² Ibid, 835. ³ Twiss' Life of Eldon, 2, 315.

mission of all vigour and efficiency. Its scope was limited; many charities were exempted from its operation, and the Commissioners were deprived of the power of enforcing attendance, and of demanding the production of documents. In short, they could take only voluntary evidence. The Commissioners were nominated by the Ministry, and the execution of the design was committed to the opponents of the bill. In the Commons the Lords Amendments were agreed to and it became law. A vehement discussion now arose respecting the enquiries of the Select Committee, and the constitution of the Commission. Brougham published his letter to Sir Samuel Romilly, in which he denounced the mangling of the bill, which completely suppressed the object of its authors. He was replied to in the "Quarterly" for July, 1818, in an article in which he was subjected to that "fierie hell" of criticism, which had been tried on Keats in the previous number with signal effect. Canning was suspected of having a hand in this article, ([1]) and the Tories hoped that Brougham would not be able "to lift up his head again." They had at last been thoroughly awakened and alarmed by the proceedings of the Select Committee, and Brougham was looked upon as the author and embodiment of all that was vicious and irregular in its proceedings. It was charged against the Committee, that whereas one enquiry was entrusted to them, they had raised five distinct issues. Their original instruction it was said, was to enquire into the condition of the lower orders of the Metropolis. To this they, or rather the Chairman, added *motu proprio*, the consideration of plans for promoting education amongst them and bettering their morals; the propriety of connecting national education with national religion, the nature and state of all charitable endowments and trusts, and the circumstances

[1] Greville's Journal, 1, 16,

and administration of the public schools and Universities. Under cover to enquire into the condition of the "lower orders," he had pushed his investigations into the circumstances of Westminster, Charter House, and St. Paul's schools. It was sufficient offence and sacrilege that some of the closest, most exclusive, and most powerful corporations in England should be thus invaded under any circumstances; but it was an inconceivable insult and exasperation, that they should be included in an enquiry with the "lower orders." The *Quarterly Review* made it the subject of a grave complaint and rebuke, that the Head Master of Winchester was examined on the same day that the evidence of a benevolent surgeon was taken concerning the amount of ignorance in St. Giles's. But Brougham's offence was greater than this. He had ventured to receive and print evidence which conveyed charges of malversation and abuse against exalted personages. His "personalities" had excited disgust, and he had not treated venerable individuals with the deference they had been accustomed to receive. He had catechised the Dons of Oxford and the Masters from Eton about their antiquated processes. ([1]) His chief offence seems to have been the wearing of his hat as Chairman, and they said that the Committee resembled the Court

> " Where England's monarch once uncovered sat,
> While Bradshaw bullied in a broad-brimmed hat."

Brougham was held convicted of disguising mis-representation and prejudice under the mask of patriotism, of an inclination to every kind of innovation, and of an insufferable habit of disparaging the most revered institutions of the country.

Even without the knowledge which has since been gained by an exhaustive enquiry into the administration

---

[1] Campbell's Life of Brougham, 338.

10

of all endowments, a strong suspicion of the existence of secret abuses would have been raised by the temper and excitement caused by this enquiry. Mere rudeness would hardly have provoked the mingled hatred and fear with which Brougham came to be regarded amongst the privileged classes. Some of the diaries of that day which have since been given to the world, contained incontestable proofs of the intense personal dislike which he had aroused. "Base," "cowardly," "unprincipled," of "execrable judgment" and "perverted morality," are some of the epithets which he earned by his public course at this time. (¹) Such a man the Tories declared they would not admit into their garden, even to weed it.

The Tory answer to the popular agitation for education then, was much the same that has been given to all demands for improvement. When reform was asked for the people were accused of desiring revolution. In like manner they were charged with pursuing not education but infidelity. The French Revolution furnished a ready argument. If any proposition could be brought within the general category of "French principles" it was enough to enlist a vast mass in society against it, and "the practical lessons of Europe for the last thirty years" were sure to be adduced as unanswerable and conclusive against all changes. The only important deduction the Tories could make from the reports of the Education Committee were, that grants for building Churches should be enlarged. Accordingly, when Brougham was compelled to bespeak favour for an education scheme on the ground that it might be had without any burthen to the State, the Chancellor of the Exchequer proposed a grant of a million for providing additional places of worship in connection with the Established Church. (²)

¹ Greville's Journal, 2, 18.   ² Pamphleteer, 1818.

The attack in the *Quarterly* was followed up in the House of Commons by Sir Robert Peel in the next session. This, however, was a tactical mistake which exposed the Government to an immediate and telling reply from Brougham. ([1])

The practical benefits resulting from the Commission of which Brougham was the author, have been great, although not always admitted. Lord Campbell sneeringly said that his efforts had cost the nation several hundred thousand pounds distributed amongst Commissioners, but that no real benefit had been derived from their labours. ([2]) There can be no doubt, however, that large sums were rescued from neglect and misapplication, and applied to charitable and educational purposes. The Endowed Schools Commissioners reported that they found little evidence of malversation in 1865 ; and they attributed the discontinuance of abuses to the enquiries of the Commissioners who reported to Parliament between 1819 and 1837, to the subsequent legal proceedings which have been taken by the Attorney General, and to the establishment of a permanent Charity Commission. ([3]) The credit of the initiation of these measures belongs to Brougham. It was a rich mine for investigation. There were four Commissions appointed between 1815 and 1837, and their reports fill thirty-eight folio volumes. The annuual income of the charities upon which they reported amounted to £1,209,395. They possessed 442,915 acres of land of the estimated value of forty-four millions, while their total wealth amounted to seventy-five millions. ([4]) The evil effect of these charities in their unreformed state in parishes were they were numerous, can hardly be exaggerated. Of one such parish it was reported :

[1] Brougham's Speeches, 2, 301.   [2] Life of Brougham, 338.
[3] Report of the Endowed Schools Commission, 245.
[4] Shuttleworth's Public Education, 161.

"Bastardy and felony have increased, beer houses have multiplied, and the population become so corrupt that the neighbouring clergy and respectable laity have declared the parish to be a public nuisance." ([1]) The proper and pure administration of these endowments, and their application in part to educational purposes has been of immense public service; but Brougham and others have been disappointed in the expectation that they would afford a sufficient revenue for the support of elementary schools, or to supply even the amount of assistance which it was thought could be prudently afforded by the State.

Brougham's next Parliamentary effort on behalf of education was in 1820. It was destined to disappoint his friends, and to stop progress for a long time. Miss Martineau refers to the Bill he introduced as the first comprehensive and definite plan for the education of the people. ([2]) This, however, is an injustice to Whitbread's proposal, which the bill followed in its main principle, relating to the local provision for schools. The management clauses were original, but to a great part of the nation, wholly unacceptable. The only explanation of such a bill, as coming from him was, that if he could get education he was comparatively indifferent as to the means. On another subject he once said, "as a man of common sense I must wish to achieve some practical good in my time," and this is the probable key to his action at this time. He had guaged the strength of the Church, at any rate, for opposition. He was aware of the close, universal, and effective organisation which the clergy possessed; and he knew that they were resolved to hold the control of the State system. His experience in introducing the Bill for a Commission had taught him what to expect from the Tories. He knew also that the Whigs in the House did not care for education, and that they

[1] Shuttleworth's Public Education, 188.   [2] History of the Peace, 1, 264.

accepted innovations slowly and reluctantly, only as they were forced on them by the growth of opinion. They were ready to disturb the official comfort of their opponents when practicable, but that was the measure of their support. In Parliament he stood almost alone. Whitbread and Romilly were dead, and although he had the qualified support of Mackintosh, he was the solitary conspicuous representative of the popular feeling which gave life to the movement. In these circumstances he concluded that he could only secure the main object of the measure by large concessions to the clergy.

The bill was introduced on the 28th day of June, 1820. It was explained to the House under four heads— the foundation of schools, the appointment of masters, the admission and teaching of children, and the improvement of educational endowments. ([1]) The authority for taking proceedings was vested in Quarter Sessions, who were enabled to act on their own finding, or on the representation of two justices of the peace, the clergyman of the parish, or five resident householders. The magistrates were thus constituted a tribunal for adjudicating and proceeding in the matter. The cost of building schools was to be provided in the first place by the Treasurer of the County, but ultimately by the Receiver General of the land tax. All other expenses were to be levied by the parish officers half-yearly. The appointment of the master was placed in the Vestry. He was required to be a member of the Established Church, and a communicant, and to have a certificate of character from a clergyman. His appointment was also to be subject to the approval of the parish clergyman, who might reject him on examination, or remove him at any time. It is curious to reflect, and it proves the demoralising influence

[1] Hansard, S. S., 2, 67.

of the monitorial system, that Brougham, who was an advanced educationist in his day, had no higher idea of the character of a schoolmaster than his bill reveals. His view was that the parish clerk would best fill the office, and that it would secure a better class of men for parish clerks.

The clergy were to have the power of visitation and examination, and were to fix the course of teaching, and the scale of school pence. There is one remarkable clause in the bill. Brougham was always afraid of compulsory attendance at the day schools as being of the nature of a sumptuary law, and not justifiable either on the principle of utility or expediency.(¹) But in this bill he provided for the compulsory attendance of children at Church or Chapel on Sundays, according to the choice of their parents. A school meeting was also required on Sunday evenings for teaching the catechism and liturgy.

In submitting these provisions to the House he said he knew he should have the "sectaries" against him, but his "object was to graft the new system on an old stock." The clergy were naturally the teachers of the poor. "The parson was a clerical schoolmaster, and the schoolmaster was a lay parson." He deprecated the anger of the Dissenters, but would not, to overcome the scruples of a few, turn his back on the clergy, "whom Providence had raised up to give strength and stability to the plan"(²)—a strange solecism in the mouth of Henry Brougham. There was one saving clause in the Bill; it provided that in day schools the Bible alone should be taught, and no form of worship allowed except the Lord's prayer.

The Bill was supported by Sir James Mackintosh, and assented to by Lord Castlereagh; but before the second reading came on a great storm of indignation had arisen amongst Dissenters and Roman Catholics, and Brougham's

¹ Quarterly Journal of Education, 1835, 239.   ² Hansard, S. S., 2, 75.

old friends, "the Saints." They declared that it was a Bill for rooting out " the last remains of religious liberty in the country." William Allen wrote " such an innovation upon the principles of religious liberty, had, perhaps, never been attempted, except in the case of Lord Sidmouth's Bill, since the days of Queen Anne. ([1])

In truth the measure satisfied no party. The clergy who wished for a compulsory catechism, liturgy and creed, received it coldly. The Dissenters were outraged and alarmed at the overwhelming ascendancy it gave to the Church. It was contended that public opinion and popular influence would be extinguished if the machinery for education were thus placed entirely under the control of the Church. A " Committee for the protection of Religious Liberty " was formed to watch its progress. To these strong manifestations of disapproval, Mr. Brougham reluctantly bowed, and did not proceed with the bill. The incident was unfortunate, both for himself and the cause of education. He weakened his own influence, alienated many of his supporters, and even caused distrust of his motives. His friends admitted sadly that he was more successful in detecting error than in devising remedies. His enemies were delighted at his failure and humiliation, and rejoiced to find, that with all his stupendous talents, he had so little efficiency and influence in practical legislation.

There now followed a long interval before the question of English education was again raised in Parliament, except on occasional petitions for the amendment of particular abuses. The notice which had been called to the endowments, had stimulated enquiry into the management of local charities. They were almost without exception in the hands

[1] Life of Allen, 294. The Bill referred to was probably that introduced by Viscount Sidmouth in 1811, for restricting the licensing of Nonconformist ministers.

of Churchmen, and the masters were generally in Holy Orders. The regulations usually required attendance at Church, and instruction in the Church formularies. Where these were not expressly imposed, the effect of decisions and interpretations generally made them compulsory. Even down to the Endowed Schools Act of 1869, ([1]) where the terms of the trust did not require that the Boards should be composed of Churchmen only, the power of self-election frequently supplied the deficiency. ([2])

In 1830 the Dissenters of Birmingham petitioned Parliament to be allowed to have a share in the government of the Grammar School, ([3]) and similar requests proceeded from other towns; but it was only in a fitful and incidental way that the Legislature was approached on the subject. Brougham's failure had made independent members cautious. The divisions between parties had been widened. The leaders on both sides hesitated to commit themselves to any definite views, upon a question made of such explosive compounds, and possibly so destructive of the repose of parties. Yet it was during this period that Mr. Stanley matured and carried his scheme of Irish Education, on the basis of which Irish Elementary Schools have since remained. ([4])

But if Parliament was halting and timid the people were not idle. Out of doors the Education question was struggling forward in company with many other objects of reform, which engaged popular attention. This was the first great era of improvement directed and stimulated by public intelligence. Parliamentary and municipal reform, the thorough re-organisation of factory labour, the abolition of the slave trade, the repeal of the taxes on knowledge, the re-modelling of the Irish Church—all these questions were exciting thought, and rapidly acquiring force. The demand for the repeal of

[1] Schools Enquiry Commission Report, 129.
[2] Ibid, 250. [3] Hansard, S. S., 24 [4] Hansard, T. S., 6, 1249.

the Corn Laws was also beginning to be heard, though it was not until some years later that it took great prominence in public discussion.

It was between 1820 and 1835 that the first era of cheap popular literature ran its course. It was a period of wonderful progress, and contributed in a greater measure than any other single event in national life to stimulate the desire for knowledge and to lead to the ultimate establishment of a State School System. Many great men took part in the movement, and looked to it to produce a revolution in morals and intelligence. The most conspicuous and active of these was Brougham, and he was known as the leader and president of the " Education-mad set." A complete list of those who were associated with him would contain some of the most brilliant and illustrous names which have adorned modern English history. Amongst them were Dr. Birkbeck, the father of mechanics' institutes, Dr. Whately, Earl Russell, Sir Rowland Hill, M. D. Hill, Mr. Wyse, Mr. Roebuck, Mr. Hallam, Mr. James Mill, Lord Auckland, Lord Althorp, Mr. Denman, Charles Knight, Sir Henry Parnell, Sir George C. Lewis, Thomas Campbell, Dr. Lushington, Dr. Thirlwall, and Dr. Arnold. It was the birth-time of labourers' and mechanics' institutes, reading rooms, penny magazines, cheap encyclopædias, education societies, and lectures on natural philosophy. Political science also was becoming a subject of popular exposition.

In 1823-24 Birkbeck and Brougham were engaged in establishing mechanics' institutes and reading rooms throughout the country. In 1827, the Society for the Diffusion of Useful Knowledge was founded, and this led to the publication of the *Library of Entertaining Knowledge*, the *Quarterly Journal of Education*, the *Penny Cyclopædia*, and many other useful works. There was at one time

11

such a demand for books of this description, that when
Constable began to issue his cheap volumes, about 1828,
he looked for a million of buyers. ([1])

In 1826 the scheme for a London University was put
before the public. A Society, which did a great work in
distributing information, was the "Central Society of
Education," of which Mr. Wyse, M.P., was President. This
Society was credited with the authorship of the Government
scheme in 1839, and especially that part of it which applied
to Normal schools. The great towns were also now taking
up the question. Between 1833 and 1837 the Manchester
Statistical Society was formed. The good resulting from the
enquiries instituted by this Society was invaluable.
Manchester has ever since occupied a most conspicuous and
honourable place in the fight for education. On the
Manchester model, similar societies were afterwards formed
in Birmingham, Bristol, Liverpool, and other places. Local
Committees of the Society for the diffusion of useful
knowledge were also established in large towns. The Trades
Unions of London were combining to resist the taxes on
newspapers. A constant kindred agitation in Scotland was
led by George Combe, Professor Pillan, Dr. Drummond, and
James Simpson, which acted powerfully on English opinion.
In 1836 the Home and Colonial Society began training
children, and founding infant schools. In 1837 many ragged
schools were established, and, about the same time, a Society
was founded in Manchester for promoting National Education,
on the plan adopted by the British and Foreign School
Society. The press too was now taking up the question, and
urging its necessity and importance. The *Edinburgh Review*
had been reinforced by the *Examiner* and the *Westminster*.
In the management of the latter the guiding mind was Mr.
James Mill. The history of his opinions on this subject has

[1] Knight's Autobiography, 1, 252.

been written by his distinguished son. " So complete was my father's reliance on the influence of reason over the mind of mankind, whenever it is allowed to reach them, that he felt as if all would be gained if the whole population were taught to read, if all sorts of opinions were allowed to be addressed to them by word and in writing, and, if by the means of the suffrage, they could nominate a legislature to give effect to the opinions they adopted." (¹)

These views were not, of course shared by all who took part in the struggle. Many were drawn into it by the danger which they thought threatened the social system by the immense extension of popular influence without commensurate knowledge ; but all recognised that education must come sooner or later. Dr. Whately wrote, " I wonder not much, considering what human nature is, that some should think the education of the poor an evil. I do wonder at their not perceiving it is inevitable. We can indeed a little retard or advance it ; but the main question is how they shall be educated, and by whom."

Notwithstanding many hopeful signs of the times, the Educators had a hard up hill battle to fight. We, who are surrounded by so many instructive influences, the result of half a century of uninterrupted progress, can hardly appreciate the difficulties under which our predecessors laboured. The penny postage system, which has acted as a most powerful incident to education, was not introduced until 1840, and up to 1836 newspapers and periodicals were under a tax, which seriously limited their circulation amongst the middle classes, and kept them from the labouring classes altogether. The majority of the journals and periodicals which existed, were bitterly hostile to the new movement; the leaders of which were obliged to contend for the right of education, for its social and

¹ J. S. Mill's Auto-biography, 106.

economical advantages, and to appease the jealousy and
alarm which its extension caused amongst a large section
of the upper classes. Knowledge was associated with
irreligion and disloyalty ; with contempt of religious
institutions, and hatred of Government. One of the magazines described the establishment of mechanics' institutes
as a plan for forming the labouring casses into a disaffected
and ungovernable faction. (^{1}) As late as 1839 the same
periodical opposed the education of the people on the ground
that it would make them uneasy and restless, that ignorance
is the parent of contentment, and that the only education
which could be fitly and safely given to them was a religious
education which "renders them patient, humble, and moral,
and relieves the hardship of their present lot by the prospect
of a bright eternity." (^{2}) The establishment of the University
of London was denounced as the " creation of a God-excluding
seminary," and it was predicted that " the worst sentiments
in politics and religion would pervade it." (^{3}) Mr. Southey
wrote, " I am no friend to the London University, or to
mechanics' institutes. There is a purpose in all these things
of excluding religion, and preparing the way for the overthrow of the Church. But God will confound their
devices." (^{4})

The Church which had never before thought that a
University was required in London, now established King's
College, avowedly to protect the religious interests which
the University was supposed to endanger. In the end
these contests and divisions produced another disastrous
effect. It was supposed that in time the conflict between
party and sectarian interests would lead to the collection
of all the children into schools under the control of different
sects. This gave rise to the political maxim of the Volun-

---

[1] Blackwood, 1825, 534.   [2] Combe, Education by Jolly, 532.
[3] Blackwood, 17, 545.   [4] Southey's Life, 5, 297.

taryists, that "education, like industry, would be better off if left to shift for itself." It has, however, been long since acknowledged, that these sectarian strifes did much to impede its progress, and to prevent combined action in Parliament.

After the passing of the Reform Act in 1832, great expectations were formed of Parliamentary assistance. It is noteworthy that on the two occasions when Parliament has taken serious action in regard to education, the movement has followed a reform in the system of representation. The grants which began in 1834, and the establishment of the Education Department, were the outcome of the Reform Bill of 1832, as the Education Act of 1870 was one result of the Reform of 1868. In each case two causes had been at work. The increased power of the democracy, and the determination to use it for their advantage was the most important; and this was seconded by the alarm of the upper classes at being in the hands of an uneducated people, and the recognition of the necessity expressed by Mr. Lowe, of "educating their masters." But the great hopes raised by the formation of Earl Grey's Ministry, in 1832, were doomed to disappointment. It was natural that extravagant expectations should be formed. Brougham was a member of the new Ministry. Two other Cabinet Ministers, Lord Althorp and Lord John Russell were on the Committee of the Society for the Diffusion of Useful Knowledge. "After the Reform era," says Charles Knight, "I have sat at the monthly dinner with five Cabinet Ministers, to whom it appeared that their duty was to carry forward that advancing intelligence of the people which had carried them to power." [1] When several Sessions had passed away, and the Ministry had been partly reconstituted, the dissatisfaction became intense.

[1] Knight's Biography, 2, 131.

The Radicals who were represented by Roebuck, Grote,
Buller, Molesworth, and Romilly, came in for a share of
disapprobation. The *Westminster Review* referred bitterly
to an Education Bill which had been postponed " on account
of the influenza or some equally cogent reason." ([1]) The
feeling as regards Brougham has been expressed by Miss
Martineau in her " History of the Peace." ([2]) He was even
suspected by his friends of having deserted the cause.
The Parliament was described as a " do nothing Parliament,
halting half-way between helplessness and mischief," which
had expended its whole force on Reform, and had no policy,
and no course of action. ([3]) Justice has since been done
to Earl Grey's Ministry. " No previous administration
had ever accomplished so many reforms as the Grey Cabinet
had effected in a year." ([4]) " They accomplished in four
years what would have done honour to any administration
in fourteen, yet they did not move fast enough for their
impatient supporters." ([5]) Mr. J. S. Mill has also now
acknowledged that too much had been expected from the
small band of Radical members who had set up on their
own account, and that their lot was cast in a period of
inevitable reaction. ([6])

Brougham's position was understood more clearly by his
enemies than his friends. They saw that by his elevation to
the woolsack as a member of Lord Grey's Ministry in 1830,
he had gone to his " political death-bed." He had lost
power rather than obtained it. His power was that of a
popular leader—not that of a parliamentary adviser. In the
House of Commons he had been the nominal leader of the
Whig opposition, but the Whigs had never trusted him. He
was not of their set. They were jealous of his superiority,

---

[1] *Westminster Review*, 1837, 27.   [2] Martineau's History, 2, 76.
[3] *Westminsier Review*, 33, 387.   [4] Walpole's History, 3, 209.
[5] English Premiers, by Earle, 2.   [6] Mill's Autobiography, 195.

distrusted his energy, and were alarmed at his influence in the country. They adopted him for their own purposes, as they had adopted Romilly and Horner, and were glad to be relieved of his presence from the House in which he spoke with authority. He saw too late that he had made the greatest error of his life. As the promoter of education, the leader of the anti-slavery movement, the chief Parliamentary representative of the Dissenting bodies, and the head of the reform party, his power and influence were immense. They were destroyed at a blow by his acceptance of the Great Seal, and he "ceased to be for ever the great popular chief." [1] From this time phrases which had been current amongst his enemies were passed about by his former friends. They began to accuse his vanity, and even to suspect his genuineness. He was "ungenerously deserted by his friends, while cruelly assaulted by his foes, he was maligned by those to whom he had been a benefactor, and all mankind seemed to be in a conspiracy against him." [2]

In the House of Commons Brougham's place, as leader of the Education party was somewhat poorly filled by Mr. Roebuck, and at times by Mr. Wyse. It is to the honour of the former that in the first year he came into Parliament he made an effort to re-open the question; and that with so much success that the Government was induced to grant a small and wholly inadequate sum for education purposes. In 1833 he moved that in the next session the House would proceed to devise means for the universal education of the people. [3] He advocated compulsion to the extent of making it an offence to keep a child away from school between six and twelve years of age. Lord Althorp objected to bind the Government by the resolution, which was not pressed to a division; but he intimated that the Government were not

[1] Roebuck's History of the Whig Administration, 1, 470.
[2] Campbell's Life of Brougham, 414.   [3] Hansard, T. S., 20, 139.

passive in the matter, and subsequently moved for a grant of £20,000 to be expended at the suggestion of the National Society and British and Foreign School Society, in aid of private subscriptions for the erection of schools. He correctly described this as the commencement of a new system, the extent of which they could not foresee. ([1]) The grant was opposed by Mr. Hume on economical grounds, and by Mr. Cobbett for the reason that schoolmasters were "a new race of idlers," but it was carried in a House of seventy-six members. Modest as this beginning was, it was not viewed without alarm, it being foreseen that Government would now be pressed to make yearly grants. There was abundant evidence of the willingness of the Government to spend money for objects which it approved. In the same session twenty millions were voted for the abolition of slavery; and one million was applied to pay arrears of tithes in Ireland. ([2]) It is perhaps also noteworthy that in the same year the education vote in Prussia amounted to £600,000.

In 1834 Mr. Roebuck re-opened the question, and moved for a Select Committee, condemning in a vigorous speech the "slavish bigotry and intolerance" that prevailed in National Schools. Again the Government showed a disposition to make concessions, and the motion was withdrawn in favour of one moved by Lord Althorp on behalf of the Government, for a Committee "to enquire into the state of education in England and Wales, and into the application and effect of the grant for the erection of schools, and to consider the expediency of further grants in aid of education." ([3]) The Committee was appointed and renewed, on the motion of Mr. Roebuck, in the next session. Lord Melbourne's first Administration was dissolved

---

[1] Hansard, T. S., 20, 730. [2] *Westminster Review*, 19, 387.
[3] Hansard, T. S., 23, 127.

in November, and after the general election Sir Robert Peel became Premier. Early in 1835 Lord John Russell brought forward a motion in regard to the Irish Church, in which he declared that the Anglican Establishment in Ireland was excessive, and that its surplus revenues should be applied to education. ([1]) Sir Robert Peel would make no compromise, and the Government was defeated by a majority of twenty-seven, and resigned. In a few days Lord Melbourne's second Administration came in. This year Lord Brougham, whose short term of office had expired, never to be renewed, submitted a series of resolutions to the House of Lords, affirming the insufficiency of the means for national education, and the necessity of supplementing them; of establishing training schools for teachers, and of appointing a permanent Board of Commissioners for guarding and applying funds left for educational purposes. In a subsequent session he brought in another bill having the same object. No progress was made with it, and he complained that his bill was unfortunate at all times, since when their Lordships had nothing to do they could not proceed with it. A practical suggestion he afterwards made found acceptance. This was the appointment of a Department of Public Instruction—the idea of which he derived from France. ([2]) About the same time the Bishop of London attacked the Central Society of Education, which was doing the work of propagandism in the country. He said that he viewed with great alarm the attempt to establish a compulsory system of education, secular in character ; and he cautioned the Christian public against it.

The grant of £20,000 yearly was continued after 1834, but its division was already causing great dissatisfaction. The first grant had been equally divided between the National, and the British and Foreign School Societies.

[1] Life of Melbourne, 2, 101.   [2] Hansard, T. S., 38, 1618.

The principle of the Government was to make grants where one half of the sum required was raised by local efforts. The British and Foreign School Society had exhausted their local funds in the. first year, and were unable to make a proportionate advance. The result was that gradually two-thirds, three-fifths, or three-fourths of the grant went to the National Society, which had superior local resources. ([1]) It also became evident that the system was defective in a most essential feature, as no provision was made in poor localities where it was most required, and where education was at the lowest ebb. These defects and inequalities were gradually turning the public mind to a rate supported system, which, however, was yet far in the distance.

The sessions of 1837 and 1838 passed without further substantial progress. Mr. Slaney moved for a Select Committee, but Lord John Russell deprecated haste for fear of exciting resentment and opposition on account of religious differences ([2]) which continued to be the great stumbling block. Mr. Wyse followed up the attack in 1838, by asking for the appointment of a Commission to provide for the efficient application of the grant, and for the establishment of schools. ([3]) The Government opposed the motion; Lord John Russell, who was the Liberal leader in the Lower House, saying that he " was not prepared to state any manner in which Parliament could aid the work beyond what it had done." He expressed his own preference for the British and Foreign Society's System, but adhered to the principle of distribution adopted by the Treasury, that the largest share of the grant should be given to those who subscribed most towards it. The motion was defeated by seventy-four votes to seventy. The lessons of this division were not lost upon the

[1] Hansard, T. S., 37, 448.   [2] Ibid, 39, 388.   [3] Ibid, T. S., 43, 710.

Ministry. They began to see that public opinion would support them in more decisive action, and therefore prepared for an important step in the next session.

92

CHAPTER III.

PERIOD.—FROM THE APPOINTMENT OF THE COMMITTEE OF
COUNCIL IN 1839 TO THE MINUTES OF 1847.

THE direct intervention of the Government for the
promotion and regulation of elementary education dates
from 1839. In the assistance which the State had given
previously to that period, it had merely stood in the position
of a subscriber to the two great voluntary societies which
occupied the ground; having no connection with schools or
their teachers, and exercising no authority over their
regulations or management. The important changes which
now took place, and the subsequent history of the question
will be better understood, after a brief review of the condition
of education and the relations of parties at this time.

The new science of statistics has played an important
part in the education controversy. From 1818, up to the
present time, many sets of educational statistics have been
published. They have been derived from all sources, and
sent forth under all manner of auspices—from the Government,
from rival education societies, from the purely statistical
societies, and from individuals for whom the peculiar investigation has had an attraction. They have been useful at times
in fixing attention upon the subject, while on other occasions,
they have tended to confuse the issue. For the ordinary
reader, at any rate, they have not raised the question out of
the depths of dulness to which it has often been condemned.
They have been employed for all purposes—to prove the value
of instruction and the reverse, the want of education and its
abundance, the necessity on the one hand for legislative

action, and on the other the sufficiency of voluntary effort. The same tables have been quoted to support precisely opposite views. In the early discussions of the question they were sometimes used to make education responsible for crime. Blackwood wrote, " It is now established by decisive evidence that public instruction has not only no effect whatever in diminishing the tendency to crime, but that it greatly increases it." (¹) No useful purpose can now be served in disinterring from the reports and pamphlets in which they are buried, the voluminous figures which have been published on the question. The accuracy of the most authentic of them has been impeached, and even where this has been vindicated, they have been subject to deductions and qualifications which cannot be represented by figures. Until recent times there has never been a standard by which educational statistics could be tried, for the reason that there was no agreement as to what education meant. They failed to convey an adequate idea, alike of the depths and intensity of the exertions which have been made for the sake of education, and of the mass of ignorance which was left untouched·

The several Government enquiries into the state of education have produced four sets of statistics, to which occasional reference may be necessary for the purposes of comparison. The first were those of 1818—the result of Brougham's Select Committee. The next are known as Lord Kerry's returns, and refer to 1833. An exhaustive enquiry in 1851 produced the elaborate figures contained in the census returns of the Registrar-General. A few years later the Duke of Newcastle's Commission of 1858, became responsible for the tables contained in their report. Since the formation of the Committee of Council the reports of the Government Inspectors have been illustrated by valuable and reliable statistics ; and the various statistical societies of London,

¹ Blackwood, 38, 393.

Manchester, Birmingham, and other towns, have contributed
to swell the proportions of this branch of the enquiry, and have
often quickened and stimulated public opinion on the question.

According to the returns of Brougham's Committee in
1818, the number of scholars in day schools was 674,883, or
one in 17·25 of the population. In 1833, as vouched by
Lord Kerry's tables, they had increased to 1,276,947, or one
in 11·27 of the population. ([1]) It has been estimated
that at the former period, for every child receiving education
three were left entirely destitute. ([2]) Lord Kerry's returns
contained no calculation of the numbers absent from school,
but they were taken as proof that the voluntary societies,
with the assistance they received from Government, were
doing satisfactory work and making promising headway.
Immediately, however, that these conclusions came to be
tested by independent enquiry as to the locality and the
character of the education provided, they were found to
convey a most fallacious idea of the progress actually made.
The earliest statistical society was formed at Manchester, and
its principal object was to verify the returns of Lord Kerry,
which were thought to do injustice to the work of the
voluntary schools in Lancashire. ([3]) Some of the early
papers were directed to correct this supposed unfairness ; but
the officers of the society and those who conducted its
investigations, became at once convinced that it was utterly
hopeless to rely upon the sufficiency of voluntary means.
The enquiries made in Manchester, Liverpool, Salford, and
Birmingham, dissipated the idea that satisfactory progress was
being made. In Manchester a third, and in Liverpool half of
the children of school age were receiving no instruction at
all ; not even that of the Sunday-school. In most of the
large towns it was found that only one in seventeen of the

---

[1] Census Returns, 1851.   [2] Walpole's History, 1, 212.
[3] Porter's Progress of the Nation, 695.

population was being educated, and in some districts only one in thirty-five. In parts of Lancashire, towns of 25,000 inhabitants were without a single school. The proportion of children who received no instruction of any kind in day or Sunday-schools was found to be in Manchester thirty per cent., Liverpool fifty per cent., York thirty-four per cent., Westminster sixty-five per cent., and Birmingham fifty-one per cent. ([1]) In 1837 the London Statistical Society reported, that the country did not afford the means of education for more than one half of those in a condition to receive it. ([2]) In other places one child in thirty-five was receiving " nominal " education. The reports from Liverpool stated that improvement was hopeless until assistance and direction came from a body vastly superior in means and intelligence to any in existence. ([3]) The quality of the education supplied was even more startling in its deficiency than the quantity. The best schools were doubtless those of the rich voluntary societies, but their results were wholly untested except by independent observation. In the evidence which Professor Pillans gave before the Select Committee of 1834, he stated his belief that in a few years the children in the National Society's schools would have lost the power of reading. ([4]) They were trained to obtain an accurate knowledge of every hard name in the Book of Kings, but no love of knowledge or of books was inculcated. The sole object of the society was to manufacture members of the Church, and not to impart information which would be useful in the pursuits of life. ([5]) " Nothing, or next to nothing, is learned, and the parents merely pay for having their children kept out of harm's way." ([6]) But the bulk of the children included

[1] Journal of Statistical Society, 3, 28.   [2] Ibid, 1, 48.
[3] British and Foreign Review, 1836, 601.   [4] Ibid, 564.
[5] Quarterly Journal of Education, 1834, 253.
[6] Memoirs of Sara Coleridge, 1, 194.

in these imposing Government returns were taught in private adventure schools kept by dames and others. They were hived in dirty, unwholesome rooms, used for sleeping or working; in garrets, and often in cellars. The qualification of their teachers was that they were unfit for anything else, though they generally united education with some other employment; such as the keeping of small shops, or taking in washing or sewing. ([1]) In the mining districts most of those who went to school at all, were taught by miners or labourers who had lost health or met with accidents in the works. ([2]) In other places persons were keeping school on account of "old age"—"to get a bit of bread,"—because they could not weave, or had lost their arms, or lamed their feet, or were short of work, or "to keep off the town." It was the usual resource of widows left without means. ([3]) The Factory Act of 1833 required the Inspectors to enforce the attendance at school of children employed in factories, and to order vouchers of attendance to be kept. ([4]) The Act required education to be given, but made no provision for schools. To meet the requirements of the Act, all manner of school-houses were improvised, "from the coal-hole to the engine-house." "The engine-man, the slubber, the burler, the bookkeeper, the wife of any one of these, the small shop-keeper, or the next-door neighbour, with six or seven small children on the floor and in her lap, are by turns found teaching in and about their several places of occupation, for the two hours required by the law." ([5]) The certificates required were usually signed with the mark of the school-keeper. The Commissioners appointed to enquire into the working of the Poor Laws reported on the frightful forms in

[1] British and Foreign Review, 1836, 589.
[2] Report of Committee of Council, 1839-40, 178.
[3] Proceedings of Statistical Society, 2, 35.
[4] 3 and 4, William IV., c. 103.
[5] Journal of Statistical Society, 2, 179.

which ignorance revealed itself. There were 60,000 children in poor-houses under influences little less injurious than those of prisons. ([1]) " I know of nothing more pathetic than a workhouse school," wrote Mr. Cumin, in one of his reports. Dean Alford wrote, at the end of 1839 :—" Prussia is before us; Switzerland is before us; France is before us; there is no record of any people on earth so highly civilised, so abounding in arts and comforts, and so grossly, generally ignorant as the English." ([2])

The particulars and extracts which have been given represent the general condition of education at this period— a condition which formed the humiliating topic of every assembly of Englishmen, and of every newspaper and publication of ordinary intelligence. Under these circumstances it was a source of the greatest discouragement and perplexity to thousands of reflecting and benevolent men, that the wide divergences of opinion prevented any united and comprehensive action. The difficulty did not spring from the people themselves. It happened then, as it has always happened since, that the classes which stood most in need of education were those who presented the smallest obstacle to the acceptance of a general plan. In the evidence taken before the Select Committee of 1834 it was well established, that the parents of the scholars were, in the majority of cases, perfectly indifferent about the tone, colour, or management of the schools, so long as they could get good secular instruction.([3]) "Hundreds, perhaps thousands, of children of nonconformists were taught religion, by considering them what they were not, *i.e.*, baptised according to the rites and ceremonies of the Church of England." ([4]) The Secretary of the National Society testified of their schools, that nine-tenths of the parents would remove their children if they could

---

[1] Quarterly Journal of Education, 9, 49. [2] Life of Alford, 121.
[3] Quarterly Journal of Education, 8, 251. [4] Shuttleworth, Public Education, 246.

13

get better instruction, without thinking at all about the religious knowledge. The children of Jews, Unitarians, and Roman
Catholics, were often found in British and National Schools.
It was not that the parents were always wholly ignorant or
indifferent upon religious questions. The compulsory attendance at church and the imposition of the catechism were often
keenly felt as a grievance and a violation of the liberty of
conscience. But where no other schools were available,
earnest Dissenters would send their children to Church schools
with the feeling that home influence would counteract the
teaching of the school and Church, and with the firm
intention to keep them in the practice of Dissent. It was a
strong proof of the value attached to education when such
conditions were acceded to. Amongst the very poorest
classes, and those outside all denominational influences, there
has been since the beginning of the century, an increasing
current of feeling in favour of school instruction, often testified by exertion and self-sacrifice even in extreme poverty.

The interdict against a united and national system came
from the moral teachers of the people, and was pronounced
necessary in the interests of religion. As new plans were
developed and discussed, several phrases have been used to
describe them. There were the exclusively denominational
schools, in which the creeds and doctrines of a particular
Church were imposed on all the children. The " comprehensive" system, and the " combined" system, are phrases which
have been used to describe other plans. Most of the schemes
which have been proposed and embodied in resolutions or
bills during the last half-century, would come under one or
the other of these three descriptions. The meaning and
object of the denominational system requires no explanation.
Under the " comprehensive" system, a school would generally
be in connection with some religious body, and definite
religious instruction would be given in the school; but the

parents of the children would be allowed to decide whether they should attend or be withdrawn from it. The " combined" system is that which was established in Ireland, the scholars receiving secular instruction from the school-master, and separate religious teaching from the ministers of the denominations. But no common ground was found upon which the sects could meet and agree and let education proceed—although, at the outset of the struggle, there was no party which objected to State assistance. The Voluntary-ists who afterwards grew into an influential party, had not yet formulated their objections to State aid and control. When the Committee of Council was appointed, the great body of the Protestant Dissenters of all sects, sustained the Ministry and approved of public grants. Mr. Edward Baines, the founder of the *Leeds Mercury*, and father of the gentleman who afterwards became the leader of the Voluntaryists, supported and voted for the Government scheme of 1839. ([1]) It was not until the administration of the Committee of Council threatened to give undue advantages to the Church, that Dissenters discovered civil and political reasons against State education, and joined in a policy of opposition to its extension.

From the beginning of the struggle to its close, the Church, while doing its utmost to extend education of its own kind, by its own methods, and for its own purposes, has been the grand and chief obstructive to any national system. The National Society prescribed tests and methods, laid down terms of union, and from the Sanctuary at Westminster claimed the right to dictate the terms upon which the educa-tion of the people should be permitted to proceed. The charter of the National Society declared that it was founded to educate the children of the poor, "without any exception," in the doctrines of the Established Church. ([2]) The position

[1] Hansard, T. S., 42, 727. [2] Notes of my Life, Denison, 137.

which the Church took up at that time is accurately stated by Archdeacon Denison, who has been supposed to represent an extreme and violent section of Churchmen, but who has merely stood up manfully for the integrity of early Church principles. " The Church can never, if it would be found faithful, have the ' comprehensive school,' in that sense of the word ' comprehensive,' in which the State employs the term. It may, indeed, ' comprehend' others than Church children in its schools, as it sees occasion, for missionary purposes ; but this exclusively upon its own terms only." ([1]) This was the exact position that was taken up by the National Society in the first instance, and which embodied its principle and practice down to the introduction of the conscience clause. In his evidence given before the Select Committee of 1834, Mr. Wigram, the Secretary of the National Society, said the doctrines of the Church were the appointed means of producing practical religion, and they were not at liberty to substitute anything else. The clerical superintendent of the Society, said he should not be justified according to the principles of the Society, in allowing their school-children to attend Dissenting places of worship. ([2]) The same view was taken by Churchmen who were remarkable for liberality towards Nonconformists. Bishop Blomfield has been instanced as a man of this character. ([3]) He had been an Edinburgh Reviewer, though afterwards his services were transferred to the Quarterly. As a proof of his liberality, it is stated that his schools were attended even by the children of Jews. His biographer omits to mention that they were compelled to learn the catechism, but Bishop Blomfield himself had no hesitation in making the admission. He told Lord Althorp's Committee that any attempt to give common education to children whose parents were of different persuasions would fail, unless the

---

[1] Notes of my Life, Denison, 105.

[2] Quarterly Journal of Education, vols. 8 and 9.   [3] Life of Blomfield, 53.

parents were content to let their children receive religious instruction according to the doctrine of the Church of England, and that the Church could not come to any compromise that the catechism should not be taught on week days. ([1]) He afterwards always "strenuously upheld the claims of the Established Church to be the educator of the people," ([2]) aud he was one of the skilful negotiators who framed the subsequent concordat between the National Society and the Education Department. The Rev. F. D. Maurice, was one of the last Churchmen whom his generation would accuse of bigotry or illiberality, yet he took the same view of the education question. " We have an education which assumes us to be members of one family, of one nation. If any persons like to be educated on that ground, we will educate them ; if they do not like it, they must educate themselves upon what other principle they may, for we know of no other and will admit no other." ([3]) The same author contended that the clergy were an order sent into the world for the express purpose of cultivating humanity.

A curious illustration of the determination of the Church clergy to make their schools religious institutions, is afforded by what was called the "blending" system. This has now gone altogether, and would probably be illegal under the time table conscience clause, but for some years it was hotly contended for. The object was to interweave doctrinal and historical religious teaching with the ordinary school lessons throughout the day. The copy books were composed of scriptural texts ; the geography was scriptural ; the arithmetic was illustrated by scriptural facts, and all were taught by teachers trained in theological seminaries, in which all knowledge was made secondary and subordinate to dogmatic learning. Mr. Milner Gibson quoted in the House of

---

[1] Quarterly Journal of Education, 9, 214. [2] Life of Blomfield, 191.
[3] Maurice on Education, 172.

Commons from the Rev. Francis Close, who said, "what they sought, was to interweave Church of England evangelical principles with all their instruction, and to diffuse them through the school room all day long." ([1]) The Rev. J. C. Wigram, Secretary of the National Society, prepared a scriptural arithmetic for the purpose. Some of the examples are curious relics of a disused method. "The children of Israel were sadly given to idolatry, notwithstanding all they knew of God. Moses was obliged to have three thousand men put to death for this grievous sin. What digits would you use to express this number ?"

"Of Jacob's four wives, Leah had six sons: Rachel had two ; Hillah had two ; and Zillah had also two. How many sons had Jacob ?"

In this way it was thought to instil morals, and to give a high religious tone to the schools,—purposes which would have been answered as well by teaching the children Bible conundrums. Baden Powell exposed the frivolity of this "blending" system. "It seems difficult to imagine any plan better adapted for making religion an object of contempt and aversion, than thus perpetually associating it in the young mind with the drudgery of school tasks. Scripture spelling surely cannot lead the learner to think scripture any better than a spelling book, nor Bible arithmetic teach him otherwise than to place christianity and ciphering on the same level. The most solemn truths mixed up with the puerile illustration of the alphabet ; the words of divine instruction made vehicles for teaching orthography ; scripture language used for conveying instruction in grammar ; the sacred events of divine revelation employed to furnish examples for arithmetic, are methods of teaching which may indeed secure a familiarity with religion, but it is the kind of familiarity which breeds disrespect."( ) Dr. Hook's proposal to have

[1] Hansard, T. S., vol. 116, 1242.   [2] Pamphlet by Rev. Baden Powell.

schools in which separate religious instruction was given, was a blow to the supporters of this system. They began to enquire whether history could be taught without enforcing the tone and principles of Socinianism or Trinitarianism. Whether " a man might teach reading, writing, spelling, and arithmetic without letting it appear whether he was a Mahomedan or a Christian." But granting it might be so, they returned to their conviction that " we who embrace with all our hearts the divinity of Christ should not allow a disbeliever even to teach our children to cipher." ([1])

There was, however, an eminent minority in the Church which dissented from the extreme pretensions of the National Society and the general body of the clergy. Distinguished amongst these was Dr. Whately, whose labours on the Irish Board of Education helped to give stability to the combined system in Ireland. Dean Hook advocated a similar plan for England, and Dr. Arnold declined to join in the proceedings of the National Society on account of the too great influence which the clergy would have over the education machine. ([2]) Bishop Stanley, the father of Dean Stanley, in the discussions of 1839, vindicated the Government plan of combined education. In more recent years the list of liberal-minded clergymen has been supplemented by the names, amongst others, of Bishops Fraser and Temple, Archdeacon Sandford, Canon Kingsley, Dean Hamilton, Canon Gover, Dean Alford, Dr. Caldicott, Mr. J. C. Cox, Mr. E. F. M. MacCarthy and Mr. Zincke.

In opposing the demands of the Church to the exclusive control of education, Protestant Dissenters took a reasonable and moderate position. They asked only for a proportionate share in school management, and that their children should not, as the condition of instruction, be compelled to learn hostile creeds. To have done less than this would have been a violation of their principles, and a step backward in the

[1] Memoirs of Sara Coleridge, 2, 31. [2] Memoirs of Sara Coleridge, 1, 213.

political and religious freedom for which they had striven, and in a great measure obtained. They had a noble history, which gave them a title to be heard as a part of the people, on questions affecting popular welfare, which it would have been ignominious to surrender. They had by immense sacrifice, exertion, and courage, defeated the design of the ecclesiastical leaders of the Reformation, that our Church government should be made to embrace the whole body of the people. From a despised and persecuted minority they had grown into a power. They had been especially the missionaries of religious and political instruction to the poor, and had defended the rights of minorities. They had obtained a paramount influence over the middle classes, and had shaken to its foundations the traditional authority which the Church claimed over the lower orders. In the Civil Courts and in the Legislature they had upheld the title of the people to equal participations and rights before the law. Their history had been one of continued progress towards religious emancipation, from the days of the Revolution to the repeal of the Test and Corporation Acts. The Church had neglected the religious instruction of the nation. That was not denied. " There has been a heavy sin somewhere—granted; let us not attempt to hide it. The clergy have had the heaviest share in that evil. Let this be confessed, too, both secretly and publicly." ([1]) " There was then, so to speak, no parish school—the nursery of the parish church—seventy or eighty years ago." ([2]) In this gross abnegation and neglect of duty the Dissenters had taken up the work, and they became naturally the instructors of the poor. Their constitution was democratic, and they had strengthened and consolidated their influence by the habits of self government which they had taught, and the political knowledge they had spread. Their life and discipline had

[1] Maurice's Lectures on Education, 238.   [2] Notes of my Life, Denison, 115.

become identified with the growth of liberal principles and the progress of all liberal measures. They felt, therefore, that the demand of the clergy for the exclusive control of education was opposed to the general spirit of the laws and the current of feeling through society. If in later struggles they committed errors of judgment which for a time retarded education, they were made honestly, in defence of principles which were sacred, no less by reason of the travail which had secured their recognition, than on account of the benefits which had resulted from them to national life. The Church had failed to recognise the growth and effect of historical changes; and her endeavour again to set up in education the rules of ecclesiastical instead of civil law, was justly felt to be an anachronism, and an attack on the hardly-won rights of Nonconformity.

Such were the condition of education and the relations of parties, when, in the Session of 1839, Lord John Russell stated the views of Lord Melbourne's Ministry upon the question. The historical reasons for the formation of the Committee of Council vary as they are considered from different aspects. It had undoubtedly been led up to by the exertions of the Central Society of Education, which, by its agitation, had increased the pressure out of doors, and compelled the Government to take action. It was the motion of Mr. Wyse, the Chairman of the Society, in the former Session, which had forced the hand of the Ministry. It had been intimated to the Society that their zeal embarrassed the Government. (¹) There were many Liberal Members of Parliament who supported it, including the Marquis of Lansdowne, Lord Melbourne, and Lord John Russell, all members of the Government. It had incurred the dislike and dread of the Church party, as likely to disturb their claim to a monopoly in the control of education; and when the

¹ *Westminster Review*, 51, 182.

Government plans were found to correspond in a measure with its suggestions, the suspicion that the Ministry was acting under its influence ripened into conviction. Bishop Blomfield declared that Ministers were acting under the advice of an association whose object was the destruction of the Church, "knowing perfectly well that through the medium of the Church, the Monarchy might be most successfully assailed." ([1]) To Archdeacon Denison the formation of the Education Department was a Whig plot for revolutionising or destroying the parish school, concocted to please the Nonconformists. ([2]) Later, it became in the eyes of a section of Nonconformists, a monstrous machine for establishing a tyranny over literature, journals, the pulpit, and for destroying the vitality and independence of national life. From its origin, however, the Committee of Council had one able and adroit defender and apologist—the first Secretary, Sir James Kay Shuttleworth. On all occasions when it was attacked, he was ready to take a brief on its behalf, and honestly could see nothing in the Department but the perfection of statesmanship and human wisdom. To him it was a grand inductive experiment. The Government recognised two principles—that of separate (Church) education, and combined (British and Foreign) education, and then left them to work themselves out and see which would predominate. ([3]) He had qualities for his position which were invaluable for the extension of the influence of the Committee. His history was sometimes at fault, and capable of an easy adaptation to the necessities of his argument, but he never failed in his estimation of the wisdom and sufficiency of his Department. That which was acknowledged on all hands to be a mere expedient, a tentative scheme adopted in utter perplexity and confusion of counsel, he magnified

---

[1] Blomfield's Life, 198. [2] Notes of my Life, 117.

[3] The School in its Relations to State, Church, and Congregation.

into a deliberate State policy, having a settled purpose and confident of its capacity to meet all emergencies.

With such a permanent officer at its helm, it was almost inevitable that the power of the Committee should steadily grow : but the truth about its formation has been told by those who were the authors of its existence. It was neither plot nor policy. The arrangement was never intended to be ultimate or permanent. It was a compromise between the necessity of education, and the difficulty of devising a general system acceptable to the country. ([1]) Lord Althorp's Committee of 1834-35 had been so fairly constituted of members of utterly opposite opinions that they came to a dead lock, and, after taking evidence for two years they shrank from pronouncing any opinion. The formation of the Committee of Council was an expedient to evade the difficulty of constituting a Board of Education.

Lord John Russell explained that no confidence would have been felt in a Board of different persuasions, and they had therefore resolved on appointing a Board from the official servants of the Crown, who would be responsible to Parliament. It was practically a Board of one persuasion, notwithstanding which it never received the confidence of any party. The definite proposition was, that the President of the Council, and other Privy Councillors not exceeding five, should form a Board to consider in what manner grants should be distributed. ([2]) The constitution of the Board has remained much the same since its formation, with the addition in recent years of a Vice-President, who has sat in the House of Commons, and occupied the post of a financial Education Minister. The members of the Committee have consisted of the principal Ministers of the Crown and have changed with the Ministry. ([3]) Lord Lansdowne was the first President of the Council, and undertook to carry out the measures of the

[1] Newcastle Commission Report, 90.
[2] Hansard, T. S., 45, 273.   [3] Newcastle Commission Report, 26.

Government. They proposed that the grant for education should be increased to £30,000, and that as a first measure, a State Normal School for the training of teachers, on the combined system, should be established.

This was the beginning of the tinkering system in education. The difficulties of the Government were no doubt great. They found the ground partially occupied, and felt it was impossible to supersede the agencies in existence. Vested interests had been created by the previous grants to the voluntary societies, and when they came to be taken away and administered directly by the Department, the cry of invasion and aggression was raised, and no common basis of opinion between Church and dissent could be discovered upon which a general plan could be established. The earlier grants to the voluntary societies had produced an unfortunate effect. Instead of standing on the principle that national education should not be converted into a machinery for perpetuating sectarian distinctions, the grants had been so distributed as to widen the differences and strengthen the distinctions between denominations, and for a long series of years this was the practical effect of every attempt by Government to extend education. The Government also had difficulties peculiarly its own. It was a time of party crises, and the Ministry felt that they were vulnerable on every side, and could not afford to lay themselves open to sectarian assaults—a difficulty which they did not escape, as events will show. Their natural enemies in the Opposition were always on the alert to seize an advantage, whilst the feeling amongst the Liberals was one of painful and petulant disappointment. It resulted that their practice on important questions had become,

> "To promise, pause, prepare, postpone,
> And end by letting things alone."

The Government were hardly open to attack on the ground of the extent of their educational operations. Thirty thousand pounds for the education of fifteen millions was not a large subsidy. It was, as Carlyle said, "a small fraction of the revenue of one day," and Brougham did n'ot forget to note that in the same year £70,000 was voted for building Royal stables. ([1]) The model school experiment was to be provided for, out of a fund for £10,000, apparently voted in 1835, but never applied.

But small as the measure was in a financial sense, it undoubtedly involved important principles. The creation of a State Department of instruction meant the assertion of civil as opposed to ecclesiastical education, and that the State grants would be administered by the Department instead of being paid as heretofore to voluntary associations. In this sense it was a significant advance, and an assault upon the ecclesiastical position. Indeed there was but one safe course for the maintenance of the exclusive and high ground taken by the Church, and that was the refusal of all State aid. The acceptance of assistance from the Government, however carefully fenced by conditions, involved eventually Government supervision, as surely as the application of local rates involves local control. This point however did not strike the Church party, and they turned their opposition against the less significant scheme for a Normal school, in which secular teaching was to be given on the combined principle, while religious instruction was to be supplied to the students by ministers of their particular denomination. Against this proposal the whole force which the English Hierarchy could command was directed.

The Dissenters received the plan with acquiescence if not with satisfaction. Macaulay credits Brougham with attempting to get up an opposition amongst the Quakers, ([2]) but if he were in earnest it came to nothing, and he resisted the

[1] Walpole's History, 3, 487. [2] Macaulay's Life, 2, 51.

attacks of the Bishops in the House of Lords. (¹) The representatives of the non-exclusive educationists in the House, Mr. Wyse and Mr. Ewart, gave their support to the proposal as a forward step, not adequate and complete, but the pledge and guarantee of a national system in time. There was amongst the Church party some little division of opinion at the outset. Sir Robert Inglis, the representative of Oxford University expressed his gratitude that the Government proposed to do so little mischief. But the suspicions of Sir Robert Peel had been aroused by the ready assent given to the plan by Liberal members. He demanded distinct information of the principles by which the Board would be guided, challenged the foundation of the Normal school, and claimed the right of the Church to establish Schools and to insist that the children should be brought up in the doctrines of the Church. (²)

In the Lords Bishop Blomfield attacked the plan as leading to latitudinarianism and irreligion and as the heaviest blow yet struck at the religion of the country. He repudiated the claim for religious equality, and said that if every sect was to have the same advantages as the Established Church, it might as well abdicate its functions. The State had delegated its functions in the matter of educating the poor to the Church, (³) and the duty of the Bishops, as rulers of the Church, was to protest against any system not connected with it, or which by implication might throw discredit on it, or raise Dissenting sects to a level with it. (⁴)

A most perverse anxiety was shown to exclude the public from forming a correct idea of the Government plan in regard to the Normal School. Viscount Morpeth said the petitions against it were offensive and mendacious. (⁵)

¹ Hansard, T. S., 47, 756.   ² Ibid, 45, 305.
³ Life of Blomfield, 200.   ⁴ Hansard, T. S., 47, 756.   ⁵ Ibid, 1383.

Placards against popery and infidelity were paraded together, and it was stated that the Government was intent on converting Church children into Socinians and Papists. The misrepresentations have survived to our own day. Lord John Russell explained, in the House of Commons, that the Government proposed the appointment of a chaplain of the Established Church, but that the children of Dissenters should be instructed in the religious opinions of their parents. This proposal, as sketched in Bishop Blomfield's Life, was "the establishment of a model or Normal School, on a non-exclusive plan, with teachers of various persuasions, different versions of the Bible, and a 'rector' of no particular religion." (¹) When after the lapse of a quarter of a century, such a distorted version could have passed current, the heat and passion of the time may be imagined. At any rate, they were so great that the Government determined to lighten their ship, and the proposal for the establishment of a Normal School was thrown overboard ; the money intended for its establishment being subsequently divided between the National Society and the British and Foreign School Society.

This concession, however, did not satisfy the Opposition. Lord Stanley, who had himself introduced the Irish system, attacked the principle of civil education, and quoted some forgotten Statute of Henry IV., to prove that education was "chose spirituelle." To give control over such a matter to a lay body would sap the foundation of all faith, and lead to general scepticism and national infidelity. (²) He also attacked the Board as unconstitutional and irresponsible.

The debate was several times adjourned. It may be interesting to note that both Mr. Gladstone and Mr. Disraeli opposed the Government. The latter in an ingenious speech said that he feared we were returning to the system of a

¹ Life of Blomfield, 194.　² Hansard, T. S. 48, 259.

barbarous age—that of paternal Government. "It was always the State and never society ; it was always machinery and never sympathy." He expected to see under the new system the wildness of fanaticism rather than the rise of infidelity, and predicted that the Roman Catholic Church would rise predominant and supreme under the scheme of the Central Board. English character would become revolutionized and we could no longer expect English achievement. ([1])

The proposal of the Government was carried in the Lower House by the narrow majority of two, and the Ministry barely escaped destruction. The fight was renewed in the House of Lords, on the motion of Archbishop Howley, for an address to the Queen, praying that no steps might be taken to give effect to the plan until the Upper House had had an opportunity of considering it. The address was carried by a majority of one-hundred-and-eleven votes, and was taken by the Peers in procession to Buckingham Palace. ([2]) The Government, however, remained firm.

The reply to the address stated that the Queen had appointed the Committee under a deep sense of duty, and that all proceedings would be laid before Parliament. The Queen had often urged Lord Melbourne to introduce some measure for primary education in England—a work on which Her Majesty had set her heart on having her reign remembered. ([3])

The Church thus " took the responsibility of resisting by the utmost exercise of its authority and influence in the country, in both Houses of Parliament, and at the foot of the Throne, the first great plan ever proposed, by any Government, for the education of the humblest classes in Great Britain."([4])

[1] Hansard, T. S. 48, 580. [2] Memoir of Blomfield, 200.
[3] Life of Melbourne, 2, 309.
[4] Shuttleworth, Public Education, 4.

At this distance of time, and in view of what has been done since, this language seems to exaggerate the importance of the occasion. It would be more correct to say that the Church opposed the smallest extension of education not under its own control. Deep offence was felt in the Church, and for a time the separation between the clergy and the Department was complete. It went to such a length that some of the clergy refused the grants for building. (¹) But the estrangement was of short duration. The Church is never beaten out of the field, and its action in regard to education is an example of its tact in turning defeats into victories. The Normal school disposed of, and the Committee of Council fairly established, it next turned its attention to the right of inspection. The clergy were apprehensive that the Inspectors would be partial to secular teaching and would make religious knowledge secondary and subordinate. Their object, therefore, was to obtain the control of inspection. In this they were so far successful, that in the next session of Parliament the Archbishop of Canterbury was able to express his satisfaction at the adjustment of the differences between the friends of Church education and the Committee of Council. (²) This arrangement was afterwards known as the Concordat of 1839-40, and while the Church derived substantial advantage from it, the Dissenters and the public began henceforth to regard the Department with great suspicion, and all subsequent attempts proceeding from it were looked upon as the result of a preceding agreement with the Church or the National Society. It became a current belief that the

¹ In the condensed account of these transactions contained in Miss Martineau's History of the Peace there are two important errors. She assumes that the £10,000 voted for a model school in 1835 was applied for that purpose. She also states that as the result of the appointment of the Committee of Council, the clergy afterwards, with few exceptions, refused to participate in the Government grants. She has evidently been misled by the statement in the *Annual Register* for the year.

² Hansard, T. S., 55, 753.

Department was "managed" by Bishop Blomfield and Sir R. Inglis. ([1])

The clergy had no intention of being permanently excluded from the benefits of the grant. Bishop Blomfield said "If the Government would grant us money, and be content, as they ought to be, with an inspection authorised by the Church, we should act very preposterously, I think, if we were to refuse their proffered assistance." ([2]) They had good reason to be satisfied with the terms which were made for them. In the next ten years (1839-50) £500,000 was spent on education. Of this £405,000 went to the Church schools, ([3]) from which all children were excluded whose parents objected to the catechism. The Committee of Council also undertook, before appointing Inspectors, to consult the Archbishops of Canterbury and York, who were to be at liberty to suggest persons for the office. This was valuable State patronage, and has, in more than one instance, proved a step towards a Bishopric. The regulations respecting religious teaching were framed by the Archbishops, and the general regulations were submitted for their approval. The Inspectors held office during the concurrence of the Archbishops, and were required to report to them. They were directed to enquire, with special care, how far the doctrines and principles of the Church were instilled into the minds of children, whether Church accommodation was sufficient, and in a proper situation, and whether the attendance was regular, and how far the children profited by the public ordinances of religion; whether private prayers were taught for use at home, and on the daily practices of the schools with reference to divine worship, prayer, and psalmody, and instruction in the Bible, catechism, and liturgy. The Inspectors became, in fact, itinerant curates, paid by the State, and were used to

[1] *Westminster Review,* 1849, 182.
[2] Blomfield's Life, 202. [3] Census Returns, 1851, xviii.

consolidate and strengthen the already powerful diocesan and parochial organisation of the Church. Under their direction the thirty-nine articles were taught in some schools, while in others the children were required to write down on Monday what they remembered of Sunday's sermon.

As if this were not enough the Department passed a Minute that, " Their Lordships were of opinion that no plan of education ought to be encouraged in which intellectual instruction was not subordinate to the regulation of the thoughts and habits of children by the doctrines and precepts of revealed religion," (¹) the result being that in a few years they had to report that the teachers were in the habit of resting satisfied with a lower standard of proficiency in reading, writing, and arithmetic, even with their best scholars, than would be tolerated in any handicraft or occupation by which children were to earn their living. (²)

The inspection became also a fruitful source of jealousy and controversy. The obvious leaning of the Department to the Church, led the Committee of the British and Foreign School Society to complain, that the arrangements for inspection were unequal and partial—that the terms were violated, and that British schools were visited by gentlemen connected with the Church, who enquired into religious instruction and reported to the disadvantage of the Society. (³) The Government refused, however, to give to the British and Foreign School Society any similar control over the appointment of Inspectors to that enjoyed by the Church.

The general result of the action of 1839 was, that the Church, " instructed by circumstances, succeeded in absorbing the greater portion of the grant, and in increasing its own influence ; and the Dissenters complained that a scheme which had been in the first instance introduced in their

¹ Minutes of Council, 1839-40, 24.   ² Report, 1857, 58, 25.
³ Ibid, 1843, 4, 516.

interests, and which had been resisted by Churchmen, was unduly favouring the cause of the Established Church." ([1])

The two fundamental principles of action laid down by the Department were, that aid should be limited (1) to cases of great deficiency and where vigorous efforts had been made to provide funds—and (2) where the daily reading of the Scripture formed part of the instruction. Preference was given to schools in connection with the National and British and Foreign School Societies, and afterwards to those which did not enforce a rule by which children were compelled to learn a catechism or attend a place of worship, to which parents objected on religious grounds.

The effect of the first requirement was to exclude the poorest districts where education was most required; that of the second was to shut out many first-class schools—such as the Birkbeck schools—the Williams school at Edinburgh, and other schools of a similar character in Glasgow, Manchester, London, and other towns, and these remained under this exclusion up to the Act of 1870.

It was not to be expected that the friends of national education would rest satisfied with these partial and insufficint means—but for many years it was almost impossible to make progress. The Central Society of education was dissolved. Mr. Wyse the chairman was taken into the Treasury, and Mr. Duppa, the Secretary died. In the patronage of methods of education, the Committee of Council were careful to exclude all which originated with men of liberal opinions or who had been distinguished as educational reformers. ([2]) It was not until the Lancashire public school Association was formed in 1847, that men of this character were able to make their voice heard, or that an active educational propaganda was again undertaken in the country.

[1] Walpole's History, 3, 490.   [2] Westminster Review, 1851, 402.

In Parliament there was a small group of men, who were intensely dissatisfied with the state of education and the tardy pace at which the Government was proceeding, and who protested against its grants as paltry and discreditable. Amongst them were Mr. Ewart, Mr. Milner Gibson, Dr. Bowring, Mr. Childers, Mr. Slaney, and Mr. Roebuck. In 1841 Mr. Ewart moved for the appointment of a minister of public instruction. ([1]) This motion was frequently renewed in subsequent sessions, and it led finally to the appointment of the Vice-President of the Council, and the annual statement on the education vote. In the same year Mr. Slaney introduced a bill to enable rural parishes to levy a school rate and make their own arrangements as to schools, with powers to the magistrates to relieve those who dissented on the ground of religious scruples. ([2]) But it did not get beyond the first reading.

The Whigs were now in opposition. Lord Melbourne had been succeeded by Sir Robert Peel, who had constructed the Ministry whose great achievement, a few years later, was the repeal of the Corn Laws. Sir James Graham, who, up to 1837, had been returned as a Liberal and professed follower of Lord Althorp, had gone over to the Conservatives, and was the Home Secretary in the new Ministry. Mr. Gladstone was also a member of the Government. The Ministry adhered to the Minutes of 1839, and carried out the policy in education of their predecessors, which had been avowedly based on a compromise dictated by the Tories and the Church. In the administration of the Department, the alliance between it and the Church was cemented by the change of Government. Sir R. Peel was a statesman after the heart of the Church party. On all matters affecting their interests he consulted the heads of the Church, and with Bishop Blomfield, who has been called an " Ecclesiastical

[1] Hansard, T. S., 57, 936. [2] Ibid, 58, 799.

Peel," he maintained the most intimate and confidential relations. ([1]) The Dissenters were disposed to look with suspicion on all measures proceeding from such a Government. Sir James Graham had earned their special distrust by his apostacy from Liberal principles. The way was thus prepared for the vehement opposition to the educational clauses of his Factory Bill, which was the prominent feature of the session of 1843.

At the beginning of the session, a profound impression was created in the House by a motion of Lord Ashley in regard to educational deficiences. He relied on the reports of the Factory and School Inspectors, on that of the Children's Employment Commission, and those of the Statistical Societies of Manchester and Birmingham, to prove the failure of the Factory Acts, the vast educational destitution, and the frightful results of ignorance.

Sir James Graham took the occasion to explain the views of the Government. He expressed their desire " to lay aside all party feelings, all religious differences, to endeavour to find some neutral ground on which they could build something approaching to a scheme of national education with a due regard to the just wishes of the Established Church on the one hand, and studious attention to the honest scruples of Dissenters on the other." ([2]) This was the preface to the famous factory education scheme, which aroused the utmost consternation and indignation amongst Dissenters, and which first taught them the extent of their power in opposing legislation hostile to their principles.

The Government bill was not in any sense a large educational measure. It provided for the compulsory education of children in workhouses, and those employed in woollen, flax, silk, and cotton manufactories. It reduced the hours of labour for children between eight and thirteen years of age, to

[1] Blomfield's Life, 218.   [2] Hansard, T. S., 67, 47.

six and a half hours per day, and required that they should attend school for at least three hours. For these purposes the Government offered to make loans for the erection of schools, which were to be maintained out of the poor rate. The trust clauses became the special point of attack. They confided the management to a body of seven trustees, composed of the clergyman and churchwardens *ex-officio*, and four others, of whom two, having a property qualification, were to be appointed by the magistrates, and two were to be mill owners. The appointment of the master, who was required to be a member of the Established Church, was placed in the hands of the trustees, subject to the approval of the Bishop. The right of inspection was reserved to the clerical trustees and to the Committee of Council. The constitution of the trust was humourously offered by the Government as a guarantee that no undue religious influence would be used, and there was a conscience clause for the children of parents who objected to the teaching of the catechism and attendance at Church.

The plan, says Sir James Kay Shuttleworth, was " received with a simple and calm acquiesence by the Established Church." (¹) But Sir Robert Inglis said that it did not give enough to Churchmen, and would prevent them from teaching what they believed to be the truth. On the part of the Opposition, Lord John Russell gave a qualified approval to the Bill on its introduction. Mr. Hawes, on behalf of the Dissenters, and Mr. Smith O'Brien, as representing the Roman Catholics, opposed it. The Bill, however, passed the second reading without a division, Sir James Graham explaining that the constitution of the Boards was a matter of detail. But the true nature and effect of the measure were quickly perceived. " It must gradually subvert and supersede the independent schools, which had been established by the

¹ The School, &c., 67.

spontaneous charity of individuals and congregations, and especially those which owed their origin and success to the working of the British and Foreign School Society. Sooner or later a uniform system of Anglican teaching would obviously be introduced, instead of that which prevailed, and which naturally reflected every diversity of creed. All sects of Nonconformists concurred in opposing the Bill." ([1]) Mr. Hume, Mr. Hawes, Mr. C. Wood (Lord Halifax), Mr. Stansfeld, Mr. M. Phillips, Lord John Russell, Mr. Ewart, Sir George Grey, Mr. Milner Gibson, and Mr. Cobden united in opposing its progress, on the grounds that it rated all classes and gave the management to one—that it imposed a rate for teaching Church doctrines, and that under the guise of education it was an attempt to recruit for the Church. Mr. Cobden ridiculed it as a proposal for national education. It would provide only for some 60,000 children, and imposed Church doctrines upon a population, the majority of which were Dissenters. ([2])

Great meetings were held in the large towns to oppose it, and resolutions pledging resistance to it were passed by all bodies of Dissenters. A mass of petitions, such as were never known in Parliament before, were presented against it. ([3]) The discussion was revived in the House of Commons on a series of resolutions proposed by Lord John Russell, demanding the adequate representation of the ratepayers, the teaching of the Scriptures, the separate teaching of other religious books, the liberty to attend any Church or Sunday School, the support of training schools, grants for teaching and in aid of voluntary efforts, and opposing the disqualification of masters on religious grounds. As the result of the debates so raised the Home Secretary undertook to bring forward amendments.

[1] Life of Graham, by Torrens, 2, 234. [2] Hansard, T. S., 67, 1469.
[3] Annual Register, 1843, 196.

The modifications proposed by the Government on going into Committee were considerable. They recognised the liberty of parents to send their children to any Sunday School, and they provided that instruction in the catechism and Church doctrines should be given at a separate hour and in a separate room, and that religious instruction might also be given separately by Dissenting ministers where it was desired. ([1]) The new plan, in this respect, closely resembled the Irish system. The only compulsory religious observances, were the reading of the Scriptures and the Lord's Prayer, and Catholics were at liberty to withdraw from this. New trust clauses were introduced. The clergyman was to be a trustee, ex-officio, and to have the power of nominating one other, the remaining five being elective—one to be chosen by the subscribers, and four by ratepayers assessed at ten pounds. But one of those cunning "minority" clauses, which are in restriction of the franchise, was introduced, and prohibited ratepayers from voting for more than two trustees; the effect being, as Lord John Russell pointed out, to keep the majority of the Board always on the side of the Church. When the Dissenters were in a minority, they would be able to elect two trustees, who would stand alone ; when Churchmen were in a minority, they would send two members to co-operate with the ex-officio trustees. The head master was still to be subject to the veto of the Bishop, but in all matters of management any one trustee was to have liberty to appeal to the Committee of Council.

---

[1] Mr. Skeats, in his History of Free Churches, gives a somewhat confused and incorrect account of these proposals. He says that Sir James Graham proposed "to attach to each school a chapel, with a clergyman." This is hardly borne out by the facts. As amended, the proposition was to establish a system of combined secular and separate religious teaching, similar to plans which Dissenters have supported before and since. The account also does grave injustice to Lord John Russell's views and motives.

16

" I am aware," said Sir James Graham, "that the waters
of strife have overflowed, and now cover the land—this is my
olive branch." ([1])

But the concession came too late,—the hour for compromise had gone by. The Dissenters had no confidence in the
Government or the Church, and they were greatly excited
and elated by their successful agitation against the bill. It
had revealed resources of numbers, powers of combination,
and ability for organized opposition which they had not
known they possessed. Mr. Roebuck now took up the
question and moved a resolution condemning all attempts on
the part of the State to inculcate particular religious opinions,
and advocating the entire separation of religious and secular
teaching. The proposition was defeated by 156 votes to
sixty. But the fate of the bill was sealed. Petitions were as
numerous as ever. In the city of London 55,000 persons
petitioned against it, and it has been represented that 25,000
petitions containing four millions of signatures were presented
against the bill. The Government confessed that they were
beaten by Exeter Hall and withdrew the measure. Sir James
Graham had now fairly established that ground for suspicion
and distrust which afterwards secured for him the reputation
of being one of the most unpopular ministers England ever
produced.

The Dissenters have been greatly blamed for their action
on this occasion, which exposed them to the charge that they
also cared less for education than for the good of particular
sects. ([2]) Miss Martineau writes that their position was
lowered more by their policy than by anything they had done
or suffered for a century before. It was a " call for magna-
nimity all round." The Church was in a " genial and
liberal mood," but the Dissenters were not equal to the

[1] Hansard, T. S., 68, 1,114.   [2] *Westminster Review*, 1853, 121.

occasion, and they erred widely and fatally. ([1])   It will be seen that their policy was unfortunate in its consequences on account of the graver defections and differences to which it led; but it is impossible to concur in this indiscriminate censure as just, or to see where the Nonconformists failed in generosity in comparison with their opponents.   The bill was a small educational measure.   It was another petty adaptation of the tinkering system.   Mr. Milner Gibson correctly described it as a pitiful proposal, and Mr. Cobden said it was not worth the controversy it would raise.   But the principles were momentous for Dissenters.   It was an attack on them on their own ground, and an attempt to arrest the growth of their influence over the manufacturing classes.   Nor can it be assumed that it was an educational loss.   If the bill had been passed it would have put off for an indefinite period any further efforts by the Government.   The Ministers and Bishops with whom they were in alliance were the real obstructives. In this as in nearly every Government scheme proposed, the control of education was given to the hereditary foes of progress and of liberal ideas.   There is reason to believe that all parties in the State might now have agreed upon a plan of National Education ; but for the opposition of the Bishops. Political economists, and men of great weight in Parliament and amongst all sections of the community were turning their attention to the " combined" system as it existed in Ireland. But the heads of the Church were resolved not to give their sanction to a scheme which did not leave the appointment of the schoolmasters in the hands of the clergy. ([2])   This was their ultimatum.   In the debates on this bill Sir James Graham declared that it was a point on which he could make no concession.   From this time the difficulties of compromise increased.   New causes of difference sprang into existence. The Education Department was in constant opposition to sections

[1] Martineau's History of the Peace.   [2] *Westminster Review*, 1840, 228.

which were themselves bitterly opposed to each other, and the educationists and men of liberal opinions, saw the day of a national system postponed, and even the principle of State Education seriously imperilled.

The errors of the Nonconformists began from this time. They had proved their power for opposition, and they too readily assumed that they were equally potential in construction. The voluntary movement now began, and large bodies of Dissenters of various denominations combined to resist the intervention of Government in education. Henceforward for many years a large section of the Nonconfomist body was fighting for the integral principle of the English and Roman Churches, that education must be kept under ecclesiastical, or congregational direction. They never avowed this in terms, and each party would have repudiated the alliance, but as a matter of fact Cardinal Manning and Archdeacon Denison on the one hand, and Mr. Baines, Mr. Miall, and Dr. Hamilton on the other were contending for the self same principle—the freedom of education from all State control. Of the two parties the latter were the pure Voluntaryists and the most consistent—since they repudiated State aid as well as State direction. The clergy with some notable exceptions who found a leader and representative in Archdeacon Denison, were willing to accept State grants, so long as their right to absolute control was not questioned. This movement, especially as proceeding from the Dissenters, became one of the most formidable obstructions to national education, although both amongst the Church and Nonconformists there was a powerful and distinguished minority which rejected the extreme pretensions of those who assumed to speak with authority for their respective sides.

The discovery by the Nonconformists that State education was hostile to sound political and civil doctrine, and to the development of national life in its highest and purest forms, was made rather late, and forces the conclusion that the position was assumed rather in defence of sectional interests than on account of any fundamental objections in principle. The Dissenters were driven to this new ground by the partiality which the State system showed to the Church, and by the supreme influence which the clergy were suffered to exercise over the Department. In 1839 the Friends, Baptists, and Congregationalists were unanimous in asking for the agency of the State, and they usually joined in supporting the schools of the British and Foreign Society. The Wesleyans also often supported British schools, and it was not until the Education Committee was appointed in 1836, that they began to establish separate schools where practicable. They never had refused the Government grant, and although they became very suspicious of the Committee of Council, they did not, as a body, embrace the new doctrines of educational free trade and the immorality of Government teaching. Up to the introduction of Sir James Graham's factory bill, the leaders of the Congregationalists, who supplied the energy for the new movement, were not opposed to State aid. In the debates of 1847, Sir George Grey quoted the *Leeds Mercury* of March, 1842, which advocated two schools in each district—one for the Church and one for Dissent, each to be equally supported by the Government. The objections to Government teaching were first formulated at the meeting of the Congregational Union held at Leeds in 1843, when the excitement of the struggle against the " partial and arbitrary measure " of the Government had not subsided. At this meeting it was decided to support separate schools, and that their future efforts should be voluntary, and wholly independent of State aid. No decided final opinion was at first pronounced on the propriety of Government interference, but doubts were expressed whether it could be allowed " without establishing principles and precedents dangerous to civil and religious liberty, inconsistent with the rights of industry, and superseding the duties of parents and of churches." From the differences acknowledged to exist between religious bodies, the meeting concluded, " without despondency or regret," that both general and religious education must be chiefly provided and conducted by various denominations of Christians.

At a meeting held in London in December, 1843, it was declared that the education given by the Congregational churches must be religious, and it was recommended that no Government aid be received for schools established in their own connection, and that all funds subscribed should be granted to schools sustained entirely by voluntary contributions. ([1])

The Baptists, while they shared to a large extent the distrust of the Education Department, never went the length of the Independents in their opposition to State aid. They recommended co-operation with the friends of scriptural education at large—that is, the British and Foreign School Society's plan, in preference to the establishment of denominational schools. They repudiated the idea which Sir James Kay Shuttleworth had put forward, that public education was the work of religious communions—" an idea which, if practically carried out, would require the impossible result that every religious communion, however small, should have an establishment of schools spread over the whole country, at least co-extensive with the diffusion of its members." ([2]) A few years later, many Baptists and Congregationalists threw their weight into the secular movement, which appeared to provide the only safe, final, and permanent basis upon which the question could rest.

The axioms laid down by the Voluntaryists, on which their propaganda was based, were:—1. It was not within the legitimate province of the State to educate the people. 2. State

---

[1] Education Tables. Census, 1851, lviii.   [2] Ibid.

education would lead to unfortunate results, of a religious, social, and political character. 3. The people were quite able to provide instruction for themselves, and were doing so as fast as could be reasonably desired.

This position was founded on reasons partly historical and religious, and partly social and political. The religious ground was old and strong, but it was not applicable to the circumstances of the case. They were opposed, as they always had been, to the acceptance of State aid for religious teaching, and rejected state interference with spiritual matters as a violation of religious liberty. The right of private judgment on religious questions—the immorality of State endowments for supporting spiritual beliefs—the entire separation of the civil from the spiritual powers, were fundamental principles of their Church policy.

But in applying them to elementary education—the teaching of reading, writing, and arithmetic—they made a great mistake. There was a consistent ground which they might have taken—the separation of religious and secular teaching. They had found no difficulty in supporting the Government plan for a Normal School in 1839, where the general instruction was to be given together, and special religious instruction separately. (¹) [In maintaining this plan they would have found ample opportunity for the logical enforcement of their principles. No doubt education, as it was administered under the direction of the Department, was a constant violation of their most sacred opinions. While it was a constant attack on their religious efforts, and especially upon their Sunday schools, it threatened, as they thought, to prepare the way for universal endowment, and the pensioning of all denominations. It was a system too in which the bribes were mostly on one side—that of the Church. The Church day school was becoming the most conspicuous

¹ Life of Baines, 256.

feature in modern institutions, and it was the rule of the Church day school that its scholars should attend the Church Sunday school. These obvious facts made splendid material for an attack upon the unjust and partial minutes by which these arrangements were carried out, and it does not speak well for the sagacity of the leaders of the voluntary movement, that instead of combining on this line of assault they should have asked the Government to do nothing at all, a request which every day made it more impossible for any English Ministry to comply with.

The political and economical principles advanced in support of the voluntary movement had an air of plausibility, but when examined they failed to stand the tests of experience, or of any political philosophy which had been through the fire of proof. It was an attempt to set up a new political economy, combined with a sectarian agitation. In fact again, it rested on the false assumption, that the teaching of the rudiments of letters cannot be separated from religious instruction. State education was denounced as an invasion of civil rights—an attempt to deprive parents of their responsibilities and duties—a recognition of Communism. It was predicted that it would establish a despotism over thought, benumb the intellect, and undermine the manly independence and self-reliance of the English character. The stagnation of Government departments was contrasted with the vigour and enthusiasm of private enterprises. The arguments of Mr. Disraeli in 1839 in opposition to machinery and routine as compared with independent agencies were disinterred. It was also concluded that State instruction was an attack on voluntary charity, and on the principles of local self-government. The enormous amount of State patronage which the system placed at the disposal of the Government was regarded as a social danger. Lastly it was said, that voluntary agencies were sufficient to supply the utmost need of education, and that the natural laws of supply and demand if left to work unfettered and unrestricted were capable of covering the land with schools, and were actually doing it as fast as was desirable. Free trade in food was beginning to be the one engrossing cry of the people, and it was a natural and an easy assumption that free trade in all matters would be a national blessing.

This controversy has been long since decided. It is now acknowledged that the extinction of indiscriminate individual charity would be a blessing rather than an evil. It is admitted, too, that the Voluntaryists were fighting not for the rights and duties of parents, but for the control of education by religious denominations—not for self-government by the people, but for the government of churches, ministers, congregations, and benevolent societies. The law of supply and demand had been at liberty to work for hundreds of years, and had accomplished nothing. It was an inoperative law, and had conspicuously failed. "Education in its simplest form, which is one of the first and highest of all human interests, is a matter in which Government initiation and direction are imperatively required, for uninstructed people will never demand it, and to appreciate education is itself a consequence of education." ([1]) It was evident the Voluntaryists did not rely upon the law of supply and demand, but on sectarian and party rivalry and zeal, which is quite a different thing.

One unfortunate result of the ardour with which the Voluntaryists championed their opinions was, that they were led seriously to overrate the efficiency of existing voluntary means. While they depreciated the amount of education needed, they were too much disposed to overlook its quality altogether, and they magnified every paltry effort at progress made by the Government into a great and elaborate scheme. As an instance of the inevitable tendency to put the require-

[1] Lecky's History of 18th Century, I., 458.

17

ment as low as possible, Mr. Baines, in 1846, estimated that one in nine was the proper proportion of scholars to population. In 1854 Sir James K. Shuttleworth had raised the estimate to one in eight, ([1]) and at a later period one in six was the recognised proportion.

The leaders of the voluntary movement advocated their views with an energy and ability worthy of a stronger cause. They published elaborate statistics to prove that there was no serious deficiency in educational means, and that the emulation of religious bodies, and the competition of private schools afforded the best guarantee for the required extension. They sent out lecturers, held meetings, and organised voluntary education societies and committees in many parts of the country. They pointed to the vast achievements of individual benevolence, the increase in churches and charitable institutions, and to the rich and half-developed energies of the people, as reasons why it was "not wise to depart from the old English system of free and independent education." ([2]) The argument was not a strong one. There was no "old English" system of education, and of the results which had been effected by such means as existed, a large proportion had been accomplished by Government assistance. The Church supplied the largest share of voluntary education, but it had been the policy of the Government, within a few years previous to this controversy, to make large and direct grants for building churches and for the augmentation of livings. But the Nonconformists were not to be daunted or denied. Galileo was not more convinced than they were, ([3]) and Mr. Baines exultingly flourished the *Leeds Mercury* before his audience, to prove the rapid advance in popular knowledge and intelligence.

[1] Census Returns, 1851, xxi.   [2] Life of Baines, 330.

[3] Crosby Hall Lectures, 92. These lectures contain the authoritative exposition of the views of the leaders of the movement. The lecturers were Mr. Baines, the Rev. A. Wells, Dr. Hamilton, the Rev. A. Reed, Mr. Miall, Mr. Henry Richards, and the Rev. R. Ainslie. A newspaper, called the *Banner*, was also devoted to the agitation.

It is a pleasure to acknowledge that the Voluntaryists did not seek to spread their opinions by words alone. They were ready to tax themselves heavily in support of their consciences. The Congregational Board of Education undertook to raise £200,000 for the purpose of building schools, and up to 1859 had collected about £180,000. ([1]) The Voluntary Board of Education was established for the same purpose. Homerton Training College was also the result of their generosity and energy, and up to 1851 they had erected 364 elementary schools, which were wholly supported by subscriptions and school pence. With all their efforts they were no match for the Church and the Government together. The inevitable consequence was that the clergy were acquiring a wider and a stronger grasp over the system of State schools.

The year 1847 marks the third period of Ministerial proposals in regard to education. Lord John Russell had succeeded Sir Robert Peel as Prime Minister. The engrossing question of the Corn Laws had been settled, and it was understood that the new Government would give special attention to education, and would bring forward a comprehensive national scheme. The proposals were introduced by Lord John Russell with an earnestness and mass of detail which indicated that the Whig Cabinet attached great importance to the question. ([2]) But the measures hardly corresponded in grasp and comprehensiveness with the speech which introduced them. The Minutes were laid before the House in April, 1847. They authorised the President of the Council to frame regulations respecting the apprenticeship of the pupil teachers. They provided for exhibitions to Normal schools, to be held by "Queen's scholars;" for payment to masters for training pupil teachers; for increased grants to Normal schools; for grants and pensions to masters trained in

[1] Newcastle Commission, 6, 273. [2] Life of Peel, by Guizot.

Normal schools; and for grants to schools of industry. The pupil teachers in Church schools were placed under the instruction of the clergy in religious matters, and were required to have a certificate of moral character from a clergyman.

The discussions upon this plan show how completely education had come to be looked at as a matter of sectional interest, rather than as a national concern. The Voluntaryists, who comprised the largest section of Protestant Dissenters, magnified it into a great and elaborate scheme, calculated to strengthen the hands of the Church, to which State Education was being rapidly abandoned by the Dissenters. It was received with grief and dread, and united the bulk of the Nonconformists in a firm opposition. The Unitarians were an exception. They supported this as they have done all measures, great or small, for the advancement of education. Meetings were held in London and in many provincial towns against the scheme. In Birmingham the Mayor called a town's meeting, at which the Rev. John Angell James proposed a resolution condemning the minutes, which was carried notwithstanding the opposition of a vigorous minority led by the Rev. G. S. Bull, and the recorder Mr. M. D. Hill. ([1]) In London between three and four hundred delegates from congregations met at Exeter Hall and tried to overcome the Ministry by threatening to withdraw their support at the elections. This menace drew a strong protest from Lord John Russell in the House of Commons.

The Church party in Parliament, and the Conservatives gave their approval to the scheme. The High Church party had not taken alarm as yet. The management clauses about which such stormy differences arose had not been brought under the notice of Parliament. Bishop Blomfield expressed his approval in the Lords, and thought it was exceedingly

[1] Langford's Modern Birmingham, 1, 127.

wise and prudent not to interfere with the existing system. ([1]) Lord Brougham denounced it as no plan, but the imperfect substitute of a measure promised and expected, but withheld, and warmly complained of the Church and the sects that they loved controversy more than education. Sir Robert Peel supported the Government in the Commons, and put forcibly before the House the condition of the Irish population of Manchester, on whose behalf he made an unanswerable appeal.

Before the vote was moved there were some pertinent questions put to Ministers respecting the positions of the Wesleyans and Roman Catholics. It was elicited that the Government were manœuvering to secure the support of both parties. The existing Minutes provided that aid should only be given to schools in which the authorised version was used. The Wesleyans had been told, on authority which they regarded as sufficient, that the Catholics would not be allowed to share in the grant, and they had also been conciliated by being allowed to use their own catechisim and to nominate their own Inspectors. ([2]) But in the House of Commons, Lord John Russell, without pledging the Government to a promise, said enough to satisfy the Roman Catholics that a new Minute would be introduced which would admit them to a share of the grant. This was actually done at an early date.

Lord John Russell, in moving the vote of £100,000, anticipated some of the objections which would be urged against the Minutes, and admitted that it would have been better if at the beginning of the century a united system had been devised. But every step taken had made it more difficult to go back. He condemned the intolerance of the National Society in insisting that all children who attended its schools should learn the catechism and go to Church. It was weakly urged, on the part of the Government, that the

---

[1] Hansard, T. S., 89, 858.　　[2] Ibid, 91, 818.

Minutes did not empower the conductors of schools to compel attendance at Church and Sunday schools—they did it on their own responsibility. The Government did not think that the making the grant entitled them to impose terms on the National schools which they would not be willing to adopt, and the Minister expressed the fear, which all experience proves to have been unwarranted—that the imposition of conditions protecting the children of Dissenters would prevent the National Society from accepting aid, and lead to the closing of its schools.

The grant was strongly opposed on behalf of the Nonconformists, and led to an animated discussion. The debate was remarkable, chiefly for the speeches of Mr. Macaulay and Mr. Bright. Mr. Macaulay, who was a member of the Committee of Council, supported the proposition of his colleagues in the Ministry. His speech, while not a strong defence of the particular Minutes, was a most able exposition of the reasons in favour of State education, and as such it gave great offence to the voluntaryists. Mr. Bright's speech was an attack on a system of education, conducted solely on Church and State principles. He showed that every step taken between 1839 and 1847 had for its tendency the aggrandizement of the Church, and that the object and result of the Minutes proposed, would be to give enormous and increased powers to the Establishment. But Mr. Bright it is clear did not share the extreme views of the voluntary party. His objections were based on the wider view of religious freedom and equality. He said,—

" Free us from the trammels of your Church—set religion apart from the interference of the State. If you will make full provision for education, let it not depend upon the doctrines of a particular creed, and then you will find the various sects in this country will be as harmonious on the question of education as are the people of the United States of America."

" Nothing tends more to impede the progress of liberty, nothing is more fatal to independence of spirit in the public, than to add to the powers of the priesthood in the matter of education.   If you give them such increased power by legislative enactments, you do more than you could effect by any other means to enslave and degrade a people subject to their influence." (¹)

The Government proposals were carried by an enormous majority, and subsequent motions by Sir William Molesworth to admit Roman Catholics (²) to the benefit of the grant, and by Mr. Ewart for a conscience clause to protect the children of the Dissenters, were lost.   A small incident in the House of Lords increased the estrangement between the Noncon-formists and the Department.   A Minute was laid on the table to relieve the managers of dissenting schools from certifying as to the religious knowledge of pupil teachers. In the explanations respecting it, the Bishop of London said that the Church was not prepared to acquiesce in modifica-tions and additions from time to time to suit the prejudices of Dissenters.   " There was nothing in the compact between the Church and the Government on this subject which would allow the latter to infringe on the Minutes of the Privy Council, which were prepared with care, and which it was understood were to be fully and fairly carried out." (³)   The suspicions of the Dissenters were confirmed, that all steps taken by the Government were made after consultation with, and with the approval of, the dominant sect.

The Voluntaryists were now determined to put their strength to a crucial test.   It was, however, abundantly clear that they did not command the numbers or the united enthusiasm which in 1843 had enabled the Dissenting body

---

¹ Bright's Speeches, 2, 509, 7.
² Roman Catholic schools were admitted to grants in 1848, and Jewish schools in 1852.
³ Hansard, T. S., 94, 666.

to defy the Ministry of Sir Robert Peel. The petitions against Sir James Graham's bill had contained millions of signatures. Against the Minutes of 1847, there were 4,203 petitions presented, having only 559,977 signatures. Notwithstanding this indication of division and defection, the Voluntaryists were as good as their word in the threatened opposition to Ministers. At the general election, which took place in the summer of 1847, they opposed many Liberals who had voted for the Government Minutes. Mr. Hawes lost his seat for Lambeth on this account. At Leeds, the head quarters of the movement, Mr. Joseph Sturge, of Birmingham, stood as the representative of the Dissenters on this special ground. He was, however, badly beaten. They were reconciled, however, by the defeat of Mr. Macaulay at Edinburgh, for which they took credit. ([1]) There were, however, many contributing causes to his defeat. The drinkers of cheap whiskey, and the opponents of the Maynooth grant, which he had supported, were offended with him. With these, and others, the Dissenters allied themselves, to humiliate a man whose whole life was a plea for enlightenment and freedom, and a protest against ignorance and its attendant superstition and narrowness.

The opposition of the Voluntaryists continued for several years, and for some time they continued to increase, and were conspicuous for their energy and earnestness. But within ten years the movement had spent itself. Some of the most eminent members of the Congregational and Baptist communions, including Dr Vaughan and the Rev. Thomas Binney, while opposing the ecclesiastical tendency of the Government minutes, and the partiality shown to the Church, had refused to subscribe to the political doctrine that the State is not entitled to interfere for the education of the people. Such an abstract doctrine of the province of Government was never

[1] Life of Baines, 336.

accepted by the wisest and strongest heads of the dissenting bodies. Their objections were limited to the State becoming a teacher of religion by means of the apparatus of the religious sects. (¹) As new phases of the question were developed, there were many desertions from the voluntary ranks. Many Congregationalists were members of the National Public School Association, and others supported the Manchester and Salford Bill. The Newcastle Commission, of 1858, on which the voluntary party was represented, was able to report that the number of persons having conscientious objections to the acceptance of State aid was greatly diminished, and that all denominations were then in receipt of grants.

Some modifications of the minutes were introduced relieving schools from reporting on religious instruction, and this paved the way for a reconciliation. But the failure of the voluntary movement was owing to the conviction, that the ignorance of the country could never be overtaken without assistance from the State. Lord John Russell quoted from Dr. Vaughan's articles in the *British Quarterly Review*, to prove that in every ten years a million and a quarter of children were thrown on society without any education. Mr. Dunn, the Secretary of the British and Foreign School Society, confessed that an examination of British schools demonstrated the utter inadequacy of voluntary means to educate the country. Sir James Kay Shuttleworth estimated in 1855 that nearly £3,000,000 was required for building schools. "There are no facts to support the hope, that unless the amount of aid from the public resources was greatly increased, and distributed upon principles applying the greatest stimulus to voluntary efforts, the existing agencies could provide for the education of the poorer classes." (²) In 1850 the Archbishop of Canterbury said the Church could never from its own funds provide accommodation for the increasing numbers of children.

¹ *British Quarterly Review*, 1847, 504.   ² Public Education, 260.

In the same year Mr. Fox stated in the House of Commons, that the Congregationalists had suspended grants to poor schools. The balance sheet of the Congregational Board of Education, presented 10th of May, 1850, showed the receipts for 1849 to be £1,734 14s. 10d., or a little more than a pound a head for the members in union. The third report of the Voluntary School Association, in 1851, stated that there were six pupils in the Normal school, and that £84 was granted during the year to necessitous schools. ([1]) At the same time three school Inspectors reported officially that numerous national schools must be shut up from the falling off of subscriptions. The "illimitable" resources of the National Society were also failing. In 1839, the Committee reported that their machinery was working well, and promised before long to embrace in its operations the whole body of the peasantry. ([2]) Ten years later the report stated that its finances were embarrassed, that it was compelled to suspend operations for building schools, and that it apprehended the necessity of diminishing the supply of teachers. ([3])

The voluntary movement was beaten by the irresistible logic of facts, which no easy improvisation of first principles, no versatility in the arrangement of statistics, and indeed no generosity of purse and service could successfully encounter. While it was in its first vigour it effectually obstructed progress, and even after its early force was spent, it was a disturbing influence of sufficient magnitude to prevent the union of parties on a common basis.

The years 1845-7 were memorable also for the beginning of a dispute between the Education Department and the High Church party which occasioned intense feeling, led to serious divisions in the Church and the National Society, and prepared the way for new arrangements and alliances of

---

[1] *Westminster Review*, 1851, 467.   [2] *British and Foreign Review*, 1840-50.
[3] Dean Hamilton on the Privy Council and National Society, 52.

parties in the country and Parliament. These differences are chiefly now interesting because of the extraordinary pretensions put forward on behalf of the Church, and because many of the men engaged in them have been conspicuous and familiar forms in the public life of the time. The first reasons for the complete severance of Mr. Gladstone from the Conservative party probably arose out of this dispute, since the opposition to him at Oxford, in 1852, was the direct consequence of the discussions. The story of this controversy has been told by Archdeacon Denison from the Church point of view in his "Notes of my Life," in a manner which must win for him respect and regard, even by those who are irreconcilably hostile to the principles he contended for. The view which was taken at the Education Department has been described by Sir James Kay Shuttleworth in "Public Education." The briefest sketch of the movement and its consequences will suffice for the purpose of this history.

The dispute ostensibly began over the management clauses, which were submitted to Church schools for insertion in their trust deeds by the Committee of Council, in cases where grants were made for erection out of the public funds. This was merely the formal laying of a venue where the dispute could be tried. The real issue involved the rights of the State and the Church respectively to the control of public education, and the object on the part of the Church was to check the growing power and influence of the State Department at Whitehall—or, as Archdeacon Denison would put it, to defeat the Whig plot for crushing Church schools.

The management clauses were not however the creation of a Whig Government. The correspondence respecting them began in 1845, when Sir Robert Peel was in power, and they were submitted to the National Society during his administration. Their object was to secure the preservation of schools for the purposes for which they were erected, and to define the authority by which they should be governed. There had been much looseness in regard to the trust deeds. Many school deeds were not enrolled in Chancery, and were found to be invalid. In others, conveyances were made to individual trustees, which involved great trouble and expense. In some deeds there were no management clauses—while in others the provisions for management comprised every form of negligent or discordant arrangement. " Often there was no management clause ; in which case the government of the school devolved on the individual trustees and their heirs, who might be non-resident, minors, lunatics, or otherwise incapable." (¹) The Committee of Council therefore resolved to make the adoption of the management clauses a condition precedent to the receipt of aid from the grant. There were several clauses adapted to the circumstances of towns and parishes. In substance, they placed the control of the school premises, and the superintendence of the moral and religious instruction, exclusively in the hands of the clergy. The government of the school, and the appointment and dismissal of teachers, were vested in a committee, consisting of the officiating minister and his curates, and a certain number of persons who were residents or contributors to the school. The latter were to be elected by subscribers, having votes in proportion to their contributions, and being members of the Church of England. The schoolmaster was to be, by the terms of the trust, a member of the Established Church, and the minister was ex-officio chairman of the committee. The Committee of Council also consented that a rigorous test of church membership should be imposed on the lay members of the committee, who were required to sign a declaration that they were members and communicants of the Church. A further demand made by the National Society for an appeal

¹ Newcastle Commission Report, 57.

to the Bishop on matters not relating to moral or religious instruction, was refused by the Department.

It will be seen that these clauses did not encroach on the terms of union with the National Society. These terms were, that the children should be instructed in the liturgy and catechism of the Church of England, that the schools should be subject to the superintendence of the parochial clergyman, that the children should be regularly assembled for the purpose of attending divine service in the parish church, unless satisfactory reasons for non-attendance were given ; that the masters and mistresses should be members of the Church of England, and that reports should be made to the diocesan board by inspectors appointed by the Bishop or National Society. ([1])

These conditions were allowed to be observed in the schools of the powerful National Society at a time when Wesleyans and Jews were compelled to adopt a conscience clause for the protection of children whose parents objected to religious teaching.

The Committee of the National Society was not satisfied, and at a meeting, presided over by the Archbishop of Canterbury, a resolution was passed that "no terms of co-operation with the State could be satisfactory which should not allow to the clergy and laity full freedom to constitute schools upon such principles and models as were sanctioned by order and practice of the Church, and that, in particular, they should desire to put the management of their schools solely in the hands of the clergy and Bishop of the diocese." ([2])

A determined effort was made by the National Society to constitute the Bishop the appellate tribunal in secular as well as religious matters. As a compromise the Committee of Council proposed that the Lord President should nominate

[1] Minutes of Council, 1847-8, lxxiv. [2] Hansard, T. S., 105, 1079.

one arbitrator and the Bishop another. The Committee of
the National Society was not satisfied and refused to join in
the recommendation of the management clauses. The
consequence was a temporary suspension of grants for
erecting Church schools. Petitions were presented to
Parliament complaining of the decision of the Department.([1])

The pretensions of the High Church party at this time,
in defiance of history, and of the forces of opinion which
were set against them, are best illustrated by a few extracts
from their speeches and writings. ([2])

" The case was this : a very simple one. So long as the
civil power would help the spiritual power to do God's work
in the world, on those terms of which alone the spiritual
power could be the fitting judge, so long the help would be as
it ought to be thankfully received." . . . . . " They
were fighting for great and sacred principles, for the
upholding of the office of the ministry in God's Church, as
charged by God with the responsibility of educating the
people." . . . . . " The parish school of the English
parish is the nursery of catholic truth and apostolic
discipline."—*Archdeacon Denison.*

" The true and perfect idea of christendom is the constitution of all social order upon the basis of faith and within
the unity of the Church." . . . . . " Let it be plainly
and finally made clear that the co-partnership between the
Church and the State in the work of education, is in the fruits
and not in the direction." . . . . . . " But that gives
the State no claim, as joint founder, to intervene in the
management of the schools."—*Archdeacon Manning.*

" We shall be obliged to go to Government and to
Parliament, not to ask for a participation in the grants of
money distributed on the present principles, but to tell them,
backed by the voice of three-fourths of the empire, of all

[1] Hansard, T. S., 109, 259. [2] See Public Education, 8-10.

denominations, that the State shall not, without a creed and without a sacrament, and without any ministerial authority from God, undertake to educate the people of the country."—*Rev. W. Sewell.*

" What he contended for was nothing less than this—the birthright of the children of God to be trained up in an atmosphere of truth, not an atmosphere of conflicting creeds and varities of opinion." . . . . " Under no circumstances whatever could I consent to admit a single child to a school of which I have the control and management, without insisting most positively and strictly on the learning of the catechism and attendance at Church on Sundays."—*Hon. J. C. Talbot.*

There was much more of the same description. The right of the Church to unconditional assistance was insisted on. The civil power was charged with forgetting God and dishonouring Christ, by proclaiming openly, that the ministers of Christ were no longer fit to be trusted solely and exclusively with the education of the people. The Divine commission of the Church to teach was reasserted. An outline of Church education was prepared by Archdeacon Denison, in which he set forth the respective provinces of Church and State. The supporters of schools were to make application through the Diocesan Board of Education to the Bishop, and the Bishop was to represent to the Government that certain schools were proposed—that others were in want of annual assistance—that certain amounts were required for training colleges and for maintaining Diocesan Inspectors. The business of the Education Department should be simply to meet the representations of the Bishop, by annual grants of money. A return of the grants to Parliament with the certificates of the Diocesan Inspectors as to efficiency, would be the guarantees for the due application of the public money.

There was a large party in the National Society and in the Church hostile to these contentions, and the annual meetings of the Society for several years were pitched battles between the High Church party on the one hand and the forces of Low Church and moderates or Liberals on the other. ([1]) The liberal clergy and laity were strongly opposed to the views of the mediæval party, and presented a memorial to the Society asking to be allowed to nominate members of the committee. ([2]) A deputation waited upon the Archbishop of Canterbury, at Lambeth, and stated that if the constitution of the National Society was not altered they would feel compelled to establish a new Society for promoting education according to the principles of the Church. The Low Church party accused the High Churchmen of preferring to keep children in ignorance rather than let them receive light not tinted by themselves. ([3]) The heat occasioned by this controversy lasted about five years. The "Church army," as Archdeacon Denison called his supporters, finally broke up in 1853, after the unsuccessful assault on the seat of Mr. Gladstone, at Oxford.

Conflicting views have been held as to the part and position which the Committee of Council played in these various struggles. Sir James Kay Shuttleworth, for whose affection for his Department due allowance will be made, claims that it was recognised as the protector of minorities, the champion of civil and religious liberty, and the opponent of exalted spiritual authority ; and that there was a gradual reconciliation towards it on the part of the Dissenters, as tending to place authority in the hands of the congregation rather than the priesthood. ([4]) Archdeacon Denison writes :—"I do not know anything anywhere so clever and so triumphant as the policy of the Committee of Council on Education since 1840, except it be a Russian diplomacy, which is undoubtedly

---

[1] Blomfield's Life, 204. [2] Shuttleworth's Public Education, 21.
[3] Memoirs of Sara Coleridge, 2, 360.
[4] Shuttleworth, pub. edn., 23.

the first thing of its kind anywhere upon record." (¹) He gives an amusing account of the weapons in the Downing Street armoury. It is strange that, with all his acuteness, and his steadfast courage to look facts in the face, Archdeacon Denison does not yet see that he was beaten, not by a committee, or a secretary, or a department, or a policy—but by the change in the spirit of the times, by the development of national life, and the growth of new forces, principles, and aspirations.

There is yet another view of the operations of the Department. " In placing funds, institutions, teachers, and pupils in the hands of irresponsible Corporations—some of them governed by the bitterest opponents of secular instruction—the Committee of Council have piled up obstruction upon obstruction to the cause of progress," (²) and this was the view taken by men who were most anxious to see the establishment of a system on some definite basis adequate to the momentous interests concerned.

A correct historical judgment of the earlier proceedings of the Department must embrace many circumstances in its consideration, and chief of all the inherent difficulties which arose out of its construction. It changed with every Administration, and drifted with every current of opinion. It had no definite principle or policy. It was an expedient adopted to evade a difficulty in the closing years of the Melbourne administration, which were marked by shifts and expedients. It was, of necessity, always on the look out for support and popularity, and inclined, therefore, to the strongest side. Its compact with the Church in 1840 was an instance of its subjection to political emergencies. It obtained the support of the Wesleyans by concessions in regard to inspection and the catechism. In the same way it bought off the opposition of Catholics by admitting their schools to

¹ Notes of my Life, 120. ² *Westminster Review*, 1854, 409.

grants. It could not be an originating department on account of its relations to different parties. The minutes adopted under one Government were subject to reversal under the next, and in more than one instance this actually occurred. Its power was immense, but it was only the power of a huge paymaster. It was popular with no party, unless it was the Low Church clergy, who were satisfied with the preponderating influence it placed in the hands of the Church. It was opposed by all who claimed the spiritual control of education—by the Voluntaryists, who objected to any State intervention, by the Dissenters who were jealous of the Church and suspicious of its designs, and by earnest educationists who disbelieved in its methods and efficiency, and saw in it only a clog and hindrance to the cause they had at heart. But this very unpopularity kept the question alive, and gave an impetus to popular movements for the establishment of a system on definite lines, subject neither to the servilities nor partialities of office, nor to the fluctuations of party politics.

CHAPTER IV.

PERIOD.—FROM THE FORMATION OF THE LANCASHIRE
PUBLIC SCHOOL ASSOCIATION, 1847, TO THAT OF
THE LEAGUE, 1869.

A NEW direction was given to the popular agitation for
education by the formation of the Lancashire Public
School Association, and by the advocacy which eminent
Churchmen and Nonconformists were giving to a "combined"
system. The apathy of the Government, the divisions amongst
religious denominations, the distrust and suspicion caused
by the policy of the Education Department, and above all
the exclusiveness and narrowness of the voluntary societies,
were leading educational reformers to look to independent
sources for the solution of difficulties which had hitherto
seemed to increase with every fresh effort to overcome them.
The National Society clung with tenacity to its exclusive
conditions, and the British and Foreign School Society was
falling under the suspicion of being on its own lines, equally
bigoted and sectarian. Roman Catholics, Jews and Unitarians
were excluded from its Normal school, and it was complained
that its day schools had a creed of their own as much as
those of the National Society. Confidence in a system so
administered, and governed at every point by party and
sectarian interests was incompatible with any comprehensive
consideration of the subject.

Local government and a larger measure of local support
were the two fundamental principles of the new agitation.
With these it was attempted to reconcile religious differences,
by looking for a common ground of opinion and action. The

new effort was, in the last respect, as fruitless for the time as any which had preceded it, but it was, nevertheless, an important step in a liberal direction. It was clear to the ablest men amongst all parties that a State system was inevitable—the always harrassing and perplexing question was, what relations it should have to the religious opinions of the country. There were trusted leaders amongst the Church party who did not despair of finding a solution which would give to the Church every opportunity it required, without doing injustice to Dissenters, and many of the most distinguished of the Nonconformists were prepared to unite with the Church in support of such a scheme.

The Irish system was taken as the basis. Dr. Hook, the vicar of Leeds, who was supposed to have the confidence of the High Church party, issued a pamphlet in 1846, in the form of a letter to the Bishop of St. David's, in which he put forward the plan of separating religious and secular teaching; excluding the former from the School, and throwing the cost of secular instruction upon the rates, and placing it under local management. Provision was to be made for religious teaching by clergymen and ministers at separate hours. This plan was advanced by Dr. Hook, not in any way as a concession of the claims of the Church—but rather as the only way in which they could be upheld, without doing injustice to other denominations, and at the same time securing education. His opinions were far in advance of those of his contemporaries in the Church—he was pre-eminently a man of just and comprehensive views—but he was an unbending and uncompromising Churchman, and he had not the smallest idea of sacrificing religious education; or even Church education, so far as the last could be promoted on principles of justice. Sir James Kay Shuttleworth has described him as desiring to relinquish on the part of the Church any desire for predominance, as seeking to place it on the same level with Dissenting bodies, and as foregoing his preference for religious education. ([1])   Such however were not his own pleas.   It was his ardent desire to preserve Church education intact in principle, which led him to the adoption of the Irish system.   He foresaw that if education were given by the State, it must stand in one of two relations to religion ;   either the education given must be purely secular, or the religious tone would become entirely colourless ; or as he expressed it " semi-religious."   The key to all his action in the matter is found in the three principles which are expressed in his speeches and writings—viz., Education must be had.   The religious education given by the Church must be on strictly Church principles.   The religious education given must be consistent with justice to Dissenters.

From the earliest agitation of the question Dr. Hook took the greatest interest in it.   Before the formation of the Committee of Council he had proposed an Education Board for Leeds, more liberal in its constitution than any subsequent proposal of either Whig or Conservative Governments. ([2]) His contention always was, secular education by the State— religious education by the denominations, on fair terms for all.   In a letter to Sir William Page Wood (the late Lord Hatherley) written in 1838, he said, " anything like a semi-religious education I deprecate, but I have no objection to let the State train children to receive the religious education we are prepared to give." ([3])   In a speech at Leeds about the same time he said " It must be obvious that when a State undertakes the education of the people, it cannot make religion its basis.   It may pretend to do so at first, but the State religion will be found on investigation to be no religion." ([4])   During the acrid controversies aroused by Sir James Graham's factory bill Dr. Hook wrote to Mr. Gladstone,

---

[1] The School, &c., 69.
[2] Life of Dean Hook, 262.   [3] Ibid, 263.   [4] Ibid, 264.

" I do really think that the Church might keep the whole of the education of the people, or nearly so, in her own hands." But this was to be done on just principles. " All that is wanted is money ; we require funds. If the thing is desirable why may not the Bishops with the Clergy of England tax themselves fifty per cent., aye if need should be, a hundred per cent. and become beggars, rather than permit the education of the people to pass out of their hands ? " "But there is not sufficient piety in the Church at present to act thus, or to make such a sacrifice as this : or rather there is the monstrous notion that our Bishops and clergy are to demand all the money they require, whether for education or Church extension, of the State. The State is to supply the funds, and the Bishops and clergy to expend those funds as they think fit. I call this a monstrous notion in a free State where there is full toleration, and where the taxes are paid by Dissenters as well as by Churchmen. If the Church supplies the funds, let the education be an exclusively Church education ; if the State supplies the funds, the State is in duty bound to regard the just claims of Dissenters." ([1])

These expressions were the preliminary to his letter to the Bishop of St. David's, "How to render more efficient the education of the people." The scheme has been described as bold and original. ([2]) Bold it was and generous in principle as proceeding from a Church clergyman, but it had no title to originality. It was merely an adaptation of the Irish system. Secular instruction only was to be given by the State .Children were to be required to produce certificates of attendance at a Sunday school. Class rooms were to be attached to the schools, in which the clergy and the dissenting ministers were to be allowed to give religious instruction at separate hours. "I do not ask," he wrote, "whether such an arrangement would be preferred to any other by either party,

---

[1] Life of Dean Hook, 347.   [2] Ibid, 262.

for each party would prefer having everything its own way; but I do ask whether there would be any violation of principle on either side? I ask whether, for the sake of a great national object, there ought not to be a sacrifice, not of principle, but of prejudice, on either side." (¹)

The pamphlet caused a sensation for a time. The High Church party regarded it with amazement as a surrender and betrayal. The National Society took offence at the strictures upon its work. The clergy were angry at the contemptuous criticism of the religious instruction given in Church schools, and the Voluntaryists, whose agitation was then at its height, were of course hostile to the scheme. It was a great honour to Dr. Hook's just and liberal suggestions that all the prevailing and established, blind and narrow incompetencies should oppose them.

A new combination in support of secular education had its rise about the same time in Manchester. Mr. Cobden had finished the task of the Anti-Corn Law League, and was already turning his thoughts in other directions. In August, 1846, he wrote to Mr. Combe, that he was in hopes he should be able to co-operate efficiently with the best and most active spirits of the day in the work of moral and intellectual education. (²) In July, 1847, a Committee was formed in Manchester for the establishment of a national system. The first intention was to show how it might be worked out in Lancashire. An address was issued to the county called " A plan for the establishment of a general system of secular education in the county of Lancaster." The movement originated with Mr. Samuel Lucas, Mr. Jacob Bright, Professor Hodgson, Mr. Alexander Ireland, Mr. Geo. Wilson, and the Rev. W. McKerrow. The programme put forward by the Committee led to the formation of the Lancashire Public School Association, which a year or two later was converted into

¹ Life of Dean Hook, 405.   ² Life of Combe, 219.

" The National Public School Association." Its object was to
" promote the establishment by law in England and Wales of
a system of free schools ; which, supported by local rates
and managed by local committees, specially elected for that
purpose by the ratepayers, shall impart secular instruction
only, leaving to parents, guardians, and religious teachers
the inculcation of religion; to afford opportunities for which
it is proposed that the schools shall be closed at stated hours
in each week." (¹) This was the first comprehensive and
elaborate scheme put forward for securing national education;
based on the principle that the cost should be thrown
on property, that the management should be confided
to local representatives, and that the people should be taught
to regard education, not as a bone of contention between
churches and sects, but as the right of free citizens.

This movement won the support of the best known
Liberal politicians in the country. Mr. Cobden devoted a
large part of his valuable life to secure its success. It had
the benefit of the experience and machinery of the Anti-
Corn Law League. The Liberal press advocated it almost
unanimously. Many eminent Dissenters gave it their
adhesion, including Dr. Vaughan, the editor of the *British
Quarterly Review.* In Parliament it had the support of
Mr. Milner Gibson, Mr. Cobden, Mr. W. J. Fox, Sir Thomas
Bazley, Sir John Potter, and Mr. Alexander Henry. Manchester now became the centre from which, under various
conditions, an agitation was maintained unceasingly until
the passing of the Education Act of 1870.

In the session of 1850, Mr. W. J. Fox, member for
Oldham, who had formerly been a popular Unitarian preacher
at the Eldon Street Chapel, Finsbury, and who in that
capacity had provoked the energetic opposition of Bishop
Blomfield and his clergy, moved for leave to bring in a bill

¹ *Westminster Review,* 54, 411.

for the secular education of the people in England and Wales. ([1]) This bill was much upon the lines of the Lancashire Association scheme, but left religious instruction an open question for the ratepayers. In a speech displaying a perfect knowledge of the subject in all its bearings, Mr. Fox demonstrated the failure of the voluntary societies, combined with such aid as Government had afforded, and the absolute necessity for a more comprehensive measure. He denied that the movement for secular education aimed at abating or checking religious instruction—its object was to ensure such secular knowledge as would make religious efforts more efficient and successful. The scheme he proposed was founded on the principles of local exertion and local superintendence. The deficiency in the parishes was to be ascertained by Inspectors, and the locality invited to supply it by means of a rate administered by their representatives. In order to conciliate the managers of existing schools, it was proposed that grants should be made to teachers according to the number of pupils efficiently instructed. No restraints were to be put on religious bodies, which would be able to erect and endow denominational schools, to be rewarded by the State for secular results. The new schools were to be free to the inhabitants of the district, without charge, without distinction in the treatment and training of their children, and without obligation to accept religious instruction; but with the right reserved and inalienable, to have at convenient times, fixed by the master, their children instructed in religion, where and by whom they pleased.

Lord John Russell, on the part of the Government, supported the introduction of the bill, but declined to pronounce any opinion on its merits. It was opposed by the Church party, and the familiar cry of "religion in danger" was heard again. Sir R. Inglis accused Mr. Fox of neglecting the

[1] Hansard, T. S., 109, 27.

eternal destiny of children, and Lord Arundel passionately exclaimed " The two armies were drawing up their forces, and the battle was now between religion and irreligion, the Church and Infidelity, God and the Devil, and the reward for which they must contend was Heaven or Hell."

Bishop Ullathorne expressed the views of the Roman Catholics to the same effect, but in more temperate language. " It involves a principle against which the Church of Christ is contending throughout Europe, and that for the most awful reasons. Awake and train out the dawning intellects of your children in this dry material way, and you will unchristianise the country. Leave the religious faculties to slumber, while the secular ones are being trained, and you leave no foundation for submission even to temporal Government." From the high priest point of view there was no good in the scheme—but only visions of Democracy ! Socinianism! Communism! and Infidelity! and all these because it was proposed to teach the alphabet !

Lord Ashley attacked the proposal as despotic in character, and likely to be prodigious in results. Its probable cost was exaggerated, and visions of immense rates were conjured up in opposition to it. The Premier (Lord John Russell) opposed the bill on account of its secular character, and the gratuity of the instruction offered. On the other hand Mr. Roebuck, with all the energy which distinguished him at that portion of his career, denounced the intervention of " meddling priests," and the principle of charitable donations for education. " You make laws, you erect prisons, you have the gibbet, you circulate throughout the country an army of judges and barristers to enforce the law, but your religious bigotry precludes the chance or the hope of your being able to teach the people, so as to prevent the crime which you send round this army to punish." Mr. Fox received valuable assistance from Mr. Milner

Gibson, Mr. Muntz, Mr. Anstey, and other members. The influence of the Church party, however, was supreme, and this, combined with the opposition of the Government, sufficed, after several nights' discussion, to reject the bill, on the second reading, by a large majority.

The defeat demonstrated the necessity of combined action out of Parliament to secure that pressure of public opinion which is the only guarantee for useful legislation. It was determined to extend the Lancashire agitation, and to give it the force of a national movement. With this object a meeting was held in Manchester in the autumn of 1850, when the Lancashire organisation changed its title to that of the " National Public School Association." Delegates attended from all parts of the country. The meeting was presided over by Mr. Hickson, who had been a prominent member of the Central Society of Education, and a resolution was proposed by Dr. Davidson, Professor of Theology in the Lancashire Independent College, in favour of free and secular instruction. It was seconded by the Rev. W. F. Walker, a Church clergyman from Oldham, and was supported by Mr. Cobden. Munificent donations, in aid of the object of the Society, were announced, including £500 from Mr. Edward Lumbe, £100 from Mr. Henry, M.P., £100 from Mr. Mark Phillips, £50 from Mr. Gardner, of Malvern, and £50 from Mr. W. Brown, M.P.

Meetings were held in all parts of the country, which were organized by Dr. John Watts, of Manchester, who has been known for thirty years as one of the most untiring educationists of Lancashire. Mr. Cobden threw himself into the movement with all his energy and ability. It is interesting now to remember that Mr. W. E. Forster was one of the supporters of the association. ([1]) Branches were formed in all the large towns. In Birmingham Mr. William Harris,

[1] Combe, Education by Jolly, 239.

subsequently one of the founders and officers of the League, Mr. H. B. S. Thompson, and others who have taken part in the recent agitation, had charge of a local branch. Statistics and pamphlets were published and circulated by the Society and a powerful influence was exerted in support of parliamentary action. The agitation was taken up in Scotland by Mr. George Combe, Mr. James Simpson, and Mr. M. Williams. It was a part of the object of the Society to demonstrate the practicability of free secular instruction, and as the result of the movement, the famous free secular school of Manchester, conducted by Mr. Benjamin Templar, and afterwards by Mr. G. E. Mellor, was founded. The Williams school at Edinburgh, Mr. Bastard's school at Blandford, and many other schools and institutes on a broad platform were the outgrowth of this agitation.

It was not to be expected that the scheme of the association would be suffered to pass without challenge. The first note of opposition came from Sir James Kay Shuttleworth, who, in response to an invitation to attend the conference, wrote—" I cannot conscientiously concur with them (the founders of the association) in seeking to establish a system of daily schools separate from the superintendence of the great religious bodies of the country." ([1])

This opposition was consistently maintained during his life, by the former Secretary to the Committee of Council. He constantly resisted the tendency to a separation between sectarianism and national education, and contended against the influence of those who were pursuing that policy. The system established by the Education Act of 1870 was in his eyes the dream of impracticable enthusiasts. He could not conceive that men of parliamentary experience could make the serious proposition that local municipal boards should be invested with power to establish rate supported schools in parishes, with whatever constitution, to compete with those

[1] Westminster Review, 54, 411.

of the religious communities; much less that the constitution of the new schools should exclude all distinctive religious instruction. ([1])

The attack on the plan of the National School Association was nominally directed against its alleged irreligious character. The fear of a representative system which should make education national, rather than sectarian, was in fact the root of the hostility. The fight at this time was not so much respecting details, as upon the principle of management. On the one side the Church, the Wesleyans, the Voluntaryists, and the Roman Catholics were contending for the management by the church or congregation—on the other hand, those who looked to education for political and social advantages were striving to secure local representation. The great service rendered by the National Public School Association was in popularising and extending the doctrine of Government by the people in matters of education. It was in no sense an Association hostile to religion. Almost without exception its members were connected with religious congregations. Nothing is wider from the truth, than that elementary education has ever been made the instrument of an attack on the religious institutions of the country. The men who have cared least about religion are those who have offered the fewest impediments to the acceptance of any plan, denominational or otherwise, which promised to embrace the whole community— and they have never been guilty of the selfishness of attempting to propagate even a negative creed at the expense of the community. The efforts for the separation of schools from the control of the religious communions, were partly owing no doubt to the growth of the municipal sentiment; but they had their origin in the differences which arose amongst the sects, and which wholly prevented any advance. The resistance on the part of the Church, the Roman Catholics

[1] Public Education, 36.

and exclusive educationists to a rate supported and representative system, arose from their repugnance to allow the direction of education to pass out of their own hands. But they made religion their shibboleth and attacked the National Association as being animated by a spirit of direct antagonism to the spread of religious opinions. So far was this hostility carried that where their influence prevailed, books and magazines which advocated the scheme were excluded from public libraries.

Several bills were introduced or supported under the auspices of the Association. They were not in all particulars alike, but in each of them a provision was made for moral teaching, and for affording the ministers of denominations opportunities of giving religious instruction to children of their own persuasion. The clauses required that there should be "sedulously inculcated—a strict regard to truth, justice, kindness, and forbearance in our intercourse with our fellow-creatures; temperance, industry, frugality, and all other virtues conducive to the right ordering of practical conduct in the affairs of life." "Nothing shall be taught in any of the schools which favours the peculiar tenets of any sect of Christians. No minister of religion shall be capable of holding any salaried office in connection with the schools." "The school committee shall set apart hours in every week, during which the schools shall be closed, for the purpose of affording an opportunity to the scholars, to attend the instruction of the teachers of religion in the various churches or chapels or other suitable places. No compulsion shall be used to enforce attendance, nor shall any penalty or disability whatever be imposed for non-attendance on such religious instruction."[1] Provisions were also contained for converting existing schools into free schools, and admitting them to the benefit of the rates, without disturbing their man-

[1] Shuttleworth. Public Education, 39.

agement, but on the condition of the acceptance of a time-table conscience clause. The terms of the clause were as follows :—" And be it enacted, that the inculcation of doctrinal religion, or sectarian opinions shall not take place in any such schools, at any time on any week day, between the hours of ... and ... in the morning, and ... and ... in the afternoon ; and that no manager, trustee, or other person shall be deemed to have committed a breach of trust, or be in any way liable to any suit or proceeding, by reason of the omission to inculcate on the scholars, during the hours appointed, doctrinal religion or sectarian opinions ; and no scholar who receives secular instruction at any such school, shall be compelled to attend the school at other times than those mentioned, or whilst doctrinal religion or sectarian opinions shall be inculcated ; and no part of the payment to be made to the managers of any such school shall be in any way applied, for the purpose of inculcating doctrinal religion or sectarian opinions." As a matter of fact therefore the National Association offered to the denominations the terms imposed by the Act of 1870—but so influential was the opposition to its plans that Sir James Kay Shuttleworth predicted that its advocates were destined to be absorbed in other parties or cease to exist. "No hope could be entertained of the acquiescence of the religious communions in the school rate, unless the constitution of the school, as respects its management, continue unchanged, and, whatever securities were given to the rights of conscience, unless the peculiarities of its religious discipline and instruction were left without interference." (¹)

In the results, and regarding these efforts and agitations from our present educational status, these predictions have been wholly falsified ; and the disingenuous and mischief-making war-cry "religion in danger" has wholly failed in

---

¹ Public Education, 43.

its scare. National progress has left comparatively but a
modicum of bigotry and superstition to work upon, and
in natural and inevitable sequence, the prophet has been
ignored, and the priest (of every sect) is being by degrees
relegated to his proper position.

The Manchester and Salford Committee on Education
was formed to oppose the National Association, and was
started under the auspices of Sir James Kay Shuttleworth,
who set himself resolutely against education as a political
object, resting on other than religious grounds. All the
influence which he could exert over the Administrations
under which he served was used to cement the union between
education and the denominations. He wrote to the Secretary
of the National Association "No evidence has transpired that,
as a political object, the education, in daily schools, of the great
masses of our fellow-countymen supported by manual labour,
had received any important impulse from the efforts of any
political class in this country; whereas, the various religious
bodies have made large sacrifices for the support of daily
schools; the Church alone claiming to have provided the
rudiments of instruction for about a million of children."

It was useless to argue with the Secretary of the
Committee of Council on this subject. He could not be
made to see that it was the working out of the democratic
principle which gave the impulse to education, and he could
not, or would not acknowledge that the objects of the
Church, in keeping its control of the question, were as much
political as religious, aiming at the preservation of dignities
and revenues depending on a political alliance. All that
came before him were the Government returns. By these,
his views, not constitutionally large, could hardly be
developed. His Department insisted that religion should be
the basis of the assistance it administered, and a certain
number of schools was provided by each of the sects which

was permitted to compete. Beyond this he did not see. He described the new scheme of the Manchester and Salford Committee as " one on a religious basis, under the guidance of ministers and communicants ; the elders, class leaders, and deacons of the Church and congregations." The new association proposed to raise funds by means of local rates—not to be applied exclusively for secular instruction. The management of the schools and the appointment and dismissal of teachers were confided to the Church or congregation, by which the school was erected. The foundation of the scheme in theory was, that all denominations should be treated impartially, though an attempt was made to impose the Protestant version of the Bible on the Roman Catholics. It was a scheme of concurrent endowment, and was supposed, on good reason, to express the sentiments of the Government of the day. Though dealing with local rates, it was not founded on any representative principle. The ratepayers were offered no control over school management. The Town Council was to collect a rate and pay it to the managers of the denominational schools. Where a deficiency of accommodation existed, the religious bodies were to have the option of supplying it in the first place, and only upon their neglect was the municipality empowered to build schools. No provisions were made to secure responsibility for the administration of public funds. On the Committee there were members of all the religious denominations, including the Roman Catholics. The harmony of this heterogeneous body was of short duration—the Roman Catholic members, who represented 100,000 of the population of the city, withdrawing on a dispute as to the use of the authorised version of the Bible.

There was yet another society in the field, the " Yorkshire Society for Promoting National Education," the secretary of which addressed a letter to Mr. Cobden on the rise and

21

progress of National Education. Its head quarters were at Leeds, and it took the secular ground, but its efforts were overshadowed by the superior energy of the Voluntaryists, who also made Yorkshire the centre of their operations.

There was thus at this time a triangular contest in which the Secular or separatist party really supplied the momentum to progress. They were equally opposed by the Voluntaryists and the Denominationalists; the former of whom would do nothing, and the latter nothing except on their own lines. The problem of the hour was how to bring national education under civil and popular control. If it took a long time to solve, and if indeed its solution is not yet complete, it is owing to the magnitude of the forces which were arrayed against it, and their traditional and historical authority, which was increased rather than diminished by the early policy of the Government in dealing with the subject.

The two schools of Manchester educationists came into conflict in Parliament in the Session of 1851. Mr. Fox, as representing the National Public School Association, moved a resolution in support of " the Establishment of Free Schools, for secular instruction, to be supported by local rates, and managed by committees elected specially for that purpose by the ratepayers." (¹) Sir Geo. Grey, on the part of the Government, opposed the motion, the Ministry evidently leaning to the rival scheme, in the preparation of which the officials of the Committee of Council had taken an active share. The Home Secretary said he had been informed by the chairman of the Manchester and Salford Bill Committee that they were maturing a plan applicable to Manchester and Salford, which was in the nature of a private bill and would be introduced in the following Session; that a

¹ Hansard, T. S., 116, 1255.

similar attempt was being made in Leeds; and that these plans held out some hope of a settlement.

Mr. Milner Gibson supported the bill of Mr. Fox. Mr. Adderley (Lord Norton) ridiculed the idea that the separation of religious and secular instruction implied hostility to religion—and Mr. Cobden showed that the local Manchester and Salford scheme had already got into difficulties. The whole body of the Roman Catholics had seceded, because the Committee made it a fundamental principle that in all schools erected at the public expense, the authorised version of the Bible should be read. Mr. Fox's bill was lost upon the first reading.

In March, 1852, Lord Derby became Prime Minister and announced that if the question of parliamentary reform was disposed of during the session, the next great measure undertaken would be the establishment of a system of public education. The statement of the Government intention was not favourable to the prospects of the Manchester and Salford Education Bill—the second reading of which was moved by Mr. Brotherton, who avowed his preference for a secular system, but which he was disposed to sink, rather than permit the continuance of street instruction. The bill was presented to the House as a private measure, and a postponement was asked for, to enable the Corporation to oppose it if they thought fit. It proposed a rate in aid of existing schools, the management of which was to be undisturbed—but subject to a conscience clause for the protection of children whose parents objected to religious instruction. In new schools the authorised version of the Bible was required to be read. The bill was supported by the Bishops, the clergy, the Wesleyans, and many dissenting ministers. It was opposed by Jews, Roman Catholics, the Society of Friends, and the teachers and superintendents of the Sunday School Union. On the second reading it appeared that the Manchester Town Council had

passed a resolution adverse to it, and that the Corporation of
Salford had approved it. It was resisted in the House by
Mr. Milner Gibson and Mr. Roebuck on the ground that it was
a public bill, and should be proceeded with as such; and by
Mr. Walpole, the Home Secretary, on the general principles
it raised. It was eventually referred, together with the bill of
the National Public School Association, to a Select Committee,
on which with others, sat Mr. T. M. Gibson, Mr. Bright, Mr.
Cobden, Mr. Fox, Lord John Russell, and Mr. Gladstone. The
Committee sat for two sessions. A large mass of evidence was
taken, but there was no report on the merits of the plans, and
the bills disappeared.(¹) In the same session the Congregationalists and the Baptist Union opposed both of the
Manchester bills.

The session of 1852 was also signalised by a dispute respecting the management clauses of the Church schools, the
stringency of which had been relaxed by Lord Derby's Government; giving increased powers over the schoolmaster to the
Bishops and clergy, both in relation to religious and moral
government. A strong opposition to this change proceeded
from within the National Society itself, and a section of the
members threatened an attempt to alter the charter, and to
suspend the issue of the Queen's letter. A large secession from
the Society seemed imminent, and was only averted by the
cancelling of the Minute by Lord Aberdeen's Government in
the next session.

The year 1853 witnessed some important alterations
by which the cost of education, as administered by the
Department, was suddenly and largely increased. The
capitation grant was a conspicuous feature in the new plans
of the Government, and the way in which it was adopted is a
curious illustration of the manner in which the power of the
Education Department was capable of extension, almost

¹ Parliamentary Report, 1852, No. 499, 400.

without the exercise of parliamentary authority and supervision. Lord Aberdeen's Government, which was formed after the general election of 1852, had put the necessity of extensive changes in our education system in the van of their professions. Lord John Russell was President of the Council in the new Ministry, and his devotion, for many years, to the details of the administration of the Education Department, and his well known interest in the question had raised great expectations. Mr. Gladstone, also, was a member of the Cabinet, and it was understood that he, with others, was pledged to bring forward a liberal measure on the " comprehensive" system. Archdeacon Denison wrote, " It is their darling project; the only idea of the method and manner of education, of which their minds appear to be capable." [1]

It was on the ground of Mr. Gladstone's association with the Whig Cabinet, and especially on the suspicion of his heresy on this question, that his re-election at Oxford was opposed in the beginning of 1853. The resolution to oppose him was taken at a meeting of the National Society. Archdeacon Denison wrote from Mr. Dudley Perceval's committee room, " it should, I think, have been sufficient to ascertain and fix a Churchman's vote, to see Mr. Gladstone in the same Committee of Council with Lord John Russell and Lord Lansdowne; who, as they sit in the Cabinet, nominally without office, but in effect as joint Ministers of public instruction, will have ample leisure, and be the better enabled to devise and mature a scheme for employing the power and influence of the Coalition Government to undermine, and finally to destroy by law the parochial system of the Church of England." [2]

Under the new scheme of the Government the school population was divided into two classes, urban and rural. To provide for the former the Borough Bill was introduced. The

[1] Notes of My Life, 101.   [2] Ibid, 101.

parishes were dealt with by a Minute of the Committee of Council.

In explaining the Borough Bill Lord John Russell went over the well-worn history of the question, the long list of attempts and failures, and the controversies which had prevented union and effective action. The Government had concluded that they ought to strengthen and improve the voluntary system rather than set up anything in its place. Some returns of the National Society, collected in 1847, showed that the school pence in the Church schools amounted to £413,004 per annum. These figures were hardly consistent with those of the Registrar General in 1851, which gave the payments of scholars in connection with all the schools of the religious bodies as £259,134. But Lord John Russell took the higher estimate, and expressed his gratification that the poor contributed half-a-million towards education. This was evidently a sum of money which, for financial reasons, the Coalition Ministry could not afford to dispense with, and it decided them against any attempt to introduce a large measure for free schools. A liberal plan was again made subordinate to the straits of office. The principle of free education was supported, at this time, by the most enlightened politicians of the day, and was becoming increasingly popular. It was a prominent feature of the bill of the Manchester and Salford Committee, which was prepared at the Education Department. But the Government dared not face the sacrifice of even a quarter of a million per year. Therefore, instead of the great measure which Lord Derby had promised in 1852, the Whigs and Peelites offered the country another instalment of the patchwork system. The definite proposal was that in incorporated towns the Town Council might, with the assent of two-thirds of their body, levy a rate, not to establish independent schools, but in aid of those in existence, and of further voluntary efforts. The rate was to be applied to pay twopence a week for each scholar, in respect of whom fourpence or fivepence was contributed from other sources. There was no provision for the erection of new schools. The Council was to have authority to appoint a Committee, partly of its own members, and partly of residents, to distribute sums raised by rate.

The bill was coldly received in Parliament. It was not actively opposed, but it was regarded by the friends of education as a half measure. No enthusiasm for it was shown in the country, and the Government made no effort to pass it into law. So little encouragement did the Ministry receive, that another measure for the regulation of education endowments which was promised in the House of Lords was also abandoned.

But while the Borough Bill collapsed, and the towns were left without provision, the rural districts were much surprised by an unexpected subsidy. This was effected by a Minute of the Committee of Council. Its operation was limited in the first instance to agricultural parishes and unincorporated towns, containing not more than 5,000 inhabitants. It provided, that on certain conditions as to attendance and teaching, and contributions from other sources, a capitation grant of six shillings per scholar in boys schools, and five shillings in girls schools should be paid to the managers. The intention was to create a premium on regularity of attendance, (¹) and to a certain extent this was probably accomplished. A much more striking consequence was the encouragement of dishonest practices in the enumeration of attendances—which later became a scandal to public administration. The education vote rose at a bound from £160,000 to £260,000, and on the extension of the Minute in January, 1856, to the whole country, another £200,000 was required. This was a great boon to the clergy, and did

¹ Shuttleworth's Public Education, 356.

more than anything to reconcile them to the administration
of the Department. It relieved them from writing begging
letters, and getting up bazaars and engaging in other
amateur speculations. Where districts were well supported,
the managers had more money than they knew what to do
with. The unbending principle of Archdeacon Denison,
always true to his ideal of the Establishment and his
Order, could make no headway against these State bribes.
" As I go about now," he writes sadly, "and hear Churchmen
talking about their schools as connected with the Council, I
hear commonly, of little else, than the number of pounds
they get by way of grant : this seems to be the test of a
good school." ([1])

In poor districts, where contributions could not be raised,
and where of necessity there was the most need for education,
nothing was effected. The perverse obstinacy with which
successive Governments adhered to the vicious principle that
assistance should be given not for education, but as an
encouragement to sectarian zeal and rivalry, is an amazing
example of the injury which may be effected by a bad
precedent.

But the manner in which the Minutes of 1853 became
law is worthy of notice, as showing the almost irresponsible
power, and the absolute independence of authority which
the Committee of Council possessed. In introducing the
Borough Bill Lord John Russell briefly referred to a new
Minute applicable to the country. He said, "this Minute,
when its provisions shall have been fully matured, will be
laid upon the table ; and the House before coming to any
vote upon it will have ample opportunity for duly considering
it." As a matter of history it was never considered in
Parliament. The Municipal Bill was not really discussed.
The grant for education was hurried through among a crowd

[1] Notes of My Life, 109.

of miscellaneous estimates, when it was not expected to come on, and the capitation grant was not discussed at all. That it was generally acceptable however in Parliament may be assumed from its subsequent extension in 1856.

During the administration of Lord Aberdeen, Jewish schools were first admitted to grants—but schools of a purely secular character were still refused participation.

The Manchester and Salford Bill re-appeared in a somewhat altered shape in 1854, under the charge of Mr. Adderley. The main principle of the bill was, to make the Corporation bankers for managers and school committees. Mr. Milner Gibson moved " that education to be supported by public rates is a subject which ought not to be dealt with by a private bill." ([1]) The Town Council of Manchester by a unanimous vote had requested the Members for the Borough to oppose the bill. The municipality naturally refused to accept the charge of a system when they had no control over its regulations, and the feeling of the people of Manchester at this time was strongly in favour of the disassociation of religious and secular teaching. The Committee to which it had been formerly referred had made no report because they could not agree on the evidence. The Corporation petitioned the House to defer legislation until some general measure was proposed by the Government. The opposition to the principle of this bill now took shape, and it was complained that it would cause the same bitterness as the church-rate controversy—since it proposed to put schools of all denominations upon public rates. It is clear that the bill involved the same principle as that which caused such a general feeling of hostility to the 25th section of the Act of 1870. Mr. Bright strongly opposed the measure and said it would necessarily import strife and retard education for many years. It was again and finally rejected.

[1] Hansard, 130, 1054.

22

The discussion on supply was notable for a persuasive and powerful appeal made by Mr. Cobden. Lord John Russell, on moving the education vote, had said it was useless to bring forward a general plan until there was a greater concurrence of opinion, and that Government must confine its efforts to improving the quality of instruction. Mr. Cobden warmly complained that the President of the Council was letting down the question, and going backward in regard to it. He maintained that they must make up their minds to local rates. They could not otherwise have a system worthy of the name. After sixteen years of trifling, they wanted something decisive. The country could not afford to have a " little national education." If they were to do anything adequate, they must raise at least three-and-a-half millions a year, and England was rich enough to do that. He suggested a permissive bill, giving power to different localities—beginning with corporate towns. He said that many meetings were held amongst the advocates of secular and denominational education, and there was a tendency to toleration and compromise. There was no occasion to be afraid that people wanted to do anything irreligious. There could not be got together a hundred men into whose heads it would enter to do anything inimical to religion ; yet no sooner was secular education mentioned, than it was declared a plot was laid to undermine religion. So anxious was he for education, on secular principles or without them, that he was willing to join in efforts for denominational education, or for secular education, or separate education ; the only condition being that it should include the whole community. He condemned the languid tone and feeble hand with which Lord John Russell had approached the question of late, and contended that an immature plan would result in a further postponement. ([1])

[1] Hansard, 134, 962.

The Crimean war necessarily diverted public attention from domestic questions; but, nevertheless, there were in 1855 four measures before Parliament proposing 'different means of dealing with education. One of these, Denison's Act, permitting Guardians to pay the fees for the education of children of out-door paupers, actually became law. The statute was practically inoperative, as shown by the evidence given before the Newcastle Commission. In nine counties only eleven children received the benefit of its provisions —and only some six or seven thousand throughout the country. ([1]) It remained ineffectual until its repeal in 1876. Its author was an advanced educationist, and one of the early advocates of compulsion.

The other bills of the session were, a Government measure, under the charge of Lord John Russell; another, introduced by Sir John Pakington; and a secular bill, promoted by the National Public School Association, and under the care of Mr. Milner Gibson. The Government bill was never put fairly before Parliament, which was distracted by discussions upon the conduct of the war. Lord Palmerston succeeded Lord Aberdeen as Prime Minister in February, 1855, and continued to hold the office until the beginning of 1868. Earl Granville was President of the Council during the whole of this time. During the early part of 1855, Lord John Russell held the post of Colonial Secretary in Lord Palmerston's Ministry, and he was entrusted with the education measures of the Government. His absence at Vienna, on a mission connected with the war, prevented progress, and on his return to England he resigned his office. One result, however, of his visit to Vienna seems to have been to enlarge his views on education, and in the following session he was roundly charged by the Voluntaryists with bringing home "a new-fangled scheme of despotism."

[1] Newcastle Commission, 380.

Sir John Pakington pressed forward his measure with much resolution and energy. The state of education as fostered by the voluntary societies was a scandal. An analysis of the imposing returns of the National Society showed that not more than 30 per cent. of their schools were legally secured for educational purposes ; 47 per cent. of the whole were neither legally nor virtually so secured, and of the 47 per cent. 50 per cent. were kept in dame's cottages, corners of churches, belfries, kitchens, or other rooms of parsonage houses. Sir John's bill was permissive in character. It proposed to place education in the hands of Boards elected by the ratepayers. Magistrates were to be *ex-officio* members, and other members were to have a ratal qualification of £30. Powers were vested in the Boards for providing schools, superintending the education of the district, levying rates and expending them under the control of the Education Depart-ment. The rates were to be supplemented by Parliamentary grants, and the schools were to be free. Existing schools were to be assisted out of the rates. A conscience clause was to be imposed on all schools. In new schools the religious teaching was to be in accordance with the opinions of a majority.

Mr. Milner Gibson's bill was for secular education. It was not put forward in antagonism to that of Sir John Pakington. They were both agreed that schools should be free, and be supported by rates. Mr. Gibson aimed at entire local management and liberty of conscience. In the state of parties and the distractions of opinion there was no hope of progress. All the measures were opposed by the Voluntaryists, and by the advocates of the existing schools which were now satisfied with the money they received. The Wesleyan Committee passed resolutions affirming that their community would never consent that the teaching of religion in their schools should be subject to restriction. (¹) Before the close of the session all the bills were withdrawn.

In 1856, Lord Granville, the new President of the Council, brought in a bill in the House of Lords for the appointment of a Vice-President of the Council, who would be responsible to the House of Commons for the distribution of the grant, now enormously increased by the capitation grant, which had been extended by Minute to boroughs. The bill passed, with slight opposition, and Mr. Cowper, afterwards known as Mr. Cowper-Temple, and the author of the clause bearing his name in the act of 1870, (²) was the first Vice-President. The President of the Council also submitted a bill enabling towns and parishes to rate themselves for purposes of education, but no effort was made to pass it.

The House of Commons was meanwhile the scene of some stirring debates. Lord John Russell, no longer fettered by the responsibilities of office, moved a series of twelve resolutions, covering the whole field of the education controversy. They affirmed the necessity of the revision and consolidation of the Minutes of Council; of an increase in the number of Inspectors; the formation of school districts; an enquiry into the available means of instruction; the proper application of charitable trusts; the power of rating; the election of school committees, with powers of management; the reading of the Scriptures; and a scheme of indirect compulsion, to be carried out by employers. In regard to direct compulsion, Lord John said:—" I do not think it would be possible, I should be glad if it were, to compel the parents of these children to send them to school. I do not think you could, by any enactment, reach the parents in such places as Birmingham, Sheffield, and others, in which, however,

---

¹ Newcastle Report, 312.
² Section 14, prohibiting the teaching of religious formularies.

we have to lament the greatest evils arising from neglect of attendance at school."([1]) But at last something like an adequate view of the necessities of the case was being taken, since the estimated cost of the plan was placed at £3,240,000.

A curious combination of parties made common cause against the resolutions. In the discussion and divisions which took place upon them, Mr. Gladstone and Mr. Disraeli, Sir James Graham and Mr. Baines, Mr. Henley and Mr. Milner Gibson, Lord Robert Cecil and Mr. Cardwell were found acting together.([2]) On the other side Lord John Russell was cordially supported by Sir John Pakington. At the outset of the discussion it was evident that a majority of the House had determined to subject the author of the motion to a humiliating defeat. The Government gave their late colleague only a half-hearted support, and would not assume the responsibility of founding a measure on his proposals. Mr. Henley moved on the discussion of the first resolution that the Chairman leave the chair. The debate was several times adjourned, and Lord John, in the hope of avoiding defeat, abandoned the greater part of the resolutions. The manœuvre, however, did not avert the catastrophe. Sir James Graham, who had been converted to Mr. Baines's views, strongly opposed Lord John Russell's plan. Mr. Gladstone spoke in favour of a system on the established basis. The Nonconformist leaders went to Mr. Henley and told him that they were going to vote for him on the ground that State education involved a danger to definite religious teaching. At this special time the Voluntaryists were making despairing efforts to sustain their failing cause, and Mr. Baines, Mr.

---

[1] Hansard, T. S., 140, 1955.

[2] Mrs. M. A. Baines, whose name is familiar in the educational discussions of this time, and who was one of the first advocates of compulsion, has sent the author a cartoon by "H. B.," which refers to the resolutions in question, and which reproduces the figures of the most prominent parliamentary advocates of education at this time.

Hadfield, and Mr. Miall were indefatigable in urging their opinions on Parliament. Mr. Henley's motion was carried by the unexpected majority of 102. As a curious illustration of the prejudice which still existed against education in some quarters it may be noticed that in the course of these debates Mr. Drummond, a member of the House, instanced two celebrated criminals of the day, Palmer and Sadleir, as the results of education, and exclaimed, " It really seems as if God had withdrawn common-sense from this House."

In the following year Sir John Pakington renewed his attempt to pass a bill for cities and boroughs, and was supported by Mr. Cobden; but the sudden dissolution of Parliament on the question of the China war interrupted its progress, and the election which followed decimated its supporters. Out of doors public opinion was supplying constant pressure, and amongst the incidents of the year was the conference at Willis's rooms, at which the Prince Consort presided. About this time Mr. Keith Johnston, the geographer, published a diagram, giving a comparative view of the percentage of the population of various countries in Europe receiving instruction. From this it appeared that England stood tenth on the list.

Sir John Pakington was a member of Lord Derby's Ministry which went into office in February, 1858. It was on his motion that the Duke of Newcastle's Commission was appointed. Sir Charles Adderley was Vice-President of the Council, but his accession to office had materially moderated his views on the question. He said, " Any attempt to keep the children of the labouring classes under intellectual culture after the very earliest age at which they could earn their living, would be as arbitrary and improper as it would be to keep the boys at Eton and Harrow at spade labour." The expression did not point to progress, but happily that was not dependent on the favour of officialism.

The appointment of Mr. Lowe as Vice-President of the Council in 1859, as a member of the Ministry over which Lord Palmerston presided until his death, and the acceptance of an inspectorship by Mr. Fraser, the present Bishop of Manchester, were guarantees, at any rate, for an intelligent investigation of the existing system. Their accession to office marks, not so much a new era in national education, as a revolution in the Government methods of management. In the many fierce conflicts which have raged around this question, there have been none more bitter than those which are associated with the name of Mr. Lowe. Of all our Ministers of education he has left the deepest impress of individuality upon the system, in its official character, and provoked a hostility more unmeasured than any other politician. For four years he was the object of the most implacable and envenomed attacks from all persons who had the smallest interest in the details of the Government administration; including those who were anxious to extend and reform the powers of the Department, and those who wished to abolish it altogether.

The reforms initiated by Mr. Lowe were wholly confined to amending the Privy Council system as it existed— and in no degree to extending it, or substituting for it a more general and comprehensive plan. Judging from the vigour and fearlessness with which he executed his task it may perhaps be regretted that he did not undertake the larger achievement of laying down the lines of a complete system. But the Government of which he was a member was not disposed for any grand or heroic measures. Lord Derby had gone out on the question of reform, and on the accession of Lord Palmerston, there set in the easy, do nothing, " rest and be thankful" period, which lasted for five years. It extended to all branches of government, and was a constant wet blanket upon the agitation for domestic improvement.

Mr. Lowe's course at the Education Department was determined by another active consideration—and that was, Mr. Gladstone's resolve to cut down the cost of government. The education estimate of 1859, Mr. Lowe's first year at the Department, was £836,920. The vote had increased to that amount from £160,000 in the preceding six years. There was a strong and just presumption that the efficiency and the utility of the system were not advancing in proportion with the cost.

Mr. Lowe, in moving the estimate, announced that the Ministry did not propose to take any new step until the Duke of Newcastle's Commission had made their report. He sketched the good and bad points of the system, though he hardly seems to have gauged the actual amount of friction and dissatisfaction which existed. The advantages, to his mind were, that it relied on an existing machinery, which was a stimulus to liberality, and had given proof of strength in tangible results. It was defective in that it did not reach districts most in need of assistance, but that could only be remedied by fundamental alterations. There was also a constant tendency to devour the Department. Another fault was, that public money was spent on schools founded on exclusive principles. The public was justified in asking that before grants were made to denominational schools, they should require in the trust deeds a conscience clause, protecting the children of parents who objected to religious formularies. This was done in many instances. ([1]) The exclusive system was wasteful, and increased the labour and cost of inspectorship by at least a third. At the then rate of progress, Mr. Lowe estimated that the grants would eventually be two-and-a-half millions per annum.

[1] About 1850, it became the practice of the Department to require the insertion of a conscience clause where aid was given to new schools. but the custom was not general.

23

Mr. Adderley, being relieved from the restraints of office, introduced in 1859 a bill for indirect compulsion, providing that children should not be employed in labour except it was certified that they had received a certain amount of instruction. The discussion was chiefly remarkable for an opinion expressed by Mr. Gladstone, who urged that the public mind was absolutely unprepared to deal with the question, which might with more advantage be the theme of speakers at statistical or social science associations.

The estimate for 1860 was the first intimation of the alterations contemplated by the Department. For the first time since 1834 the vote for education was reduced. The Vice-President complained that the system had a tendency to grow more wasteful rather than more economical. Comprehensive schools were the truest economy, so that one school sufficed instead of two—but he said the country had been retrograding, and foundation deeds were more exclusive than thirty years before. The British and Foreign Schools which were open to all classes except Roman Catholics, were replaced by denominational schools, chiefly Wesleyan, and the antagonism between the sects became sharper and more defined. The Committee recognised the necessity for a strict appropriation of the grant. They reduced the building grant, and determined to withdraw further grants for the erection of Training Colleges. They had suspended the capitation grant in Scotland, and had resolved on a reduction of pupil teachers. The voluntary party alone, amongst the various sections of educationists, received these changes with great satisfaction. The re-action in favour of their principles, which they had so long predicted, had now, they thought fairly set in.

The Duke of Newcastle's Commission, which was gazetted in 1858, presented their report in March, 1861. The result of their three years' enquiry is comprised in six bulky volumes, containing reports and evidence on all branches of the subject, and furnishing a most complete history of State education. The most important part of the enquiry was that which related to the education of the "independent poor." Other matters dealt with, were the education of paupers, vagrants and criminals, military and naval schools, and the application of endowments. The investigations extended also into the character and ability of teachers—the instruction in Training Colleges, the quality of teaching, and the attendance. The enquiry was principally devoted to the labours and results of the Committee of Council; but was also illustrated by valuable reports by the Rev. Mark Pattison, and Mr. Matthew Arnold on education in Europe; and by Dr. Ryerson on Canadian education. Taken with the reports of the Schools Enquiry Commission relating to higher education, and Mr. Fraser's report on the common schools of the United States, they form probably the most comprehensive account of education in all its branches, both at home and abroad, which has yet been put before the public. The accuracy of the statistical details of the report of the Newcastle Commission has often been disputed, and it has been made abundantly clear, that from some cause they greatly underrated the deficiency of education in the country. The report, perhaps on account of the endeavour to reconcile the conflicting views of the Commissioners, was characterised by considerable looseness of statement, and by wide differences of opinion between the Commissioners and the witnesses and school inspectors.

The general conclusions of the Commissioners can only be indicated very briefly. The leading object of the schools was found to be, as a rule, the care of religious instruction on the part of the managers—while they were sought by the parents principally for secular instruction. The evidence of the Assistant Commissioners was conclusive as to this. Jews and Roman Catholics were commonly found in Church schools, and Church children in Unitarian schools. In

Church schools the catechism was taught to all the scholars, and they were often compelled to attend Sunday School or Church. "There can be no doubt that this sort of interference engenders the bitterest feeling of hostility to the Established Church." ([1]) The difficulty of introducing a comprehensive system lay with the founders of the schools, and not the people. In Sunday Schools, reading and writing were incidentally taught, but their primary object was religious instruction, and by this machinery religious denominations increased the number of their adherents. The gross amount of education was subject to large qualifications and deductions, on account of irregularity of attendance, and the quality of instruction. It was assumed that half the children between three and fifteen ought to have been on the books of some school —in actual numbers, 2,655,767. The real numbers on the books were 2,535,462—leaving a deficiency of 120,305 who received no education. The children of the poorer classes receiving instruction were estimated at 2,213,694. ([2]) Of this number 917,255 were under inspection, the remainder being in private adventure schools, dame schools, and charity schools. With the exception of the children of out-door paupers or vicious parents, nearly all the children in the country capable of going to school received some instruction. The general conclusion arrived at was, "There is no large district entirely destitute of schools, and requiring to be supplied with them on a large scale." ([3]) "The means of education were diffused pretty generally and equally over the whole face of the country, and the great mass of the population recognised its importance sufficiently to take advantage to some extent of the opportunities afforded to their children." ([4]) The attendance was distributed over about four years, as to most children, between six and twelve. About one-third attended less than 100 days, 43 per cent. attended 150 days,

[1] Report, 36.　　[2] Ibid, 79.　　[3] Ibid, 86.　　[4] Ibid, 86.

and 41 per cent. attended 176 days, entitling them to the capitation grant. ([1]) Only 10 per cent. attended the same school between three and four years. " This state of things leaves great room for improvement, but we do not think that it warrants very gloomy views, or calls for extreme measures." ([2]) Compulsion was not recommended. The demands of labour could not, in the opinion of the Commissioners, be resisted. There was an increasing tendency to the employment of children, and they were of opinion that independence was of more importance than education. ([3])

The inspected schools were found to be much superior to others, but there were great complaints of the mechanical character of the teaching. The inspection was not valuable as a criterion of results. The schools were judged by the first class. Three out of four left school with such a smattering as they picked up in the lower classes. " They leave school, they go to work, and, in the course of a year, they know nothing at all." " We are successfully educating one in eight of the class of children for which the schools were intended." " The mass of children get little more than a trick of mechanically pronouncing the letters, and the words which they read convey hardly any ideas to their minds." ([4])

The suggestions of the Commission amounted, in substance, to an effort to supplement the system which had grown up under the Privy Council, without having recourse to such a measure of local rating as would disturb the management, or give the general body of ratepayers any control over the schools. They advised that assistance should be given by means of two grants; one out of general taxation, dependent on attendance, and one from the county rates, based on examination. For the rural districts it was advised that County Boards should be appointed. Quarter Sessions

[1] Report, 173.   [2] Ibid, 173.   [3] Ibid, 188.   [4] Ibid, 250.

were to elect six members, being in the Commission of the Peace, or Chairmen or Vice-Chairmen of Boards of Guardians, and these members were to elect six others. In towns containing more than 40,000 inhabitants the Town Council was to be authorised to appoint a Borough Board of Education. The Committee of Council was to appoint an Inspector as a member of each Board, and the Boards were to choose their own examiners.

The Commissioners declined to recommend a compulsory conscience clause, which they thought would give a dangerous shock to the existing system.

The suggestions of the Commissioners, being evidently the result of a compromise between conflicting opinions, gave very little satisfaction to any party. ([1]) The conclusions and recommendations were alike attacked. Lord Shaftesbury impugned the accuracy of their reports on ragged schools. Mr .Dillwyn complained of their injustice to Dissenters. The school Inspectors denied that the conclusions on the general results of the teaching were trustworthy. Grave doubts were also raised as to the accuracy of the enumeration of schools and scholars. For this purpose the Inspectors had chiefly relied on returns from voluntary societies and religious bodies, a method of enquiry which the statistical societies had previously condemned as untrustworthy. In a subsequent debate on the returns made to the Commissioners by the National Society, Mr. Lowe demonstrated their inaccuracy, and said, "It would be paying too great a compliment to those figures to base any calculation on them." ([2]) But they were a great consolation to those who objected to any change,

---

[1] The Commissioners were the Duke of Newcastle, Mr. Justice Coleridge, the Rev. W. C. Lake, the Rev. William Rogers, Mr. Goldwin Smith, Mr. Nassau W. Senior, and Mr. Edward Miall. The report was signed by all the Commissioners. Mr. Senior also presented a separate paper containing Heads of a Report.

[2] Hansard, 170, 1199.

and ten years later they were circulated throughout the country to prove that the system of education, as it existed in 1860, was perfectly adequate to all needs. They have since been conclusively falsified by experience in the working of the Education Act.

It at once became evident that the division of opinion which the Commissioners hoped to avoid by their report could not be averted. Sir John Pakington appealed to the Government to bring forward a measure, for which the circumstances appeared to be favourable. The Duke of Newcastle was a member of the Cabinet, as well as Earl Russell. But the very moderate suggestions of the Commissioners had already given rise to alarm. Mr. Henley said there was very much in the report which gave sanction to secular education. " The Committee appointed to watch proceedings in Parliament with reference to grants for national education," of which the Duke of Marlborough was Chairman, and several Bishops were members, had met and declared their fears that the radical changes proposed would prepare the way for bringing schools at no distant period under the control of the ratepayers, and extinguishing the religious element altogether. The National Society also saw in many parts of the report a grave danger to the maintenance of religious teaching.

The Ministry of Lord Palmerston was not inclined to face the dangers which threatened any attempt to solve the question. The Prime Minister with easy nonchalance postponed all attempts at reform, and the Chancellor of the Exchequer did not exempt even the education vote from the rigorous economy he practised. In moving the estimates for 1861, Mr. Lowe entered upon an exhaustive criticism of the report of the Commission and explained the views of the Government. He admitted that the system was expensive, that the instruction was deficient, and the machinery complicated. But he said it was not the intention of the Government to infringe on the organic principle of the system; its denominational character, its foundation on a broad religious basis, and the practice of making grants in aid of local subscriptions. The Government were asked to propose a bill on the basis of the report, but they would rather some one else did it. Such reductions as would not impair efficiency would be effected by a Minute of Council, but it was promised that no innovations would be made until the end of the next financial year. The capitation grant was not given on sufficiently stringent conditions. They ought to be satisfied that the children had been properly taught. They did not propose to base payment simply on results. The capitation grant would still be paid on the number of attendances above a certain number, but the Government went a step further. They proposed that an Inspector should examine the children in reading, writing, and arithmetic. If a child passed in all subjects the full capitation grant would be paid. Failure in one subject involved a reduction of the grant by a third, in two subjects by two thirds, and in case of complete failure the whole of the grant would be withheld.

This was the foundation of the "Revised Code," and the system of "payment by results." The Minutes were submitted to Parliament at the end of the session, and during the recess were the subject of animated discussion and agitation. The vested interests, which had been gradually entrenching themselves for a quarter of a century, took alarm, and raised the cry of invasion and confiscation. The system which professed to be doing so much, and to be capable of such vast expansion, and productive of such admirable results, shrank with the self-consciousness of inherent weakness and incapacity from any real test of its quality. Mr. Buxton quoted Spencer,—" They raised a most outrageous, dreadful, yelling cry." Pamphlets appeared, "not in single files, but in battalions." The arguments against the proposed changes are summed up in a letter from Sir James Kay Shuttleworth to Earl Granville. An attempt was made to show that the character of the education would deteriorate, but also and beyond, that the State had no moral right to make the changes without the consent of the other contracting parties—the managers and the schoolmasters. "The character of a system of public education thus created ought not to be abruptly and harshly changed by the fiat of a Minister, without the consent of the great controlling bodies and communions, who have expended twice as much as the State. Even were Parliament to make such a change, it would be a national dishonour. It would be an act of repudiation ever to be remembered with shame." (¹)

In the session of 1862, Mr. Lowe brought up the projected amendments of the revised code—the result of the labour of six months which he had spent in the perusal of pamphlets and papers. In fixing the limits of the controversy he said that the religious element underlay the whole system ; aid was only given to schools in connection with religious denominations. The Order in Council of 10th of May, 1840, which provided that the Inspectors should be approved by the Archbishops, was in full force, and no attempt was made to disturb it.

Formerly there were three grants—the capitation grant, the augmentation grant to teachers, and a grant to pupil teachers. The Commissioners had advised the abolition of these grants and the substitution of a capitation grant, part payable on attendance and part on examination. The Government had considered their report and stated their conclusions in the revised code. The existing system was tentative, provisional, and preliminary, and the grants were

¹ Letter to Earl Granville, 72.

established at a time when it was believed that the educational question would end in a system of rating. They had to consider how such a system could be made final and definite, on which the country could repose and find peace after so many stormy epochs. They did not attempt to renovate on its foundations. It had been introduced as an experiment, but had passed out of the experimental stage. It had struck roots into the country and they had no wish to disturb its fundamental principles. The great defect was its partiality—that it did not permeate through the whole country—it followed the lead of managers, and was regulated by wealth and public spirit rather than by the need of education. They must accept the situation—they had no power of altering it.

He admitted that the inefficiency of the system was not questioned, and the strong and startling evidence of incapacity was not refuted. Inspection, as opposed to examination, was not a test of a system. It dealt with abstract phases, general efficiency, average, moral atmosphere, tone, mental condition, and not the result of the labours of the teacher. The managers were afraid of this test, and said that the examination would be ruinous. They must choose between efficiency and a subsidy. There was a conflict between the Commissioners and Inspectors. The first said that one-eighth were properly educated—the second, 90 per cent. The Government would examine the children, and see which was right. Then many persons thought they had acquired a continuity of interest. The Training Colleges thought that the system in all its integrity must be kept up for them for ever. There was a danger that the grant should become, not a grant for education, but to maintain so called vested interests. The Government could not agree with the Commissioners as to county rates. They decided that there should be one grant, and that it should rest on examination—except in the case of infants, who would be entitled to the capitation grant on attendance. There was a strong case against the Training Colleges. They were established as voluntary institutions—but the Government paid 90 per cent. of the cost. ([1]) It had been proposed that there should be a reduction of teachers, but as they were in a position of great difficulty, the Government were willing to let them stand as they were, with the alteration of slight details. There was no reason to suppose that a loss was impending over schools. They offered a spur to improvement—not a mere subsidy. They could not say that it would be effectual or economical, but it would be one or the other. "If it is not cheap, it shall be efficient; if it is not efficient, it shall be cheap." The new principle was a searching one. It exposed the faults of the system, and had elicited confessions of bad attendance and inefficient teaching.

In the House of Lords, Lord Derby objected to grouping by age. The Bishop of Oxford did not wish to see education committed to Government management entirely, or private or charitable exertion superseded, for the " direct blessings given to it from above depended upon the work being the direct work of charity." He objected that the code provided for mere inspection in the mechanical part of training; reading, writing, arithmetic. Every child was to be examined. " The examiner in a hurry, the pupil in a fuss." It was introduced suddenly, harshly, and without due appreciation of the system. The Bishop of London urged that two grants should be given, one for attendance, and one for examination. If this were conceded, public opinion would change in regard to the code. He asked for one third to be given for attendance and two thirds for examination.

[1] The Duke of Newcastle's Commission reported that out of £4,378,183 contributed by Government towards education, £2,544,280 had gone for training teachers. Report, 25.

On the adjourned discussion in the Commons, Mr. Walpole moved a series of resolutions against making the whole of the aid depend on examination, against grouping by age, and the examination of children under seven. He referred to the length and breadth and strength and depth of feeling which agitated the country, and declared that religion would go to the wall. Mr. W. E. Forster opposed the code, which he said would destroy the system, and blamed the Government for forsaking the recommendations of the Royal Commission. After a long debate Mr. Lowe replied in a splendidly luminous argument, but expressed the desire of the Government to meet the wishes of the House. They were willing that a substantial part of the grant should depend on the general report of the Inspectors, and they gave up grouping by age. Mr. Walpole accepted the alterations proposed and withdrew his resolutions.

After the acceptance of the revised code there was a general disposition to wait until its results could be tested. But for several sessions proof was afforded of the bitter personal hostility its author had raised against himself, by his interference with what had come to be regarded as proprietary rights. He was the object of attack from all quarters—from school managers to monitors in the country, and from Inspectors to office boys in his own Department. It had been the practice of the Education Department, in certain cases, where extraneous matter was introduced in the reports of Inspectors, to send them back for revision. A difference arose between one of the Inspectors and the office in regard to this practice. Upon this Lord R. Cecil moved a resolution "that the mutilation of reports and the exclusion of matters adverse to the views of the Committee of Council, were violations of the understanding on which the Inspectors were appointed." The disappointed and angry faction of Tories and Denominationalists combined to make a personal attack on Mr. Lowe, in which they were joined by some professed Liberals. The subordinates of the education office were induced, in violation of discipline and trust, to communicate some official matters to the leaders of the Opposition. Mr. Lowe was weakly defended by his colleagues, and the Tories were allowed to snatch a division, in which the resolution was carried by a majority of eight. Mr. Lowe, who had made the question one of personal confidence, resigned his office. A Select Committee was afterwards appointed to enquire into the circumstances, and they entirely exonerated him. On the motion of Lord Palmerston the previous resolution was rescinded. The authors of the attack, however, had the personal gratification of driving from office the most able Minister who has yet held the post of Vice-President; who, if he initiated no large measure for the establishment of education on a broad and liberal basis, brought the system which existed to a practical test of usefulness, and converted a pretentious, but delusive plan, into an actual educational experiment.

Mr. Bruce succeeded Mr. Lowe at the Education Department, and in moving the estimates of 1864, insisted on the right of the Department to refuse grants for building where a conscience clause was not accepted. This now became the regular practice of the Department, and led to many differences between the office and the National Society. The first effect of the revised code was to lessen the money voted for education by Parliament. In 1865 the grant had fallen to £693,078; and in 1868 to £511,324.

With the death of Lord Palmerston in 1865, a new movement for domestic reform began; but for several sessions the question of the franchise occupied the first place. At the beginning of 1866 the liberal party was strong and united, Earl Russell being at the head of the Government;

but before the end of the session its majority of seventy was scattered and disorganised. Lord Derby succeeded Earl Russell. The Duke of Marlborough became Lord President, and Mr. Corry, Vice-President. The new Government on their accession brought forward no projects for the extension of education—but they raised the grant on examination, from two shillings and eightpence to four shillings. Mr. Bruce introduced a permissive bill to enable boroughs to levy rates for education. It proposed to trust a school committee with the management of the funds. The Committee was to be chosen in corporate towns from the Town Council, and in other places from the general body of ratepayers.

In 1867 the controversy was renewed in the House of Lords. The Queen's speech had said, " The general question of the education of the people requires your most serious attention, and I have no doubt you will approach the subject with a full appreciation both of its vital importance and its acknowledged difficulties." Parliament had been summoned in November, on account of the Abyssinian war. Earl Russell took the occasion to move a series of resolutions on education, but the Lords declined to enter upon the consideration of the subject in the brief limit for which they sat. On the reassembling of Parliament, the Duke of Marlborough introduced a bill to regulate the distribution of sums granted by Parliament for education. It was proposed that Her Majesty should be empowered to appoint a Secretary of State, who should have the whole range of educational matters under his consideration and control ; should administer the grant, and propose to Parliament such schemes as he might think fit, to promote education. The terms of the revised code were to be put into an act of Parliament. The Government proposed to admit secular schools to a share of the grant, and to impose a conscience clause on all schools. Compulsory rating and compulsory attendance were avoided. The bill passed the second reading, but was afterwards withdrawn.

Mr. Bruce also re-introduced his bill of the previous session, which was supported by Mr. Dixon. This measure emanated from the Manchester Bill Committee. Its provisions were extended to meet the case of local authorities who neglected their duties. It was made applicable to the whole country, and the important provision was added that all schools should be free. From the parliamentary discussions of the time, it would appear that Mr. Lowe had put forward during the recess a scheme for secular education by means of rates. The session was also memorable for the recantation of Mr. Baines, who brought up the deliberate and revised judgment of the Congregationalists, who had determined to place their schools under Government control and assistance.

Through the exertions of Mr. Melly and Mr. Dixon in 1869 an enquiry was obtained into the educational condition of Leeds, Manchester, Liverpool, and Birmingham, and resulted in the valuable reports of Mr. Fitch and Mr. Fearon. The Endowed Schools Act was also passed this year. In the same session the Marquis of Townshend brought forward a bill for compulsory attendance, and secular instruction in day schools. This was the last of the numerous abortive schemes which during the preceding half century were placed before Parliament.

CHAPTER V.

PERIOD.—FROM THE FORMATION OF THE LEAGUE, 1869, TO
THE PASSING OF THE EDUCATION ACT, 1870.

IN the new political movement which began upon the death
of Lord Palmerston, it became at once apparent that the
education question would take a foremost place. In the
discussions upon the reform of the representation, Mr. Bright
had predicted that the inevitable consequence of an extension
of the franchise would be, that the people would at once demand
an education system worthy of the country, and adequate to
its needs. The strong current of feeling in favour of a comprehensive law was beginning to be manifested on all occasions
throughout society. It was impossible to take up a newspaper
or magazine, or to follow the public life of any large town,
without discovering how deeply the attention of a part of the
community was engaged upon the subject. It was evident
also that public opinion was taking a much more intelligent
and comprehensive grasp of the question. The people were
tired of the tinkering process, and of half measures. Permissive legislation which was so fashionable in Parliament, was
in disrepute in the country, and there was an earnest call for
a measure based on the two principles of compulsory rating
and compulsory attendance.

At the conference held in Manchester on the 15th and
16th of January, 1868, strong expression was given to these
views. This meeting was called by the Manchester Education
Bill Committee, and was attended not only by the group of
Lancashire men who had led the way in all agitations of the
subject for thirty years, but by educationists from many other

districts, and by the Parliamentary leaders upon the question. The Manchester Education Bill Committee had grown out of the Education Aid Society, in the same city. The Committee had prepared the Bills introduced by Messrs. Bruce and Forster in 1867 and 1868, and they naturally exercised a considerable influence over the Government measure in 1870 ; though the ministerial proposals fell far short in important particulars of the resolutions passed at the Manchester conference The Government bill in short, as will be seen, was a compromise upon a compromise which had been already proposed. The Bill Committee had its origin in compromise. The Manchester Educationists were tired of the long conflict between rival schemes, barren of satisfactory results. They found they could do nothing and advance nothing apart. There was a great work to be done, ready to their hands, in getting the waifs and strays of Manchester into school. At a low estimate something like 20,000 children were without any instruction in this city, which in the matter of education, had the reputation of being the most advanced and intelligent in the United Kingdom. To accomplish this work the advocates of religious education, and those of secular education, came together; and the result was the formation of the Manchester Education Aid Society in 1864. This Society undertook a double duty,—to test the educational condition of the city, and to get children to school, either by paying their fees, or using other inducements and persuasion with their parents to send them. The result was that in two years only, 10,000 children were taken off the streets and sent to existing schools. But the investigations of the Society had elicited the painful fact that these were not half, perhaps not even a third or fourth part of those who were not receiving any regular instruction. The labours of the Society demonstrated conclusively to its members that voluntary means, however generous and earnest, and however carefully organised, were

25

powerless to combat effectually against the mass of ignorance. The consequence was that the Education Aid Society developed into the Bill Committee, under whose auspices the National Bill of Mr. Bruce was brought forward in 1867. The Bill Committee was a purely local body, and although it attracted much attention amongst educationists, it did not seek to extend its organisation or influence by combining with other kindred centres. The relation which it held to the League at a short time later, is explained in a letter addressed by Mr. Dixon to the Editor of the *Manchester Examiner*. A proposal had been made for joint action by the two bodies, and, in a circular issued by the Bill Committee, and signed by their Chairman; Mr. Francis Taylor, an opinion had been expressed that it would be wiser for the League to join in urging upon the Government the adoption of the bill proposed by the Committee, rather than to waste valuable time in discussing a new one. To this Mr. Dixon replied, " that not only was the bill of the League a more complete measure than that of the Education Bill Committee, but, also, that the operations of the League extended far beyond the enforcement of certain views upon a Minister." He added, "The work we have set our hands to, is to arouse the whole country to a sense of the extent and dangers of our present educational destitution ; to create and guide a strong public opinion : and thus to make possible a bold and comprehensive measure. However desirous the five members of the present Government, alluded to by Mr. Taylor, may be to pass such a measure, they will be utterly unable to do so, unless they are backed by the determined attitude of an active, powerful, and growing party in the country. The Education Bill Committee is composed of gentlemen to whom the friends of education owe much, but their numbers are insignificant, and, as a body, they are scarcely known beyond their own locality. It was my desire that they should extend their organisation, so as to become national instead of local, but I was informed that this could not be done. Had my suggestions been favourably received by the gentlemen to whom they were made, Birmingham would not have originated the League, but would have followed Manchester, which in my opinion, ought to have headed, and was entitled to lead a national movement."

It has been already explained that the first bill supported by the Bill Committee was for permissive rating, but such a measure was behind public opinion. This was made evident at the Conference of 1868, where a much more decisive course was advocated, and adopted in the new draft which was prepared. The Education Bill Committee was appointed at this Conference and was not dissolved until after the passing of the Act of 1870. ([1])

The movement in Birmingham, which led up to the formation of the League, began during the mayoralty of Mr. George Dixon. In the first instance it took the form, as in Manchester, of an effort to remedy a local evil. Mr. Dixon had long taken a great interest in the subject, and when on the death of Mr. Scholefield, Member for the Borough, he consented to become a candidate for the vacant seat, it was understood that he was largely influenced by the hope of being able to make some effectual effort for the establishment of a general system. During his mayoralty he had called several private meetings to consider the state of education in Birmingham. Eventually it was determined to form an Education Aid Society for the town, on the model of that at

[1] Amongst the Manchester men who took part in the movement were Sir Thomas Bazley, Mr. Jacob Bright, Mr. R. N. Philips, Mr. Cheetham, Professor Christie, Rev. Canon Richson, Rev. F. W. Davies, Mr. O. Heywood, Mr. Alderman Bennett, Dr. John Watts, Mr. W. R. Callender, Professor Jack, Mr. Francis Taylor, Dr. Pankhurst, Mr. W. L. Blacklock, Mr. A. Aspland, Mr. A. Milne, Mr. B. Armitage, Professor Greenwood, Mr. R. Fowler, Mr. S. Robinson, Mr. E. R. Le Mare, Mr. Herbert Philips, Mr. John S. Mayson, and Mr. J. A. Bremner.

Manchester. At a public meeting held in the Town Hall, on the 14th of March, 1867, a series of resolutions were passed with that object. Mr. Dixon was elected President of the new society, and Mr. Jesse Collings its Honorary Secretary. Its constitution was wholly independent of party politics or sectarian bias. On the Committee were the names of many who took part on opposite sides in the subsequent agitation. (¹)

The Society undertook, as a part of their duty, to thoroughly investigate the educational condition of the town, and to prepare statistics on the subject. A house to house canvass was undertaken for this purpose, and it brought out some remarkable results; demonstrating the inability of many parents to pay school fees, the absence of proper provision, and the necesity of compulsion to secure attendance. The figures were compiled with great care and tested in a variety of ways. Their accuracy was impeached by Lord Robert Montagu in the House of Commons, who suggested that they had been exaggerated by agents whose interests depended on making out a harrowing case in order to get subscriptions. When challenged, however, to support his accusations, he altogether failed to do so. The observation and experience of the members of the Society convinced the majority of them that only stringent legislation could put the education of the town upon a satisfactory basis.

In the general election of 1868 the question was widely discussed. In Birmingham it was prominently put forward by Mr. Bright, Mr. Dixon, Mr. Collings, and by the Liberal press.

¹ The Hon. and Rev. Grantham Yorke and Mr. R. W. Dale were Vice-Presidents. The first committee consisted of Mr. J. Thackray Bunce, Rev. Dr. Burges, Mr. Joseph Chamberlain, Mr. R. L. Chance, Rev. Charles Clarke, Mr. J. A. Cooper, Mr. George Dawson, Rev. Charles Evans, Mr. Sebastian Evans, Rev. Canon Gover, Mr. William Harris, Mr. Hawkes, Rev. Micaiah Hill, Mr. J. S. Hopkins, Mr. John Jaffray, Mr. T. C. S. Kynnersley, Mr. William Kenrick, Mr. Alderman Manton, Rev. Canon O'Sullivan, Mr. Alderman Ryland, Mr. W. L. Sargant, Mr. Sam. Timmins, Rev. Charles Vince, Rev. A. Ward, and Rev. Dr. Wilkinson.

The League had its origin in a conversation between Mr. Dixon and Mr. Collings, when it was resolved to call a private meeting to consider the advisibility of organising a National Association for the purpose of agitation. A meeting was held at Mr. Dixon's house early in 1869. There were present, Mr. Dixon, Mr. Chamberlain, Mr. Collings, Mr. Bunce, Mr. Harris, and many others, who afterwards joined the Provisional Committee.

All these gentlemen took an active share in the struggle which followed, and many of them during the succeeding eight years devoted themselves, without reserve of time or energy, to secure the objects of the Society.

A circular was shortly issued inviting adhesions to the League on the following basis :—

OBJECT.

The establishment of a system which shall secure the education of every child in the country.

MEANS.

1.—Local authorities shall be compelled by law to see that sufficient school accommodation is provided for every child in their district.

2.—The cost of founding and maintaining such schools as may be required, shall be provided out of local rates, supplemented by Government grants.

3.—All schools aided by local rates shall be under the management of local authorities, and subject to Government inspection.

4.—All schools aided by local rates shall be unsectarian.

5.—To all schools aided by local rates admission shall be free.

6.—School accommodation being provided, the State, or the local authorities, shall have power to compel the attendance of children of suitable age not otherwise receiving education.

This was, with slight alteration, the basis which had been proposed by Mr. Collings in his review of the American common school system.

The response to the circular proved that public opinion was ripe for the movement, and that there was a deep-seated conviction on the subject throughout society, which was only waiting to be led. In a few months, and before any public demonstration had been made, 2,500 persons, including many of the best known politicians, thinkers, and writers in England had joined the League. A provisional committee was appointed to make arrangements for a general conference of members, and to transact the preliminary business of the organisation. Mr. Dixon was elected chairman, Mr. Chamberlain, vice-chairman; Mr. Collings, honorary secretary; and Mr. Jaffray, treasurer. At a somewhat later period the author was appointed secretary, a post which he held until the dissolution of the League. [1]

The movement was embraced with great avidity in all the large towns, and in the autumn local committees were formed in London, Manchester, Bradford, Bristol, Leicester, Sheffield, Liverpool, Leeds, Huddersfield, Exeter, Bath, Warrington, Devonport, Carlisle, Merthyr Tydvil, and Wednesbury. From this time the agitation rapidly increased in influence, and the first meeting was looked forward to with great interest and enthusiasm from all parts of the country.

The programme for the general meeting included the formal constitution of the League ; the discussion of Parliamentary procedure, and of the general principles advocated

[1] The members of the first Committee were—Henry Holland (Mayor); Aldermen Hawkes, Osborne, Ryland, and Wiggin; Councillors George Baker and William Harris; the Revs. Charles Clarke, Charles Vince, and H. W. Crosskey; Messrs. W. J. Beale, J. Thackray Bunce, J. H. Chamberlain, R. L. Chance, George Dawson, A. Field, T. P. Heslop, W. Holliday, G. J. Johnson, T. Kenrick, J. A. Kenrick, G. B. Lloyd, C. E. Mathews, W. Middlemore, Follett Osler, Wm. Ryland, S. Timmins, [a]   J. S. Wright.

as the basis of the agitation; a soiree to the members by the Mayor, and a demonstration in the Town Hall.

Mr. Dixon took the chair at the Exchange Assembly Rooms on the 12th October. The report of the provisional committee, stating the origin and purpose of the League, was read by Mr. Collings. Archdeacon Sandford moved that the report should be adopted, and in doing so he warned the members that they must be prepared for opposition. He said, " I am quite satisfied that very many severe things will be said of your platform. We shall be told no doubt that it is a godless scheme; that it is a revolutionary scheme; that it is a scheme utterly unsuited to the taste and feeling of the British people; that it cannot succeed; and that if carried out it will flood the land with atheists and infidels." He strongly opposed, as leading to perpetual divisions and dissensions, the scheme of concurrent denominational education, to support which a conference had been held at Willis's Rooms in the preceding year; which was in fact the final effort of Archdeacon Denison.

Mr. Dawson seconded the resolution in a speech which will be long remembered by those who heard it for its argument, its eloquence, and its humour.

Mr. Edmund Potter, M.P. for Carlisle, moved the appointment of the Officers, Council, and Executive. This was seconded by Dr. Hodgson, who had been one of the founders of the National Public School Association, and an Assistant Commissioner in 1858. He said, " The President's reference to the Manchester Association leads me to say that although death has thinned the ranks of those who composed that Association for obtaining secular, rate-paid education, there still remain a large number, who, instead of looking upon the labours of the League with jealousy, will hail its co-operation with the greatest earnestness and enthusiasm, not even desiring to meet it in friendly rivalry." Mr. Dixon was chosen chairman of the Council, Mr. Jesse Collings hon. secretary, and Mr. Jaffray treasurer. The Council was a consultative body, consisting of all members of Parliament who joined the League, donors of £500 and upwards, representatives appointed by the branches, together with nearly 300 ladies and gentlemen chosen from the general body of members. ([1])

During the eight years of the agitation there were many changes in the constitution of the Executive. Before the conclusion of their labours death had removed from the Committee some of their most trusted and able colleagues, including Mr. Dawson, Mr. Vince, and Alderman Rumney.

[1] The Executive Committee appointed at this meeting consisted of— Messrs. J. T. Bunce, Joseph Chamberlain, J. H. Chamberlain, Charles Clarke, H. W. Crosskey, George Dawson, Alfred Field, William Harris, Henry Holland, William Kenrick, William Middlemore, E. C. Osborne, Follett Osler, Arthur Ryland, Charles Vince, and J. S. Wright, of Birmingham ; Mr. Charles Booth, Liverpool ; Rev. Dr. Caldicott, Bristol ; Major Ferguson, Carlisle ; Edward Huth, Huddersfield ; Canon Kingsley, Eversley ; Mr. Maxfield, Leicester ; Captain Maxse, Southampton ; William Simons, Merthyr Tydvil ; Rev. S. A. Steinthal, Manchester ; Rev. F. B. Zincke, Ipswich ; Angus Holden, Bradford ; and the Hon. Auberon Herbert, Dr. Hodgson, George Howell, and Herbert Fry, London.

During the continuance of the organisation the following names were added to the Committee :—R. Applegarth, London ; Rev. J. J. Brown, Birmingham ; Professor Fawcett and Mrs. Fawcett, Cambridge ; G. B. Lloyd, Rev. M. Macfie, R. F. Martineau, S. Timmins, C. E. Mathews, Rev. J. Renshaw, Rev. J. M. McKerrow, Dr. Langford, Birmingham ; Thomas Webster, Q.C., Sir C. W. Dilke, F. Pennington, Edward Jenkins, R. Williams, London ; C. H. Bazley, William Cheetham, Alderman Rumney, Harry Rawson, Manchester ; William Bragge, J. Taylor, Councillor Hibberd, H. J. Wilson, John Muscroft, Sheffield ; W. F. Collier and William Adams, Plymouth ; Joseph Cowen, Newcastle ; James Kitson, Rev. J. Haslam, Rev. H. W. Holland, Leeds ; S. S. Mander, Wolverhampton ; F. G. Prange, Liverpool ; G. B. Rothera, Nottingham ; Stephen Winkworth, Bolton ; Bancroft Cooke, Birkenhead ; J. C. Cox, Belper ; Alderman Hutchinson, Halifax ; Rev. R. Harley, Leicester ; Isaac Holden, Keighley ; Captain Sargeant, Bodmin ; Rev. J. Marsden, Taunton ; John Morley, Tunbridge Wells ; Thomas Nicholson, Forest of Dean ; James Hanson, Bradford ; S. C. Evans Williams, Rhayader ; and John Batchelor, Cardiff.

There were a few secessions on questions of policy. Mr. Simons went over to the Welsh Committee, which decided in favour of purely secular teaching ; Canon Kingsley gave his support to the Education Act ; and Professor and Mrs. Fawcett withdrew on the ground of the opposition to the 25th section. But with few exceptions the members of the Committee remained loyal to the principles and policy of the League, and gave the Officers an undivided trust and support during the most trying years of the agitation, and notwithstanding the strain on party loyalty, which was caused by the opposition to the policy of a Liberal Government.

It was determined to make parliamentary work a prominent feature in the League programme. Accordingly, at the meeting on the twelfth of October, Professor Fawcett moved, and Professor Thorold Rogers seconded a resolution that a bill, embodying the principles of the League, should be introduced during the next session. Papers were also read by Mr. Dixon on " The best system for National Schools, based upon local rates and government grants ;" by Professor Rogers on " Secular Education ;" by the Rev. S. A. Steinthal on " Local Educational Rating ;" by Mr. Pentecost on "Compulsion ;" by Dr. Rowland Williams on "The legislative enforcement of attendance ;" by Alderman Rumney on " Compulsory attendance ;" by Mr. Alfred Field on " Free schools ;" by the Rev. F. B. Zincke on " Unsectarianism ;" by the Hon. Auberon Herbert and Mr. G. J. Holyoake on "Secular education ;" by Mr. H. J. Slack on " Denominational schools ;" and by Captain Maxse on " Free and compulsory education." The following gentlemen took part in the discussion which followed. Mr. Simons, Merthyr ; Mr. Applegarth, Mr. Green, Sir C. Rawlinson, Sir William Guise, the Hon. George Brodrick, Mr. Follett Osler, the Rev. Septimus Hansard, the Rev. H. W. Crosskey, and the Rev. Dr. Caldicott. The Conference was brought to a conclusion by a great meeting in

26

the Town Hall, not the least enthusiastic and striking of the many celebrated gatherings which it has witnessed. The speakers were Mr. Dixon, Professor Fawcett, Mr. Mundella, Mr. J. Chamberlain, Mr. Cremer, Mr. Carter, and Mr. Collings.

It is necessary to notice one incident which took place at the first meeting, which while it did not disturb in an appreciable degree the harmony of the proceedings, and did not divert attention for a moment from the ultimate object, yet pointed to a difference of opinion within the League, and was prophetic of future difficulty. Then, as ever, it was the religious difficulty which raised its head to confront progress. The Chairman was challenged by the Rev. Mr. Dowson of Hyde, to say whether the League supported secular education or the British school system. Mr. Dixon replied, "We do not use the word 'secular'; but we exclude all theological parts of religion, and I am sure that what is left is what even Mr. Dowson himself would call secular." In answer to further questions on the same subject Mr. Dixon stated that the word "unsectarian," excluded all dogmatic and theological teaching, and all creeds and catechisms, and also that if the Bible were read it must be without note or comment. ([1]) Concisely stated the programme of the League as to religion in school, was Bible reading or not, at the option of the ratepayers. As events proved it might have been wiser to have gone at first for the absolute separation on all points, of religious and secular teaching. Bible reading was satisfactory to no considerable party; and the permissive use of the Bible did not prevent the members of the League from being denounced on Church and Tory platforms as the enemies of religion, of government, and of morals.

The financial prospects of the League were, from the outset, of a very encouraging character. It was thought probable by the founders of the League that the agitation

[1] Report First General Meeting, 187-194.

might extend over a period of ten years, and a guarantee fund was therefore arranged, of which a tenth part was to be called up annually. (^{1})

Of this fund eight instalments were called up; but as special funds were raised during the struggle for electoral purposes, to which the ordinary subscribers were contributors, the sums originally promised were, in many cases, actually exceeded. The total amount of the guarantee fund was £60,000, showing an annual income of £6,000—which was occasionally raised by special donations to between £7,000 and £8,000. These sums did not include subscriptions for purely local purposes, which were also large. On the day after the introduction of the Government Bill, a full list of the subscribers to the central offices was advertised in the *Times*, and covered a page of that newspaper.

Immediately after the first meeting the business of the League began in earnest, and its progress was unexampled in the history of public organisations. The work of the central office was of a very absorbing and exacting nature. It is proper to record that by far the greatest share of the labour was wholly voluntary, and was undertaken by men who inevitably sacrificed their individual pursuits and private interests in its performance. Even when the magnitude of

---

[1] Theie were many generous subscriptions to the fund, including those of Mr. Dixon, M.P., £1,000; Mr. A. Brogden, M.P., £1,000; Mr. R. L. Chance, £1,000; Mr. J. Chamberlain (Moor Green), £1,000; Mr. Joseph Chamberlain, £1,000; Mr. G. B. Lloyd, £1,000; Mr. A. Field, £1,000; Mr. Follett Osler, £1,000; Mr. William Middlemore, £1,000; Mr. A. Kenrick, £1,000; Mr. J. H. Nettlefold, £1,000; Mr. Alderman Phillips, £1,000; Mr. F. S. Bolton, £1,000; Mr. Isaac Holden, £1,000; Sir Titus Salt, £1,000; Mr. C. Paget, £1,000; Mr. Thomas Thomasson, £1,000; Mr. Edmund Potter, M.P., £500; Mr. T. Kenrick, £500; Mr. J. A. Kenrick, £500; Mr. John Jaffray, £500; Mr. Clarkson Osler, £500; Mr. F. Pennington, £500; Mr. William Kenrick, £500; Mr. Hugh Mason, £500; Mr. Edward Ashworth, £500; Mr. Joseph Cowen, £500; Mr. John Leech, £500; Mr. William Leech, £500; Mr. Haslam (Bolton), £500; and Mr. Harold Lees, £400. Sir Charles Dilke was also an annual subscriber, for several years, of £100.

the operations compelled the appointment of a large staff of stipendiary assistants, they were drawn from the ranks of men who were willing to make personal sacrifices for the success of principles which were dear to them, and in the performance of a public duty.

It may be interesting to note the division of labour which was maintained as a rule, for eight years, amongst those who were chiefly responsible for the direction of the agitation. Mr. Dixon was Chairman of the Council and the parliamentary leader and adviser of the League until his retirement from Parliament in 1876. For eight years he devoted himself without reserve to the service of the organisation. In the interval between the constitution of the League and the introduction of the Government Bill in 1870, over a hundred public meetings were held in different towns to advocate and explain the platform. Mr. Dixon's attendance at these meetings was always eagerly sought. After the Parliamentary struggle began, his attention was necessarily more confined to the proceedings of the House of Commons, but at all times, and wherever and whenever they could be best employed, his services were at the disposal of the Executive. The pains which he has since bestowed upon the local administration of the Education Act, and the development of the resources and powers of School Boards, are well known throughout England. It is perhaps the best refutation of the calumnies which were heaped upon the League, that the leader of those who were branded as sectarians, revolutionists, irreconcilables, sciolists, infidels and communists, has devoted himself unremittingly for fifteen years with many of his colleagues, in the first place to secure an efficient education law, and afterwards to derive the largest possible product which able administration is capable of yielding.

Mr. Chamberlain was the head of the Executive Committee, and the acting Chairman of the League, and as such was chiefly responsible in originating and conducting its policy in the country. In this department he was earnestly seconded by Mr. Collings, the honorary secretary. For the general policy, all the Officers were jointly responsible, under the direction of the Executive. As a matter of convenience and efficiency however, it was found advisable to place an Officer at the head of each department of work. Mr. Bunce was Chairman of the Publishing Committee, and in that capacity he had not only the supervision of all the publications, the variety and extent of which were great; but he drew up most of the important circulars which were issued to the members and branch committees, and to the parliamentary supporters of the League. Mr. Martineau, as chairman of the Branches Committee, undertook to overlook and direct the local organisations, a post involving a great amount of correspondence, investigation, and advice. Mr. Harris was chairman of the Parliamentary Committee and Mr. Clarke of the Finance Committee; positions which involved a large amount of administrative labour, and often the decision of important matters of policy. Mr. Jaffray was treasurer for several years, and was succeeded in the post by Mr. Mathews. Meetings of the Officers' Committee were held always twice a week, often more frequently, and as a rule one or more of the Officers attended at the central office daily. At the beginning of the agitation an immense amount of public speaking was thrown upon the Officers. But in that branch of the work they were greatly relieved by the assistance of Mr. J. H. Chamberlain, Mr. Sam. Timmins, Mr. Dale, Mr. Dawson, Mr. Vince, Mr. Zincke, Mr. Herbert, and other members of the Executive.

This notice of the personal services which were rendered to the League is necessarily most imperfect. There were at every local branch, members who were working in their districts with the same degree of earnestness and disinterestedness—the mere record of whose names would fill many pages. But in mentioning those who took a prominent share in the agitation, it is impossible to overlook the services of Mr. Steinthal, who undertook the organisation of the Manchester district, and who with the assistance of Mr. Winkworth of Bolton, Mr. Dowson of Hyde, and others, induced the people of Lancashire to take a part in the work worthy of the fame of the foremost educational county of England.

An idea of the progress made by the League, and of the hold which its principles had taken on the public mind, may be obtained, if its position at the end of four months is considered. By the end of February the guarantee fund amounted to £60,000 : there were in connection with the central office 113 branch committees in different towns, and many of these had local auxiliary committees in correspondence with them. Trade societies, representing a large section of the working population, had joined the League and subscribed to its funds. Nearly two hundred public meetings had been arranged from the central office, and nearly all of them had been attended by one of the Officers or members of the Executive. A quarter of a million copies of different publications had been put in circulation, including 7,000 copies of the Report of the general meeting, and 10,000 copies of Mr. Collings' Essay on American Common Schools. In December a monthly paper was started. This was continued during the existence of the League, and had an average circulation of about 20,000 copies.

In regard to the political constitution of the League, it was composed, without exception, so far as the author's knowledge goes, of members of the Liberal party. But all shades of religious opinion, except Roman Catholicism, were represented on the Committee and amongst the members. The first list of members comprises the names of four hundred clergymen and dissenting ministers, including many eminent

Liberal Churchmen, and the best known and most trusted Nonconformists.

The prophecy of Archdeacon Sandford, at the first meeting, was speedily fulfilled. Notwithstanding the strong religious element in the personal constitution of the League, it did not escape the charge of being animated by hostility to religion. If the authors of the accusation had contented themselves with saying that every liberal movement in the way of education must necessarily come into conflict, not so much with religion, as with the pretensions of the directors, professors, and exponents of theology, there might have been room for an admission, that the League came under the common indictment. It is hardly necessary to say that there was no foundation whatever for the charges that the Officers, the Executive, or the members of the League were thinking of anything but the best way of getting children into school. But the success of the early operations gave alarm to the Church and the Conservatives. They saw, in fancy, their cherished preserves invaded, and their vested interests in danger. Two " Unions" were immediately started in opposition. One had its head quarters in Birmingham, the other in Manchester, the latter being the most prominent and representative. The avowed object, as expressed in authentic documents, was stated to be " To counteract the efforts of the Birmingham League, and others advocating secular training only, and the secularisation of our national institutions."

The new programmes were put forth under the sanction of a long array of Archbishops and Bishops, Dukes, Earls, and Tory Members of Parliament. While the League could hardly boast a Coronet, the " Unions " had very little else to boast of. Their lists were wholly uncontaminated by any association with popular institutions, or their representatives. They were Conservative organisations, as much as the League was a Liberal and Democratic organisation. A feeble effort was made to relieve the aspect of Toryism by parading the names of Mr. Cowper-Temple, Mr. Baines—and some more doubtful Liberals, but it was not very successful. What is essentially to be noticed in regard to these Unions is that they were called into existence to obstruct and not to construct. But for the League they would never have been heard of, and education might have languished for another half century. The Bishop of Manchester, at one of the Union meetings, after referring to the educational destitution of the country, said, "Now to this educational destitution, without meaning to ignore the labours of the Manchester Education Aid Society, or of those gentlemen who have prepared the Manchester Committee Bill—I wish to give them all credit for what they have done,—I think the Education League was the first to call, prominently, national attention ; and I suppose if it had not been for the existence of the Education League, and the programme they put forth, this Education Union, which has assembled us here to-night, would have had no existence." ([1])

It was into the arms of a Society thus constituted and originated, that Mr. Forster the Radical and Puritan precipitated himself, and attempted to drag after him the Liberal party.

The contest between the rival societies was conducted with much animation, and before the assembling of Parliament there was not a town of any importance in England where meetings or conferences had not been held. In Wales, also, the excitement was intense. These discussions had their natural effect upon the Government, and in January Mr. Forster, the Vice-President, announced their intention to bring in a bill.

Acting upon the resolution passed at the first meeting of members, the Executive Committee had prepared instructions

[1] Report of Meeting, Free Trade Hall, 1870, 6.

for a League bill, and the draftsman had nearly completed his work. Early in the session, Mr. Dixon had expressed his intention to proceed with this measure, but on the announcement of the Government bill he consented to suspend action until the proposals of Ministers were made known. Great expectations had been raised amongst the people and the Nonconformists by the committal of the education question to the care of Mr. Forster. He was regarded as the Radical representative in the Ministry. He had been used to pride himself on his ultra-liberalism, and his alliance with the extreme section of the popular party. He had given for many years considerable attention to the subject, and had taken an active share in the agitation of the National Public School Association. He had also backed Mr. Bruce's bill in 1868, which was a Free School bill—the feature of an education programme dearest to Radicalism. There was another circumstance upon which the popular party founded their hopes—Mr. Bright was a member of the Cabinet. But, most unfortunately, before the education question came under the notice of Parliament, he had been attacked by the distressing illness which robbed the country of his services during this critical period.

The Government measure was submitted to the House on the 17th of February, 1870. Its author bespoke for it the favour of the House, divested from considerations of party. It was a bold request to make, remembering that this had been a critical question with all Ministers for forty years, and had kept alive the most intense and acrimonious divisions in the country. The demand that it should be suddenly raised above the region of passion, and feeling, and self interest, suggested to practical minds a political impossibility, and awakened amongst earnest Liberals a corresponding feeling of distrust. But although Mr. Forster was courageous, he

27

was not original. A greater Minister, when about to surrender the traditions and principles of his party on a crucial question, had suggested that the time had come when it ought no longer to decide the fate of parties. But the Radical's imitation of the Conservative was inappropriate and infelicitous, because there was the important distinction that Mr. Disraeli was struggling in a hopeless minority, while Mr. Forster was member of a Cabinet supported by a great parliamentary majority, and backed by a nation enthusiastic for searching legislation. There was all the difference between resignation to unavoidable surrender, and the desertion of principle when its triumph might have been won. It will no doubt be pleaded that the difficulties of the Government were great, and had been piled up year by year since the formation of the Committee of Council. They had to interweave a new and efficient system with one which was inherently defective, and had been discredited by results. No doubt this was the case; but if Mr. Forster had possessed the courage of Mr. Lowe, there was no insuperable difficulty. The opportunities of 1870 were such as few Ministers enjoy. The people had been sickened by living for six years in an atmosphere of unworthy compromises and of tinkering legislation, and they would have gladly supported the Government in passing a thorough measure on distinctly Liberal lines. No one asked at this stage of the agitation that the existing system should be destroyed, but the people had a right to ask that a system which had proved itself incapable, should not be riveted upon the nation, and entrenched behind new privileges and larger subsidies. They had a right to expect a Liberal measure from a Liberal Government. As a matter of fact, the clergy and the Tories had never ventured to hope from any Ministry such concessions as those which were offered to them by Mr. Forster. There were two courses open to the Government — to make old and admittedly imperfect plans bend to the necessities of modern life, or to sacrifice efficiency in favour of custom and authority. They chose the latter. The bill was studiously framed to secure the support of the existing managers, and through them, of the Conservative party.

As explained by Mr. Forster, the provisions of the bill he introduced were :—

The Country to be divided into School districts— (Municipal Boroughs and civil parishes).

The Government to take powers for ascertaining the deficiency of school accommodation.

The abolition of denominational inspection.

The imposition of a conscience clause (the benefit to be claimed by the parent in writing).

The removal of restrictions against secular schools.

The denominations to have a year's grace to supply the deficiency of accommodation.

On the failure of the denominations, School Boards to be elected, with powers of rating to establish schools.

School Boards to be elected by the Town Council in Boroughs, and by select vestries in parishes.

School Boards to have power to remit school fees on the ground of poverty, and in special cases to establish free schools, the consent of the Education Department being first obtained.

School Boards to have power to assist existing schools out of the rates.

No restrictions to be placed on School Boards in regard to religious instruction, except the observance of the conscience clause.

The School Boards to have powers to frame bye-laws for compelling the attendance of children between five and twelve years of age.

The precise effect of the bill was hardly perceived upon its introduction, and it was received with a chorus of satisfaction from the Liberal benches, which reflection greatly modified. Mr. Dixon while giving a general assent to the principles enunciated, criticised its provisions. He condemned the year of grace allowed to denominational effort, and complained that instead of meeting the religious difficulty by the separation of religious and secular instruction, the bill threw it upon the School Boards to decide. He also strongly opposed as weak and inefficient, the permissive compulsion on which the Government relied.

A circular was at once issued by the Officers of the League to the branches and members, pointing out the particulars in which the bill appeared to be defective, and inviting the expression of local opinion. Replies were received from sixty-eight branches, and were laid before a meeting of the Executive Committee on the 24th of February. Great disappointment was experienced at the incomplete character of the Government proposals. It was resolved to withhold the bill which had been drafted, and to use the whole force of the League in pressing for amendments in the ministerial bill which was held to be inefficient in the following points.

The only means proposed for enforcing attendance was through the agency of School Boards. Therefore unless such Boards were generally established, great irregularities and inequalities would exist. There would be the anomaly of abundant provision, and imperfect attendance. The bill was wasteful, to the extent that it required school provision, and took no security that it should be used.

Great and unnecessary delay was encouraged by the bill. It was estimated that three years, or even half a generation of school life might be lost before it came into operation. There was first of all to be an enquiry to ascertain the deficiency—then a year's grace was to be allowed to the denominations—and upon the formation of a School Board, another year might elapse before operations were begun.

The proposal to extend the denominational system was in itself objectionable. The country had a right to ask that the new system should be of a public character, under public management, and conducted on unsectarian principles. The extension of the denominational system was a direct restraint on the establishment of a national system.

The election of School Boards by select vestries was strongly opposed, as an attempt to restrict the free exercise of the ratepayers rights, by confiding the election to bodies consisting of self-chosen, and *ex-officio* members, usually representing two interests—the land and the Church. The ballot was also demanded as a security against coercion.

The illusory provisions in regard to compulsion were objected to, it being evident that " permissive compulsion " was wholly inadequate. The uselessness of such legislation had been recently demonstrated by the failure of the Workshops Act. It was clear also, that influences and interests which were opposed to education might seek representation on School Boards with the object of preventing the exercise of their powers.

On the subject of free schools, the Committee pointed out the injustice of taxing the working classes to provide for schools partly free, and imposing an additional tax in the shape of school fees. They were also opposed to the pauperising influence of the Government provisions, and to the obstruction to attendance which would be created.

The provisions in regard to religious instruction were condemned. The bill threw the question of religion to the constituencies, to be fought out in every borough and parish. In order to avoid a parliamentary conflict it was to be transferred to electoral platforms throughout the country. The League demanded the time table conscience clause, and the exclusion from state-aided schools of catechisms, formularies, and doctrinal teaching.

The proposals for granting aid out of the rates to existing denominational schools were opposed, as creating a scheme of concurrent endowment, the chief effect of which would be to enrich Church schools.

The amendments resolved upon were :—

1.—School Boards to be established in all districts, instead of only in those districts in which education is declared to be unsatisfactory after enquiry by the Privy Council.

2.—Such Boards to be elected immediately on the passing of the Act, and to be required to provide without delay for the educational necessities of their districts.

3.—In districts not included in boroughs, School Boards to be elected by the ratepayers generally, voting by ballot.

4.—Compulsory attendance of children at school to be made imperative, instead of being left to the discretion of School Boards.

5.—Admission to schools established or maintained by School Boards to be free.

6.—No creed, catechism, or tenet peculiar to any sect to be taught in schools under the management of School Boards, or receiving grants from local rates. In all other schools receiving Government aid the religious teaching to be at distinct times, either before or after ordinary school business, and provision to be made that attendance at such religious teaching should not be compulsory, and that there should be no disability for non-attendance.

In a statement of the provisions and amendments, they were thus summed up :—" The bill provides, in a feeble, hesitating, tentative way, for the application of certain principles—local rating, local management, direct compulsion, free schools, and unsectarian teaching. The amendments of the League propose to carry these principles into full operation, by dealing firmly with them, and providing that their application shall be rendered certain, instead of being left to accident or caprice. In a word, the League proposes that Parliament shall legislate, giving to local bodies only administrative powers."

Mr. Forster's idea of raising the question above party considerations was to throw himself into the arms of the Opposition, and to rivet an intensely sectarian and party system upon the country. He had approached a subject which had baffled Ministers for half a century with too light a heart, and too easy a conviction of his ability to " canter over " the religious difficulty. He ended by over-riding some of the most cherished convictions and principles of the party to which he belonged. From the beginning of the parliamentary discussion he was adopted as the *protégé* and instrument of the Tories and the clergy, a position which ought not to have been a comfortable one for a strong Liberal statesman. The Executive Committee of the League therefore determined to make a direct appeal to the Prime Minister.

On the 9th of March, a deputation waited on Mr. Gladstone at his official residence. Mr. Dixon introduced the deputation—probably the most numerous and representative which had ever visited Downing Street. It comprised 46 members of Parliament, and 400 members of the League, representing 96 branches. Mr. Chamberlain, as Chairman of the Executive, stated the views of the League. He described its origin, its rapid growth in numbers and influence, and its claims to fairly represent Liberal opinion throughout the country. In stating the objections of the Committee to the bill, he said they were opposed to the year's delay, which would give to the denominations opportunities to run a race of wasteful expenditure, and to increase sectarian bitterness. They objected, also, to the permissive recognition of great principles, to permissive compulsion and permissive sectarianism, and also to the retention of school fees. The conscience clause proposed was entirely unsatisfactory : no parents would dare to make use of it, or to place themselves under the ban of the parson and the squire by signing such a document. If the Government entertained any doubt as to the opinion of the country, and would give them a little longer time, they would make that opinion sufficiently manifest. In conclusion, he asked that the Government which secured the support of Liberal Churchmen, and of the leading Dissenting bodies, in their efforts to carry out the principles of religious freedom and equality in Ireland, should not reject their petition for the application of those principles in England, and that they would remove from what was otherwise a noble measure, clauses which would inflict intolerable hardship and oppression upon a large class of the community.

Sir Charles Dilke spoke on the conflict between the principle of permissive, and of direct and general compulsion : Mr. Mundella described the application of compulsory laws in foreign States : Mr. Applegarth represented the views of the working classes : The Rev. S. A. Steinthal advocated the abolition of school fees : Mr. Illingworth, the Rev. F. Barham Zincke, and the Rev. Charles Vince explained the views of the deputation on the treatment of religion.

Mr. Gladstone expressed a hope that a basis was afforded upon which, by united efforts, they would be able to work out a satisfactory result. On the same day the Premier also received a deputation from the Welsh Educational Alliance—a body working in sympathy with the League.

On the second reading of the Government Bill, Mr. Dixon, at the request of the Executive Committee, moved " That this House is of opinion that no measure for the elementary education of the people will afford a permanent or satisfactory settlement, which leaves the question of religious instruction in schools supported by the public funds and rates, to be determined by local authorities." Mr. Dixon explained that his amendment did not cover the ground of his objections to the bill, which might be improved in many respects. He could have wished to show reasons for the general establishment of School Boards, and for their free election by the ratepayers ; also for the immediate and general application of compulsion, and for the abolition of school fees. He was also opposed to the granting of a year's grace for the establishment of new denominational schools. But he confined himself to a review of what was called the religious difficulty, which would be greatly aggravated by the bill. In the course of time School Boards would become universal, rates would be levied everywhere, compulsory attendance would be generally enforced, and members of different sects would have to pay for, and to send their children to schools of other denominations. The minority would have to pay for the religious teaching of the majority. Denominationalism would thus be increased, rather than lessened, as he held it ought to be. If the Irish system had been adopted there would have been no opposition to the bill. He believed they could not reach a solid foundation short of separate religious teaching. If the agitation should be continued there would arise in the country, a party who would ask for exclusively

28

secular education. The Vice-President of the Council had misunderstood the nature and extent of public feeling on the question. A contest between the Church and Nonconformists already seemed inevitable. Looking at the lessons of history he had no doubt which would prevail. If the bill should pass, at future elections of Town Councillors, to be a Dissenter would be a qualification for office, to be a Churchman a disqualification, amongst Liberals. The conscience clause had been tried and found wanting. Parents would not avail themselves of it. The time-table conscience clause was the only one that would work. There ought to be separate religious instruction apart from secular teaching. He hoped that the Government would modify the clauses, and that it would not be left to School Boards to decide this question after a conflict involving much strife and religious animosity. He had taken the unusual and grave step of moving an amendment to the second reading, because it was the only way in which he could gain for the subject the importance it deserved. There would have been a deep feeling of disappointment in the country unless the first opportunity had been taken for giving expression to the strong and decided feeling which existed. If the Government should not think it right to make any declaration of opinion in compliance with these views, it would remain for the constituencies to express their opinion in a manner which would leave no doubt as to public sentiment.

Mr. Illingworth seconded the resolution.

Mr. Forster complained that an amendment had been proposed on the second reading—a course generally taken by members hostile to the Government and the measure. He quoted from proceedings of the League, the Welsh Alliance, and the Congregational Union, to show that they were not agreed on the question of religious instruction. Remarking on his Puritan blood, and his connection with the Radical school, he asked, with a strangely distorted sense of Puritan and Radical principles, that religious questions should be submitted to the decision of municipal bodies ; the inevitable effect of which would have been to introduce into their discussions, subjects of dispute and contest which had been excluded since the repeal of the Test and Corporation Acts, and to restore the tyranny of majorities in matters of religion. He gave great praise to the Opposition for the concessions they had made in the acceptance of a conscience clause and the abolition of denominational inspection. He asked that the House should go into Committee, his speech containing no indication that the Government were prepared to make any concessions.

The debate was continued on the following evening by Mr. Winterbotham in a speech of marked ability. Mr. Auberon Herbert, Mr. Vernon Harcourt, Sir Henry Hoare, Mr. Jacob Bright, Mr. James Howard, Professor Fawcett, Mr. H. Richard, and Sir Charles Dilke also supported the amendment. The Liberals who opposed it were Sir Roundell Palmer, the Chancellor of the Exchequer (Mr. Lowe), Mr. Mundella, Mr. Cowper-Temple, and Mr. U. Kay-Shuttleworth. A number of Conservatives also gave their support to the Government; being determined apparently by the general agreement which existed below the gangway on the Liberal benches.

As the result of three nights discussion, Mr. Gladstone indicated that certain modifications would be considered by the Government—such as those referring to the popular election of School Boards, and the separation, in time, of religious and secular instruction, with other provisions to give to the minority equal privileges with the majority. Under these circumstances Mr. Dixon said he felt it his duty to withdraw the amendment.

The alterations proposed by the Government were not laid on the table of the House until the 26th of May.

During the interval, although much uncertainty was caused by the delay—there being many rumours that the measure would be withdrawn—the country was not idle in giving expression to its views. The opinion that nothing but a thorough measure would be of use was strengthened and confirmed by the publications of the reports of Mr. Fitch and Mr. Fearon on the elementary schools of Birmingham, Leeds, Liverpool, and Manchester—verifying, as they did, the conclusions of the Education Aid Societies. In March a large number of petitions were presented, praying for more decisive and perfect provisions in the bill. As an illustration of public feeling, though perhaps not the most conclusive one, it may be noticed that the signatures to the League petitions amounted to 277,651, while those on the opposite side were only 18,822.

A meeting of the Executive was held on the 24th of March, when the following resolution was passed:— "That the Executive Committee regards with satisfaction the spirit of concession manifested by Mr. Gladstone in his speech on the second reading of the bill, but desires to reiterate its unshaken conviction that no amendments can be satisfactory in reference to the religious difficulty which do not provide that no creed, catechism, or tenet peculiar to any sect shall be taught in schools under the management of School Boards, or receiving grants from local rates, and that in all other schools receiving Government aid the religious teaching shall be at a distinct time, either before or after ordinary school business, provision being made that attendance at such religious teaching shall not be compulsory, and that there shall be no disability for non-attendance. That this Committee is further of opinion that the whole of the League amendments should be moved in Committee."

Amongst Nonconformists the bill had created feelings of mingled surprise, anger, and dismay. They were startled to receive such a blow against their most cherished principles from a Government to which they had rendered such loyal service. Almost for the first time since 1839, all sections of Protestant Dissenters were found closely united in support of common views. There were individual exceptions, amongst whom Mr. Baines was the most prominent; but such men admittedly did not represent the opinions of any considerable or important section of the Nonconformist body, either in respect of numbers or authority.

The Central Nonconformist Committee, which was formed in Birmingham, and was in connection with Dissenting Committees throughout the kingdom, took an active and important share in the agitation against the objectionable provisions of the bill. The Chairman of the Committee was Mr. Middlemore. Mr. R. W. Dale and the Rev. H. W. Crosskey were the Honorary Secretaries, and Mr. Schnadhorst, who has since acquired a national reputation, was the Secretary. The Committee at once called meetings of Dissenters in every part of the country to consider the religious clauses. Petitions were presented to the House of Commons praying for a reconsideration of the proposal to give local boards unrestricted power to determine the religious character of schools supported by local rates. This petition was signed, in a few days, by over two thirds of all the Nonconformist ministers in England and Wales, of all denominations. On the 11th of April a deputation waited on Mr. Gladstone and presented to him personally a protest in the same language and representing the same bodies. The deputation comprised Mr. Dale and Mr. Crosskey, the Rev. J. G. Rogers, of the Congregational Union Committee; Rev. W. Brock, President of the Baptist Union; Rev. J. Hargreaves, of the Wesleyan Methodists; Rev. G. Lamb, of the Primitive Methodists; Rev. J. S. Withington, of the United Methodist Free Churches; Dr. Cooke, President of the New Connexion Methodists; and the Rev. W. Gaskell, President of the Provincial Association of Lancashire and Cheshire Unitarian Churches.

But perhaps the most earnest, formidable, and unanimous opposition to the bill proceeded from Mr. Forster's own borough—and from his own constituents and friends. At ten open public meetings convened in the town in the month of May, resolutions were passed in favour of a compulsory, unsectarian, and free system. Petitions were forwarded to Mr. Miall for presentation to the House, and a memorial was addressed to Mr. Forster, begging him to reconsider his course. This agitation was, perhaps, stimulated by the strong support which the clergy and Conservatives gave to Mr. Forster, and it was encouraged and promoted by the great majority of the Liberal party.

The Manchester Corporation also appointed a deputation to wait on the Premier to advocate more stringent provisions for procuring attendance, to protest against assistance out of the rates to denominational schools, and to urge the Government to settle the religious question at once by deciding what should be taught, instead of leaving it to be contended for amongst municipal bodies.

In the course of the discussions on the bill, the Manchester Bill Committee, which had been in favour of leaving the religious instruction to local decision, and under whose advice Mr. Forster had acted in drawing up his clauses, became convinced that public opinion would not tolerate such a method of dealing with the question, and advised that it should once for all be settled by the Legislature.

Earl Russell also wrote to Mr. Forster confessing that he had changed his views, and thought it would be impolitic to remit religious questions for local decision. He also strongly advocated the time-table conscience clause, and the prohibition of catechisms and distinctive religious teaching in rate-aided schools. He added, "such men as Mr. Miall and Mr. Winterbotham ought surely to be conciliated by justice and not overpowered."

There was during the same period, a steady growth of the League branches, of the number of members, and of the funds placed at its disposal. Repeated warnings were addressed to Ministers from all sources, that persistent adherence to the objectionable features of the bill would result in a formidable breach in the ranks of the party. In several Parliamentary contests which had occurred, the League had made its power felt; and this feature of the agitation promised to become much more prominent.

The first batch of Government amendments—those indicated by Mr. Gladstone on the second reading—were laid on the table, on the 26th of May. They provided, 1. That where select vestries were not popularly chosen, the School Boards should be elected by the ratepayers generally, voting by ballot. 2. That a time-table conscience clause should be imposed on all schools receiving Government aid, or assistance from local rates: and 3. That Government Inspectors should not examine the religious teaching in any school.

Great disappointment was felt at the imperfect character of these alterations. At a meeting of the Executive Committee, held on the 3rd of June, resolutions were passed declaring the Government amendments inadequate and unsatisfactory, and expressing the view that if no further amendments could be secured it would be desirable to postpone legislation until the next session. It was determined to raise a special fund of £10,000 for the purpose of continuing and extending the agitation, which had grown to dimensions making a heavy strain upon the resources of the central office.

The Central Nonconformist Committee also adopted resolutions complaining of the unsatisfactory character of the ministerial proposals, and advocating an organised opposition to the passage of the bill in the form which it presented.

The critical position of affairs induced the officers to summon the Council of the League—a body which by the constitution was entitled to be called together only on special occasions—the object being to make the most formal and impressive protest which they could put on record. The meeting was held at Willis's Rooms on the 16th of June, Mr. Dixon presiding, when there were present members of the Council and representatives from all parts of England. This body sustained the action of the Executive—and resolved that the amendments proposed to be introduced by the Government were wholly insufficient to meet the requirements of the country, as expressed in public meetings and petitions.

Mr. Vernon Harcourt had given notice of an amendment on going into committee, to the effect that provision should be made to secure that in all schools deriving assistance from the public rates, the religious teaching given should be undenominational in character, and confined to unsectarian instruction in the Bible : and that no measure of National Education would be effectual which did not provide for the compulsory attendance of all children of school age, to be enforced by School Boards established in every district. As an amendment to this resolution Mr. Cowper-Temple intended to move, " that in all schools established by means of local rates, no catechism or religious formulary which was distinctive of any particular denomination should be taught." (¹)

---

¹ Mr. Cowper-Temple was Chairman of the Education Union. He explained, however, during the debates in Parliament that he did not put his amendment on paper at the request, or as the representative of the Union. The wording of the clause is somewhat ambiguous, and might be interpreted to admit catechisms and formularies which are distinctive of more than one sect. Mr. Cowper-Temple is said to have stated that he intended it to allow the use of the Lord's Prayer, the Ten Commandments, and Apostles Creed. But I believe that in practice the interpretation of its author has been considerably narrowed.

But on the order of the day for going into committee Mr. Gladstone rose to make a further statement. From this it appeared that the Government had decided on adopting Mr. Cowper-Temple's amendment—and on the time-table conscience clause. They had also resolved to strike out clause 23, which authorised School Boards to give assistance out of the rates to voluntary schools. In lieu of this clause they proposed to raise the grant to denominational schools out of the consolidated fund, so that it would be equivalent to fifty per cent. of their expenditure. They also proposed to discontinue the building grant after the period of grace allowed to the denominations to establish new schools.

These proposals could hardly be satisfactory to the League or to Nonconformists. The Ministry, in fact, threw themselves into the arms of their enemies. They adopted the clause proposed by the Chairman of the Union, and the suggestion made by Lord Robert Montagu that they should return to the former liberal scale of grants. The building grant was discontinued in such a manner as to give a stimulus to the foundation of denominational schools. The grants which were applied for before the end of the year would, at the normal rate of application, have extended over from fifteen to twenty years. In the schools thus established and endowed, any kind of religious instruction might be given at the pleasure of the schoolmaster—excepting the use of catechisms and formularies. Mr. Disraeli charged the Government with creating a "new sacerdotal class." They also refused to concede the principle of direct and general compulsion, upon which public opinion chiefly relied to secure an efficient system.

Mr. Henry Richard gave notice of a motion "That grants to existing denominational schools should not be increased, and that in any national system of elementary education the attendance should be everywhere compulsory, and the religious instruction should be supplied by voluntary

29

efforts, and not out of the public funds." It was resolved by the Executive to support this amendment. The most representative Nonconformist bodies also passed resolutions in its favour. The debate upon it occupied four nights, and extends to 250 pages of Hansard. Sixty-two Liberals, representing many of the largest constituencies in the kingdom, went into the lobby against the Government upon this motion.

A still larger defection occurred on the discussion of clause 17, providing for the regulation of public elementary schools. To the Government clause (that adopted from Mr. Cowper-Temple) Mr. Jacob Bright moved a further amendment—that in rate-supported schools in which the Scriptures were taught, the teaching should not be used or directed in favour of, or against the distinctive tenets of any religious denomination. The division upon this amendment ought to have conveyed a sufficient warning to any Ministry not absolutely blind, or bent upon rushing on its own destruction. One hundred and thirty-three Liberals walked out of the House without voting, while 132 Liberals, representing 1,063,579 electors, voted against the Government. The clause proposed by the Government was carried by the union of 121 Liberals (including 25 Government officials) and 132 Conservatives. The Liberal minority included members of every section of the party, representing constituencies of all diversities of character, from the city of London to the West Riding.

From this time, although the League did not relax its efforts, it was felt that the struggle in Parliament was nearly a hopeless one. In the progress of the bill through Committee the Government steadily resisted all amendments, whether proceeding from the League or the Church party. Where attempts were made to give a more reactionary character to the measure the adherents of the League gave a cordial support to the Ministry, but only in their turn to be crushed by an alliance between the Ministerialists and the Tories.

Mr. Walter's amendment for the establishment of School Boards in all districts was defeated, but as an evidence of the importance which the country attached to the representative principle in educational management, it is worthy of notice that 112 Liberals voted against the Ministry. As a partial concession to the strong feeling which existed Mr. Forster consented to introduce a provision for the creation of School Boards on the application of the inhabitants.

Sir Stafford Northcote made an effort to omit the words prohibiting the use of catechisms and formularies in rate-supported schools, and Sir John Pakington moved to make the reading of the Bible compulsory. Both proposals were lost.

Mr. Dixon's motion to secure free admission into rate-supported schools was equally ineffectual.

Sir Charles Dilke moved that the School Boards should be elected by the ratepayers instead of by Town Councils and Vestries. The amendment was opposed by the Government and rejected by the narrow majority of 150 against 145. The lesson of this division, however, was not lost, since at a later stage the Government accepted the proposal.

Lord Frederick Cavendish is responsible for the cumulative vote, which Mr. Gladstone, with some impetuosity, accepted on the part of the Government.

One of the most remarkable circumstances in the progress of the bill is, that clause 25 permitting the payment by School Boards of fees in denominational schools, was agreed to without discussion or division. The explanation however is obvious. The clause was grouped with clause 23 of the original bill, which provided for assistance out of the rates to existing schools. The greater clause over-shadowed the lesser, and it was not discovered that the latter involved a similar principle. It was therefore overlooked. Considering the feeling which was afterwards aroused by the attempt to enforce the 25th section, it is worth while to reflect what would have happened if clause 23 had been allowed to pass.

A further effort was made by Sir Thomas Bazley to insert clauses providing for direct and general compulsion, but it was defeated.

On the motion of Mr. Candlish that the parliamentary grant should not be extended to schools not then in existence, unless they were provided by School Boards, Mr. Dixon entered a formal protest against the course pursued by the Government, which he predicted would end in creating religious dissensions, disastrous both to religion and education. With a fine sense of casuistry, Mr. Forster replied that the money offered by the Government was intended for secular and not for religious teaching ; and this notwithstanding the admission of the voluntary managers, that their schools could not continue to exist without aid from the Government. In considering the conduct of the measure by the Vice-President, one of the least satisfactory features is, that while professing to change the principle upon which grants were made, allocating them for secular instead of religious instruction, he did it in such a manner as to strengthen and encourage the foundation of schools, whose chief object was, by their own admission, to foster denominational interests. In 1839 Lord Melbourne and Lord Russell, in the name of the Queen, declared that education must have a religious basis, and they consistently refused aid to schools in which religion was not taught. In 1870 Mr. Forster professed that the sole object of the Ministry was to provide secular education, yet he was careful to carry it out in such a way that sectarian schools would receive the largest share of the advantages offered by the Government.

On the discussion of the parliamentary grant Mr. Trevelyan, who had resigned his post in the Ministry, addressed the House. He said that private members stood in a happier position than members of the Government, for they were justified in voting for the bill under protest, at a future time opposing the increased grant; but it would be the duty of the Government to press forward the increased grants, for which every member of the Government would be bound to vote, however much it might be against the Liberal creed. He was not prepared to incur such an obligation. Politicians of his standing had formed their beliefs and aspirations during the Irish Church Agitation of 1868, and during that period, Scotland and Wales and many of the large towns of England, pronounced against denominational education. That election was, in large portions of the country, a crusade in favour of religious equality. Very great was the responsibility of confusing ideas of right and wrong by repudiating denominational ascendancy in Ireland, and then pouring out the public money like water in favour of denominational education in England. He felt bound to oppose the increased grant, and this was why he had taken the painful step of leaving the Government.

In the House of Commons, the ballot in School Board elections was stoutly contested by the Conservatives, but was carried by the Government after an all-night sitting. The House of Lords subsequently expunged the clause, to which the Government assented.

On the third reading of the bill, Mr. Dixon said that he had not offered to it a factious opposition, or attempted to delay its progress, but it must not be concluded that he was satisfied. It was his intention to give notice that early next session he should move for leave to bring in a bill to amend the act. It owed its success in the House mainly to two causes, which would not be forgotten in the country. The first was the constant and earnest support given to it by the Opposition, and the other was the statement, made over and over again by the Government, amounting almost to a threat, that unless their usual supporters went into the same lobby with them, they would run the risk of losing the bill, and incur the condemnation of the country. He regretted that the success of the bill had been purchased at such a heavy price, for he could not hide from himself that it had roused the suspicion, the distrust, and the antagonism of some of the most earnest supporters of the Government. He thought it was a great disadvantage, if not a positive evil, that those who had done so much to place the Government in the position it occupied, should be accustomed to an attitude of opposition, and to make appeals that would be repeated to the Liberal party outside the House, against the action of a Ministry which had hitherto received from them the most unvarying, loyal, and enthusiastic support.

The concluding debate was also marked by a passage of arms between the Prime Minister and Mr. Miall, who spoke as the Nonconformist representative in the House. The latter complained that he and his supporters had been made to pass through the Valley of Humiliation. The Administration was in power mainly in consequence of the support given by the Nonconformist body to the policy announced by the first Minister of the Crown two years before. They gave whatever new impulse was given to the Liberal cause, then and for years to come. When this question was brought forward they did not expect anything immoderate, or demand anything that was selfish ; but they thought that some consideration would have been paid to their objections— which, however, had been increased and aggravated by the remedies applied. He suggested that there would in future be a diminution of the confidence which they had formerly reposed in the Ministry, and greatly incensed the official Liberals by using the expression, " once bit, twice shy."

Mr. Gladstone made an impetuous reply, in which he justified the course which had been taken by the Government. He said, " my honourable friend thinks it worthy of him to resort to a proverb, and to say that the time has come when he is entitled to use the significant language, ' once bit, twice shy.' But if my hon. friend has been bitten, by whom is it ? If he has been bitten, it is only in consequence of expectations which he has himself chosen to entertain, and which were not justified by the facts. We have been thankful to have the independent and honourable support of my hon. friend, but that support ceases to be of value when accompanied by such reproaches as these. I hope my hon. friend will not continue that support to the Government one moment longer than he deems it consistent with his sense of duty and right. For God's sake, sir, let him withdraw it the moment he thinks it better for the cause he has at heart that he should do so." The language used on both sides proves how intense was the exasperation which existed between Ministers and a large section of their supporters ; and the subsequent history of the Administration shows how ready the Nonconformists were to take the Prime Minister at his word. A subsequent portion of his speech may be adduced in proof of the political honesty of his character, but at the same time it exhibits the wide gulf which existed in feeling between himself and the mass of those who had returned him to power. He made no pretence that the Education Act was a measure for secular education only, or even that it was impartial in character. He said, " it was with us an absolute necessity—a necessity of honour and a necessity of policy—to respect and to favour the educational establishments and machinery we found existing in the country. It was impossible for us to join in the language, or to adopt the tone which was conscientiously and consistently taken by some members of the House, who look upon these voluntary schools, having generally a denominational character, as admirable passing expedients, fit indeed to be tolerated for a time, deserving all credit on account of the motives which led to their foundation, but wholly unsatisfactory as to their main purpose, and therefore to be supplanted by something they think better." These expressions wcre consistent at any rate with the course which Mr. Gladstone had always pursued in relation to education, though they did not exhibit great sagacity in estimating the weight and direction of public opinion.

In the concluding stages Mr. Forster made light of the threat of an agitation against the act—but this did not deter Mr. Dixon from giving notice of his intention to move in the next session for its amendment.

The act received the Royal assent on the ninth of August, 1870.

The Denominationalists were allowed up to the 31st of December to make application for building grants. The Church papers demanded immediate and energetic action on the part of Churchmen. Not a moment, they declared, was to be lost. They were advised to ascertain the educational need in every district, and to report "schools in progress" to the Department. The Roman Catholics took the same course, the Duke of Norfolk and Lord Howard leading the movement. These appeals to purely sectarian interests resulted in 3,111 applications ([1]) to the Department for building grants in less than five months—the normal rate of application being about one hundred and fifty per annum.

If any doubt had been felt as to the effect of the act in stirring up sectarian feuds, it was soon dissipated by the action of the country. Everywhere the introduction of the law was the signal for the revival of disputes of the most painful

[1] Of these applications 1,332 were afterwards withdrawn.

character, which previously had slumbered, and which it was hoped were gradually dying out. Mr. Forster's reward for passing the act, which he accomplished by means of an ability and persistency which are not denied, was a seat in the Cabinet. But his relations with his constituents, or more correctly with the Liberal party in Bradford, were embittered for the next ten years. In January, 1871, he went to Bradford to deliver an account of his stewardship. He was met by a vote amounting to one of want of confidence.

Mr. Alderman West moved, and Mr. Alderman Scott seconded, a resolution,—

"That this meeting tenders its congratulations to the Right Hon. W. E. Forster, M.P., on his having obtained the high and honourable position of a member of Her Majesty's Cabinet, and begs, at the same time, to thank him for the full and clear account of his parliamentary experience during the past year, which he has given this evening."

Mr. Charles Turner moved as an amendment,—

"That this meeting having heard Mr. Forster's account of his parliamentary experience during the past session, and fully recognising his previous services to the Liberal cause, regrets its inability to approve of the educational measure passed mainly by his exertions, and deplores deeply the means resorted to, to secure its adoption in a Liberal House of Commons."

Mr. Elias Thomas seconded the amendment, which was carried. The Vice-President, however, had his consolations in the confidence and praise of the clergy, the Tories and their press. On a rumour of his removal from the Education Department, the *Guardian* remarked, " We should be glad to see his advancement to any post of greater dignity, but certainly it will illustrate very unhappily the necessities of parliamentary government if, just as he has shown himself master of the situation in one most important Department, he

30

should be transferred to another in which he has everything to learn. The work of the education bill is not done ; on the next two or three years everything will depend. We doubt whether Parliament would have given such unexampled autocracy to the Department if they had not fancied that Mr. Forster was to preside over the inauguration of the new work."

With these ill omens, the Education Act of 1870 entered upon its work.

CHAPTER VI.

PERIOD.—FROM THE PASSING OF THE EDUCATION ACT, 1870,
TO THE ADOPTION BY THE LEAGUE OF THE SECULAR
PLATFORM, 1872.

NOTWITHSTANDING its defects in important particulars, the
Education Bill, as it was sent up to the House of Lords,
was a very different measure from the draft which Mr. Forster
had introduced. The separation of religious and secular
instruction effected by the time-table conscience clause was
only partial—it was as Mr. Gladstone said, a separation in
time alone. Yet it was the acceptance of a principle, which,
step by step, with a persistency which never yields, has been
gradually asserting itself in the practice of our legislature
and government for a century past. Ten years before the
passing of the Act the justice and practicability of any
conscience clause was denied by nine-tenths of the school
managers; and the general imposition of a time-table
conscience clause would have been felt to be the most complete
and disastrous defeat which Denominationalism could sustain.
It is not desirable to over-estimate the value of the concession. The time will probably come when such a badge of
toleration will not be required. It is very doubtful indeed
whether in the existing state of society, any conscience clause
which ingenuity could devise would prove effectual. The
actual experience under the existing clause has not been
satisfactory; but still something was gained. Mr. J. S. Mill
said, "I should be glad to forget as soon as possible what the
bill would have been without it. Though brought in by a
Government which has earned such high distinction as the

destroyer of religious inequality in Ireland, a more effectual plan could have scarcely been devised by the strongest champion of ecclesiastical ascendancy, for enabling the clergy of the Church of England to educate the children of the greater part of England and Wales in their own religion at the expense of the public." [1] The integrity of the denominational teaching was broken by the clause. The principle of the division in time between the two branches of instruction once admitted, the complete separation in other respects has become a question of patience.

In some other points the denominational character of the bill had been successfully attacked. The proposed year of grace was reduced to about five months ; the direct power to subsidize denominational schools out of the rates had been negatived; and the teaching of catechisms and formularies in rate-aided schools had been prohibited.

The amendments in the civil clauses of the bill, striking also against denominational influence, were even of greater value. These provided chiefly for the free election of School Boards by the ratepayers, and the power of localities to acquire School Boards on application to the Department. These amendments brought more freely into play the principles of local rating and local management. The permissive power to establish Boards by the vote of the School district, became in practice of the highest value, for it was by this means that the best results of the Act were produced.

As soon as the bill became law, the Executive Committee decided on a double line of policy. It was resolved in the first place to make the most of the Act as an educational measure, by encouraging the application of the representative principle, in the formation of School Boards, the provision of schools, and the adoption of

[1] Speech at St. James's Hall, March 25, 1870.

compulsory bye-laws. While the Act was yet passing through its final stages, the Town Council of Birmingham, at the instigation of Mr. Dixon, took steps for acquiring a School Board. This example was immediately followed in Leeds and Sheffield, and at a short time later by the Corporations of Manchester, Liverpool, Middlesborough, Leicester, Nottingham, Oxford, Bolton, Coventry, Canterbury, Blackburn, and other important boroughs.

It was also determined to agitate against the proposed increase of grants to denominational Schools, and to strive for other amendments calculated to make the educational operation of the Act more universal and efficient.

A circular was issued by the Officers to the local branches, explaining how the Act might be put into operation without waiting for the formal notices and enquiries, and urging the adoption of this course in all districts where there was an obvious deficiency of accommodation. With the same object, a letter by the Chairman of the Executive on the advantages of School Boards was circulated, and a legal hand-book containing an Analysis of the act, for the use of members, was distributed.

At a meeting of the Executive Committee, held on the 7th of September, it was resolved to maintain and extend the organisation of the League for the following purposes :— " 1. To assist in putting the Education Act in operation, so as to secure, as far as possible, the establishment of unsectarian, compulsory, and free schools. 2. To promote amendments in the Act by converting the permissive into obligatory clauses, and securing the recognition of the principle of religious equality in rate-aided schools. 3. To resist the increase of parliamentary grants to sectarian schools. 4. To watch the progress of educational legislation in reference to the Irish system. 5. To influence public and parliamentary opinion by meetings, publications, petitions, and all other available means, in favour of a national, unsectarian, and free system of education ; and with this view to secure the return of members to the House of Commons pledged to support the principles of the League."

With these objects, renewed efforts were made to extend and re-invigorate the organisation. A large number of travelling and local agents were appointed, and an active canvass of the constituencies was undertaken, with the result that in a short time the branches and adherents of the League were doubled.

The electoral policy of the League was as yet undeveloped, but in the action taken at Shrewsbury, Newark, and other towns, there were distinct indications that principle would not be sacrificed for the sake of party cohesion. Speaking at Shrewsbury, Mr. Dale had called upon the constituencies not to vote for candidates who were unprepared to resist a denominational system, and the increase of grants to sectarian schools. " Nonconformists must make it clearly understood that there were certain terms by which their allegiance to the Liberal party stood or fell, and that they meant to take some part in Liberal counsels."

The deep-seated distrust which the policy of the Government had created amongst Dissenters, was illustrated by the action of the Central Nonconformist Committee. This body had been appointed to watch the progress of the Education Bill in Parliament, but it was not dissolved on the passing of the Act. At a meeting held at Carr's Lane, on the 19th of October, Mr. Chamberlain in the chair, it was decided to continue the existence of the Committee, to obtain the amendment of those provisions which violated the principles of religious liberty, to secure the refusal of national aid to new denominational schools, and its gradual withdrawal from schools under sectarian management—to prevent the development of the denominational system in Ireland and Scotland, and to resist legislative encroachments on the rights of Nonconformists.

A new departure in the movement was now taken. The Chairman said that the Committee were of opinion that they had previously been a little too moderate, and whereas they had formerly asked that there should be no increase of aid to denominational schools, they now asked that all grants of national money for denominational purposes should gradually be withdrawn. The Committee proposed to assist in a movement which had already obtained many supporters in Scotland, and still more in Ireland, to resist any alteration of what was called the mixed system of education.

The second annual meeting of the League was held at the Queen's Hotel, Birmingham, on the 25th of October, 1870. In moving the adoption of the report presented by the Executive, Mr. Dixon sketched the progress which had been made. Since last year they had gained an Education Act, which, notwithstanding its defects, would set the country in motion. It depended greatly upon the League that the movement should not cease until every child in the country was efficiently educated, and he trusted they would be animated to still greater exertions. They had not worked in vain in the past, but it was to the future that they must look for results. They had merely prepared the ground on which they might hope to labour successfully. He referred to some of the defects of the Act which they might hope to amend. One of the greatest was the sanction of an increase of grants to existing denominational schools. He felt it to be a bitter thing to swallow, that they should have to listen to the leader of the Liberal party—a man to whom they owed the Irish Church Bill—and to accept from him a clause which was a deviation from the principles of religious liberty and equality. He urged the members earnestly to promote the establishment of School Boards, and the enforcement of compulsion.

Mr. Vernon Harcourt in seconding the motion, strongly condemned permissive legislation, which he described as a complimentary phrase for parliamentary cowardice. The word " efficient," crept in, in only an obscure manner in the clauses of the Education Act. The foundation of the Act was School accommodation, which many people understood to mean a question of bricks and mortar. The party opposed to the League seemed to think that National Education consisted in eighty cubical feet of space ; whether it contained a child, and whether the child could read and write, did not seem to be considered. It was argued that schools being provided there was to be no School Board. He trusted this was not the true interpretation of the Act, but a great many people held that opinion, he might almost say, cherished that hope. The consequence was that there was a great rush on the building grants, quite irrespective of what was to be done with the schools when they were built.

A motion was made at this meeting to substitute the word " secular " for " unsectarian " in the programme of the League. The proposition received considerable support, but it was withdrawn on its being explained by Mr. Chamberlain that the general body of subscribers were not prepared for it, and that it would impair the efficiency of the organisation.

Sir Charles Dilke proposed a resolution advocating the establishment of School Boards, and the execution of the permissive powers of the Act, which was seconded by the Rev. Mr. Steinthal.

The Rev. J. W. Caldicott proposed and Mr. R. W. Dale seconded a resolution, recommending resistance to the increase of grants to voluntary schools.

On the motion of Mr. Vince, seconded by Mr. Wilkinson, the following resolution was carried, definitely pledging the League to assist in maintaining intact the Irish system :— " That this meeting has heard with satisfaction that an Education League has been formed for Ireland, on a basis similar to that of the National Education League, and strongly sympathises with its promoters in their efforts to prevent the overthrow of the present system in Ireland, and the substitution of the denominational system in its stead."

During the autumn and winter the agitation of all public questions was in a measure suspended, so completely was attention engrossed by the Continental war then raging. But in many boroughs preparations for a struggle were beginning ; while in nearly all the parishes the clergy and Tories were making superhuman efforts to provide school accommodation, and thus prevent the formation of Boards. The most flattering, exaggerated, and fallacious estimates of existing accommodation were prepared for the Department. The National Society's paper said the clergy were doing in one year " what, in the ordinary course of things, would have been done in twenty years." Begging letters were sent out on a scale never practised before ; visitors at holiday resorts were hunted down by collectors ; and every sort of misrepresentation was used to exaggerate the cost and the inconvenience of School Boards. These efforts were so far successful that it was estimated by the officials of the National Society, that some six thousand applications for building grants had been sent in, four-fifths of which were on behalf of Church Schools. On no previous occasion

31

242

had the clergy ever shown a greater fear and distrust of popular control. They had not forgotten the warning of Bishop Wilberforce, " Immediately you introduce the rate-payer, you must give him the real direction of the instruction furnished by the rate."

The opposition to School Boards was led by the Bishops. The Bishop of Salisbury publicly returned thanks that there was only one School Board in an important part of his diocese. The Bishop of Chester headed the attempt to prevent the formation of a Board in his Cathedral Town. When the regulations were issued by the Department for the formation of Boards in rural districts, there were some populous parishes in which steps were taken at once to secure a poll of the ratepayers. These contests were marked by every kind of intimidation, misrepresentation, unscrupulous influence, and false cries, employed to maintain sectarian supremacy, and prevent popular representation. ([1]) The clergy were suddenly and newly inspired with a great horror of rates, which, to say the least of it, was suspicious. The Bishop of Hereford, with sly humour, told his clergy that although the farmers might fear God, it could be taken for granted that they feared a rate more. The ratepayers were urged to vote against a Board unless they wanted their rates raised and their wages reduced. Pressure was put on tenants to secure their votes ; they were taken by their landlords to the poll; and in some instances they were evicted where they voted for a School Board. The terrors of compulsion, threats of the prison, and the cat-o'-nine-tails were put before the labourers. These tactics were in many cases successful, and the much dreaded institution was often rejected ; a result frequently secured by the votes of illiterates. The parish

[1] For details see the Monthly Paper of the League ; also papers by Mr. Bunce, Mr. J. C. Cox, and Mr. Sonley Johnstone, read at the third Annual Meeting, 1871.

having decided against a School Board it was sometimes found an easy matter to collect what was called a "voluntary" rate; or more frequently to throw an extra charge upon the parents by raising the School fees.

The attitude of the clergy towards School Boards, where they were found to be inevitable, was characteristic and consistent. There had been much talk, when the bill was before Parliament, about the liberality of the Church, and her willingness to accept and work the measure in an undenominational sense. In the discussion on Mr. Jacob Bright's amendment, which sought to prohibit the teaching of distinctive tenets in rate-aided schools, Mr. Forster had said, that "it mattered little how the clause was worded, because, whatever its precise terms might be, undenominational religious teaching would be given (in Board Schools). The Government had already given the strongest indication, in a general way, that the religious instruction was not to be sectarian or dogmatic." The Church, however, had no intention of accepting Mr. Forster's interpretation of the clause. The object the clergy set before themselves was to get the largest amount of distinctive Church teaching which was possible under the conditions of the Act. At a meeting of the Saltley Training College, held after the Act was passed, Bishop Selwyn said, "The foundation of all teaching was the gift of the Holy Spirit in baptism. All school teachers should be communicants, and by their example lead their scholars to the Holy altar. In fine, let all schoolmasters first learn, and then teach all others they could, the grand truths of that Catholic faith once for all delivered to the Saints."

On the same occasion, Lord Lyttleton, in advising schoolmasters to do the best that was possible under the fetters imposed upon them, said, "The Act of Parliament put no restriction upon schoolmasters in teaching from the

Bible, and, though he did not say they would be able to teach the full amount of distinctive doctrine, he defied any one to say how much they would be limited to teaching."

The Bishop of Winchester told his clergy that although creeds·and catechisms were excluded, it would be easy for the schoolmaster to teach all the distinctive doctrines of the Church without the use of those standards.

The Bishop of Ely said, "he would rather see Mahometanism taught in the country than have that undogmatic Christianity, which really meant Christianity with no doctrine at all."

The Bishop of Peterborough said, "the position of the Church in relation to rate-aided schools was, that an attempt was about to be made to solve the problem, which he believed to be impossible, of teaching an indefinite Christianity."

Mr. Disraeli advised that Churchmen "should omit no opportunity and no occasion to maintain and increase the legitimate and holy influence of the Church."

The National Society declared that it was more necessary than ever that pupil teachers should be taught dogmatically, in order that they might give the religious lessons in schools which had been built, principally for that object. The Monthly Paper of the Society said: "If by a time-table, religious instruction be limited to a single hour a day, the more need is there, that the teaching given in that hour should be pointed, dogmatic, and unmistakable. All that is happening in the matter of education, is a call to the Church to put out her strength, and to do valiant battle for her principles in her schools."

"Our work is to teach children the facts of our religion, the doctrines of our religion, the duties of our religion. We must teach them the facts of our religion, that they may be intelligent Christians, not ignorant as Heathens; the doctrines that they may not be Christians only, but Churchmen; the duties, that they may not be Churchmen only, but communicants. This last, in fact, is the object at which we are uniformly to aim, the training of the young Christian for full communion with the Church; and, as preliminary to that, a training for confirmation. The whole school time of a child should gradually lead up to this."

" They (the children) ought to know why they should be Churchmen, and not Dissenters; why they should go to church, and not to meeting; why they should be Anglicans, and not Romanists."

" The time has come when probably the whole fate of the Church of England, humanly speaking, will turn upon the hold she may have upon the rising generation. Political changes are giving more and more power to the people. If the Church have the people with her, she will be beyond all danger from adverse legislation. Let her, then, educate the children of the people in her principles." ([1])

A Church clergyman, Mr. Gace, the vicar of Great Barling, improved upon these instructions and put them into the practical shape of a catechism for use in parochial schools. A specimen will suffice.

" *Question.*—We have amongst us various sects and denominations who go by the general name of Dissenters. In what light are we to consider them?"

" *Answer.*—As heretics, and in our litany we expressly pray to be delivered from the sins of false doctrine, heresy, and schism."

" *Q.*—Is, then, their worship a laudable service?

" *A.*—No, because they worship God according to their own evil and corrupt imaginations," &c.

" *Q.*—Is Dissent a great sin?"

---

[1] Monthly Paper of National Society, August, 1871.

"*A.*—Yes, it is in direct opposition to our duty towards God."

"*Q.*—Is it wicked then to enter a meeting house at all ? "

"*A.*—Most assuredly ; because as was said above, it is a house where God is worshipped otherwise than he has commanded, and therefore it is not consecrated to his honour and glory."

This was the kind of teaching which might be given in substance, if not in form, in Board Schools, and the precise words of which might be taught in schools receiving aid from the rates, under section 25. There were doubtless many clergymen of sufficient liberality to shrink from putting the Act to the purposes suggested ; but as ninety per cent. of all Church Schools were in union with the National Society the extracts given may be taken as fairly representative of the intentions and views of the great body of the clergy.

At the second stage of the conflict caused by the operation of the Act—the election of School Boards—the divisions and hostilities of parties were more strongly marked than ever. The disappointment, the confusion, and the bitterness of feeling were greatly intensified by the working of the cumulative vote, with its curious and anomalous results. Whatever may be the ultimate decision upon the advantages of this method of election, about which there was much difference of opinion, even amongst the members of the League ; it must be admitted that the choice of the education question as the subject of the first experiment was unfortunate. The Goverment of Sir Robert Peel had introduced into the Factory Bill of 1843, clauses based on a somewhat similar principle, having the like object of fettering the majority ; but Lord John Russell at once exposed the insidious nature of the device. If any expectation was now entertained that election by the cumulative vote would smooth the working of the Act, and lead to compromise and harmony, it was speedily negatived. The immediate result was to exasperate the majority, to widen the breach, to encourage the spirit of sectarianism, and to make the Act the most unpopular measure of modern times. The avowed principle of the Act was to leave the decision of important questions of policy and administration to the judgment of localities. The effect of the cumulative vote was, in the greatest number of instances, to deprive the majority of the power of laying down any broad principles of action. Worse than this, in many cases, it enabled the minority, brought together by the combination of sectarian interests, to impose a policy and conditions absolutely repugnant to the views of the majority. In the working of the vote everything depends upon accurate knowledge of proportionate strength, upon the nice manipulation of numbers, upon the absolute obedience of the voters, and upon skilful electioneering. Under such circumstances, it was an easy matter for a drilled, compact, organised minority, or a combination of sects, amenable to discipline, to obtain a victory over an undisciplined and independent majority, who were practically disfranchised by the difficulty of securing an equal distribution of votes. In execution the new franchise became a Church and Chapel franchise, giving power to a number of discordant sects, which had the resources of electioneering at their command, and whose last thought was the promotion of general education. In the first elections the Tories and the Church party, reinforced by the narrowest and most exclusive sects, achieved greater successes than they had done for generations in parliamentary and municipal contests.

To add to the embarrassments of the cumulative vote, the early elections were taken under a system of voting papers, which was unintelligible to the great mass of the rate-payers. The result was that in the large boroughs, one-half of the electors took no part in the struggle. This happened in London, Manchester, Birmingham, Sheffield, and Nottingham. While the denominationalists, Churchmen, Roman Catholics, and the representatives of cliques and interests were polled to a man, the majority of the community who care little about isms, were virtually disfranchised.

To show how a minority may thus secure a triumph over the majority, the case of Birmingham may be taken. There was never any doubt that Birmingham was liberal, and was with the League. There was not an assured Liberal of reputation in the town who publicly dissented from the League scheme. The party was absolutely united and was in a vast majority. At the parliamentary election in 1868, the Borough had refused to be fettered by the minority vote, and by means of an able organisation had broken through its restrictions. The Liberal leaders now refused to acknowledge the principle of the cumulative vote, and determined to nominate fifteen candidates—that is the whole Board. This has been generally regarded as a tactical error, but if the Liberals had been able to poll their full strength, there was good reason to believe that they could have carried fifteen candidates against eight Conservatives. If it was a mistake for the Liberals to run fifteen candidates, it was a greater mistake, considering the proportion of parties, for the Conservatives to run eight candidates. In the result eight Churchmen and Tories were returned, with one Roman Catholic and six Liberals. A careful examination of all the circumstances leads to the conclusion that the Liberals were beaten, not because they attempted too much, but because the party was not sufficiently organised, and because the managers had not mastered the difficulties and intricacies of the new method of voting. It is a matter of notoriety that the Liberal party at this time, though united on the question of principle, was not as highly organised as it had been before and has been since. Too much confidence was placed in the known superiority of numbers, and too much reliance on the prestige of 1868.

Although the fifteen Liberal candidates secured a majority of 4,462 voters, and of 66,934 votes, they were defeated—and a Church majority was returned. As a curious result of the first election under the cumulative vote the figures deserve to be recorded—but in estimating their significance it must be remembered that a large portion of the Liberal strength was left unpolled—a fact which could be easily demonstrated by a reference to the statistics of previous and subsequent elections.

The voting was as follows:—

For the Fifteen Liberals,

	Voters.	Votes.
Chamberlain, Joseph (Unitarian)	13,861	15,090
Dale, R. W. (Independent Minister)	14,394	16,387
Dawson, George (Dissenting Minister)	14,238	17,103
Dixon, George (Churchman)	14,435	16,897
Vince, Rev. C. (Baptist)	14,138	15,943
Wright, J. S. (Baptist)	13,567	15,007
Baker, George (Friend)	13,399	14,101
Collings, Jesse (Unitarian)	13,432	13,873
Crosskey, Rev. H. W. (Unitarian)	12,917	13,314
Holland, Rev. H. W. (Wesleyan)	12,955	14,359
Lloyd, G. B. (Friend)	13,461	14,642
Middlemore, William (Baptist)	13,446	14,332
Radford, William (Baptist)	12,284	12,515
Archdeacon Sandford (Churchman)	12,790	13,202

The first six were successful.

32

For the Eight Conservatives and Churchmen.

Burges, Rev. Dr. ...	...	...	...	10,065 ...	21,925
Dale, Rev. F. S. ...	...	...	...	8,807 ...	17,465
Elkington, A. J. ...	...	...	...	8,010 ...	14,925
Gough, J.	...	...	...	8,461 ...	17,481
Hopkins, J. S. ...	...	...	...	8,344 ...	15,696
Lloyd, S. S.	...	...	..	11,134 ...	30,799
Sargant, W. L. ...	...	...	...	8,520 ...	15,683
Wilkinson, Rev. Dr.	...	...	...	9,601 ...	19,829

The whole eight were returned.

The Rev. Canon O'Sullivan, the Roman Catholic representative, headed the poll with the smallest number of voters, and the largest number of votes — voters 3,171; votes 35,120.

Numerical Result.

Votes for the " Fifteen "	...	...	220,637
Votes for the " Eight "	...	...	158,703
Majority of votes for the " Fifteen "			66,934
Voters for the " Fifteen "	...	...	14,709
Voters for the " Eight "	...	...	10,247
Majority of voters for the " Fifteen "			4,462

These figures sufficiently demonstrate that the cumulative vote gives the control, not to numbers, but to organisation. In other towns the anomalies were quite as glaring, and the general result of the first elections was, that in most Liberal boroughs in England the Tories and the Church secured the control of the School Boards for the first three years, with the power of taxing the majority to teach the religion of the minority.

Much has been said in disparagement of the " Caucus,'' but the caucus, which is simply another name for electoral organisation, was the offspring of the cumulative vote and the minority vote.

The system of voting papers adopted in the first School Board elections has, happily, been abolished. While it existed, it was the parent of every description of trickery, deception, and fraud. Mr. Swinglehurst wrote from Kendal : " I have seen something of voting in half civilised States, but Mr. Forster's School Board voting has no equal in fostering falsehood and trickery."

This electoral chicanery was accompanied by a revival of sectarian quarrels in their most objectionable form. Accusations of bigotry and intolerance on the one side, and of infidelity and irreligion on the other, were freely exchanged amongst candidates. The Bible was brought into the fray, to serve as an election rallying ground. The Church party in Birmingham declared that the question was one of " Bible or no Bible," notwithstanding that their opponents advocated the reading of the Bible ; and this hustings' cry was advertised by huge placards, on posting stations, from the windows of gin palaces and beer houses, and on the backs of cabs. The Church rate controversy was renewed under another semblance, and with more intense passion and irreconcilable hostility. No parliamentary or local contests had for generations previously been known to provoke the same amount of bitterness and division between parties.

Protests against the cumulative vote were sent to the Government from the Birmingham Liberal Association, and other Liberal centres. An exhaustive analysis of the results of the early elections, with an able essay on the subject, was prepared for the League by Dr. James Freeman, of Birmingham, and was widely circulated. In the next session of Parliament, Mr. Dixon introduced a bill for the alteration of the law. He met, however, with little support, and the bill, which was opposed by some members of the League, who belonged to the school of philosophic Radicals, and who were anxious to experiment in forms of proportionate representation, was withdrawn without a division. The working of the system has since been greatly improved by the abolition of voting papers, and the application of the ballot; but it still depends upon nice calculations of strength, upon perfect organisation, and upon implicit submission to discipline. The natural tendency of such artificial forms of voting is to make electioneering a science, and to reduce political arrangements to machinery. By the practice of these means a more equitable balance of parties on the School Boards has been secured at recent elections. If evidence were wanted to prove how completely the majority were baffled and misrepresented in the first contests, it is only necessary to compare the results with those of single elections to supply the vacancies which arose. In many places Liberals were returned without effort, and by large majorities, where Tories had obtained the control of the Boards.

The effect of remitting religious questions to the decision of School Boards was exhibited the moment they began operations. The choice of chairmen, clerks, school visitors, and other officers, was determined by theological qualifications, and on sectarian grounds. The system of proportionate representation had no influence in restraining sectarian majorities from administering the Act, in matters alike of principle and detail, to their own advantage. The School Boards were the arenas in which solemn questions of religion and delicate matters of doctrine were made the shuttlecock of debate. No better device could have been imagined for encouraging a spirit of irreverence. Candidates for the post of schoolmaster were publicly examined respecting their interpretation of selected passages of Scripture. The doctrines of the Trinity, the Atonement, the Inspiration of Scripture, of Eternal Punishment, of the Actual Presence, became subjects of dispute. Extracts were read from the lesson books of the Catholic Church, to the cry of " No Popery," and sometimes a Jew would possess himself of Watts's hymns from which to quote " specimens of Christian charity." There was no cohesion upon the majority of the Boards, except that of sectarianism. Acrimonious personal disputes were frequent. It was not an uncommon thing for a minority to leave the room in a body, or to refuse to serve on committees with members of opposite opinions. The first meeting of the London Board was marked by a long and heated discussion as to the propriety of having private prayers before the opening of business. It was eventually decided that a room should be set apart for the purpose for the use of those members who desired it. But at the next meeting the whole of the requisitionists were absent, and the chairman, Lord Lawrence, was left to his solitary devotions. The first chairman of the Birmingham School Board published a pamphlet, in which he indulged in personal reflections and criticisms upon the characters, abilities, and conduct of his colleagues in the minority.

It is notable that these discussions arose in towns which had been remarkable for liberality of thought and toleration upon religious questions. If the occasion sometimes seemed trivial, and if the personal feeling evoked was at times little short of scandalous, it was the more evident that nothing but very ingrained convictions could provoke divisions of such extent, in a society where different denominations had worked harmoniously together for many years for the promotion of social happiness and improvement. The conflict, though fought out on matters of detail, was throughout one of principle. On the one side it was an attempt to revive and

re-enact religious privilege and prerogative, and on the other
to preserve and advance the fullest measure of religious
liberty and equality.

The signal for the conflict was given at the Birmingham
School Board, and for the following three years the proceedings of the Board were watched with intense interest throughout the country. The Rev. F. S. Dale, the most able and
persistent member of the Church majority, gave notice of two
resolutions, one for the enforcement of the powers of compulsion, and the other for the payment of fees in existing
schools. The motion was brought forward before there was
any school under the control of the Board, and its object, as
generally received, was to fill and to assist the denominational
schools at the cost of the ratepayers. The resolution took
the form of empowering the remission of fees under Sec. 17.
It was shown that this could not be done, as the Board had
no Schools ; but it was discovered that fees could be paid at
existing Schools under Sec. 25, and it was to the powers
of this section that the subsequent debates had special
reference.

Mr. Chamberlain led the country agitation against the
25th section. At the School Board he moved an amendment
to Mr. Dale's resolution declaring that the payment of money
out of the rates to the denominational schools would be an
infringement of the rights of conscience, and would delay the
establishment of free schools. At a later stage of the discussion the special reason advanced in support of the 25th
section, was the alleged " right of choice " which it gave to
the parents. But, as Mr. Dixon pointed out, the clause was
introduced when there was no right of choice—the only
schools being those of a denominational character. The party
which opposed compulsion as un-English and unconstitutional
was now trying to use the law to force children into sectarian

schools. In some parts of England the law was administered in this manner. For several years the Manchester School Board had no schools under its control. The Board did precisely the same work, and occupied the same position which the Education Aid Society had done, with this difference—that instead of voluntary subscriptions the rates were used, and instead of persuasion a compulsory bye-law was enforced. It was not until several years had passed that the Board asked for any right of inspection in the schools which were assisted. The Board was in fact merely a relief agency for the denominational managers.

A similar course would have been followed in Birmingham if it had not been opposed by every device of controversy which the Liberal leaders, backed by three-fourths of the ratepayers, could employ. The six Liberals on the Board—Mr. Chamberlain, Mr. Dale, Mr. Dawson, Mr. Dixon, Mr. Vince, and Mr. Wright—were the acknow-leged leaders of the Liberal party in the borough, and the ablest speakers and debaters which the town could produce when it was celebrated for a wealth of talent amongst public men. The fortnightly meetings of the Board were looked forward to with the greatest interest and zest, partly because of the principles at stake, though no doubt also because of the intellectual enjoyment they afforded. They were always inconveniently crowded by the public. The successful resistance which the minority offered to the enforcement of of the 25th section, against a united and resolute majority, is unique in the proceedings of public bodies. For nearly three years the question was fought resolutely, step by step ; at the Board, in Parliament, in the Town Council, at the Education Department, in the Queen's Bench, and at every election and public gathering of Liberals in every ward of the borough. When at last the majority, by Mandamus from the Queen's Bench, compelled the Town Council to honour the precept of the Board, they did not venture to enforce the bye-law they had made; since it was well understood that the levies would have been resisted in the homes of the ratepayers, and distraints, on a scale wholesale and unparalleled, would have been necessary to collect the rate.

It must not however be understood that the first Birmingham School Board did nothing but wrangle about first principles. At the Committees of the Board much solid work was done, in estimating the school requirements of the borough and in arranging for its supply. In the first three years the foundation was laid for the system of splendid schools which are now conducted under the administration of the Board.

It has been sometimes objected that the 25th clause was a small matter to cause such an unusual amount of feeling. The total payments made by virtue of the clause in 1872 were a little over £5,000, of which about two thirds was voted in Manchester and Salford. This sufficiently indicates the extent to which the subsidy might have grown if it had not been checked by public agitation. If the example of Manchester and Salford had been generally followed in parishes having a complement of school accommodation, the country might have had imposed upon it a free and compulsory system in denominational schools alone, with School Boards established for the single purpose of paying fees out of the rates and enforcing compulsion. It has always been surprising how easily the objections of denominational managers to free education disappear, when the school fees can be provided with advantage to, or without embarrassing their financial arrangements.

But the 25th clause was merely the key of a position, chosen upon which to fight the issue, whether the country was prepared to accept in perpetuity the system of sectarian schools supported by public rates. Mr. Disraeli saw the position. He said, "The 25th clause may be called the symbol of the question; those who are in favour of the 25th clause are in favour of religious education, and those who are against it are in favour of secular education." Mr. Chamberlain accepted the situation. He wrote, "It is futile to allege that the practical results are small, and that the grievance is sentimental, for Dissenters are almost unanimous in their conviction, that a grave principle is involved, and that now or never they must take their stand against what they affirm to be a retrograde policy."

Outside the School Board the agitation was conducted by the League, reinforced by Liberal associations and by the various combinations of Nonconformists, and of Working-men. The movement amongst the Dissenters was strikingly active and earnest. A conference of the Nonconformist Committees of Manchester, Liverpool, and Birmingham was held at Manchester in April, 1871, at which it was arranged to call a general conference, and also to appoint a deputation to represent to the Prime Minister their insuperable objection to the 25th clause. This deputation represented all sections of Protestant Nonconformists, and comprised representatives from various parts of the country. At Mr. Gladstone's request, their case was stated in writing and submitted for his consideration. A part of their contention was that he had undertaken, in striking out clause 23 of the original bill, that a distinct and definite line should be drawn between School Boards and voluntary schools—that the tie between them should be altogether severed. Instead of the direct subsidy contemplated by clause 23, the grants had been increased to them by fifty per cent., but the payments under the 25th section, though nominally for fees, were in the nature of a subsidy.

33

The managers and supporters of the Nonconformist day schools in Birmingham declined to receive the fees, and in a memorial to the Board protested against their payment to other schools. At an immense gathering of Dissenters in the Town Hall, an appeal was made from the School Board to the constituency. At meetings of the Congregational and Baptist Unions it was declared to be a new form of the old Church-rate, to be resisted more resolutely than ever. A representative gathering of the London Nonconformists was held at the Cannon Street Hotel, at which a most emphatic protest was adopted. At every meeting of Dissenters throughout the country, and at the annual meetings of the Associations of Nonconformist churches, resolutions were adopted, encouraging the League in the continuance of the agitation. There was no division or disunion amongst the Dissenters on the question; and the meetings at which the subject was to be discussed were as remarkable for their numbers as for their unanimity.

The feeling was intensified by the partiality shown at the Education Department, and the pressure put upon School Boards to make them adopt bye-laws under section 25. In cases where a power was taken to remit fees under section 17, Mr. Forster said "it would not be just" for the Boards not to avail themselves of section 25. Thus, the Liberals had to contend not only against the Tories, the Church, and the disadvantages of the cumulative vote, but against a Liberal Government, an adverse administration of the Act, and against the moral weight of the Education Department. The Department had often been unpopular in the country, but never so much out of favour as now. The feeling which Mr. Lowe's action upon the revised code had aroused, was of a very different character to that inspired by Mr. Forster. The former had provoked the personal hostility of a few thousand school managers, teachers, and monitors, upon whose vested interests he was supposed to have encroached. There was a large admixture of personal spite in the antagonism, which was based upon no principle, but upon selfish considerations. But the opposition to Mr. Forster had nothing personal in its nature. It arose from the conviction that he had betrayed the principles which had been entrusted to him, and had thrown back the cause of progress. The respect which he had professed for municipal opinion was in strange contrast with his attempt to make localities accept a forced interpretation of the Act. The usefulness of the Education Department was greatly undermined. It is desirable that a State Department having such extensive and various ramifications should be able to command the respect of the country. This could not be the case when the School Boards flatly refused to obey the instructions of "my Lords." A conflict between a central board and the local governing bodies, backed by the people, could have but one issue. The School Boards at Southampton, Portsmouth, Wednesbury, and other towns refused to be dictated to by the Department. Opinion was still further outraged by the partiality with which the Endowed Schools Act was administered, the tendency of which was to throw the secondary education of the country entirely into the hands of the clergy.

The result was that very early in the course of the agitation, the relations between the Government and their Radical and Dissenting supporters were seriously imperilled. Some attempts were made to check the disintegration ; but no concessions were offered on the part of the Government, who held with obstinacy rather than with firmness to the policy they had laid down. Appeals were made to the leaders of the country movement not to endanger the union of the party. Mr. Winterbotham and Mr. Melly were both strongly opposed on principle to the payments in question, but they held that the matter was settled by the Act of 1870, and that the position must be accepted. This idea was repudiated by the leaders of the agitation, and by the rank and file of the party, and open revolt from the first was only restrained by the strong sentiments of affection and esteem which the Prime Minister had inspired amongst all sections of the party.

The plea of the "right of choice," supposed to be guaranteed by the 25th section, whether put forward by the clergy or the Department—it was never put forward by the parents—was disingenuous. The clause was enforced where there were only denominational schools, and where there could be no right of choice. The very men who set up the cry of the right of choice were those who had made it impossible that there should be any choice in three-fourths of the school districts. Mr. Bright said "I suppose there are probably thousands of parishes in which there will scarcely be any schools but Church schools." This was the state of things which the Act was aimed to produce. The "right of choice" was a pretence and was advanced in the interests of the denominational schools. But if the cry had been ever so genuine it was one which the temper of the country would not have acquiesced in. If it meant anything it meant that parents should have the right to have the religion of their choice taught out of the public rates—a claim wholly opposed to the tendencies and principles of modern legislation.

The Act had hardly been a year in operation—scarcely a Board school had been opened, when distraints were being made for the recovery of rates, upon the goods of persons who refused to contribute to the support of denominational schools.

New complications were introduced by the movements in Scotland and Ireland. The Scotch Bill of the Government, introduced in 1871, was more sectarian in character than the English Act, as it had been amended. The conscience clause, if not a sham in purpose, would have been in practice the merest delusion. The time table was given up. Creeds and formularies were permitted throughout the daily instruction. The universal formation of School Boards, with powers of compulsion, became, under these circumstances, a concession to the Denominationalists, and made it a certainty that wherever compulsion was carried out, sectarian instruction might be forced on every child.

From Scotland attention naturally turned to Ireland. In any case this was inevitable, but it was quickened by the appeals which came to the English Nonconformists from the Protestants of Ireland. The members of the disestablished Church, with those Protestant sects who had helped to procure disestablishment, were already fearful of seeing another religion established in its place. The agitation of the Roman Catholic hierarchy for the overthrow of the combined or mixed system had been stimulated by the definite extension of the sectarian system in England, and there was a growing distrust amongst Protestants in all parts of the kingdom as to the intentions of the Government. In a debate on a Bill of Mr. Fawcett for the abolition of tests in Trinity College, Dublin, Mr. Vernon Harcourt called attention to the reserve and mystery with which the Government shrouded their opinions on the question, and, with great sagacity, predicted that it was the subject which would probably cause the shipwreck of the Liberal party. The uneasiness which was felt had led to the formation of the Education League for Ireland, which was in union with the English League. The objects were, to maintain non-sectarian education in Ireland, to oppose changes in the national system, and to raise the status of teachers and improve the quality of education. If it had not been for the agitation against the English Act, there would have been great danger of an anarchy of opinion on this subject, caused by the want of candour on the part of Ministers, and their demoralising concessions to Denominationalism in England. While the *Times* supported denominational education in England, it thought it was high time the Government informed the Roman Catholic prelates that their demands could not be complied with. The *Spectator*, with more even-handed justice, thought that what was fair for England was fair for Ireland. There was probably some doubt and division in the Cabinet, and it was well known to be a ticklish question. Some Ministers were openly advocating State supported denominational colleges. Mr. Goschen, and Mr. Chichester Fortescue, the then Chief Secretary, proclaimed their desire to extend the denominational system. Mr. Gladstone's speeches left his opinions in doubt, and this very uncertainty was the cause of much anxiety.

The changes demanded by the Roman Catholic heirarchy, as put before the Irish Royal Commission which reported in 1871, were great, startling, and aggressive. The manifesto of the Bishops required "all restriction upon religious teaching to be removed "—" the fulness of distinctive religious teaching to be permitted to enter into tbe course of secular instruction "—" full liberty to be given to the performance of religious exercises, and the use of religious emblems." ([1]) The intention to push their demands to the extremity by means of religious and political organisation soon received confirmation. At a meeting of Roman Catholic Bishops held in October, 1871, a series of resolutions were drawn up and ordered to be read at public masses of the Roman Catholic Church throughout Ireland. Amongst other things the Bishops " declared their unalterable conviction that Catholic education was indispensably necessary for the preservaiton of

[1] Report of Mr. Laurie, Assistant Commissioner, par. 40, 3.

the faith and morals of the Catholic people." "In union with the Holy See and the Bishops of the Catholic world they renewed their often-repeated condemnation of mixed education as intrinsically and grievously dangerous to faith and morals." They drew from Irish history evidence that "godless education was subversive of religion and morality, of domestic peace, of the rights of property, and social order." In all future elections of Members of Parliament they pledged themselves to oppose the return of candidates who would not uphold the principle of denominational education for Catholic children. Cardinal Cullen said, "they pronounced for Catholic schools, Catholic teachers, Catholic books, everything Catholic in the education of their children;" and they claimed "an adequate share" of patronage and endowment.

No one will deny to the Roman Catholic Bishops the merit of candour and honesty. They did not cloak their design under the pretence that the subsidies they demanded were for secular instruction. In the plainest language they asked for the endowment of the Roman Catholic religion out of the public funds. They required that the Roman Catholic Church in Ireland should be placed in the same position of paramount authority towards other sects which the Church of England occupied in regard to English and Welsh Dissenters. The religion of the minority had been disestablished, and they now asked that the religion of the majority should be put in its place.

These were demands which, if there was any principle or stability in the professions of English and Scotch liberalism, could not be conceded. Here began a new step in the disintegration of the Liberal party. The Liberals had given to the Roman Catholics religious equality; and they now asked for religious preference. Most Liberals had looked forward to a time when the alliance between the Roman Catholics and the Liberal party would be severed by a natural divergence of policy and feeling, and the hour appeared to have arrived. The Dissenters of Great Britain had not lent their aid to the disestablishment of one religion, with the view of elevating another, to which they were more hostile, in its stead. The appeal therefore from the Irish Protestants of all sects for assistance in resisting these threatened encroachments, was taken up with much cordiality, and was supported and encouraged by the Radicals and Nonconformists of England, in numbers and weight, which left no doubt that, with the exception of a few Ministerialists and the Roman Catholics, all but a fraction of the Liberal party was opposed to any tampering with the existing Irish system.

The Parliamentary action this year was confined to an attempt to amend the new revised Code which was issued in February, and which gratified the Denominationalists by the large increase of grant. In the discussion of its provisions in the House of Commons on the 10th of March, Mr. Dixon moved " That an address be presented to Her Majesty praying that she would be graciously pleased to direct that such alterations be made in the new Code of Regulations issued by the Committee of the Privy Council on Education, and now lying upon the table of this House, as shall prevent any increased scale of grants of public money to denominational schools." There was much fluttering and indignation amongst the Tories and the clergy when the intention to move this resolution was made public, and they denounced in no measured terms the " unblushing and unprincipled persistence " in. opposition to the grant. There was, however, no cause for their alarm, for in spite of the efforts which were concentrated against the proposal, it was carried by the now familiar combination of Ministerialists and Tories. Sixty-six Liberals, representing the most influential and populous constituencies in the Kingdom, voted against the Government, while a much larger number absented themselves from the division.

A joint deputation from the League and the Central Nonconformist Committee waited on the Vice-President to protest against the increased grant, and to suggest some additions to the Code for securing more effectual teaching, and a more economical administration of public funds. The chief suggestions were that there should be a graduated system of grants, with larger payments for passes in the higher standards ; that a certain proportion of subscriptions should be required in voluntary or denominational schools ; that the balance sheets of the latter schools, as well as those of the Board schools, should be published ; with other provisions to prevent so-called voluntary schools from being conducted wholly at the public cost—a result easily attainable by the combined action of the Education Act and the new Code. The extreme tenderness felt at the Education Department for the views and interests of the Denominationalists prevented the adoption of these recommendations.

In other respects the code was a small step towards proficiency. The number of attendances required to obtain a grant was increased, and the standards of examination were raised. All amendments intended to improve the quality of instruction were heartily supported by the League.

The events which have been noticed made 1871 a busy year for the League, which was the head quarters and centre of advice, instruction, and encouragement for all who were striving for an efficient national system based on unsectarian lines. The promotion and election of School Boards ; administrative work upon the Boards ; resistance to the sectarian tendencies of the act, and agitation for its extension and amendment so as to secure higher educational results,

34

fully occupied the members of the branches, acting under the direction of the Executive.

The influence and operations of the League in the country were of a more extended character than in the previous year. At the Annual Meeting in 1871, the Committee reported that the branches had increased to 315. Agents, resident and travelling, had been appointed for each division of the country. A great number of publications were issued, designed to show the deficiencies of the Act, and to promote the formation of School Boards, and the enforcement of compulsion. Papers on Normal schools, the Scotch bill, the cumulative vote, the defects of the Act, the cost and results of denominationalism, the revised code, and the 25th clause, were widely distributed during the year. The special work undertaken in the constituencies with a view to parliamentary elections, was also of a very important and suggestive character. The breach was not so wide as it afterwards became, but the League had no intention to decline the challenge of Ministers to appeal to the country, and action was being taken in many boroughs which was much to the discomfort of the Whig supporters of the Government, and laid the foundation for that unpopularity at St. Stephens' which the organisation afterwards acquired.

The serious nature of the disruption in the party, and the intense dissatisfaction caused by the persistence of the Government in their policy of retrogression, were manifested at the third annual meeting of the League, held at Birmingham on the 17th and 18th of October, 1871. The meeting was attended by specially appointed delegates from various sections of the party, representing especially the Labour organisations and the Nonconformist associations. Probably no gathering of Liberals, so numerous and representative, coming from every part of the kingdom, had ever met together to protest against the action of a Liberal administration. There were present in large numbers earnest Liberals who felt that Liberal principles were endangered, and Educationists of note who remonstrated against a policy which had obstructed education by mixing it up with the question of religious establishments.

Mr. Dixon presided, and in his opening address exposed the defects of the Act as an educational measure, and the danger of the sectarian struggle which it had aroused. He said that the Government had been warned against their policy, but the warning had been unheeded. Referring to the future he said, "in the Scotch Education Bill which the Government are to introduce next session, the Denominationalists may be again triumphant; and when the Irish Education question is dealt with, the Ultramontane Roman Catholics may be equally successful in gaining a victory over the champions of united secular and separate religious instruction; but the pages of history tell us that the spirit of religious freedom and equality in this country is unquenchable, and rises more vigorous from defeat. And the reports which the Officers of the League receive from all parts of the country induce me to believe that forces are now silently gathering which will undermine the power of the strongest Government, and overthrow the political fabric of the most time-honoured of Churches."

Sir Charles Dilke moved the adoption of the report of the Executive. In the course of his speech he said, "such a pass have things come to that every gathering of Liberals in the kingdom is a meeting for the denunciation of the Liberal Ministry, except in Scotland, in which happy country the effect of this bill has not been felt." "I think the only men who can look with confidence to the future are those who take the view that these difficulties will never cease until the Government confines itself to giving facilities for teaching that which can harm the conscience of no man, and leaves the religious teaching to be given, at their own time, by religious men. If we can look with confidence to the future, we cannot look with any feelings but those of horror, and almost of despair at the present, because compulsion is being very nearly forgotten during the sectarian strife; and, whilst the bigots are endeavouring, not only to preserve but to extend their stronghold, the children go untaught."

Mr. Alfred Illingworth seconded the resolution and described the sectarian struggle in the Borough of Bradford. He touched a subject which was very prominent in the minds of those present. " I am glad to see we have gentlemen present from Scotland and Ireland. I am watching with a great deal of interest and somewhat of a mischievous feeling, to find out how the supporters of Denominationalism will act, when asked to apply the principle to Ireland."

Mr. Colefax of Bradford moved the appointment of the Council, the Officers, and the Executive Committee. He contended that the Act created a new Church-rate. If he were asked to pay a shilling rate in some of the districts of Lancashire, he would be paying something like sixpence towards the maintenance of the Church of England, and fourpence or fourpence halfpenny towards the Church of Rome.

Mr. William Middlemore, Chairman of the Central Nonconformist Committee, seconded the motion.

Mr. Chamberlain, then moved on behalf of the Executive Committee, " That Mr. Dixon be requested to give notice of a motion to the following effect, at an early period of the next session—'that, in the opinion of this House, the provisions of the Elementary Education Act are defective, and its working unsatisfactory, inasmuch, as it fails to secure the general election of School Boards in towns and rural districts; it does not render obligatory the attendance of children at school; it deals in a partial and irregular manner with the remission and payment of school fees by School Boards; it allows School Boards to pay fees out of the rates levied upon the community to denominational schools, over which the ratepayers have no control; it permits School Boards to use the public money of the ratepayers for the purpose of imparting dogmatic religious instruction in Schools established by those Boards, and by the concession of these permissive powers, it provokes religious discord throughout the country, and by the exercise of them it violates the rights of conscience.' "

Mr. Chamberlain proceeded to justify this early attempt to amend the Act, and accepted the onus of proof that parliamentary action was opportune and desirable. In a convincing argument he showed that when the Education Act was introduced, the condition of the country was disgraceful and dangerous, perilous to morality, and the welfare of the State. The semi-public, semi-private system, after a trial of thirty years had failed, and for a great national want, a complete national system was the only remedy. So much was admitted by Mr. Forster. The bill had been in operation fourteen months and what had been its results? More than half the boroughs, and 98 per cent. of the parishes, had not taken the first step towards the provision of a national system—the formation of a School Board. Under the conditions of the act a national system was rendered impossible, when a single sect was allowed to provide accommodation in excess of its numbers and importance. Education had become the monopoly of one denomination. The major part of the act was a dead letter. In a bill of a hundred clauses the working of two or three operated against all the rest. Vast sums of public money were pledged for denominational objects. Three thousand new vested interests were created, which were three thousand fresh stumbling blocks in the way of a national system. The bill had revived sectarian animosities and religious feuds in their worst form. The School Board election in Birmingham had caused more ill feeling than all the political contests for a quarter of a century. Under the partial operation of compulsory bye-laws a new crime had been created, so subtle in character that it evaporated with a parochial boundary. What was a penal offence in Birmingham, might be committed at Smethwick with impunity. What was a misdemeanor at Liverpool was none at Birkenhead. The last anomaly was that " voluntary " schools might be supported solely by enforced contributions, levied upon persons who dissented from the doctrines which those institutions were primarily established to maintain. The principle of municipal government was violated, and the money of the ratepayers was applied in support of institutions over which they had no control. Not a school had been built, and not a child owed its education to the Act. Time had been wasted and temper tried in disputing principles which ought to have been settled by the legislature. Money had been squandered in contests which might have been rendered unnecessary. The call for their action was the more urgent because of the animus with which the act was administered. It was perfectly intolerable that they should have a denominational act, denominationally administered. The Education Department had gone out of its way to admonish and advise School Boards, and make them conform their decisions to denominational interests. The League had never ceased to protest against the measure. They had not been a party to the so-called compromise, and would not be bound by compromises which violated principle. Great principles were at stake and endangered. The cause of National Education was gaining very little—but the cause of religious equality was losing much. There was another consideration. To-morrow they would discuss the questions of Scotch and Irish Education.

The system adopted in those countries would depend on the decision of England. If they acquiesced in a denominational system for this country, they could not in justice and consistency refuse a similar system to Ireland and Scotland. They were not influenced by sectarian motives. The League was an educational organisation. Compulsion and free schools were their key stones—with unsectarianism as a necessary condition precedent, in a country situated as theirs was. In seeking these things they believed they were seeking the true happiness and welfare of the land in which they lived.

Mr. Joseph Cowen seconded the resolution. He advised Nonconformists not to pay the school rates. He said he had no hope of gaining anything from Mr. Forster, but he had hopes of the Prime Minister. Mr. Gladstone was a sincere and earnest man, and when he was once satisfied that his principles were correct, he had courage and ability to carry them out.

The resolution was supported by the Rev. H. C. Leonard, Mr. George Howell, the Rev. H. W. Crosskey, Mr. Giles, Mr. P. W. Claydon, the Rev. J. J. Brown, Rev. Mr. Tilly, Mr. Snowdon, and the Rev. W. W. Jubb.

Mr. Bunce, chairman of the Publishing Committee, read a paper on the " Working and defects of the Education Act." Mr. Bunce's paper was founded on statistical information supplied to Parliament, and facts collected and collated for the purpose by the agents and secretaries of the League. It was an exhaustive enquiry and comparison, demonstrating the operation of the Act during the fourteen months of its existence, and exposing its patchwork character, its delays, and the embarrassment caused by the bitter controversy it had aroused. In summing up, Mr. Bunce wrote, " As to its working the Act is imperfectly applied ; large portions of the country being left without a single School Board, and the Boards already established are few in number and most unequally distributed. Though the Act has been more than a year in operation it has not produced a school; but it has evoked a storm of religious bitterness, and developed incessant conflict; it has inflicted great injustice upon the opponents of sectarian teaching at the public expense, by taking their money and giving it to the maintenance of denominational schools; and thus it has precipitated ecclesiastical and political questions of incalculable magnitude, and pregnant with vital issues. As to the defects of the Act, these are described in the original objections of the League, which experience has confirmed to demonstration—namely, that it is defective in leaving to decision by localities, essential points which should have been settled by Parliament for the whole country; and that it suffers from the influence, at once enfeebling and irritating, of permissive adoption, permissive compulsion, permissive freedom, and permissive sectarianism."

Mr. R. W. Dale read a paper on " the payment of School Fees." After describing the effect of section 25, Mr. Dale said, " How this invasion of the religious rights of the community, under the pretext of guarding the religious rights of the individual, is to be resisted, I will not now discuss. Seizures for church-rates are too recent for some of us to forget that it was only by a persistent refusal on the part of Nonconformists to pay the rate that the sentiment of public justice was aroused to the inequality of the law under which church-rates were levied. But there is yet another course which I trust every member of the League will adopt. Every representative now sitting in Parliament for a Liberal constituency, every new candidate for Liberal suffrages, should be asked whether he is prepared to vote for the repeal of clause 25 of the Elementary Education Act, and the amendment of clause 74. A refusal, or an ambiguous

promise, should be met with a clear and definite declaration that he cannot have our vote." . . . .
"This may lead to the breaking up of the Liberal party: When the Liberal party is false to its noblest principles, it is time that it should be broken up. The 'Liberal party,' which carried the most objectionable clauses of this Bill by Conservative votes in the House of Commons, must either be willing to retrace its steps, or else must depend for continuance of power upon Conservative votes in the country."

Mr. J. Charles Cox, of Belper, read a paper called "Blots in the Bill." In the course of his paper, Mr. Cox said, "Though an ardent supporter of the Government at the last election, I refuse to see the slightest difference between this present injustice, and the old Church-rate question, which we thought had been finally stifled. The matter is beyond argument, and I for one, though a magistrate of my county, have made up my mind to refuse to pay one farthing of any such rate, in the same way that I refused to pay the old Church-rate, and I believe that the truest policy of the League would be to advise all its adherents to do the same."

The Rev. Sonley Johnstone described the working of the Act in Wales, and the excessive rancour and virulence which its introduction had caused.

The Rev. J. W. Caldicott, Head Master of the Bristol Grammar School, characterised the Act as a bundle of compromises, combining the utmost possible magnificence of promise, with the utmost possible shabbiness of performance. The Act said, "every child ought to be educated; but if the majority in any place so pleased, they might allow the children to remain ignorant. The Act said the parent who was proved to have neglected the education of his child ought to be punished; but it left the proof of the offence in the parents hands. The Act said inefficient schools ought not to be allowed to exist, but they might have as many as they

35

chose, and they might cram them full of children. The Act said the State ought not to intermeddle in matters of religion; but yet every ratepayer might be taxed to pay for the teaching of his neighbour's creed."

The second day of the meeting was devoted chiefly to the discussion of the Irish and Scotch systems. The Rev. David Wilson, D.D., of Limerick, a member of the Commission appointed in 1868 to enquire into the condition of primary education in Ireland, described in an elaborate paper the working of the mixed system in Ireland. He impugned the fairness and impartiality of the report presented by the Commissioners. The Rev. John Scott Porter of Belfast, a member of the deputation from the Irish League, pleaded for the maintenance in its integrity of the Irish system, as the only guarantee for the religious freedom of the minority.

Mr. Miall, Mr. Walter Morrison, and Mr. J. H. Burges took part in the discussion. Mr. Morrison cautioned the meeting against the well-known proclivities of some of the Cabinet in favour of a denominational system for Ireland.

Papers were also read by the Rev. Robert Craig, of Glasgow, and by Professor Nichol, from the Scotch Education League, on Education in Scotland; and by Sir Charles Dilke and Mr. Collings on Free Schools. The Rev. William Binns, Birkenhead, Rev. Mr. Gould, Norwich, Mr. Cremer, London, the Rev. J. Haslam, Leeds, Dr. Lunge, South Shields, and the Rev. S. A. Steinthal, continued the discussion. The Chairman announced, at the close of the meeting, a large increase of subscriptions. The proceedings were closed by a Soirée in the Town Hall, given by the Mayor, Mr. G. B. Lloyd, to the members of the League.

A full report of the meeting was widely circulated. The papers and speeches contain an admirable exposition of the lines of the controversy at the period.

The agitation was immediately followed up in all the large towns, and within the next three months a hundred and twenty meetings were held in England and Wales, which were attended by the Officers or deputations from the Executive. These meetings were almost without exception, free and open to the public, and though they were often scenes of great excitement, and sometimes of disorder, they convinced the leaders of the movement that the great preponderance of public feeling was on their side. Amongst the new adherents was Earl Rnssell, who wrote to Mr. Dixon publicly joining the League, and strongly condemning the Government policy.

The beginning of 1872 marks a new period in the growth and direction of the agitation, which may be more conveniently described in a separate chapter.

CHAPTER VII.

PERIOD.—FROM THE RECOMMENDATIONS OF 1872 TO THE
GENERAL ELECTION, 1874.

THE Government, in bringing in the Education Bill had
professed a desire to supplement the denominational system.
But the controversies of 1870-71, and a year's administration
of the Act, had convinced the most sceptical that their real
purpose was to perpetuate, strengthen and extend it. The
large increase of annual grants, the thousands of new
denominational schools endowed with building grants, the
undisguised administration of the Act in the interests
of Church schools, admitted of no other interpretation.
There was also, in the background, a suspicion, always on
the alert, that a similar system would be extended to
Scotland and Ireland. These new conditions threw upon
the Executive the responsibility of considering how the
original scheme of the League could be adapted to the
altered circumstances, in such a manner as to secure efficient
local control over the public schools, to promote the observance of sound principles in public expenditure, and at the
same time to afford to all denominations the fullest opportunity of giving religious instruction to their own scholars,
at their own labour and cost.

The step now taken by the League was the sequence of
the aggressive coalition between the Ministry, the Clergy, and
the Tories. Until the Denominational system had been
encouraged to claim fresh privileges, and to usurp new
ground, the League had been content that it should be left
pretty much alone, to merge by degrees, and as experience
should suggest, in a national system. The idea of gradual

extinction was now abandoned for that of active conversion, having regard, of course for just privileges, and the interests of religion.

At a meeting of the Executive Committee held on the 18th of January, 1872, it was resolved to submit the following recommendations for the approval of the members.

" 1.—The compulsory Election of School Boards in all districts.

" 2.—No schools to be recognised as public elementary schools but those under the control of elected School Boards.

" 3.—Existing School buildings to be placed by consent under the control of such Boards, for use during the hours of secular instruction, to be given under the direction of School Boards; the buildings to be retained for all other purposes by the denominations with which they are connected.

" 4.—Any school in respect to which such control is declined, to be excluded from participation in the annual Government Grant.

" 5.—In all schools provided by School Boards out of local rates, periods entirely separate and distinct from the time allotted to ordinary school teaching may be set apart for instruction on week days. Such religious instruction to be given by denominations at their own cost, and by their own teachers appointed for that purpose, but no privilege to be given to one denomination over another. In cases of dispute appeal to be made to the Education Department."

Thus by the logic of facts, and in pursuit of elementary principles of justice, the " combined " system was once more placed before the nation. The old accusation of following "godless" and "irreligious" education was raised more vehemently than ever ; but the people were getting a little used to this cry of " wolf." The League had been denounced as godless and irreligious when it advocated Bible reading ; and it was now condemned as infidel and atheistic in upholding a system which the Primate and Bishops of the Established Church in Ireland had supported, and which Irish Protestants, without exception, regarded as the chief safeguard of their religious freedom. That which on one side of the Channel was preached as the palladium of liberty, was denounced on the other as an intolerable tyranny, and this by members of the same sect.

The members of the League, almost without exception, adopted the proposals of the Committee, and there was a considerable increase in numbers and subscriptions. The only member of note whose decided views they contravened, was Earl Russell, who had joined on the express ground of his warm approval of Bible reading as part of the ordinary school work. The change, however, did not lessen his interest in the question, or his disposition to advance the work of education ; and he became, before his death, a convert to the doctrine of free schools, which twenty years before he had stifled in Parliament.

The great Conference of Nonconformists, held at Manchester early in the year, comprising delegates from nearly two thousand churches, accepted the principle ; and it was widely advocated by the liberal press, as the only means by which a complete and efficient system could be brought into general use. The educationists of the old Manchester school especially, felt that they were standing on firm ground again.

At the annual meeting in the autumn, Mr. Collings moved the adoption of the suggestions, and explained the reasons which had led the Executive to recommend them as the only practical solution of the difficulties created by the new Act. Mr. Charles Vince seconded the resolution. His argument was a forcible illustration, not only of his strong common sense and power of persuasive reasoning, but of the absolute impartiality, justice, brightness, and purity which were the distinctive features of his mind. He upheld the scheme as one of equal justice to all creeds and classes, and asserted that having regard to the divisions and differences in English Christendom, strictly unsectarian religious teaching was impossible.

Mr. Chamberlain in speaking upon the proposed change, said that Bible reading without note or comment, offered as a compromise in 1869, had not given satisfaction. It did not please the religious bodies or conciliate the Roman Catholics or Secularists, towards whom it was certainly sectarian. Moreover the Act of 1870 had altogether altered the circumstances under which it was put forward. It had stimulated denominational schools, and made their existence easy at a minimum of cost to their supporters. In considering the increase of these schools, their "suitability" was an element in the discussion. The Act provided that schools must be "suitable" as well as efficient. It had been held by the Department that Roman Catholic Schools were not suitable for the children of Protestants. On what principle then was it considered that a Protestant school was suitable for the children of Roman Catholics, or a Church school for the children of Nonconformists? Under such arrangements compulsion was only possible at the sacrifice of every principle of justice. The League put forward this scheme as the proper solution of the educational difficulty.

It is a matter for surprise that the advantages which this scheme offered, in educational, religious and social aspects, were not more accurately appreciated outside the ranks of the Dissenters. There were guarantees for efficient education, under wiser management and with larger means and better appliances, which should have made it welcome to education-ists of whatever party. There were opportunities given for religious teaching, which religious men of all sects ought ardently to have embraced. It was a protection for conscience which would have satisfied every principle of justice, and it was a social peace offering which the country, and especially the interests of the children stood sadly in need of.

There were certain direct and obvious benefits offered to the Church, as the denomination in possession of the vast majority of schools and buildings, which it was folly for Churchmen to overlook. While preserving the use of their buildings, and an active and in most instances preponderating share in the school management, they could have thrown the entire cost of secular instruction on the rates. The clergy at once and for ever would have been relieved from writing begging letters. Some of the secular papers which usually advocated Church interests, cautioned the clergy not to reject the scheme, while they were in a position to make terms, without considering whether the difference between them and their opponents was fundamental or superficial. The Bishop of Manchester, whose services to education throughout these discussions were of inestimable value, told Convocation that, under the scheme, " if they were only faithful to their own convictions, if all they had been saying about religious education in their different parishes had any meaning at all, and was not merely talk, they certainly had still, as managers and teachers of schools, ample scope and opportunity for indoctrinating their children with that sound religious teaching they thought most conducive to their welfare." The clergy however, with some conspicuous exceptions, were blind and deaf to any merits of the proposal, apparently on no other ground than their jealousy of the intervention of a School Board, in matters where by custom they were invested with supreme rule.

To Dissenters, as such, the advantages of the plan would have been great. New avenues for social and educational work would have been opened to them, and a more real and effective guarantee for the free exercise of opinion would have been established. The time-table conscience clause was defective in essential qualities. In its very nature it was but a half-provision. It professed to guard the conscientious convictions of parents; but it did not recognise the conscience of the ratepayer. As a matter of fact the agitation against the Act proceeded from citizens rather than from the parents of scholars. But even in its express design, as a defence for parents and children, it was illusory. Its terms enabled children to be withdrawn from religious instruction without forfeiting any benefits of the school. When religious instruction was given it required that it should take place at certain hours, specified in the time-table, either before or after the secular business. It also contained a provision that no scholar should be obliged to attend, or to abstain from attending any particular Sunday School or place of religious worship, as a condition of admittance to a day school. Mr. Forster said that the advantage of the clause was that it was self-working, and required neither notice on one side nor claim on the other. It was certainly an improvement on the first draft which required a claim to be made in writing. Perhaps a more stringent clause might have been devised, but the fault did not lie so much with the clause as with the circumstances. From the nature of the case it was impossible that general advantage should be taken of the clause. There was the same difficulty about it, as there was about voting before the ballot was introduced. Of necessity there could be no secresy in withdrawing children from religious instruction, and without secresy the clause was practically worthless.

36

It may be urged that men, who, having objections based on conscience, fail to avow them on account of some social disadvantage they may entail, are not entitled to very much sympathy. That is an insidious view ; especially for the large class who have no great faith in conscientious objections. But it must also be acknowledged that there are persons, even amongst the humblest classes, who while they might be willing to suffer themselves for opinion, would naturally hesitate before they would subject their children to the same kind of endurance.

However, the fact remains, that the Dissenters did not avail themselves of the clause. The general testimony of the Inspectors was, that practically the whole of the children attended the religious instruction. In the few instances in which the parents took advantage of the clause its working was not satisfactory. We put aside the cases of actual violation of the time-table. In regard to its observance, the public, without the supervision of School Boards, was absolutely in the hands of managers and teachers. That the law is frequently broken is well understood. One Inspector reported that he found upon his visits of surprise, that the time-table was unobserved in ten per cent. of the schools. But assuming that the letter of the law is generally obeyed, it is still pertinent to enquire how far the spirit is fulfilled, when the legal right of withdrawal is insisted on. A few out of many cases reported to the officers of the League will serve as illustrations.

It was a custom in some Church schools to assemble the children at holy days or festivals, and to march them to service in hours which, according to the time-table should have been devoted to secular instruction. The Department held that this was allowable, so long as the day was not reckoned for attendance in the computation of the grant, and notice was given to the parents. The consequence was that any school able to earn an excess grant, might, without being fined at all, devote a number of spare days to religious exercises. A verbal message to the children to come to school clean and tidy on the morrow, as they were going to church, was held to be sufficient notice; and the notice was equivalent to a command.

Down to the formation of the League, the National Society enforced its rule in many parishes, that children attending its schools should also attend Church and the Church Sunday-school. When the conscience-clause came into force there were many parents, who, while they did not withdraw their children from religious instruction on week days, were glad to avail themselves of the privilege of taking them to their own Chapels on Sundays. In such cases, without infringing the actual letter of the law, there was room for the exercise of a petty social tyranny; which in the rural districts especially could be practiced with impunity.

In one village notice was given to the parents that the day scholars must also attend the Church Sunday-schools, or they would be excluded from the benefits of the clothing club. It was also stated that if the parents did not wish the children to attend Church the reasons must be fully explained to the minister.

A Dissenter, whose children attended a National School, sent them to a Dissenting Sunday-school. Their school fees were at once raised from 5d. to 1s. 6d. per week.

In another town notice was given that attendance on Sunday would be a special qualification for prizes. The vicar wrote, "You must bear in mind that these schools were founded and partly endowed for the express intention of teaching the principles of the Established Church." He had no difficulty in satisfying "my Lords" that he was within the law in confining his prizes to Sunday scholars.

The following seductive advertisement, designed to fill the Church schools of a country town, was issued at the beginning of the cold weather:—" Coal, shoes, bread and beef charities. Persons with families will take notice that they will receive nothing from any of these charities unless their children are sent regularly to the National or infant school on week days, and to the Church Sunday-school on Sundays."

It is a favourite copybook text that example is better than precept. The children attending the National school of a Wiltshire village were invited by the vicar to the school-room on Christmas-eve. Being assembled they were grouped as Churchmen and Dissenters. The prizes were then distributed—amongst the Church children only. This seemed to the spectators a strange proceeding, but was intelligible on the ground that the Church children might be the best scholars. But when the awards were over, the little dissenters were dismissed, while the more fortunate orthodox ones were rewarded for their virtue with tea and buns. The sequel is almost as sad. A huge Christmas tree was subscribed for in the town, the Dissenting children were mustered, marched round with a band of music, and taken to enjoy themselves, while the small upholders of the Establishment were left out in the cold. In this way Christianity was taught.

In another instance the anniversary of a Baptist chapel was celebrated. The Sunday-school children were invited to tea. Some of them attended the Church day-school. To the parents of these the vicar sent notice that he had made up his mind that "those parents who could afford to send their children to the tea party could not want help, and that the children could not come to the school treat in August."

Many other examples might be . quoted to show the partiality with which the law worked, and which could only be redressed by the extension of the representative system, and by drawing a strict line of demarcation between the business of the State and that of the Churches. In considering the suitability of schools, no account was taken of the character of the population where it would have told against the pretensions of the Church to control education. In parishes where three-fourths of the inhabitants were Dissenters Church schools were enlarged to prevent the formation of School Boards. Even when Boards were established they were frequently made subsidiary to denominational purposes. Masters were advertised for and elected to Board Schools, on the ground that they were Churchmen or communicants, or "of thorough Church principles." In addition to their school duties, they were often required to assist in the Church service—to play the organ or to instruct the choir. The master of one Board School was dismissed for not attending Church, the vicar writing to him that they intended to have a schoolmaster "who would be helpful in Church matters." Another was discharged for attending a lecture on Oliver Cromwell in a Methodist chapel. In several instances the Catechism was taught in Board Schools in open defiance of section 14.

It is difficult to convince the members of dominant Churches that more is gained by toleration than by persecution. It was the hereditary tendency of the clergy to grasp at every morsel of power, and to entrench themselves behind walls of prescription and privilege which drove the Dissenters to the conviction that their only safeguard was in the final separation of religious and secular teaching. But all the advantages in the struggle were on the side of the Church. They were in possession. They were backed by the whole Conservative force, and they had succeeded in disuniting the Liberals. They aimed, also, at dividing the Dissenters, and in this move they were partially successful.

In the matter of tactics the Dissenters might wisely take a lesson from the Church. Whatever their secret differences may be, and however much they may enjoy abusing each other privately, the clergy present a firm and united front to the common enemy. On the other hand it is never difficult for a Minister or a Bishop to find Dissenters who will assist in pulling the nuts out of the fire for the Church.

It was so in 1870, and because of the secession of a few, the Nonconformists were twitted with not knowing their own minds. The same device was resorted to in 1872. Not long after the Manchester Conference had declared for the League recommendations, a declaration appeared called " The School and the Bible," protesting against the exclusion of the Bible from the school. It was signed by nearly six hundred laymen and ministers, unconnected with the Established Church. Most of them were unknown, but there were a few representative names, including those of Mr. Samuel Morley, Mr. Charles Reed, Mr. Spurgeon, Mr. Newman Hall, and Dr. Stoughton. The protest was speciously drawn to catch signatures. As a matter of fact there was no party which was striving to exclude the Bible from national education. It was already excluded by Act of Parliament from the ordinary work of the day. Under the plan of the League it might have been taught more freely, fully, and explicitly — but at the cost of the denominations. In reference to this declaration, Mr. Dale wrote, " A careful examination of the names that are known to us, shows that in nearly every instance they belong to men who, from the first, have upheld the Government policy, and opposed the Nonconformist agitation. They do not represent any secession from the great and growing party, which, for the last two years, has been contending for religious equality in education." ([1])

[1] The Report of the Manchester Conference, and the debates on religious instruction at the Birmingham School Board, contain the most authentic accounts of the position taken by the Dissenters at this time.

However the declaration answered its design, by making it appear that the Nonconformists were divided, and thus playing into the hands of the National Society.

The Parliamentary session of 1872, was a dismal one for the Liberals, who were passing through a creeping process of disintegration which was anxiously watched, and carefully promoted by the Tories. Tumultuous cheers from the Opposition benches greeted the appearance of Mr. Forster, especially when he could be drawn on to snub a Leaguer or a Radical, the temptation to which was great, and the opportunity frequent. Mr. Dixon's motion, [1] which covered the whole ground of the League exceptions to the Act of 1870, was met by a skilfully conceived amendment, to the effect that the time which had elapsed and the progress made were not such as to enable the House to enter with advantage on a review of the operation of the Act.

The amendment was a harbour of refuge for both positive and doubtful politicians. It was supported by all who were opposed to further change, including the phalanx of Whigs and Tories ; by those who shrank from pronouncing a definite opinion on the League scheme; by those who placed party loyalty above principle—and by the numerous section who prefer delay to action. The speech in which Mr. Forster moved it was also calculated to propitiate Liberals who were strongly opposed to his policy. He did not deny that the Act needed revision, and he prompted the belief that in the next session the Government would be prepared for alterations. It was gathered that they had under consideration the formation of Boards in all districts, the universal enforcement of attendance, and a modification of the 25th clause. These assurances detached a number of votes from Mr. Dixon's following, but nevertheless over a hundred liberals voted against the Ministry, while an equal number refused them

[1] See page 268.

their support. Comparing the division with that of the preceding year, it showed that the League strength in the House had exactly doubled.

In the same session Mr. Candlish brought in a bill to repeal the 25th section. The straits to which the Government were now reduced, were exemplified by the voting on this occasion. One hundred and thirty-two Liberals supported the bill. The Ministerial majority was composed of 123 Liberals and 195 Tories. Eleven members of the Government, including three Cabinet Ministers, took no part in the division. In the meantime the irritation in the country was intensified. The Nonconformists were exasperated by the policy of the Ministry, and were preparing for electoral action. Refusals to pay rates, followed by distraints, were common, while School Boards and Town Councils were at open war.

As an educational measure the Scotch Bill of this year was an improvement on the English Act, since it provided for universal School Boards and compulsory attendance. It was, however, intensely sectarian. The time-table conscience clause was given up. Denominational instruction might be given at the cost of the ratepayers without restriction or limitation. The payment of fees in voluntary schools was made obligatory. These provisions were taken to foreshadow the views of the Government in regard to Ireland, and the suspicion daily gained ground that a coalition of Ministerialsts and Tories had resolved to enforce a compulsory system of denominational education throughout the United Kingdom.

The Government was now (1872) in its fourth session, and had therefore reached more than the average age of Parliaments. The serious divisions of the party rendered it the more probable that a dissolution might come abruptly. For these reasons much attention was given to electoral

organization. The details of this department are not of a
character to make public. Many public meetings were held,
and conferences between members and their constituents
were promoted. In some places the League was strong
enough openly to assert the right to take part in the counsels
of the party, and to make its own terms. In others the
work was of a more delicate nature; but in the end the
organization contrived to make its influence respected, often
where its presence was least suspected. A large electoral
fund was subscribed to meet the special expenditure which
these operations demanded.

In view of the expected amendments of the Government it was determined that the whole strength of the
League should be devoted to assist in carrying them. Therefore at the annual meeting of 1872 it was resolved that the
Parliamentary action should be confined to three points—
universal School Boards, compulsory attendance, and the
unconditional repeal of section 25.

There was some ambiguity in the utterances of
Ministers respecting this clause. That there might be no
mistake on the part of the League, the Executive took
pains to make it clear that nothing but unconditional
repeal would satisfy them. Mr. W. H. Smith had given
notice that he should move that the power to pay fees should
be transferred from School Boards to Guardians of the
Poor. Whether the motion was a trap for the Ministry,
or was sincerely designed to help Mr. Forster in his perplexity
may be a little doubtful. It led, however, to more formidable differences between the Government and their natural
adherents. Mr. Hebbert, the Parliamentary secretary to the
Poor Law Board, took up the idea, and during the recess
expressed his approval of it. This was in time for the
League to make it clearly known that no such solution of
the difficulty would appease the quarrel. Mr. Chamberlain,

37

representing the Executive, characterised the idea as a proof of the incompetency of its authors to understand the scruples of Dissenters. While it would not remove a single ground of their hostility, it would create evils fatal to the spread of education and the independence of the people. It was a pretended concession, ignoring principle, and would carry sectarian conflict into the election of another group of public bodies, placing Magistrates, Guardians, and School Boards in constant antagonism. Where it secured the education of a child, it would be at the price of the degradation of the parent. Rather than any such shifting of the cards, Mr. Chamberlain advised that the question should be left alone.

It may be objected to the action of the Dissenters that they had never opposed Denison's Act, which enabled Guardians to pay the fees of the children of out-door paupers in denominational schools, and which involved the principle of the 25th clause. But, although Denison's Act had been on the statute book for fifteen years, it was inoperative and unknown. The new proposal was that it should be enforced, and should be widely extended in its application. The Boards of Guardians had never liked the Act, and the Manchester Board on the motion of Mr. J. A. Bremner, now passed a strong resolution against its extension.

In opening the fifth session of Parliament the Queen's speech announced an amending bill. Mr. Dixon also gave notice of his bill for School boards, compulsion and the repeal of section 25. In March Mr. Gladstone asked that the League bill should be postponed until the Government measure was introduced, and as there was a general expectation that the latter would follow the same lines, this was readily conceded. In the meantime there was a ministerial crisis on the question of Irish University education, and a dissolution seemed to be imminent. But the difficulty was bridged across, and after repeated delays the Government brought forward their Bill in June.

A bitter sense of betrayal was produced amongst Educationists and Nonconformists by the statement of the Vice-President. The Act of 1870 had been three years in operation, and the Education Department had not yet sent out the whole of the notices to provide the deficiency of accommodation. While education languished the sectarian conflict was incessant. Energy which might have been employed in execution, was occupied in the struggle over first principles. In these circumstances the Government made no proposal calculated to advance education a step, or to give peace to the distracted country. They made no provision for School Boards, or attendance ; and in regard to the religious question they precipitated themselves into the arms of their enemies. The authority to pay fees was transferred from School Boards to Guardians, with this difference, that where it had been permissive, it was now to be made compulsory. Where a hundred pounds had been spent before, thousands might now be applied for precisely the same purpose.

The Opposition were in ecstacies ; but Mr. Dixon and Mr. Richard warned the Government of the feeling which would be aroused in the country. The Executive declared the Bill to be an aggravation of the evils complained of. It was a further concession to denominationalism, and its pauperising influence would be a national calamity. The Guardians of Birmingham, Manchester, Sheffield, and many large towns condemned it in the strongest terms. The Nonconformists refused to accept it as any alleviation of their grievances.

Just before the bill was introduced a vacancy had occurred in the representation of Bath. Captain Hayter, the Liberal candidate, had stated in his address that the Act required amendment, and had expressed the hope that Mr. Forster's promised bill would prove satisfactory. But when it appeared he carefully avoided any reference to its provisions; and the local wire pullers, who were anxious to secure every vote, were cautious not to introduce any element of discord. But while the disappointment was fresh and keen, Mr. Paynter Allen, who was one of the confidential agents of the League, was instructed to visit Bath, to ascertain Captain Hayter's views, and to obtain his support for Mr. Dixon's bill. This was not an isolated proceeding on the part of the League. It had been the habit of the Committee to "interview" Liberal candidates; and, on several occasions, active support or opposition had been given to particular nominations. In some of the bye elections, which had recently occurred, the League had made its power respected by the Whig element of the party.

The Liberal candidate for Bath, acting probably under the advice of his Committee, excused himself from seeing the agent of the League. The local leaders of the party took very high ground; though one which, under ordinary circumstances, would have been reasonable enough. They were committed to Captain Hayter, whatever his opinions might be; they were in the thick of the fight; and they were indisposed to allow, if they could prevent it, any side influences to come into operation. Most of them were Nonconformists and were wholly at one with the League in principle. But it is noticeable that while Dissenters will go to a Conference and pass resolutions with acclamation not to support candidates opposed to their views; yet when the practical issue has to be tried, and the party has to be transfixed for its own good, they generally find local reasons why their own particular constituency should not be selected as the worthless object for the experiment. In this instance they denied the right of the League to make any requisition on the subject of their candidate's opinions.

In this conjunction the officers invited Mr. J. C. Cox,

a member of the Executive, to come forward as the representative of the League. At much personal inconvenience, and with great moral courage, Mr. Cox accepted the invitation. But it was felt to be highly undesirable to intervene in the contest if any ground of accommodation could be found. With this view, the author, with Mr. Thompson, Mr. Cox's agent, went to Bath to make a further effort to ascertain Captain Hayter's opinions, which, at this period, were of abnormal importance. His Committee peremptorily declined to make any statement on the subject, or to allow their candidate to be approached. The representatives of the League then offered to withdraw, without exacting any public statement which would jeopardise his success if they had the private assurance that Captain Hayter was generally favourable to the principles of Mr. Dixon's bill. But this also was denied.

Mr. Cox then issued his address to the electors. For a few days the city was in a state of great excitement. On making an attempt to hold a meeting Mr. Cox and his friends were assaulted and temporarily blinded by the free use of cayenne pepper. The Liberal leaders, in an interview which they sought with Mr. Cox, refused to make any concession, and denied his right to interfere in the contest. On the part of the League it was contended that Mr. Cox stood on the same footing as Captain Hayter, and was equally entitled to solicit the suffrages of the electors. The commotion increased when it was known that Mr. Cox was nominated. There had been some difficulty in securing the nomination. The Ballot Act was newly in operation and required the names of ten electors. So great was the pressure put upon Liberals that the names were not easily procured. When the nomination paper was sent in, it was discovered that some of the assenting electors were on the Committee of the Conservative candidate. The mistake was owing to the ignorance of Mr. Cox's agents of local politics, but in any case it was only following the example of the Liberal Ministry, which relied on Tory votes to carry its policy. Mr. Cox and his friends were now loudly denounced as emissaries of the Carlton.

Terms of compromise were at last arranged through the intervention of Dr. Caldicott, of Bristol. Captain Hayter publicly declared himself in favour of School Boards and compulsion, and against the payment of fees by Guardians; thus making, in the end, larger concessions than were asked at the outset. The Liberal Committee had, throughout the contest, played the game of the League. Mr. Cox now withdrew, but the split in the party had gone too far to avert the defeat of the Liberals.

This election was the cause of much excitement in political circles, and especially in the clubs and the lobby of the House. The political Committee of the Reform Club was set in motion, and other important agencies were invoked to reconcile the quarrel. The managers at the Treasury began to suspect that the country was in earnest. The election was followed by a Conference of Liberals at the Westminster Palace Hotel. The announcement that the League intended to pursue the same policy in other constituencies was received with acclamation. Mr. Bright made his first public appearance, after his long illness, at this meeting, and while deprecating the division of the party, he characterised the Education Act, as in some respects, " the worst measure passed by a Liberal Government since 1832."

The Bath policy was followed up at Shaftesbury, Greenwich, and Dundee; and, in prospect of a general election, League candidates issued addresses in other towns where the sitting members were hostile to the League platform. In this action we incurred much odium for dividing the party. The accusation was ably rebutted by

Mr. Harris in an article called " Who divides the Liberals ? "
The elections in which we took part demonstrated that the
League was in a great majority in the party.· In Parliament
the Government had only been able to go on by means of
the Tory vote. The Treasury candidate at Dundee,
Mr. Fitzjames Stephen, was the strongest to be found; yet
Mr. Edward Jenkins, a member of the League Executive,
polled three times his number of votes. The same results
happened elsewhere. Mr. Harris wrote, " If concession is to
precede union, it must be clear from which side it ought to
come. It may be doubtful if a tardy recognition of this
truth would save the present Ministry, or preserve the
prestige and power of the Liberal party ; it is absolutely
certain that without it further defeats and humiliation are
inevitable." Mr. Chamberlain said, " The majority will not
always yield to the minority, and the principle of religious
equality must be accepted as part of the programme of any
party which in future seeks our support and alliance.
Therefore you may expect to see the lesson of the Bath
election again and again repeated."

The session which had been looked forward to with hope
was barren of results. The hostility provoked by the
Government bill led to its withdrawal. But Denison's Act
was made obligatory, and it was estimated that about 100,000
children of paupers would receive some sort of education
under its provisions. An Act for indirect compulsion in the
agricultural districts was also pushed through Parliament by
a private member. It provided that no child under
eight should be employed in agriculture, and no child under
twelve who had not made in the preceding year a certain
number of attendances at school. But no securities were
taken for carrying it into effect, and it remained on the
statute book a dead letter. The 25th section continued in
force, and distraints were constantly levied on the goods of

Magistrates, Town Councillors, Members of School Boards, and ministers of religion who refused to comply with the law. In Parliament the Government still adhered to its Palmerstonian policy of playing off Conservative votes against those of its own adherents. This course was pursued both upon the Education Bill, and the Endowed Schools Act Amendment Bill; and the Tories were only too pleased to assist in widening the breach.

Towards the end of the year the Radicals enjoyed a brief hour of triumph, and much consternation was produced in the Tory and Whig confederacy by Mr. Bright's re-entrance into the Ministry. His acceptance of office after his severe judgment upon the Education Act, was received as an assurance that the ministerial policy would undergo important modifications. The Executive of the League at once suspended their electoral action, and prepared to sustain the Ministry in any measures they might take for the redress of the grievances complained of. Mr. Bright's address to his constituents confirmed the opinion that some substantial alterations were under consideration. He wrote " I hold the principles when in office that I have constantly professed since you gave me your confidence sixteen years ago. When I find myself unable to advance those principles, and to serve you honestly as a minister, I shall abandon a position which demands of me sacrifices that I cannot make." In speaking to the vast meeting in Bingley Hall which welcomed his return to public life, he declared decisively for a national in preference to a denominational system. He said the fault of the Education Act was " that it extended and confirmed the system, which it ought, in point of fact, to have superseded." The 25th clause contained an evil principle, " and one that· should not be continued." " With regard to this question of educating through the sects, I believe it is not possible to make it truly national or truly good. The fact is, I think we all feel, that the public do not take great interest in Denominational schools. The Church cares nothing for Dissenters : and in regard to this question, Dissenters care just as littlé for the Church. The people regard these schools as Church schools, as Chapel schools. They do not regard them as public and national, and general schools, and as part of a great system, in which the whole people unite for a great and worthy national object. Then again, the School Board! I do not know that the Government of that day were responsible for the mode of electing School Boards. It was not certainly in the original memorandum of the Bill, which I was permitted to see ; but the mode of electing appears to me about the very worst for purposes of general and national education which could possibly have been devised. When a contest for a School Board arises, the question of real education seems hardly thought of. It is a squabble between Church and Chapel and Secularists, and I know not how many other ' ists '; and when the School Board meets there is priest and parson and minister and other partisans. There is no free breeze of public opinion passing through the room, but rather an unwholesome atmosphere of what I call sectarian exclusiveness, and sometimes of bigotry, in which no good can thrive." In conclusion he said, " I apprehend, I cannot but believe that further experience, and something like failure, will before long force on Parliament and the country a general reconsideration of the question."

But notwithstanding these strong expressions and the expectations they created, it was soon made abundantly clear that no real unity or harmony upon the question existed in the Cabinet. In taking a new pilot on board they had not dismissed the old one. While Mr. Bright was denouncing the 25th section, as containing an evil principle, Mr. Forster was still using all the moral pressure of his department to compel School Boards to adopt bye-laws for its execution

38

In October Mr. Bright came to Birmingham to censure the Act, and in November Mr. Forster went to Liverpool to defend it. In this hopeless muddle and confusion of counsel there could be nothing but discouragement before the party, and no wonder the Tories won the elections. How greatly the Liberals were broken and disheartened was shown when the dissolution came.

But while the Liberals were losing the Parliamentary contests, they were winning all round in the School Board elections, which came on again in the autumn of this year. However disunited and demoralised in regard to Parliamentary policy, they were compact enough for other purposes, and having mastered the intricacies of the cumulative vote, they were in most cases able to reverse the decisions of three years back. In Birmingham a liberal majority was returned by a vast preponderance of votes. The candidates stood on the League platform of separate and voluntary religious teaching, and this plan was carried out in the Board Schools of the town during the next six years. A Religious Education Society was formed to give religious instruction. The teachers were volunteers and were admitted to the Board schools at certain hours in accordance with the time-table, to instruct the children whose parents wished them to attend. (¹)

The annual meeting this year was of a formal character, owing to the uncertainty respecting ministerial intentions. At an Executive meeting held at the close of the year it was decided to draw a more distinct line between the polemical and educational work of the League. With this object

¹ The clergy, with a few exceptions, refused to take any share in this work, and owing to the insufficiency of teachers amongst the Dissenters it was but a partial success. The religious communities were forced to admit their inability or their disinclination to teach religion without state assistance. To avoid a contest in 1879, it was agreed that the Bible should be read in the schools by the ordinary teachers without note or comment.

Mr. Dixon was asked to confine his bill to School Boards and compulsion only, while Mr. Candlish undertook the repeal of section 25.

During the two years under review a vast amount of educational work was done by the members of the League, in connection with School Boards and the enforcement of attendance. Although this department of the work was not so prominently before the public, it was never lost sight of by the officers, and it constantly engaged the close attention of the staff. Amongst the publications of the year may be noticed "The Struggle for National Education," by Mr. John Morley, and Mr. Dale's articles in the *Contemporary Review.*

Although a dissolution of Parliament had not been unexpected, its precise hour took everyone by surprise. Members and candidates were scattered abroad; constituencies were unprepared; plans were not matured, and differences were unreconciled. For a fortnight all was confusion and scramble, out of which came the Liberal party, a shattered wreck. It went into the contest, weakened, distracted, and divided. The main wing, composed of Dissenters, was suspicious and sullen. The Prime Minister's manifesto offered them no rallying ground. In regard to education he thought that "no main provision of the measure could advantageously be reconsidered without the aid of an experience such as we had not yet acquired." He also suggested that the uneasiness caused by one or two points was out of proportion to their importance or difficulty. He did not fairly estimate the temper of the Dissenters, and offered them, instead of principle the abolition of a tax.

The chief issue in the election was the school or the publichouse. The Tories went for restricted education and unlimited drinking. With the latter they coupled religion, as a matter of course, and "Beer and Bible" made a telling election cry.

The League took immediate action in the election. The address of the Prime Minister was taken as indicating a serious misàpprehension of the gravity of the situation. The Executive asked that a national system of education should be made a distinct feature of the Liberal programme. The Branches were advised to press candidates for definite pledges on this head. The result was so far satisfactory that out of 425 English, Welsh, and Scotch candidates, 300 were pledged to the repeal of the 25th section, which was accepted by Liberals and Conservatives as the "symbol" of the controversy. In the new Parliament there was a large gain of members in favour of League principles.

The results in particular constituencies were curious. Mr. Gladstone was again returned for Greenwich, but this time "as junior colleague to a gin distiller." He would have been invited to stand for Manchester, but for the threatening attitude of the Nonconformists.

The prominent members of the League had various fortunes. Mr. Dixon's seat was of course assured. But the Chairman of the Executive was defeated at Sheffield. In the selection of candidates there had been a test ballot between Mr. Chamberlain and Mr. Allott, a popular local politician. It was decided in favour of the former, but Mr. Allott's supporters were disappointed at the result, and did not accept it with loyalty. This, coupled with the dissertion of the Whigs and Moderates, who looked upon Mr. Chamberlain as a firebrand, led to his defeat. This was the most serious blow which the League had sustained. Several other members of the Executive were unsuccessful, including Mr. Cox, Admiral Maxse, and Captain Sargeant. On the other hand Mr. Cowen, Sir Charles Dilke, Mr. Jenkins, and Mr. Pennington were returned.

Mr. Candlish retired from the representation of Sunderland on account of failing health, and the charge of the 25th clause passed to Mr. Henry Richard.

Mr. Forster was opposed by the Liberal Committee in Bradford. He was however ostentatiously and avowedly supported by the Conservatives, and with the aid of the Catholic vote, and a small proportion of Liberal votes, was returned at the head of the poll.

Mr. Baines lost his seat for Leeds on account of his views on the Education question. In some twenty other constituences Liberal upholders of the 25th clause were beaten, owing mainly to the defection of the Nonconformists. It must be said however, that generally the Dissenters had the greatest difficulty in breaking away from their traditionary support of the Liberal party, and many obstinate adherents of the Government policy were sent back to Parliament from constituencies where the absence of the Dissenting vote could easily have turned the scale.

The defeat of the Liberal party, calamitous as it proved in some respects, was not an unmixed evil. It has taught the country that no Government will be allowed to juggle with great principles with impunity. It also prepared the way for the re-union of the party on a more liberal basis, with more assured purposes, and with infinitely superior organisation. It is impossible also not to believe that the events recorded will have a marked influence on the educational and ecclesiastical legislation of the future.

CHAPTER VIII.

PERIOD — FROM THE GENERAL ELECTION, 1874, TO THE PASSING OF LORD SANDON'S ACT, 1876, AND THE DISSOLUTION OF THE LEAGUE.

THE political revolution which has been described threw upon the Executive the duty of reviewing their policy. The change of Government found their work but half done. The object they had placed before themselves—" the establishment of a system which should secure the education of every child in the country "—was far from being realized. The provisions made by the Liberal Government were incomplete, inefficient, and illusory. Securities were wanting for the instruction of half the children of the nation. Under such circumstances there could be no thought of relinquishing the purpose for which the League was instituted.

There were, by common confession, great difficulties before the Committee, but they had to ask themselves in what manner and degree these had been increased by the defeat of the Whig party. During the election struggle the Tory leaders had accepted the defence of the denominational system as an integral part of the Conservative creed. But in this respect they did not differ from the Liberal Government which they followed. The League could be under no greater disadvantages now, than when it had had to contend against a coalition of Whigs and Tories. In one respect the committee were relieved from great embarrassment. They could no longer be accused of endangering the existence of a Liberal administration ; and as a matter of choice it was far preferable to them to contend against avowed enemies rather than professed friends. They did not accept the late ballot as a verdict of the country against the proposals of the League, but rather as a vote of no confidence in the Whig policy, and they believed that in the reconstruction of the party their principles would assume greater prominence, and take a firmer hold upon the attachment of the nation.

The immediate objects aimed at were resistance to any further extension of the denominational system, and the acceptance by the party of a national system, as a distinct and leading feature of the Liberal programme of the future. The means proposed were the continued propagation of opinion as to the necessity of School Boards and compulsion, the ultimate absorption of the denominational system under representative management, and the completion of the structure by universal free schools. It was also determined to pay increased attention to the non-political details of the system, such as greater efficiency of instruction, the extension of school age, the encouragement of the higher standards by a graduated scale of grants, and the elevation of the status and qualifications of teachers.

The actual state of education was defective and humiliating to a degree very imperfectly realized, notwithstanding the efforts which the League had made to enlighten opinion.

Beginning with the Training schools, the fountain-head of the system, it was throughout wasteful, unproductive, and inefficient. One of the primary requisites of a fruitful system is a staff of trained and skilful teachers. The Normal schools afforded no guarantee for an adequate supply. The case against them, both in point of cost and efficiency, was a strong one. Starting as voluntary institutions under exclusive management, and with sectarian aims, they had in course of time, contrived to throw 75 per cent. of their expense, on the public ; and this without investing Parliament or the Education Department with any powers of effective supervision.

At the beginning of the League agitation the voluntary subscriptions to the Normal schools amounted to about two per cent. of their cost, the remainder being made up of Government grants, students' fees, endowments, and the sale of books; and the managers were still appealing for larger subsidies. Of the total accommodation which they afforded three-fourths was in the hands of the Established Church; and Dissenters were then, and are still being taxed out of all just proportion to pay for the theological training of Church teachers, with the prospect of being afterwards compelled to send their children to them for instruction in Church doctrines. Neither was this grave injustice counter-balanced by any reasonable anticipation that the scholars would be made to receive sound and lasting secular knowledge. For national purposes, and as national institutions, the Normal schools were an imposition and a delusion. The chief object of their managers was to qualify the students to teach dogma. The catechism and the liturgy were the corner-stones of the system, and attention was devoted to them to the neglect of mental exercise, and effectual training in the science of teaching. Their tendency also was to grow more extravagant and more exclusively sectarian.

It is not a matter for surprise that under such conditions the general status and attainments of the teachers were of an inferior order. The only wonder is that any good teachers were produced under a system not calculated to stimulate independence of character, or to raise intelligence into prominence. The social position of the Church teacher in the country districts was that of a menial Church officer. A Church schoolmaster wrote that many teachers of his class were subjected to a worse slavery than the most dependent labourer in the parish. Rest and relaxation, except for brief periods of the year, were almost unknown to them. After an exacting week's work in the school, they were generally compelled to undergo a similar drudgery on the Sunday. Fifty per cent. of the advertisements for Church teachers stipulated that they should assist in Church offices. From quasi-curate to beadle and gravedigger, there was no employment which the schoolmaster was not expected to undertake. Some of the inducements offered to them may be gathered from the advertisements in the National Society's Paper. "To officiate as parish clerk;" as "collector of charity and Church funds," as "choirmaster and precentor." "To attend Sunday school and take charge of the children at Church, and to and from Church." "An organist, willing to assist in Church matters." "Parish clerkship, with liberty to take private pupils." "Clerkship and sexton." "Ability to manage and train a surpliced choir indispensable." Situations were offered to certificated mistresses whose husbands or brothers "followed agricultural pursuits," or could undertake, "at stipulated wages, the management of a kitchen garden and two or three cows." The social standing of the rural schoolmaster was little above that of the agricultural labourer, and the only ambition he was encouraged to entertain was that of "the charity boy who longs to be a beadle."

And even of their kind the staff of trained adult teachers was wholly insufficient for national requirements, so that the mass of scholars were left under the care of mere boys and girls. The pupil teachers of 1870 were little better qualified than the monitors of Lancaster's and Bell's day. The method was an off-shoot of the discredited monitorial system, which had the one recommendation of cheapness, for the sake of which true economy was sacrificed. The pupil teachers were generally badly instructed, often of low intelligence, and the common standard of their attainments was below a decent average. Far from being efficient teachers and helpers, the Inspectors found their attempts

39

to express their own knowledge, such as it was, were lamentably poor, meagre, and childish.

If anyone thinks that this picture is overdrawn let him study the education blue books. The reports of the Inspectors are a standing record of the humiliating but inevitable results of teaching so conducted. In the upper classes of a very few of the best schools there might be found a fair amount of intelligence and information. But such schools were rare exceptions. The ordinary condition of the scholars in the higher standards was that of comparative ignorance, and they were, as a rule, incapable of expressing by word or writing any minimum of knowledge they might possess. The sixth standard does not stand for a large amount of knowledge for a child to take out into the world as a weapon in the battle of life; yet there was not one scholar annually to every other school who passed this standard. And if this was the plight of the children in the highest classes, what was to be expected of those who never got beyond the lower standards. The Committee of Council reported in 1869, that of " four-fifths of the children about to leave school, either no account or an unsatisfactory one, was given by an examination of the most strictly elementary kind." In the overwhelming majority of cases the children took away from school no knowledge which they were likely to retain. The largest percentage of passes was in reading, but it was seldom indeed that the scholars understood what they read, or that the words which they pronounced mechanically and by rote, conveyed any meaning to their minds. The Bishop of Manchester, an old Inspector, having an intimate knowlege of every detail of the system, applied to the results produced, the terms " inconceivable," " disgraceful," " discreditable," and "miserable," and said "it filled him with great shame when he realised it." Mr. Kennedy, another Inspector of great experience, wrote " We are contented with little more than a pitiful counting of heads, and that we call education."

It would be a grave injustice to the schoolmaster to hold him responsible for the whole of this lamentable failure. By general admission, irregular attendance and migration from school to school were concomitant causes. Reasonable progress, under such conditions, was impossible. The regular scholars were thrown back and discouraged by the irregular ones; the masters were disheartened and perplexed and made to despair of any excellent standard. It is difficult to convey in figures an adequate idea of the extent of this evil. In 1873-74 the Committee of Council estimated that there were two-and-a-half millions of children who ought to have made the 250 attendances—which might have been completed in half a year—required to qualify them for examination. But only 752,268 were presented to the Inspectors. Of the rest no account was given. A third of those who were examined in the lower standards ought to have been in the higher. And in all cases the percentage of passes was lamentably low.

For seven years the League strove without relaxation to put the actual state of the school system fully and fairly before the public, and to rouse the nation to a sense of the danger and discredit which were involved. With the same object the systems of foreign countries were carefully examined, and their methods and results stated and tabulated for comparison. The energy and persistency with which these views were urged produced their inevitable effect upon the public mind. In all meetings of workmen the free school platform was received with enthusiasm, ([1]) and notwith-

[1] On the Free School system, see papers and addresses by Mr. Chamberlain, Sir Charles Dilke, and Mr. Collings, published by the League. Also a series of articles in the Monthly Paper of the League by Mr. Allen. On American Free Schools, Bishop Fraser's Report, and the author's " Free Schools of the United States" may be consulted. Later contributions to the same branch of the subject are contained in the speeches of Dr. Cameron, M.P., and in papers by Dr. Watts, of Manchester.

standing the temporary disadvantages to which it subjected them, compulsion was not only acquiesced in, but demanded. The natural and the most earnest allies of the League were amongst the class who were most affected by the changes proposed. But the desire for compulsion grew amongst all parties, and the chief difference of opinion was as to how it should be carried into effect. The early working of the compulsory bye-laws of School Boards had demonstrated that so far from injuring the voluntary schools, the enforcement of attendance was of great advantage to them. This experience reconciled the clergy of the towns to compulsion, but in the parishes progress was greatly retarded by the clerical distrust and jealousy of School Boards, and the farmers' dislike of rates. The idea of a possible system of compulsion in connection with denominational schools had not taken shape during the existence of the Liberal Government, or if it had, there was no one with sufficient hardihood to give expression to it.

The School Boards increased in number from 344 in 1872, to 1769 in 1876. The first Boards were formed in the Boroughs and were with few exceptions granted on the requisition of the locality. Many of the large parishes also made application for Boards. But the great proportion of the rural Boards were formed by order of the Department to supply deficiencies of accommodation. In all cases however they might have been prevented by local exertion; ample opportunity for which was always given by the Education Office. On the subject of School Boards there was a marked difference of feeling during the latter years of the League agitation. The section of the public which holds itself independent of party, had been partially awakened to the truth about educational results, and was revolting against the illiberality of the clergy, who having proved themselves unable properly to educate the people, were unwilling to let any other agency into the field. That portion of the press too, which acts as a barometer of public feeling amongst certain classes was gradually coming round. The Bishop of Manchester warned the clergy to prepare for a universal system of School Boards, within a quarter of a century, whether they liked it or not. Other leaders of the Church party concurred in this view; but the rank and file of the country clergy held fast to their objections. Lord Francis Hervey called the dissenters "unclubbable" people; but in this matter the clergy better deserved the description. They would permit no association on the part of the community in this sphere of their work. Had they not fought for years against the co-operation of Church laymen in the management of their schools ; and was it likely they would now permit the formation of a School Board, upon which by chance, there might be an inquisitive or cantankerous Dissenter ? They had one tremendous weapon ready to their hands, and they wielded it with great energy and effect. It was the no-rate cry. The impost was not so very terrible in reality. The average rate for 1874-75 did not exceed threepence. But it was capable of expansion. Some amusing examples of exaggeration came under the notice of the Officers. The Government returns gave the rate for each district, stating its amount in pence and decimals. In this manner a rate of three halfpence would be given as 1·5d. This was easily convertible into 1s. 5d., and in this form was placed before the dismayed agriculturists. Even small farmers were made to understand that a School Board would cost them from £20 to £50 a year. No wonder they threatened to reduce wages if the labourers voted for a Board.

Upon the formation of the new Ministry it was not seriously anticipated that any attempt would be made to confer new advantages upon sectarian schools. It was whispered that compulsory powers might be given to magistrates or guardians, or even to voluntary managers, but no great attention was paid to suggestions which were generally acknowledged to be opposed to the spirit of modern legislation. The Church party seemed to be thinking more of repeal of the Cowper-Temple clause, which restricted the use of their catechism. It seemed possible also that Ministers might think themselves justified in extending the operation of the 25th clause which had been made a test question in the election.

The issue between parties was first raised in the new Parliament on Mr. Dixon's Bill for compulsion and School Boards. Mr. Talbot, the member for West Kent, gave notice of an amendment supposed to embody the views of the denominationalists, which declared that the House could not entertain the universal establishment of School Boards, until perfect liberty of religious teaching was secured, and unless the Boards were empowered to contribute to the support of voluntary Schools. No overt action was taken in this session by the leaders of the party to give effect to the amendment, but the voting on the main question was of a character which made all sections of Conservatives desire that it should be taken out of Mr. Dixon's hands, and settled by their own Government, on their own lines.

The beginning of 1875 was emphasised by Mr. Gladstone's formal retirement from the leadership of the Liberal party, and for several sessions he only appeared in the House on special occasions. The disorganisation of the party was now more than ever complete. But the incident gave to the Executive Committee an opportunity of restating the terms on which alone reconstruction was possible. They declared their conviction that there could be no union under any leader who was pledged to the continuance of a policy which encouraged denominational interests in opposition to national education, and which was objected to by the majority of the

Liberal electors. Similar resolutions were passed by the representative Nonconformist bodies, and by important Liberal Associations, including that of Bradford. For a time the Liberal leadership was put into commission, under the immediate direction of Earl Granville and Lord Hartington.

Mr. Dixon's bill appeared again before Parliament in the session of 1875. It had become the more urgent because of the admitted failure of the Agricultural Children's Act. The Conservatives were more generally recognising the necessity of compulsion, and Mr. Salt, the member for Stafford, had prepared a bill to give leave to municipal and urban authorities in towns where no School Boards existed, to exercise the power of Boards for enforcing attendance.

An earnest appeal was made to the country to support Mr. Dixon's bill, which, in spite of the foreshadowing gloom of foreign politics and the hopeless discomfiture of Liberals in Parliament, was advocated by crowded meetings convened by the League. A special enquiry had been made by Mr. Allen into the education of the rural districts, and Mr. Dixon was able to adduce on behalf of its principle a mass of new and striking evidence, which appealed in the strongest way to the sympathy and intelligence of the House. The result of the divisions in this and the preceding session was that over two hundred Liberals, including all the members of the former Government, except Mr. Gladstone and Mr. Lowe, had now voted for the bill, and the Officers had the satisfaction of feeling that its ultimate fortunes were bound up with those of the Liberal party, whatever they might be. The Marquis of Hartington, the titular head of the party said, " I think there is a disposition on the part of the Liberal party, to sink their differences whether great or small, in consideration of the great object which all are beginning to recognise—

namely, that there is a paramount necessity that a secular system of education may exist and extend throughout the country at large."

Another feature of the year was Lord Sandon's new code. This was an educational surprise. The conditions of the grant were made more stringent, and greater encouragement was offered for better results in the higher standards. There was a loud protest from the voluntary managers against this process of "stringing up." The question with them was the old one, and yet one which is ever new to them —not what was desirable in the interests of education generally, but what would suit their schools. The stringency of the code had to be relaxed in response to their piteous appeals, but it still recognised in its amended form a principle for which the League had hitherto vainly contended, the graduation of the scale of grants, dependent on results and efficiency.

In other respects, however, Lord Sandon was very gracious where denominational interests were concerned. Under Mr. Forster's administration there had been grievous complaints of the partiality shown to the Church. On Lord Sandon's succession the evil was aggravated. Whitehall was crowded by clerical wire-pullers and friars of all colours, and the Department was interviewed and memorialized without cessation. A clerical minority unable to carry its policy on a School Board had nothing to do in order to frustrate the majority but to hold a private meeting, and pass resolutions and forward them to the Department. The wishes of the representatives of the ratepayers were coolly ignored. Many flagrant instances of centralized dictation occurred, and under the adminstration of Mr. Disraeli, the country was treated to the system of paternal Government, which Mr. Disraeli himself had prophesied and denounced in 1839. School Boards were not allowed to fix the fees desirable in the interests of schools and scholars, for fear they might unduly compete with sectarian schools. The Birmingham Board were ordered to double their fees. They were strong enough, however, to resist, and ultimately established a number of penny schools. In the selection of sites, the wants and conveniences of localites were made subordinate to the interests of denominational schools. In the provision of accommodation the opinions of the School Boards were ignored. The Department consulted the Inspector, the Inspector consulted the Clergyman, and between them they settled the matter. Renewed opportunities were given to the voluntaryists to take possession of the ground. Grants were made to new Church schools when there was ample accommodation under School Boards. The formation of Boards was obstructed on every pretext. The Town Council of Winchester applied in the usual way for a Board for the city. The clergy got up a petition against it, and on an exparte statement, the Department refused a Board to the locality. In another case, " My Lords " ordered a School Board to confine the instruction in their schools to infants, leaving the elder children to the denominational schools. The Board flatly refused to obey, and the Department was obliged to retire from an untenable position. The Manchester Board passed a reasonable resolution refusing to pay fees to schools which refused to admit the Inspector of the Board. The Department interfered and addressed a strong remonstrance to the Board. A most unwarrantable interference was attempted in regard to elections. A regulation was made that in borough elections there should be only one polling station for each ward. It had been found by experience that it was not possible to poll a thousand electors at one station during the seven hours allowed for polling. But the electors in the wards of large boroughs ranged from five hundred, to five, ten, fifteen, and twenty thousand. The average in Birmingham was four thousand voters to each

40

ward. If this regulation had been submitted to, it would have disfranchised three-fourths of the borough electors. The spirit of dictation in these matters was carried to such an extreme, that Mr. Dixon was asked to bring the subject under the notice of Parliament.

The question of attendance continued to press with irresistible force on public judgment, and it became clear that it could not be left long in abeyance. The League Bill introduced for the third time in 1876, was supported by the powerful advocacy of Mr. Bright, which brought a fresh accession of Liberal strength. The process of conversion to compulsion amongst Conservatives was rapid, and was accelerated by the desire to secure it on their own terms, while they had the opportunity. As the Ministry settled into harness there were many speculations current as to their intentions. Great pressure was put upon them to take some decisive step in the interests of Church Schools. On the change of Government the National Society had threatened a reactionary agitation, the objects of which were fuller liberty of sectarian teaching in Board Schools, and fresh subsidies to denominational Schools. The modest request was that the Church Catechism should be taught in the schools of the ratepayers, that payments out of the rates should be made to denominational schools, and that powers of compulsion should be vested in voluntary managers. These proposals were supported by convincing arguments, for those Churchmen, who are first Churchmen and then citizens. " For the Church to cease to contend for the Education of her own children in her own faith, would be a betrayal of a religious trust which must eventuate in the loss of temporal privileges." ([1])

Other proposals were to allow ratepayers to allocate their rates to particular schools, on the Canadian plan, or to relieve subscribers to voluntary schools from the payment of rates.

[1] Monthly Paper of National Society.

Many alternatives were put before the Government by interested advisers, and immediate action was urged from all quarters. The pretext that it was not a party question, which had answered their purpose admirably at one time, was now roughly put aside. " If a Conservative Government will not listen to the voice of Churchmen, what is it fit for ?" was not unnaturally asked by the clergy. The *Guardian* wrote, " The opportunity before Lord Sandon is a great one, it can hardly recur, and advantage should be taken of it to the utmost." There were many other indications that the Church party and the Tories finding they could not baffle a state system of education were bent upon getting it into their own hands.

Lord Sandon's bill in its earliest shape raised no great expectations in any party. It was not a vigorous measure, calculated to reconcile educationists, nor did it satisfy those who had been clamouring for greater freedom to teach dogma at the public cost. So far as its provisions went it promised to benefit denominational schools by forcing children into them and securing a more regular attendance. It gave leave to Town Councils and Boards of Guardians in non-School Board districts to make bye-laws for attendance. The power to pay fees was transferred from School Boards to Guardians. There were also provisions for indirect compulsion, similar to those which had been so often tried with such imperfect success. No child of a fixed age was to be employed in labour who was not furnished with a labour pass—that is, a certificate of having passed a certain standard, or made a stated number of attendances at school. But while children were to be prevented from working, there was no security taken that they should be instructed. Canon Girdlestone said that in rural districts the bill would prove a mere sham and dead letter, and the feeling grew that its provisions were illusory, and were intended as a sop to the public conscience, to appease the agitation.

The position of the Liberal party did not encourage the hope that they would be able to carry any thorough amendments, but it was necessary to find a rallying ground. The Executive Committee therefore restated the principles on which they conceived a satisfactory solution could be based.

In the first place it was declared that no measure could be permanently acceptable which did not provide for direct compulsion in all cases.

It was also held desirable that local authorities entrusted with the administration of compulsion should have powers for the provision and management of schools.

The strong objections to the payment of school fees by Guardians, which was equally unsatisfactory on social and religious grounds, were recapitulated. The Committee advocated a large extension of the free school principle, as the proper means of meeting the case of parents unable to pay fees.

An extraordinary provision was contained in the bill enabling the local authority to delegate their powers to Committees, not of their own body. This was strongly opposed as a violation of representative principles, the effect of which would be to place compulsory powers in the hands of irresponsible persons. It was suspected that this was an indirect way of vesting such powers in the managers of voluntary schools.

The Committee also criticised the financial clauses which lessened the proportion of voluntary subscriptions needed for maintenance, and rendered it probable that many schools under private management would be conducted wholly at the cost of the parents and the public.

They also protested against the large exemptions from attendance, and the low standard of proficiency set up.

On the second reading Mr. Mundella moved a resolution in favour of direct compulsion, and this being lost, Sir Charles Dilke moved the rejection of the bill, which was now regarded as a measure for increasing the powers and privileges of the Establishment.

At this·stage the League lost the parliamentary services of Mr. Dixon, who, for domestic reasons, was compelled to retire from the post which he had occupied from the formation of the League. Mr. Chamberlain, who succeeded him in the representation of Birmingham, strongly censured the principle of the bill, which he regarded as a long concession to denominational interests, and which, had the Liberal party been united, would not have been suffered to pass ·the House of Commons.

Mr. Henry Richard gave notice that, on going into Committee, he should move " That the principle of universal compulsion in education cannot be applied without great injustice, unless provision be made for placing public elementary schools under public management." A large meeting of Dissenters was held at the Westminster Palace Hotel to back up the motion, and many meetings of Liberals throughout the country also supported it ; but, in the state of parties, its defeat was a foregone conclusion.

When the bill got into Committee its progress was attended by surprises. The Tories, on the second reading, had rejected the principle of direct compulsion when moved by a Liberal, yet when the bill emerged from Committee it embodied a more vigorous compulsory law than any Liberal had ventured to propose to Parliament. It was a bill for magisterial compulsion, under which proceedings might be initiated by any person. The conversion of the Conservatives had been rapid. They had originally opposed compulsion on the ostensible ground that it was a violation of the liberty of the subject ; but in reality, as had been strongly suspected, and was now demonstrated, because they did not believe that their own schools could continue to exist under such a law. As soon as it was found that the popular desire for education was greater than the fear of sectarianism, their opinions developed at a wonderful rate. By virtue of the bill before the House the country was to be placed under a compulsory law without the safeguard of public representation, and without the co-operation of the class affected by it; a law which might be set in motion by informers, and enforced by magistrates in one class of denominational schools where there was but the flimsiest protection for the rights of conscience. This law was passed by the party which had refused compulsory powers under School Boards in the name of liberty, and which had taken for its motto, "the right of the parent to choose the school."

A clause moved by Mr. Pell, enabling School Boards to be dissolved on certain conditions, was strongly opposed by Mr. Bright, but was carried. ([1])

In regard to school grants Lord Sandon avowed that the effect of the Bill would be to enable schools to be maintained by the childrens' pence, combined with the money received from Government.([2]) The necessity for local subscriptions was thus dispensed with, and with it the last guarantee for the influence of public opinion upon the management.

[1] The Tories, backed by the clergy, made a strong fight for this clause, and evidently looked to important results from it. But not more than two or three Boards have been dissolved under it during six years.

[2] There are no means of ascertaining the number of schools which, under these clauses, have been able wholly to dispense with voluntary subscriptions. As the general result of the clauses the subscriptions fell from 8s. 8½d. per child in average attendance in 1876 to 7s. 3¼d. in 1880. Dr. Watts estimates that a good school should earn 17s. 6d. per head on the average attendance, when the cost of elementary instruction would stand thus: Government 17s. 6d., school fees at 3d. per week 11s. 6d., plus 2s. 6d. for those who do not count in average attendance, 14s., or a total, without any voluntary contributions, of 31s. 6d. per head. (Transactions of Manchester Statistical Society, 1879, p. 64.) The total expenditure per scholar in average attendance in voluntary schools in 1880 was 34s. 7¾d. The tendency of recent legislation has been to give the Denominationalists a stronger hold upon the school system, and at the same time to make their schools a heavier charge on the national exchequer.

A motion of Lord Robert Montagu, making the payment of fees by Guardians compulsory and universal, was carried with the assistance of Mr. Forster.

It may be doubted whether in their fondest dreams, the National Society had ever looked for success like this. The prospect held out to them by Lord Sandon's Act was this. In the rural districts they were given supreme control over the school system. They were relieved from the harassing necessity of canvassing for funds. The pence of the children always an uncertain source of income, were secured by the rates. The Government grants in good schools were sufficient for the rest. They had no competition to fear now, and lastly they had powers for compulsory attendance. The title of the Act should have been "An Act for compelling attendance in denominational schools, under private management, supported out of the rates and taxes." In brief, it was in the parishes a new Act of Appropriation and a new Act of Uniformity.

A final effort was made by the Liberals to rally their weakened and disordered forces against the principle of this legislation. A representative deputation had an interview with the Marquis of Hartington at Devonshire House, who consented to move the following resolution upon the Report, " That in the opinion of this House principles have been introduced into this bill which were neither mentioned nor contemplated on the second reading, and which have a tendency to disturb the basis on which education now rests, to impede the formation of new schools, to introduce discord and confusion, and to place the management of schools in the hands of persons who neither contribute to their support nor are elected by the ratepayers." The resolution was rejected by a strictly party majority, but it reserved the right, and marked the determination of the Liberal party to re open, when occasion should serve, the whole question of education by means of schools under private management.

The effect of this act was to destroy the *raison d'être* of the League as an Educational Organisation. It put all parents under a legal obligation to have their children instructed, and subjected them to a penalty in default. It threw upon local authorities the duty of seeing that parents obeyed the law. It was not obligatory upon the School Attendance Committees to make bye laws for attendance, but the ancillary clauses declared their duty to see that the law was enforced; while a final power was reserved to the Education Department to supervise the work of the local authorities, and to compel the observance of their duty. Much of the strength of the measure was frittered away by the saving clauses and exceptions; but, nevertheless, it professed to provide for the object which the League was founded to secure, " the education of every child in England and Wales;" and only on the treble default of the parent, the local authority, and the Education Department could it fail in its purpose.

I propose, in conclusion, briefly to state the reasons which led the Executive to advise the dissolution of the League, and to review the operation of the law since that event.

CHAPTER IX.

CONCLUSION.

IT was not without mature deliberation that the Officers took the decisive step of advising the dissolution of the League. They felt that it was not a course to be taken lightly. Whether judged by the following it had secured, or the resistance it had provoked, the Organization had occupied a conspicuous place in public attention for eight years. Its object had been earnestly taken up in the country, and the leaders of the movement had received a generous support and allegiance through an exacting conflict, in which it became necessary to sacrifice party loyalty for the preservation of principle. The influence and prestige which it had acquired were not denied by its opponents, and the eagerness with which the Conservatives seized the first opportunity to fasten the education system on their own lines was sufficient proof of the apprehension with which they looked upon any further development of a national scheme. Their avowed object was to take the question out of the hands of the League, and this accounted for the seemingly drastic nature of the measure which they passed.

The Executive Committee could not fail to perceive that while the functions of the League, as an Educational Assocation, were materially affected by the legislation of 1876, the course of the previous agitation had also altered its political relations towards the Whig or official element of the Liberal party. If Lord Sandon's act were carried out with integrity, and zealously enforced in the country, it promised to secure universal schooling. If on the other hand it should

41

fail, the entire Liberal party was pledged to carry the work forward to a fitting conclusion. The Committee had therefore to consider what had been the result of the movement, and what remained to be done which required the continued existence of a distinct organization.

When the League was established the public mind was comparatively uninformed, both as to the extent of educational destitution, and the principles upon which a national system should be based. Notwithstanding the efforts of many thoughtful and earnest men who had exerted themselves to create an enlightened opinion, ignorance, apathy, and indifference in regard to the question prevailed through a large portion of the country. The previous societies which had been formed to promote education, after brief periods of agitation, had either yielded to the discouragements and opposition they encountered, or had been silenced by some trifling concession from Governments whose convenience or existence were endangered by the controversy. There had been a political bias upon the question, but no section of politicians having control of the legislative machinery, had ever adopted it as a distinct feature of a party programme. The Whigs, with some honourable exceptions, of whom Lord John Russell was the most distinguished, had distrusted the advance of popular intelligence almost as much as the Tories, and the Radicals were too weak to prevail against the combined forces of inertion. Many Governments had taken up the question to quiet a troublesome demand or subdue a sectional opposition, and had patched it here and there, but none had undertaken the establishment of a general system. The subject had been played and coquetted with by sects, and interests and cliques, but it had never got down to the people, and the men who were really in earnest and were pursuing education for its own sake, had not been able to gather the impetus which was requisite to carry the movement to a successful conclusion.

Looking back on half a century of procrastination and trifling, it may seem paradoxical to hold that the Act of 1870 was introduced prematurely, yet there are grounds for the belief that a stronger and more liberal measure, and one which, in an educational sense would have been economy of time, could have been passed if legislation had been delayed for another year. The time was no doubt opportune for a compromise with the Church; but compromise with ignorance, inefficiency, and sectarianism, which were the characteristics of the existing system, was not desirable. Nor was it necessary. The Church party would have accepted any settlement which did not make a direct attack on the institutions in existence. They had been alarmed by the resources which the Nonconformists had shown in 1868, and they certainly did not look to the Liberal Government for reinforcement and indulgence. Then followed the League agitation which created the popular enthusiasm for education. These were the circumstances which enabled the Government to approach the question with a prospect of success; but it was not necessary that they should turn the weapons which had been forged by their own supporters against them.

The Act of 1870 was thorough in one particular. It promised, sooner or later, to place efficient schools within reach of the entire population. The process has been needlessly slow. Canon Warburton, one of the Inspectors, writing in 1880 enumerates twenty-six parishes or hamlets in the fragment of a county, which are still " outside our national system of elementary education." (¹) But the supply of schools has kept far ahead of the arrangements for their use. In other respects the Act was pretentious and illusory, and

¹ Blue Book, 1880-81, 409.

was speciously drawn to catch votes, to reconcile conflicting interests, and to smother opposition. The Church was conciliated by large concessions to a sectional interest, and an attempt was made to propitiate the popular party by embodying in a perfunctory way the principles of the League. The sects were offered the first chance, and the Nation was invited to follow and pick up the crumbs. Overlooking all the lessons of history, the Government relied on the power of sectarian competition as the principal factor in the construction of a system which by courtesy was called national.

The very opposite principle was the foundation of the League scheme. Instead of relying on sectarian jealousy and rivalry, on denominational patronage and private charity, the members of the League appealed to public spirit, to local Government, and National resources, and to the co-operation of the parents and people. The scholars of the preceding era had been mainly those who came under denominational influences. It was now proposed to bring a much larger class under instruction, and to introduce new and stringent experiments in execution. The laws of compulsion and of local rating were of this character, and it was insisted that they could only be successfully worked by recognising Liberal methods of administration. These were the extension of local government and the direct representation of the class affected by the law; the removal of all taxes on attendance, and perfect freedom and security for opinion and conscience. A law based on these principles would not have been felt as the imposition of harsh conditions by a superior authority, but as a Liberal contract between the Government and the people. The experience of eleven years has demonstrated that the Education Acts have been successful in proportion only as these principles were adopted.

The best justification of the objections taken by the League to the Act of 1870 is to be found in its results. Even since it has been supplemented by the peremptory clauses of Lord Sandon's Act, and after the school life of more than a generation of children has elapsed, the law has failed to embrace the school population of the country. In estimating a measure of such pretensions and magnitude it must be judged by what it has left undone, as well as by what it has done. After five years of permissive compulsion there were children to be counted by the million, who might and ought to have been at school, and who were not there. In 1876 the Committee of Council estimated that there were two-and-a-half-millions of children above seven years of age who might reasonably have been expected to make 250 attendances in the year, to do which they would have only been required to attend regularly for 25 weeks. The actual numbers who accomplished this feat were 1,141,892. At the same period the children of school age (between 3 and 13) were estimated at 4,606,544. Of these 1,862,244 were not even on the school registers, and did not see the inside of a school from year's end to year's end. The average attendance, which is the best test of success, fell short of the school population by 2,769,364. Taking the lower and inadequate estimate of seven years (from 3 to 10) as the proper school life, there were still 1,387,400 children practically outside the system. ([1])

Of the results which have hitherto been obtained, the largest are due to concessions made to the League in 1870, which strengthened the educational features, and moderated in some degree the virus of sectarianism. The most important amendment was the power to acquire School Boards by the vote of the district. This gave scope for the greatest activity in putting the Act into operation, and it was taken advantage of by the League to the utmost extent. Out of 2,051 School Boards established in ten years, 967 have been formed under this provision, bringing a third of the population voluntarily

[1] Blue Book, 1875-76.

under compulsory bye-laws. This indicates also where the Act was weak. It failed in the same manner and for the same reasons that the Privy Council system failed. In districts where public spirit and intelligence abounded it succeeded, but elsewhere neglect and apathy were left to take their course. Notwithstanding the improvements which were secured, it remained an Act for bolstering up a discredited and unproductive system, which has never attained any high standard of excellence. If the amendments suggested by the League had been adopted years of slow transition might have been years of active construction.

The evil of such partial measures is that they deaden public movements, smother the inclination for improvement, and become the obstructives they are designed to remove. Interests which feign to be harrassed appeal for rest, and there is the invariable demand that the " experiment " shall have a fair trial. This disposition exists to such an extent, that Ministers who pass mere stop-gap measures are generally in a position to deride, for a time, all further agitation for reform. If the League had been dissolved in 1870, there was every likelihood that the question would have slept for another generation, with the result, that at the end of that time the country would still have found itself without a system adequate to national requirements.

The controversy of the next five years was productive of great good in several ways. The whole country was at last awakened to the glaring deficiencies and contemptible results of the system which had been jointly administered by the Education Department and the denominations. On the showing of the Inspectors themselves, a vast number of the schools which they visited produced results little better than those of the dame schools. The conviction grew that education needed improvement in quality quite as much as in quantity. Both parties in the State were converted to compulsion as the first necessity of the situation. But beyond this the Liberal party became united upon the desirability of placing education under public administration, and enforcing attendance through the machinery of School Boards.

The rapid growth of these opinions, and the influence which they exercised on Parliament, were manifested in the Session of 1876. The new Code introduced by Lord Sandon was the first indication that the Conservative Government had been penetrated by the imperfection and inadequacy of the system they were called upon to administer; but their well-meant attempt to raise the standard of acquirement was frustrated, in a large degree, by the resistance of the voluntary managers, who came forward again as the champions and apologists of weak methods and poor results. The Code, however, was, in some respects, an improvement, and considered in connection with the Act which Lord Sandon subsequently passed, it promised to effect important changes in the educational condition of the country. At the end of 1876 a law for universal compulsory education had been embodied in the statute books.

The aspect which the question had now assumed placed the Officers and Executive Committee in a position of considerable responsibility and difficulty. In advising as to the future of the organisation they had to take several circumstances into consideration. The object for which the League was established was now guaranteed by legislation. On the other hand, the means by which it was to be secured fell so far short in efficiency, simplicity, and liberal qualities of those proposed by the League, that serious doubts were raised as to the easy and successful working of the law. While an amount of school attendance might be obtained which would satisfy the statutory requirement, the Officers were unable to see how the steady and regular attendance, on which efficiency so much depends, could be secured as long as the payment of fees was enforced. They also doubted whether education could be raised to a proper standard under other than public management. It was evident, moreover, that in the administration of the new Act the principles of religious liberty and equality, for which they had contended, would be subject to constant violation.

But the League was founded as, and had remained throughout the struggle, an educational organisation. While there was entire unanimity as to the object, much latitude had been allowed to the members in the advocacy of means. The position, in this respect, was put clearly by Mr. Chamberlain at the annual meeting in 1872. He then said " Our one object, as stated in our programme, is to secure the education of every child in the kingdom, and in seeking to solve that problem, our experience, and the evidence we receive from other countries, lead us to the conclusion that the only possible way is by universal and efficient compulsion. That is the great point in our scheme. The other things are mere corollaries, and part of the necessary machinery for carrying compulsion into effect." By virtue of the new legislation an attempt was now to be made to carry out the same object by different machinery. To a considerable number of members, who cared comparatively little for the side issues of the controversy, this was a sufficient satisfaction of the motives with which they had joined the League. The polemical aspect which the discussions had sometimes assumed was owing to the attempt made by a Liberal Government to impose reactionary principles upon the country ; but the Liberal party was now pledged to a review of the whole subject. So far as the legislation of 1870-76 was an attack upon Liberal principles its amendment passed naturally and legitimately to the Liberal party, and to have maintained a separate organisation for the purpose would have been to preserve an appearance of divisions, where none in reality existed. It was felt, besides, that after the experience of 1870 and 1873, no strong Liberal Government could be again formed in which the principles of the League did not find representation.

The subject was fully discussed at a meeting of the Executive Committee held on the 11th January, 1877, at which it was resolved to recommend to a special meeting of the subscribers that arrangements should be made for the gradual closing of the organization and the transfer of its remaining work to the Liberal associations as part of the general policy of the party.

The final meeting of the League was held on the 28th day of March, 1877.

It may be useful to those who have followed the preceding pages to have before them the outcome of the last ten years of labour in the field of education. The writer has not space at his disposal to enter upon an exhaustive enquiry, but it is hoped that the tables in the Appendix will indicate with sufficient clearness the general result, and supply materials for the most interesting points of comparison. A brief explanation of the provisions of the Act passed in 1880, under the Vice-Presidency of Mr. Mundella, will complete the story of educational legislation down to the present time.

The public hears too much of the vast progress and magnificent results which have followed the legislation of 1870 and 1876, and too little of the region which remains unreclaimed. It is the interest of the partisans of one part of our composite system to prevent any further disturbance of its main principles, and therefore to make the most of its capabilities. The " amiable philosophy of optimism " which

42

prevails largely in society comes to their support. Since the dissolution of the League only one side of the shield has been on exhibition. There can be no object, especially on their part who originated the movement, in disparaging the substantial gain which has been obtained, but nothing so surely threatens the future of education as the public disposition to rest satisfied in the conceit of a presumed success. Without doubt some remarkable changes were produced by the Act of 1870. The mental energy and intelligence infused by the establishment of School Boards has acted like a new inspiration. If the returns made to the Government were put before the public in a shape which admitted of complete analysis, it would probably be seen that of real educational results, the vast proportion, almost the gross quantity of those of a high order, have been produced by the action and influence of School Boards. Yet the members of the School Boards, except those who are elected mainly as a drag on the machine, will be the first to acknowledge that their work is still in an embryotic state, and that neither in regard to methods of instruction or principles of administration, can the education controversy be considered as a closed chapter. If this is true of the great towns where education is under the constant stimulus of public energy and criticism, how much more is it true of the country districts, where every breath of independent opinion and every shred of local influence are, as far as possible, carefully excluded.

The Reports of the Committee of Council are a stereotyped admission of very partial success. The Blue Book for 1873-74 referred to "the large number of children who were not attending efficient schools, the small number even of those who attended such schools who did so with anything approaching to regularity, the large proportion of these last who were not presented to the Inspector to give proof of the results of their instruction, and the meagre nature of the results attained by many of those who were examined." The Report for 1880-81 repeats the same story in almost identically the same words, omitting only the sentence which relates to the proportion presented for examination. Any one who will take the trouble to go into the vast array of figures contained in these Blue Books and carefully balance and weigh their meaning will come to the same conclusion—that non-attendance, irregular attendance, and meagre results are the most striking characteristics of the system.

Perhaps the best test of the merits of a school system is the average daily attendance compared with the population of school age. It is not a perfect test, but it is the best measure we have of the amount of irregularity and absenteeism combined. Applying it to the Government returns it will be found that in 1871 the population of school age (between three and thirteen) was 4,606,544, and the average attendance was 1,231,434, the percentage being 26·73. To give an idea of the status which these figures represent it may be mentioned that at the same time a dozen of the American States had in average attendance from 54 to 40 per cent. of scholars, calculated on a school age of sixteen years, or between five and twenty-one. Yet there were Englishmen in numbers who denied that our case was bad, or that there was urgent necessity for improvement. In 1880 the school population had risen to 5,151,781, and the average attendance to 2,750,916, the percentage being 53·39. That is to say, in ten years the average attendance has been doubled. There is much reason to be thankful for this measure of progress, but in judging of its value two things have to be kept in view—first, what was the previous condition, and secondly, how the advance compares with what the nation has a right to expect, and with what is possible under a system subject to less friction. What is left undone is as important to our judgment of the results as what has been done. It is a good thing to congratulate ourselves on the 1,519,482 more children brought into school, only so long as we do not overlook the 2,400,865 who are still outside. Estimating on the basis of the present school population the average attendance in 1871 amounted to 23·90 per cent. The percentage of gain is 29·49 ; the percentage of non-success is 46·60. There is another light in which the figures can be put which appeals strongly to people of economic instincts. Our present school accommodation is for 4,240,753 scholars, but on the average there are 1,489,837 places vacant throughout the year. Counting the cost of the schools alone at £8 per scholar and without including the expense of other machinery, about twelve millions sterling is lying absolutely unproductive. And this happens in a country in which one of the principal obstructives to the adoption of a national system of education is the question of cost.

In the United States the school age extends over later and longer years ; from 10 to 15, 6 to 16, or even to 20, which is in itself an enormous advantage. In some of the most important and populous States of the Union, the average attendance of children between 5 and 15 ranges from 56 to 77 per cent.— in others the proportion of the school population between 6 and 16 in average attendance varies from 57 to 87 per cent. In some States an average attendance of 60 and 65 per cent. is obtained on the population between 4 and 20. These results it must be observed are produced where there is no compulsion or at the most the mere show of compulsion, but where the schools are absolutely free, where they belong to the people and are administered by the people, where education is not a matter of patronage and charity, but of right. The experience of America taken with our own is conclusive that free admission as a means of attendance is more productive than compulsion. But the American people are not satisfied with the results they have obtained, and are continually pressing for better attendance, and for compulsion as the complement of the law.

Is it not a fair deduction that if the means which were proposed by the League had been tried, something approaching to these higher results might have been obtained, the school life of hundreds of thousands of children have been turned to fair account, and the heavy charges for machinery which has remained idle have borne a fruitful interest?

The exact product of Lord Sandon's Act in the shape of additional attendance is not known. The increase in the average attendance between 1876 and 1880 was 753,139, but the returns do not distinguish between the numbers brought in by School Boards and the Attendance Committees. But quite enough is known of the Act to justify the judgment that it has been a dismal failure. The authorities to whom its execution was in the main entrusted had not been remarkable for large ideas upon education, and they justified their reputation by doing just as much as they were compelled to do and no more. The Act required that each local authority (Town Council or Board of Guardians) outside the jurisdiction of a School Board should appoint a School Attendance Committee. This was very much a formal matter, and was performed with an alacrity that raised great hopes at the Education Department. In about one-half the Unions, bye-laws were adopted on the requisition of some of the parishes, but only in fifteen Unions did the bye-laws extend over all the parishes. But this proved to be a matter of comparatively small consequence, since when the bye-laws were made they were very rarely efficiently enforced. In short this seemingly stringent Act, which Sir Charles Dilke described as the most tyrannic measure that had ever become law in any country, was laughed at and disobeyed by parents, employers, and local authorities alike. And the Education

Department stood in the background and saw the law defied and neglected with unruffled equanimity.

Where the Act was operative its effect was unfortunate. It set up a low standard of education, and has habituated the rural classes to that idea. The labour certificates enabled children who passed the second standard in 1877 or 1878, or the third standard in 1879 or 80, or the fourth standard in any subsequent year to finish their schooling and go to work, the certificate being good for all time. When the law was obeyed at all, the object was to obtain the lowest qualification for work. It was an encouragement to get as little education as possible as quickly as possible. More than half the children above ten are presented in standards suitable for a lower age. Forty per cent. of all the scholars leave school as soon as they have passed the fourth standard.

One of the first tasks of the new Liberal Ministry was to bring in a bill to compel the adoption of bye-laws throughout the country. This was accomplished by the short and vigorous Act of 1880. ([1]) By the end of that year there were only a few defaulting authorities, and for these the Department at once proceeded to make bye-laws, thus bringing the whole population under local compulsion.

The vigour with which the new Education Ministers are conducting the work of their Department, and Mr. Mundella's well-known views upon compulsion, afford the hope that some improvement in attendance may be secured, but the serious failure of Boards of Guardians as education authorities must suggest grave doubts as to the propriety of pushing the experiment any further. The powers of the Department for dealing with defaulting authorities are great, but their exercise on a wholesale scale has never been contemplated. Yet if every defaulting authority under the Act of 1876 is to become subject to these powers, it will require the permanent

[1] 43 and 44 Vict., c. 23.

location of a branch of the Education Department in the largest number of parishes.

The testimony of the Inspectors, which is practically unanimous, and which is the stronger because their bias would probably be in favour of the machinery created by the Act of 1876, affords no hope that education in rural districts can be effectually carried out under the present arrangements. The law, worked under pressure, may produce, for a short time, a fluctuating and spasmodic attendance, but it will never secure regularity. Indeed its penalties are aimed not against irregularity, but habitual neglect. But every one understands that irregular attendance is almost as bad as complete non-attendance.

The general conclusions to be gathered from the fifty or sixty reports upon the rural districts contained in the Blue Books of 1878, 1879, and 1880, are as follows :—

1. Regularity has been very little improved since 1870. Irregular, convulsive attendance is still the great evil which managers, teachers, inspectors, and all who are engaged in the work have to struggle against.

2. Illegal employment is common. It is the rule and not the exception. Employers do not ask for certificates. The law is often unknown, or, when known, it is disregarded by employers, parents, and the local authorities. Members of school attendance committees frequently employ children who have not complied with the requirements of the Act.

3. The regulations as to certified efficient schools are inoperative. Dame schools and private adventure schools exist in large numbers, and are encouraged by the local authorities. Where attempts are made to enforce the law, these schools often enable parents and employers to baffle it. Cottages are opened to receive children, who are badly housed and worse taught.

4. The attendance officers are of the worst description. They are ill-paid for this special work, and are generally fully employed with other duties. In most cases the relieving officer is appointed to the post, and a small addition is made to his salary. As a rule his compliance with his duty is nominal. If he is energetic at the outset he soon discovers that his superiors are not in favour of too great a display of vigour, and he takes his cue accordingly.

5. There is a general disinclination on the part of magistrates to convict. Sometimes they are afraid of unpopularity, often they are indifferent, they are generally disposed to accept frivolous excuses, and they inflict fines at which the parents laugh, while the ratepayers grumble at having to pay the heavy costs. Their administration of the law has brought it into contempt.

6. But the chief obstacle lies with the School Attendance Committees. They make a show of enforcing the Act, and having adopted bye-laws and appointed a nominal attendance officer, they leave the rest to chance. They are always slow to prosecute and very often they employ children in contravention of their own bye-laws. Sometimes they instruct the attendance officers to do as little as possible. They are the largest employers of juvenile labour and their duties and interests are in antagonism. They do not meet for months at a time, and owing to the wide area over which their jurisdiction extends, a great part of the district is unknown to the majority of them.

This picture is relieved by occasional lights, which only serve to make the shadows more conspicuous. Taken altogether the reports of the Inspectors are one long indictment against the rural local authorities of apathy, indifference, neglect or open violation of duty.

This is the state of affairs in regard to rural school attendance, which Mr. Mundella has to face. If he can succeed in improving it, as well as in raising the standard of instruction, and placing the administration of the Government grant on a sounder basis, his career at the Education Department will be fortunate for the country, and in the highest degree honourable to himself. But with the material he has to work upon the difficulties before him are obviously great.

It is manifest indeed that whatever temporary modifications and adaptations the system may undergo, the battle of National Education will have to be fought over again before a durable basis is found. The so-called compromise of 1870 was never accepted by the popular party, while the Act of 1876 was passed in the teeth of the strongest resistance which the Liberal opposition could offer, and under the express reservation of their right and intention to re-open the question at the first fitting opportunity. While the hands of the Government are full and overflowing, there is no disposition to press them, but if there was any sincerity in the agitation of 1870-1876, the present conditions cannot continue to exist indefinitely.

The struggle of the immediate future will be over the " Proposals " of the Education Department for a New Code, the objects of which are to raise the standard of instruction, to make the principle of payment for results more favourable to intelligent methods of teaching, and to eliminate the wasteful provisions by which the Government grant is given away on the average attendance of scholars in infant schools, who are not efficiently taught. The " special merit " grant which is a prominent feature of the " proposals " is a great step forward. The absence of some such money payment for methods as opposed to mere mechanical results was strongly animadverted upon by the Rev. E. F. M. MacCarthy in a paper published by the League in 1876. (¹)   In

---

¹ Analysis of Elementary Education Statistics, by the
Rev. E. F. M. MacCarthy, 11

In carrying out these reforms Mr. Mundella will be supported against the outcry of the vested interests, and the inefficient schools, by all who are earnest in the pursuit of a better education.

But more searching alterations are demanded in the interests of thorough efficiency. The points on which educationists chiefly rest their hopes for the future are (1) the readjustment of cost and the entire remission of school fees, and (2) the placing of education under the direct control and administration of the representatives of the ratepayers.

Compulsion, attended by the exaction of school fees, has broken down, except in regard to a select class, and in large towns such as Birmingham, where the school fees are low. The requirement of fees is the parent of irregularity, which in its turn is the fruitful source of unsuccessful teaching. With short sighted wisdom the Legislature insists on attendance on the one hand, and then raises obstructions on the other. Expensive machinery is created to enforce attendance, and then a direct tax is placed on every week's schooling; and this additional impost was placed on parents in originating an experiment which compelled them to make severe sacrifices in another direction. The difficulties of the parents have been increased. They were obliged to lose the services of their children, and their school fees were raised at the same instant. The children's pence have risen from 8s. 6d. per child in average attendance in 1870, to 10s. 4d. in 1880. And while this burden was thrown on the class least able to bear it, the tax on comfortable benevolence has declined. The voluntary subscriptions have decreased in about the same proportion that the school fees have been raised. The parents are directly taxed to bolster up a system of proved inefficiency, and one for which its advocates are increasingly unwilling to tax themselves. There is a meanness about these arrangements of which a wealthy country ought to be ashamed. If the clergy are excepted, the subscribers to voluntary schools generally contribute because the system costs them least. A small subscription saves a larger rate, the tax on parents is raised, and then the subscribers come before the public and pose in an attitude of benevolence.

But the free school question has assumed a more serious aspect than this. The tendency of recent legislation has been to bring the school into conjunction with the workhouse, and for a large class of parents to make the one a stepping stone to the other. This is no longer theory. The Boards of Guardians have had to pay school fees for five years. It is a duty which the Boards in the large towns dislike, and which they have protested against as tending to the degradation and pauperization of a large class of the community, but it is a duty which they have to perform, and the payments go on increasing from year to year. To complete the unnatural alliance the rural Guardians have made the relieving officer the school attendance officer.

There is another reason why the incidence of cost will have to be reconsidered. The 25th clause was repealed to quiet the Dissenters. But it was re-enacted in another form and with a wider application. Where hundreds of pounds were paid by School Boards for fees in denominational schools thousands are now paid by Guardians. The tax upon the rates has risen from about £5,000 in 1873 to £16,000 in 1878, £23,000 in 1879, and £32,000 ([1]) in 1880. The amount is not large at present, but it bids fair to become large, and to afford the denominational schools a fruitful and a certain source of revenue. But it was not the amount that the Nonconformists were concerned about; it was the principle. The principle of section 25 of Mr. Forster's

[1] Of this amount about £5,500 is paid to Board Schools. It is difficult to understand why the School Boards do not remit the fees in their own schools, and thus save the necessity, so far as they are concerned, of application to the Guardians.

Act, and of section 10 of Lord Sandon's Act, are one and the same, and even the language of the two sections is almost identical. The Nonconformists are no doubt indisposed to add to the present embarrassments of the Government, but it is idle to suppose that these payments will be permitted to go on for ever.

The necessity for universal School Boards is pushed again to the front by the failure of the Guardians as an attendance authority, and by the increasing efficiency, intelligence, and thoroughness of board-school work. Making all deductions for the sectarian squabbles they have witnessed, which were owing to the method of their election and the questions remitted to them for settlement, Mr. Forster's Act has reached its highest point of success in the administration of the Boards. They have brought a new energy and capacity into the field of education, they are sustained by the inspiriting influence of public representation, and they have enlisted a class of workers who pursue education for its own sake, and who had little sympathy with the narrow aims and antiquated methods of the voluntary schools. They have borne the heat and burden of the day for the last ten years, and have helped to fill the voluntary schools as well as their own. They have elevated the status, the emoluments, and the prospects of elementary school teachers. They have raised the ideal of national education. The tables in the Appendix will show how rapidly they have overtaken the voluntary schools. Notwithstanding the social tendency which has made the voluntary schools the select schools, and filled the Board Schools with the refuse of the streets and courts, they supply a better education, obtained through higher methods and superior teachers. But they cost more, it will be said. That is true. The time may come, however, when the common sense of the Nation will teach it that the cheapest article is not always the truest economy. If this is true of anything it is pre-eminently true of education. Mr. Cobden's wise words will be recalled—that "England cannot afford to have a little National Education." The motto of the School Boards is "Excelsior," and their work alone lightens the dejection with which otherwise our attempts after National Education would be regarded.

There is one final consideration which cannot be too often insisted on. Bishop Temple, in giving evidence before the Newcastle Commission said, "Everything I think which would tend to encourage local interest would improve the school," (¹) and he advocated giving to parents votes in the election of managers of the voluntary schools. It is only by direct representation that you can enlist the interest of the people and secure their co-operation in the work of their own instruction and elevation, in the absence of which no system of education can be a great or a permanent success.

¹ Newcastle Commission Report, 6, 331.

APPENDIX 1.

COMPARATIVE PROGRESS BEEWEEN 1871, 1876, AND 1880.

Year ending 31st of August.	Children of school age, between 3 and 13, less one seventh not supposed to attend Public Elementary Schools.	School Accommodation.	No. on Registers.	No. present at Examination.	No. in average daily attendance.
1871	4,604,544	2,085,414	(Not stated separately for England and Wales.)	1,509,288	1,231,434
1876	—	3,426,318	2,943,794	2,412,211	1,984,573
1880	5,151,781	4,240,753	3,895,824	3,268,147	2,750,916

Percentage in average attendance in 1871 (calculated on present school population) ... ... } 23·90.

Percentage of gain between 1871 and 1880 ... ... 29·49.

Percentage not in average attendance ... ... 46·60.

APPENDIX 2.

PERCENTAGES OF ATTENDANCE IN SOME OF THE AMERICAN STATES.

Average attendance on School Population between 5 and 15.

Massachusetts	77 per cent.	Maine	76 per cent.
New York ...	56 ,,	Illinois... ...	61 ,,
Pennsylvania.	66 ,,	Michigan ...	66 ,,

On School Population between 6 and 16.

Connecticut...	66 per cent.	Indiana ...	57 per cent.
Ohio	59 ,,	Kansas ...	87 ,,
Iowa	69 ,,	Columbia ...	56 ,,

On Population between 4 and 20.

New Hampshire ...	...	65 per cent.
Oregon	...	60 per cent.

44

APPENDIX 3.

COMPARISON OF RESULTS BETWEEN 1875 AND 1880, AND RELATIVE POSITION OF BOARD AND VOLUNTARY SCHOOLS.

NOTE.—The figures in the following Tables, so far as they relate to 1875, are taken from an "Analysis of Elementary Education Statistics," prepared by the Rev. E. F. M. MacCarthy, and published by the League. The comparative figures for 1880 are based on the returns in the Blue Book for 1880-81.

PERCENTAGE OF SCHOLARS IN ALL SCHOOLS WHO PASSED COMPLETELY (IN THREE SUBJECTS IN THE SIX STANDARDS).

YEAR.	I.	II.	III.	IV.	V.	VI.
1875	63·43	63·2	49·35	53·55	58·38	46·52
1880	65·23	66·57	59·91	55·61	58·75	58·56

PERCENTAGE OF SUCCESS ABOVE THE AVERAGE IN THE BOARD SCHOOLS.

YEAR.	I.	II.	III.	IV.	V.	VI.
1875	·57	3·09	3·94	2·73	1·61	·17
1880	2·41	3·24	4·51	4·80	5·01	5·79

APPENDIX 3.—*continued.*

In 1875 the Board Schools had the highest percentage of complete passes (*i.e.*, in Reading, Writing, and Arithmetic) in Standards II., III., IV., and V., and were second only to Roman Catholic Schools in Standard I., and to British Schools in Standard VI. In 1880 they were first in all Standards except I., and in this were second only to Roman Catholic Schools. In Reading they were second to Roman Catholic, British, and Wesleyan Schools.

PERCENTAGE OF PASSES IN EACH SUBJECT SEPARATELY IN ALL SCHOOLS.			
YEAR.	Reading.	Writing.	Arithmetic.
1875	88·28	80·04	70·91
1880	88·25	80·44	74·9

The Board Schools were in 1875 :—

·92 below the average in reading.
2·6 above the average in writing.
and 3·03 above the average in arithmetic.

And in 1880 :—

·11 above the average in reading.
2·39 above the average in writing.
and 3·39 above the average in arithmetic.

APPENDIX 3—*continued.*

HIGHER SUBJECTS.

NUMBER OF PASSES FOR EVERY 100 SCHOLARS EXAMINED.

(100 scholars may make 200 passes.)

In Denominational Schools.

| 1875 | ... | ... | ... | ... | ... | 105·5 |
| 1880 | ... | ... | ... | ... | ... | 86·29 |

In Board Schools.

| 1875 | ... | ... | ... | ... | ... | 112·08 |
| 1880 | ... | ... | ... | ... | ... | 97·61 |

NOTE.—The requirements for a pass have been somewhat raised.

Deductions from grant for higher subjects under Code Article 21 c (that is for Schools in which 75 per cent. of the passes attainable in the Standard Examination are not made) :—

In Denominational Schools.

| 1875 | .. | ... | ... | 11·31 per cent. |
| 1880 | ... | ... | ... | 5·52 ,, |

In Board Schools.

| 1875 | ... | ... | ... | 9·71 ,, |
| 1880 | ... | ... | ... | 2·87 ,, |

DEDUCTIONS FOR FAULTS OF INSTRUCTION.

Denominational Schools.

1875 Mulcted in 1·45 per cent of total grant.
1880 Ditto 0·81 ditto

Board Schools.

1875 Mulcted in 0·88 per cent. of total grant.
1880 Ditto 0·40 ditto

APPENDIX 3—*continued.*

INFANT SCHOOLS.

Denominational Schools.

1875   20 per cent. more infants taught in separate Departments under specially qualified teachers than
in classes attached to upper Departments.

1880   37·2   ditto   ditto   dttto

Board Schools.

1875   130 per cent. ditto   ditto   ditto
1880   276 per cent. ditto   ditto   ditto

PROPORTION OF ADULT TEACHERS TO PUPIL-TEACHERS.

Denominational Schools.

1880   One Adult Assistant to 3·03 Pupil-Teachers.

Board Schools.

1880   One Adult Assistant to 1·77 Pupil-Teachers.

APPENDIX 4.

RATE OF GRANT PER SCHOLAR IN AVERAGE ATTENDANCE.

Denominational Schools.

1875   ...   .   12s. 10½d.
1880   ...   .   15s. 5d.

Board Schools.

1875   ...   .   11s. 5¼d.
1880   ...   .   15s. 7¼d.

COST OF MAINTENANCE PER SCHOLAR IN AVERAGE ATTENDANCE.

1880   Board Schools £1 17 5¾
  „   Voluntary Schools £1 14 2

APPENDIX 4—*continued*.

SCHOOL BOARD RATES.

1880 Total average rate in England ... 5·1d.
" Ditto ditto in Wales ... 5·7d.

PROPORTION OF POPULATION

1880 Under School Boards 13,318,492
" Ditto School Attendance Committees 9,393,774

£22,712,266

EDUCATION GRANTS.

1880 To Voluntary Schools ... £1,681,684 3 10
" To Board Schools ... 627,081 3 3

THE STRUGGLE

FOR

NATIONAL EDUCATION.

BY

JOHN MORLEY.

LONDON:
CHAPMAN AND HALL, 193, PICCADILLY.
1873.

LONDON :
PRINTED BY VIRTUE AND CO.,
CITY ROAD.

NOTE.

ABOUT three-fourths of the following pages have already appeared in the *Fortnightly Review*. This portion has been carefully revised.

The remaining part—beginning with Section XIV., page 133—in which the writer discusses the expediency of making the elementary schools free, has not been printed before.

In an Appendix the reader will find extracts from the Elementary Education Act of 1870, as well as from the regulations of the Education Department. This may help to make the features of the existing system clearer to those who are not already familiar with it. Finally, as a means of financial comparison, the education budget of the city of Chicago has been placed at the end of the volume.

October 25, 1873.

CONTENTS.

THE STRUGGLE FOR NATIONAL EDUCATION.

I.

WE are constantly told by supercilious and inconsiderate Liberals that the present aspect of the question of national education in England is only a new version of the old quarrel between conventicle and steeple-house. The complaints against the Twenty Fifth clause are set down to the resentment of a religious faction. The cry for universal School-boards is explained by the spleen of dissent. The denunciation of Mr. Forster as a renegado from the principles of those Puritan ancestors of whom he made such untimely boast, is traced to the mortifications of nonconformist vanity and arrogance. The whole controversy is narrowed to the ancient story of rival churches and wrangling sects. Even Mr. Fawcett, in his new and slightly diverting character of "moderate churchman," is refreshed by a Conservative cheer for imputing sectarian aims to the very men who advocate national education and the absolute exclusion of denominational interests.

B

Now even if this were a true account of the matter, a Liberal might still think twice before making up his mind that there is no more to be said, nor any reason why he should take sides with one of the disputants more than with the other. He would do well to reflect that it is as unsafe to bring an indictment against a whole sect as against a whole nation. If dissenters and churchmen have thus drawn themselves off into two great camps, now both of them alive with the hum of war and giving dreadful note of preparation, there is presumably some very real and substantial prize at issue. Energetic dissenters and energetic churchmen know very well what they are about. No great body of Englishmen will take trouble and spend money and face the wear and tear of forming an army and conducting a long campaign, just to gratify a resentment or air a grievance. Those who assert that all this is done at the bidding of a clique must, in the face of all history, believe the dissenter to be a man of much docility and very little common sense. They can moreover have paid no attention to the actual evidence of the universality of the movement. As a body, the nonconformists are staunch and active in their hostility to the measure which a sounder and an older Liberal than Mr. Gladstone has described as the worst measure passed by any Liberal government since 1832.

A second reflection naturally suggests itself to any one who looks at the controversy seriously. Supposing that the present struggle is primarily and on

the surface a fresh outbreak of the old feud between
church and chapel, which of the two parties to the
feud is from its antecedents the more likely to be now
fighting on the side of political progress? We are
not talking of the minor social graces, nor of literature, nor of speculation, nor of æsthetic contributions
to our national life, nor of anything else except
purely political action. Putting all the polemics of
theology and ecclesiastical discipline aside, which of
the two parties has done most for freedom and good
government and equal laws in England? Apart from
the present issue, is the political tradition of nonconformity or the political tradition of the state church,
the wiser, the nobler, the more enlightened, the more
beneficent? Let history answer. Its voice is clear
and beyond mistake. There is not a single crisis in
the growth of English liberties in which the state
church has not been the champion of retrogression
and obstruction. Yes, there was one. In 1688,
when her own purse and privilege were threatened,
she did for a short space enlist under the flag which
the nonconformists had raised in older and harder
days; immediately after, when with their aid and
on their principles the oppressor had been driven out,
she reverted by a sure instinct to her own base doctrines of passive obedience and persecuting orthodoxy.

Yet this is the brightest episode in her political
history. In every other great crisis she has made
herself the ally of tyranny, the organ of social oppression, the champion of intellectual bondage. In the

sixteenth century, the bishops of the state church
became the joyful instruments of Elizabeth's persecution, and in their courts the patriotic loyalty of the
Puritan was rewarded with the pillory, the prison,
the branding-iron, the gallows.   In the seventeenth
century, the state church made her cause one with
the cause of the Star Chamber and the Court of High
Commission, with prerogative and benevolences, with
absolutism and divine right.   The nonconformists
shed their blood for law and ordered freedom.   The
church, when she returned to 'exalt her mitred front
in court and parliament,' retaliated on them for their
services in the great cause which she has always persecuted when she could, and always denounced when
she could not persecute, and bitterly suspected when
she has been unable to persecute and ashamed to
denounce, by urging on the most vindictive legislation
that defaced the English statute book even in the
evil days of the Restoration.   She preached passive
obedience with an industry that would have been
apostolic, if only its goal had been the elevation
instead of the debasement of human nature.   When
that doctrine became inconvenient, she put it aside
for a while, but as we have seen, she speedily relapsed
into the maxims of absolute non-resistance when
power and privilege once more seemed safe.   The
Revolution was no sooner accomplished than the
state clergy turned Jacobite, deliberately repudiated
the principles of the Revolution which they had
helped to make, and did their best to render the

Hanoverian succession impossible before it came to pass, and unpopular after. When George III. came to the throne, and politics took a new departure, the state church clung to her pestilent tradition. Her chiefs were steadfast aiders and abettors in the policy which led to the loss of the American colonies; and then in the policy which led to the war with the French republic. The evil thread of this monotonous tale has been unbroken down to the last general election. That election turned upon the removal of an odious and futile badge of ascendancy from the Irish nation. The dissenters were to a man on one side, and the dignitaries of the church almost to a man on the other. All this, it may be said, is an old story. It is so; but if we are told that the present struggle for national education is only a repetition of an old battle, it is worth while to steady our judgment by reminding ourselves what that old battle has been about. The story may be trite, but the moral is not yet out of date.

Nobody pretends that the state church alone is answerable for all the iniquities and follies of legislation and policy in which she has taken a leading part during the three centuries of her existence. The majority of the nation must share the responsibilities of the laws of the Restoration, of such outbreaks as the Sacheverell riots, of the war against freedom in America, and the war against freedom in France. The active leaders of the state church had no monopoly of intolerance or coarseness or ferocity or hatred of light. No one asserts anything so extravagant as this. What is true, and a very important truth, is that the state church has never resisted or moderated these coarse, ferocious, intolerant, and obstructive political impulses in the nation; that, on the contrary, she has stimulated and encouraged them, and where she could, has most unflinchingly turned them to her own profit. The clergy have not been the only enemies that freedom and light have had in our country; but the enemies of freedom and light have always found the clergy ready to lend unction to their own bad causes, and eager to dress up obscurantism and servility in preacher's phrases and Bible precedents. Nor again, does any one pretend that either high forms of spiritual life or noble sons have been wanting to the Anglican establishment. Human nature is a generous soil, even in the baleful climate of a state church. But it is her noblest sons, from Jeremy Taylor down to Maurice, who have ever found their church the most cheerless of stepmothers. It is not they who have shared her power, or shaped her policy, or exalted a mitred front in court and parliament. They have ever been inside the church what the nonconformists have been outside. Alas, they have been too few and too weak. Their names are rightly held in honour among men of all persuasions, but they have been neither numerous enough nor powerful enough to turn aside the verdict of the impartial student that the political history of our episcopal establishment, alike in England, in Scotland, and in

Ireland, has been one long and unvarying course of resolute enmity to justice, enlightenment, and freedom.

Dissent, it is true, offers little that touches the fastidious and sentimental love, which is so much in fashion in our times, for the picturesque, the gorgeous, the romantic, the sweetly reasonable. Its creeds are said to be narrow, its spirit contentious, its discipline unscriptural, its ritual bleak, its votaries plebeian. As politicians we need not greatly exercise ourselves in these high matters. Intellectual coxcombry and social affectation are welcome to expatiate upon them at length. The dissenters have not been favourably placed for the acquisition of the more delicate graces. To stand in the pillory, to have your ears slit, to lie in bishops' prisons, to be driven forth by the hundred from home and sustenance, to be hunted with Five Mile Acts, Conventicle Acts, Test Acts, Schism Acts, —the memory of these things may well leave a tincture of sourness in the descendants of those who suffered them, and a tincture of impatience with the bland teachers who invite them to contrast their pinched theology and sullen liturgies with ' the modest splendour, the unassuming state, the mild majesty,' of the church that afflicted and persecuted them. Dissent is not picturesque, but it possesses a heroic political record. It has little in the way of splendour and state, but it has a consistent legend of civil enlightenment. It may lack mild majesty, but it has always shown honest instincts.

II.

If this, then, be a true reading of the past, as it is assuredly the reading of our most competent students of the past, there is a fair reason why we should expect to find the dissenters on the right side in the issues of the present. If in old days war between the churchman and nonconformist was often in reality a war between the forces of political progress and the forces of political reaction, we may perhaps find on looking a little more closely that it is the same conflict which rages now. It is worth while to penetrate below the surface of an agitation that at first and on the top does not appear to go beyond recalcitrancy against the Twenty Fifth section of the Education Act of 1870. This section, as everybody now knows only too well, enables School-boards to pay the school-pence of the children of indigent parents at whatever school, denominational or otherwise, the indigent parents may select. Now the total amount contributed to the support of denominational schools under the Twenty Fifth clause in the year 1872, was no more than the trifling sum of £5,070 and a few shillings, and of this £5,070 no less than £3,405 were paid in Manchester and Salford alone, leaving some £1,665 as the amount devoted to the obnoxious purpose for all the rest of England. We may be sure that there would be no such storm as has raged about this paltry sum, unless it represented a principle which would sanction the devotion of far more portentous amounts to sectarian teaching. In truth it is only the key to a position. It is a small matter. So was the yeoman's house at Hougomont, and so were Hampden's twenty shillings. The sophists of the press ridicule the dissenters and secularists for raising such pertinacious clamour over so insignificant a payment. They do not choose to see that the insignificance of the payment is just as much a matter of reproach to those who insist upon it, as to those who protest against it. If it is frivolous and absurd to breed feud and disturbance in order to suppress it, why is it any less so to breed feud and disturbance in order to maintain it ? There is no better proof of the lethargy and indifference which the long growing decrepitude of the government has thrown over the spirits of politicians outside the two sectarian camps, than the fact that it is possible for writers or speakers to maintain that hostility to the Education Act has no wider or more positive foundation than the cession of five thousand pounds per annum to denominational schools. As we shall see in another place, the opponents of the Act are not wholly to blame for this most unfortunate misrepresentation of their real aims and substantial objections. The Twenty Fifth clause is the tiniest element in an enormous process of denominational endowment. The concentration of hostility upon this minor piece of injustice and impolicy —a concentration that was perhaps inevitable under the circumstances—has given the defenders of the Act a pretext for forgetting that we complain of the

injustice and impolicy of the whole. Such curtail-
ment of the true proportions of the controversy has
robbed it of all interest to an immense number of
those who would have been inspired with zealous
interest, if they had seen in the struggle for national
education, what it really is, one of the highest and
widest issues in the public policy of our own or any
other modern state.[1]

[1] I append a statement of the case for the agitation against the Twenty
Fifth clause :—

"The fortress to be stormed is sectarianism in education. The government
policy has immensely strengthened the position of our opponents : 1st, by
the temptation of the six months' grace, in consequence of which *the number
of sectarian schools has been increased about* 30 *per cent. ;* and, 2nd, by the
additional grants allowed under the New Revised Code, by which the
expense of maintaining these sectarian schools is rendered much less onerous
to their clerical friends and managers.

"The building grants are irrevocable. The annual education grants cannot be successfully attacked at present, as the government insist, with the
approval of the House, on equality of position as between the Board and
sectarian schools, and to reduce the state grant to the former would be to
increase the local expenses and make education unpopular. The whole system
is only vulnerable at present through the Twenty Fifth clause.

"Again, this clause is a practical grievance, which raises the whole question locally. The annual grants from the Consolidated Fund are confused in
the general taxes, and are not present to the mind of the individual when he
pays income-tax or drinks beer or tea.

"Further, the importance of this 'detail' is seen when we consider the
alternative. Mr. Forster says truly, 'If you mean to have compulsion you
must provide for the payment of fees for the poor, and while, as in most
country districts, there is only one kind of school, and that a sectarian school,
you must pay the fees to these denominational institutions.'

"The answer is : Place these schools under the management of popular
representatives during the hours of secular instruction ; and if you give
religious instruction at all, let it be at the cost of those who provide and
control it, and under a separate teacher at a distinct time, and then all
objection to the Twenty Fifth clause disappears.

"No one will refuse to remit or pay fees in the case of Board schools under
the control of the ratepayers ; and hence the settlement of this particular controversy can only be effected by the League scheme."

Here again is Mr. Dale's way of putting the matter :—
"As soon as School Boards were established it was discovered that the

It is worth while to make an attempt to extricate the question of the educational system of the country from this narrow rut, in which the mere party spirit of some and the indolence of more are well contented that it should be left. It was a very common opinion among Liberals in 1870 that the government had lost one of the most magnificent opportunities that any government ever had, of carrying the nation a long and distinct step in the forward way. Has anything

denominationalists were far more eager to pay the fees of children attending denominational schools than to provide additional school accommodation. The Twenty Fifth clause opened a new source of income for the managers of schools connected with the Church of England and the Church of Rome, and in every part of the country they tried very hard to avail themselves of it. Mr. Forster sustained them. If School Boards provided in their Bye-laws for remitting the fees of poor children attending their own schools, but not for paying the fees of poor children attending denominational schools, the Bye-laws were approved, but the approval was accompanied with a strong letter bearing Mr. Forster's own signature, and declaring that Justice required that the Boards should enable the poor parent to send his child to a school where it would receive the theological teaching the parent desired. On this principle the League joined issue with him. Had Mr. Forster contended that where the Board school was distant from the child's home, and the denominational school near, it would be reasonable to pay the fees, the controversy would have assumed a very different character. Had he said that where there was no Board school at all within an easy distance, it would be impossible to enforce compulsion unless the Board were willing to pay the fees for attendance at a denominational school, there would have been no grave difficulty. But these were not the grounds on which Mr. Forster contended that School Boards were bound to use the powers which the Twenty Fifth clause conferred on them. There might be a Board School within twenty yards of a poor child's home, the denominational school to which, probably under the instigation of a clergyman, a priest, or a Scripture-reader, the parent desired to send it, might be far less efficient, and might be half a mile away, but Mr. Forster contended that Justice required that the Board should pay the fees at the denominational school, in order that the child might receive denominational teaching. To accept denominational schools as a temporary necessity, and to send poor children to them in cases where there are no other schools in which they can be taught, is one thing; but to claim as a matter of justice that these schools should receive aid from the rates, when the children might be taught as well or better in schools under the control of the ratepayers, is a different thing altogether."

happened since to weaken the grounds of such an
opinion ? On the contrary all that has happened since
goes to strengthen them, and the fact that so many
thousand children have been got into the schools in
consequence of the legislation of 1870, does not in the
least affect the contention that they have been got
there in the worst possible way, and that the system
which sends them there is the least favourable to good
instruction, to social concord, to religious equality,
and to the sense of public duty and national responsibility. The Panglosses of politics are incessantly cry-
ing that all is well now that a slightly larger fraction
of the children are finding their way to school. All
would still not be well even if that fraction were a
great deal larger than it is.

In 1870 there was an opportunity for a thorough
settlement of the question, which might not have
wholly satisfied the Conservatives, but which would
at least have had the merit of carrying out the principles on which the ministerial majority had been
returned. Even the Conservatives and churchmen
expected such a settlement in a sense contrary to their
own wishes. They were prepared to meet and accept
it. They knew that this was one of the things which
had been meant by their defeat at the polls, and they
were ready to make the best of it. The English
Liberals, even the most exacting and impatient among
them, were fully sensible of the great difficulty and
complexity of the subject, but they remembered that
the government had already achieved two great

exploits, the Act disestablishing the Irish Church, and the Irish Land Act, each of them more difficult and more complex than the third great task which remained for them to perform. The cabinet did not shrink from dealing with Purchase and the reorganization of the Army as a whole; yet this too was a matter which called for the utmost delicacy towards powerful vested interests, the highest constructive power, and the maximum of administrative skill. People expected the reorganization of education to be dealt with as a whole. It was felt that a minister who had threaded his way with triumph through the two very arduous Irish questions was fully competent to manifest equal grasp, completeness, and firm command of the principles which had stirred the enthusiasm of the constituencies, when he came to the third question, the English question, about which the majority of the new electors cared a great deal more than they cared about the grievances of Ireland.

We know how these expectations were disappointed. An immense agitation had gone on for many years for the purpose of extending the franchise. Vast enthusiasm had been shown at the subsequent elections for the principles and persons of men, whose great cry was religious equality. The victory had at length been achieved, and those who had fought the battle expected to enter into the fruits. Yet the first great English measure which followed all this excitement and all this effort was a bill which Mr. Gathorne Hardy might have devised, and which a Conservative

chamber would not have rejected. Instead of con-
structing a system which would lean upon public
responsibility and duty, the minister gave to the
denominational system the most valuable help it has
ever had. As if to compensate the Anglican church
for the loss of prestige she had sustained by Irish disestablishment, he did his best to hand over to her the
elementary education of England.

The original Bill, as Mr. Dale has recently described
it, ' provided for the establishment of School-boards,
but they were not to be universal; it conferred on
School-boards the power of enforcing attendance at
school, but that power was permissive, and School-
boards might decline to use it. It contained a very inefficient conscience clause, and it permitted the School-
boards to make their schools intensely sectarian; there
was nothing to hinder the teaching of the Church
Catechism or the formularies of the Church of Rome.
*It enabled School-boards to give assistance to denomina-
tional schools from the rates.* It placed *no limit on the
time during which new denominational schools might
obtain building grants;* nor did it prevent *new denominational schools* from receiving the same annual grants
that were made to existing schools.'

Permissive School-boards, permissive compulsion,
permissive supremacy of the strongest sect, proved the
feebleness and want of confidence in themselves and
the nation, with which the government had shaped
their law. But the enormous subsidies which this
law gave, and was intended to give to the state

church, showed something worse than feebleness. The ministers professed to make the Board schools unsectarian, and then they encouraged the sectarian schools against them. What was hardly less important, they left the training schools mainly in the hands of the sects, so that almost the only teachers to be procured by the model unsectarian schools were persons brought up in the lines of active sectarianism. To save bare appearances they declared in name for undenominational schools, and then they did their best to enable denominational schools to win a permanent triumph over them. The statesmen who had roused the country by denouncing the ascendancy of a denomination in Ireland, forsook their own cardinal principle in a system for cherishing the ascendancy of a denomination in England. There was a political obliquity in this which far surpassed that of the Conservatives in establishing household suffrage. And Mr. Disraeli had the satisfaction of dishing the Whigs, who were his enemies. Mr. Gladstone, on the other hand, dished the dissenters, who were his friends. Unfortunately he omitted one element of prime importance in these rather nice transactions. He forgot to educate his party.

The result of this one slight oversight has been a serious disaster. It is absurd to charge those who disapprove irreconcilably of the education policy of the government with breaking up the party. It was broken up by the government itself in 1870. The party, as the parliamentary votes of its representatives

in the House of Commons attest, was hostile to the
extension of the denominational system. Liberalism
in 1868 meant this hostility more than any one other
thing. The assumption by the nation of duties which
had hitherto been left to the clergy, came foremost
among the hopes of those who had been most ardent
in the cause of parliamentary reform. It was the
first article in that programme of improvement and a
higher national life, for which, and for which only,
parliamentary reform had ever been sought by sensible
men. This was the centre of the party creed. The
break-up which we shall see openly consummated in
the course of the next few months, was practically
effected by the men who came into office to resist
denominational ascendancy, and then passed a measure
which gives to the schools of the Church of England
about 73 per cent. of the total sum provided by the
state for the primary instruction of children.[1]

No one in 1870 was so blind to the difficulties of
the problem, or so bent on symmetry at the expense
of waste, as to expect the government to introduce a
scheme that would thrust aside what had already been
achieved for primary instruction under the voluntary and denominational system—a system called

---

[1] The Education Grant for the year ending 31st March, 1871, was distributed thus:—

	£	s.	d.
Church of England	513,302	8	1
Roman Catholic	44,533	14	5
Wesleyan	45,552	10	4
British	100,064	11	2
	£703,453	4	0

voluntary, although, let us remark in passing, it had received some £10,000,000 sterling from parliamentary grants between 1839 and 1868.[1] But no one among Liberals suspected, nor did any one among Conservatives hope, that a deliberate invitation would be given to this system to extend and consolidate itself. Yet the half year of grace in itself constituted an invitation of this kind, of which the persons concerned availed themselves with prudent expedition, hardly believing in their own good fortune.[2]

But a still more decisive step than even this was taken, not only for the extension but for the perpetuation of the old system. The annual grants were increased, to the amazement and delight of the Conservatives, who had never wished for so unnecessary a concession. The increase of annual grants under the New Revised Code was an expedient as fatal to secular instruction of an advanced kind, as it was encouraging to the views of sectarian managers. On the one hand it lessened the cost of maintaining schools, so that a large and fairly managed school may be

[1] Of this £10,000,000 about six and a half millions have been paid to the church schools; add to this the church share of the cost of central administration, and the total of the church share of the ten millions will be seven.

[2] The Building Grants, during the six months' grace, were, in 1871:— 3,330 applications. Of these, 2,282 applications had been approved by the 14th June, 1872. It was estimated by Mr. Forster that the Building Grants would amount to £400,000.

Of the 3,330 applications there were—

Church of England .	2,885
Roman Catholics .	82
Other denominations .	128
British and unsectarian .	235

The total number of applications previously was only 150 per annum!

quite or nearly self-supporting; a Church manager
may thus retain the control of one of these "nurseries
of church principles," without any sacrifice being
required from the subscribers. On the other hand,
the extreme grant (half the total income), may be
obtained with only a moderate exertion, and teachers
have no inducement to increase the efficiency of the
school beyond a very low standard.

III.

Before going further, let us briefly examine the
nature of the policy of making the clergy the administrators of the fund devoted by the state to purposes
of primary instruction. Why do we object to this
policy ? Why do we assert that the maintenance of
this system of leaving elementary education in the
hands of priests is a fatal blow to our best hopes of a
higher national life ? This is a question which should
be answered in the largest way. It involves at
bottom our conception of some of the deepest problems which are destined to try the strength of societies
for perhaps two centuries to come. Before touching
this fundamental part of the controversy, let us remark
one or two more obvious, but still very important,
sides of it.

To begin with, the instruction which is given in
the denominational schools has been almost worthless,
and if it does not continue to be so, the reason of the
change will be the competition of the unsectarian
schools. We hear a great deal of the wonders that

have been wrought for education in England by the system of which the clergy have been the chief promoters. It is worth while to bear in mind the exact extent of the sacrifices made by the Church. The subscriptions to Church of England schools, according to the last published report of the Privy Council (1871-2), amounted to £343,084 13*s*. 4*d*. Whether that is any very prodigious sum, we shall presently consider. It would be ungenerous to speak of the efforts and sacrifices made by the clergy on behalf of their schools in a too critical spirit, if such efforts and sacrifices in the past did not happen to be made the ground of utterly disproportionate claims to educational control in the future. Nothing would be more ignoble than any attempt to disparage the services of the clergy in the spread of instruction. Still it is rather hard that the fact of the clergy having done a little in the past, should prevent the nation from doing a great deal in the future. When we hear the denominational system extolled as a magnificent and unparalleled monument of Christian charity and Christian energy, and when it is made to stand in the way of public policy, it would be a feeble postponement of justice to generosity, if we did not ask what after all is the outcome and upshot of this magnificent and unparalleled monument. It is this. " Of four-fifths of the scholars about to leave school, either no account or an unsatisfactory one, is given by an examination of the most strictly elementary kind."

This was under the old system. Let us pass to the new. What is that state of things which any one who knows the value of instruction finds so deplorable, and any one who knows the value of public money finds so wasteful? The last blue-book may tell us, and in a very few words. This is the key sentence to the right reading of the whole system:—" Considering the large number of children who leave school for work at ten years of age, it is not satisfactory to find that of the scholars above that age who were examined, as many as 46,916 were presented in Standard I., 74,654 in Standard II., and 81,602 in Standard III." (P. xii.) I subjoin in a foot-note the qualifications required by the New Code, so that the reader may see for himself what ability to pass in the Third Standard amounts to.[1] Consider then, first,

	I.	II.	III.	IV.	V.	VI.
(1) READING.	Short paragraph from book used in school, not confined to words of one syllable.	Short paragraph from elementary reading book.	Short paragraph from more advanced reading book.	Few lines of poetry selected by inspector.	Short ordinary paragraph in a newspaper or other modern narrative.	To read with fluency and expression.
WRITING.	Copy in manuscript character a line of print, and write from dictation a few common words.	Sentence from same book slowly read once, and then dictated in single words.	Sentence slowly dictated once by a few words at a time, from the same book.	Sentence slowly dictated once by a few words at a time, from a reading book.	Short paragraph in newspaper or 10 lines of verse slowly dictated once by a few words at a time.	Short theme or letter, or easy paraphrases.
ARITHMETIC.	Simple addition and subtraction of numbers, of not more than 4 figures, and the multiplication table to 6 times 12.	Subtraction, multiplication, and short division.	Long division and compound rules (money).	Compound rules (commonweights and measures).	Practice and bills of parcels.	Proportion and fractions (vulgar and decimal).

that only 27.14 per cent. of the whole number of children in the schools are over ten years old, and 1.32 per cent. over fourteen years old; second, that a large proportion of the children go out of the schools at ten, and learn no more as long as they live; third, that of all the children over ten who were examined in the year ending Aug. 31, 1872 (namely, 318,934), only 122,704 passed in all the subjects of even the three lower standards. Now make as many allowances as you will for those who were absent from the inspection for other reasons than non-qualification; for those who were qualified by attainments but not by attendances; for those who were for economic reasons presented in a lower standard than their attainments would have justified; for those who passed in two out of the three subjects and only failed in one: the broad result is still this,—that the mass of the children leaving school at ten or eleven, do so without any real, effective, or lasting facility in the use of the simplest intellectual instruments.

Figures and standards convey only one part of the evil. Another question remains, to which the answer is still more unsatisfactory. Even when a child can pass the new Third Standard, what does that mean? " As regards the actual amount of education which is got in our schools," writes one inspector, " by the children who are examined in the provisions of the New Code, I believe that a considerable number learn to write a fairly legible hand; but that *few learn to read without effort such books as children of their age*

ought to read with perfect ease. For example, I have
heard every child in the first class of a school read
without difficulty a paragraph of the book which the
class was being trained to use, and every one of them
break down signally even over the simple words of a
sentence in a book of a similar stamp which had not
been seen before." [1] Such children, therefore, might
pass in their standard and yet their passing would be
no guarantee that they could read ten lines away from
the book with which they had been crammed.

"At present," writes another inspector, "vast sums
of public money are granted on the examination of
children, who by reason of the disproportion between
their age and attainments, offer little or no promise
that their so-called education will be of any lasting
benefit either to themselves or the State." That is to
say, "vast sums of public money" are simply wasted.

Speaking of the half-timers, the same inspector
gives this account:—"At ten or twelve years of age
the unhappy children make their first appearance at
school, knowing nothing, and practised in all manner
of bad habits. The teachers do what they can; force
them perhaps through one or two standards; then
arriving at thirteen these ripe scholars pass full time,
leave school, and their education is over. That this
is no exaggeration is evident from comparison of the
numbers presented in any factory school in Standards
I. and II. with those in the upper standards, and from
observation of the age of the children in lower stan-

[1] Mr. Stewart's Report, p. 150.

dards. I give for illustration the only school I have examined during the week in which I write. In it 48 children were examined in Standards I. and II., and 14 in III., IV., V., and VI. Throughout the whole of Preston, which has an average attendance of more than 11,000, I do not think that 100 children have been *presented* this year in the 6th Standard. Yet it is obvious that *unless a child can show an amount of knowledge something like the higher standards of the Code, he holds out very meagre promise that any permanent effect will follow from his school career.*" [1]

Nearly every other inspector tells the same story of the ultimate worthlessness of those results for which we are paying so disproportionately. One of them even says this:—" I don't wonder that even the most intelligent parents take away their children from the elementary school after ten or eleven years of age; perhaps it is their very intelligence that makes them do so. Where there is little or perhaps nothing taught save reading, writing, and arithmetic, the school is in truth merely an infant school grown to undue and monstrous proportions." [2] " A really good reading-lesson I do not often hear," says one. [3] " I cannot conceal from myself," says another, " that the general instruction under the New Code is meagre and formal. . . . . I see this strongly in the reading exercise, where children of the higher standards who read fluently and with accuracy are often unable to

---

[1] Mr. Steele's Report, pp. 145-6.   [2] Mr. Kennedy's Report, p. 102.
[3] Mr. Syng's Report, p. 177.

answer fair and simple questions, either as to the meaning of the words used, or to the subject-matter of the lesson. I have always been of opinion that a child who cannot answer such questions ought not to be allowed to 'pass' in the exercise. For the reading is really no reading to him; it is only an exercise in sound and not in sense; it gives him no information."[1] This, let us observe, is an account of the higher and best children. "Teaching, in its highest sense," writes a third, "is almost extinct, and teachers seem inclined to think that their responsibility is now limited to training children to 'pass' the examinations prescribed in the New Code."[2]

All this is the natural consequence of entrusting public money to persons whose chief interest in the matter is something quite apart from the purpose for which that money is entrusted to them. We are thinking of the nation, of giving a chance to the poor, of improving those intellectual resources on which as a people of skilled trades we depend for so much of our prosperity. The little knots of managers on whom we so irrationally devolve the duty are not thinking of this, but either of their sect and its dogmas and shibboleths, or else of nothing at all. Mark then how little fruit we get for all our labour and money.

To pass in Standard VI. a child must be able to read with fluency and expression, to write a short letter, and to work rule-of-three sums and fractions.

[1] Mr. Watkins, p. 217.   [2] Mr. Stewart, p. 155.

These are no immoderate acquirements. Yet in this standard only 15,031 children were presented, and of these 1,236 failed in reading, 3,755 failed in writing, and 6,212 in arithmetic. That is to say, of the two million children on the school registers, only 8,819 passed without failure in the three subjects of the sixth standard.

We should never allow ourselves to forget what Mr. Mundella told the House of Commons in 1870, that the English sixth standard (in the Revised Code, not the New Code), our highest, is below the lowest Saxon, Prussian, or Swiss standard even for country schools. " Arithmetic was taught in the schools in Germany to an extent far beyond that which was deemed necessary here. In Saxony, the pupils before leaving school, were not only called upon to read fluently, and write a good readable hand, but they were also required to write from memory in their own words a short story which had been previously read to them ; and the children besides were instructed in geography, singing, and the history of the fatherland, as well as in religion. We had never yet passed 20,000 in a population of 20,000,000 to the sixth standard in one year; whereas old Prussia without her recent aggrandisement passed nearly 380,000 every year." [1]

Let this be an answer to those who remind us that eligibility for examination in the new Standard VI. practically implies, (1) that the scholar is fourteen

[1] Speech in the House of Commons, March 18, 1870.

years old, (2) that he has never missed his examination during five preceding years. Many children, I am told, who could easily pass in Standard VI. have not fulfilled these conditions, and are therefore classed for examination in IV. or V. Say 10,000 children come into this category—probably 1,000 would be nearer the mark—what then ?

This, therefore, is the first ground why we should not do anything to encourage or extend the denominational schools. Their secular instruction is bad. They do the work, for which they claim an eternal and substantial gratitude, so ill that the result hardly deserves any gratitude at all. Two-thirds of the children turned out by them come out in a condition of ignorance practically unbroken, and with a quantity of instruction so small as to be practically worthless. As was well said by Dr. Lyon Playfair, " What we call education in the inspected schools of England is the mere seed used in other countries, but with us that seed, as soon as it has sprouted, withers and dries up, and never grows up into a crop for the feeding of the nation." [1] Politicians who tell us that the one great object of their lives is to secure general compulsory education, seem never to think it of any importance whether the education is good or bad. They deafen you with the statistics of increased attendances, with the jargon of the register and the time table. To them instruction is instruction, and every hour at school is assumed to be fruitful. We hear how many

[1] Speech in the House of Commons, June 20, 1870.

thousands of schools are open, how many thousands of certificated teachers, assistant teachers, and pupil teachers are employed in them, how many thousands of pounds are required to defray the cost, how many thousands of children attend, and with that portentous numerical demonstration we are expected to be content. Yet a mere mouse comes forth from this labouring mountain. The children no doubt receive a certain amount of drill in cleanliness, order, punctuality, obedience; more than this, they are made in a silent and unconscious way alive to the presence of social interest and duty around them. They are not left in that half-wondering desolation, that forlorn abandonment, which stamps itself in the weird features of the gutter children of great cities. All this is true and it is important. But such drill is not enough, and no one seriously contends that it is enough. It is essential that the children of the workmen and of the poor should be admitted a little further within the gates of civilization than this. The denominational schools, as the figures of the results of the examinations prove, have taken no pains to admit them further.

It is hard to see why people insist so eagerly on compulsion, and declare that universal compulsion is the one thing for which they care, when the fare of which you are going to compel the children to partake is of this beggarly and innutritious quality. Hence the fallaciousness of Mr. Lowe's assertion that "we should endeavour to get to school the million and a

half of children who do not attend, rather than enter
into competition with instruction already given."
That is, we are to leave the quality as it is, and devote
all our efforts to augmenting quantity.   There can be
no more gross illusion.   Yet these denominational
schools, with all their bad instruction against which
we are warned not to compete, are the only schools
accessible, and according to the present law, the only
schools that ever will be accessible, to one half or more
of our population.   The gentleman's son at nine is
barely supposed to have begun his education, yet this
child at nine possesses an amount of knowledge that
represents more than the whole educational stock in
trade which is thought sufficient for four-fifths of the
children of the workmen.

Contrast this wretched, illusory, starved outcome of
your magnificent monument of Christian energy,—
Christian energy, mark, that has been substantially
supplemented by building grants and capitation grants
from the purse of the state—with the state of things
in Scotland.   " Every peasant in Scotland knows that
it is his own fault if he does not acquire such knowledge in his own school as will enable him to aspire to
the university.   Out of 3,500 students at the Scotch
universities, about 500 are the sons of wage-making
artisans or peasants." [1]   The common schools of the
United States are probably not so good as those of
Scotland.   Yet a professor at a university in one of
the great towns of the West lately told the present

---

[1] Dr. Lyon Playfair's Speech, June 20, 1870.

writer that among the lads in his university classes are some who rise at four or five in the morning to make their day's bread by distributing the morning papers; others who light the lamps in the streets; while one of the best students this year is a youth who goes down to the town every afternoon to earn a dinner by shaving at a barber's. In answer to a question where these strenuous pupils had previously been able to pick up instruction enough to enable them to profit by professors' lectures, my informant said it was the fault of any boy who had been to a common school if he had not picked up instruction enough for this. Of how many of the schools accessible to the corresponding class in England will their most admiring champions contend that this is true?

Mr. Forster has always, to his honour, expressed a peculiar anxiety that there should be as many ways opened as possible by which boys from the working class, who had shown special capacity and promise, should have a chance of higher secondary instruction. No other politician has spoken with such fervour of this most desirable consummation. Not all the politicians together could have done more than he has done to make it impossible. The instruction in the bulk of the denominational schools which he is bent on preserving and feeding, is so wretched that the children who can get no other are wholly debarred from ever being fit to profit by the higher instruction.

The children are being got into the schools, but what of that? Who that has had to do with the evening classes of a Mechanics' Institute does not recognise the deplorable truth of this picture which is given us of one of them, in a district where the provision of elementary instruction is counted unusually satisfactory :—" Apprentices come expecting to take up the sciences. Young joiners, masons, mechanics, and representatives of other trades come, knowing that a knowledge of building construction, practical and theoretical mechanics, and other subjects treating of the strength of materials, the erection of buildings, and the making of machinery, would be of great advantage to them. They find to their bitter disappointment, when they really have to face their work, that they have come to learn mathematics, knowing next to nothing of arithmetic ; that their spelling is so bad that some of them cannot write out the problems dictated to them by the master. Throughout all the sciences, from chemistry downwards, and to a great extent in the case of drawing also—which has been pronounced ' the mainspring of a technical education '—the same difficulty of want of foundation and groundwork is experienced." Thus the attendant at the night class after a day of hard labour has to vex himself with the harassing and cheerless drudgery of multiplication and division, of writing and spelling, instead of being fitted by an efficient discipline in his earlier youth to come direct to the higher work, whose practical interest would at once improve, refresh, and animate him.

It is no wonder that of the young men who come to

learn the special knowledge connected with a certain trade, and then find that they know nothing of the simple rudiments of the subject, while " some go back manfully to the three R's, not a few give up the whole thing in despair, and leave the classes altogether. It is precisely the same in elementary classes. Young men and women flock to the Institute when these classes commence. Scores of them can scarcely read, some can neither write nor cypher, and after a few weeks the difficulty of learning, shame of their ignorance, and temptations of one sort or another take a large percentage away." No doubt a percentage would fall away in any case, but it is too lamentable that public indifference nursing a public delusion should leave us contented with a system whose results are so disastrously useless and inefficient as this kind of story proves them to be.

Certainly no child below the sixth standard could do any real good in a secondary school. It is clear then that the present system and standards of primary instruction exclude all but a very small minority from so much as the bare chance of partaking of those vast means of educational endowment which lie open to the sons of the middle and upper classes. It will not do to say that the children of the poor have neither capacity nor industry nor time enough to come up to Standard VI. Nobody in his senses will believe that there is any disqualification about English poverty so fatal as this. It is not fatal in Scotland. It is not fatal in the United States. It is not fatal in Germany.

It would not be so in England, if the instruction of
the young were recognised as one of the highest of
national duties, instead of being a superfluity left to
the sects, and if the superintendence of the discharge of this duty were rescued from the control of
clerical managers.

The denominational schools can never make the provision of good secular instruction their main object,
for the excellent reason that the provision of good
secular instruction is a secondary object with those
who work them. These persons meant, and still
mean, sectarian instruction to be the first thing, and
secular instruction the second, and second it has been
and will be. Here is a recent advertisement from the
Church Times:—" WANTED, at once, £50 to rescue
200 souls from Dissent. Of your charity help!" On
further inquiry we learn that this means that it is
proposed to establish a church school in order to sup-
plant a dissenting school in a district at Swindon.
Yet the people who give this fifty pounds for the purpose of rescuing two hundred souls from dissent will
in due time be extolled and cherished by Mr. Forster
as persons who have made a sacrifice for education.
"In the present condition of church schools," we are
told by the National Society, "it is more than ever
necessary that they should be made the nurseries of
church principles. . . . This last [that the children
may grow up to be not churchmen only but commu-
nicants] is the object at which we ought uniformly
to aim—the training of the young Christian for full

communion with the Church; and as a preliminary to that a training for confirmation. *The whole school time of a child should lead up to this.*" [1]

Of course therefore secular instruction goes to the wall, and the greater the zeal of the churchman, the more surely will this be the case. We have no right to blame the sectarian managers for that. But we have a right to ask for the discontinuance, on the very swiftest terms compatible with practical expediency, of a system which has shown itself so deplorable a failure. Instead of that, the grants were increased— a step neither more nor less than fatal to educational progress. Those who were anxious that the quality as well as the quantity of education should be attended to, urged Mr. Forster to reduce the grants in the lower standards, even if he increased them proportionately in the higher. This most wise suggestion was rejected in the same spirit as most other suggestions likely to be disagreeable to the partisans of sectarian teaching.

Many clerical managers frankly confess that the withdrawal of religious knowledge from the subjects of the inspector's examination has quenched their interest in the whole process. They thoroughly distrust secular instruction. Their organs abound in the well-known nonsense as to its dangers, and solemnly warn us that writing and arithmetic do not make loyal citizens or virtuous men, that there is no moral power in grammar, that geography does

[1] *Monthly Paper* for August, 1872.

not implant generous aspirations, nor does spelling lead us to flee from iniquity. People who had only learnt to read and write, to spell and do sums, "would probably proceed in some such way as many did in Paris ; when they felt overawed by the superior power of authority, the people, trained under a system of secular education (*sic*), petitioned for the state to find them whatever capital was needed to convert artisans into manufacturers. When defeat had crushed the power of the state, they inaugurated the rule of the Commune, and by violence appropriated the property of the wealthy, and destroyed whatever could remind them of men in superior position." [1] This marvellous amalgam of wilful falsehood in fact with unconscious folly in inference comes from the official organ of that very important body, the National Society, and it is a fair account of the point of view from which most of the clerical managers in their hearts regard that secular instruction which the nation has to so large an extent placed in their hands.

IV.

The secular instruction in these schools is bad for another reason, besides the comparatively small value —beyond the attainment of the grant—set by the managers on secular knowledge. The teachers are bad. The most important of all the persons concerned in perfecting what ought to be treated as the most fundamental of national duties, have no ani-

[1] National Society's *Monthly Paper*, May, 1873.

mating conception of this duty, and no attainments proper for its efficient discharge. This is the inevitable result of the denominational system, for it is that system which stunts the training of the schoolmasters and schoolmistresses, limits their knowledge to scanty and unfruitful elements, and checks that independence and high self-respect which is one of the first conditions of influence over the young. " In Scotland," says Dr. Lyon Playfair, " the teachers of our elementary schools are University-bred men, and they bridge over the chasm between the lower and upper schools by their learning and zeal. It is wholly to this connection that we owe the position which Scotch artisans and the middle-class take in occupations where intelligence is a condition for success." Contrast men of such a training and such a temper with the corresponding class in England. Where are these men to find learning? Most of them come from the denominational training schools. And what is the notion of learning in them? Something most disastrously different from that of a Scotch university. Here are some specimens from recent reports made by the government inspectors :—

Battersea.—" The students of the second year [the last year of the course] fell below a fair standard of proficiency in grammar and mental arithmetic. They did very well in Holy Scripture, arithmetic, school management, and political economy."

Chelsea.—" The students of the second year passed with credit in Holy Scripture, arithmetic, English composition, and school management. They did not reach a fair standard in mental arithmetic, English grammar, geography, and Euclid. Their penmanship, also, was of very low quality."

Cheltenham.—" The students of the second year passed with credit in Holy Scripture and school management. They did not acquit themselves creditably in English grammar, Liturgy, mental arithmetic, English composition, and geography."

Culham.—"The students of the second year passed with credit in Holy Scripture. They were below a fair standard in mental arithmetic and English grammar."

Exeter.—"The students of the second year did not reach a fair standard in these subjects :—Mental arithmetic, English grammar, geography, history, Euclid."

Peterborough.—"The students of the second year did not reach a fair proficiency in mental arithmetic, English grammar, geography, history, or Euclid."

It is the same story throughout—narrow range of subjects, low standards, and lower proficiency. Why, there is scarcely one of these reports in which the inspector has not to complain that even the poor art of penmanship has not been properly mastered. We can hardly wonder that if these be the teachers, most of the learners leave their hands very nearly as ignorant as when they first went to school. You do not want Porsons or Newtons to teach rustics how to read, or handicraftsmen how to count. That is true. But the example of Scotland shows, as the common sense of any one who has thought about the art of education will tell him apart from the example of Scotland, that the work of primary instruction will never be well done by men and women who have themselves only gone a very little way beyond primary instruction. If the school-masters had, like the Scotch schoolmasters, acquired learning enough to know its value and significance, to feel a zealous interest in its diffusion, to think it one of the worthiest objects of human devotion to give the young a chance of entering into the treasures of human knowledge, we should not find four-fifths of their pupils coming away from them practically unable to read. But in England the schoolmaster is not taught either to acquire or to value learning. That is not the desire of his employers. They plainly tell us so. "There is need now more than ever," says the organ of the National Society, "that our teachers should be more thoroughly fitted for the religious side of the work; they should not only be religious people, but sound church people. . . . . Is it too much to hope that the Church will furnish from her earnest communicant members an abundant supply of really devout young people, who will give themselves earnestly to the work of school teaching, in the belief that there is no more effective way of benefitting their fellow creatures than by giving them a sound education in the theology of the Church of England?" There is no doubt an additional gusto in doing this, if your education happens to have been largely provided at the cost of fellow-creatures who repudiate the theology of the Church of England.

Of this we shall have something to say by-and-by. The present point is that bad secular instruction for the teachers is the natural result of the denominational system. "The tabulated results of the examination at Christmas last," runs the report of an inspector of Church of England Training Schools, "show continued weakness in the answers of the first-year students upon English history and geography. . . . . No subject has been taught in our Training Schools

¹ The National Society's *Monthly Paper* for February, 1872.

up to the present time with greater care and attention than the Holy Scriptures and the Book of Common Prayer, and there is no subject in which the students have more universally improved." The consequence is that while a Scotchman and an American can tell us with pride that it is the peasant boy's own fault if he does not carry away knowledge enough from the parish school to fit him for a college course, an Englishman has the sorry tale to tell that four-fifths of the children leave our schools unable to read with comfort, to spell, to write, or to count to any practical purpose. And let us add one point more. The sacrifice of mere secular knowledge to knowledge of the Scriptures does not even procure its own end. A Scotch schoolmaster would not have much chance of holding his own if he were not a hundred times better instructed in the Bible than the average English schoolmaster. And he knows a great many other things besides, and knows them well, while the English schoolmaster generally knows very few other things besides, and knows them extremely ill.

The Inspector who now undertakes the religious examination of training colleges which the state abandoned in 1870, assures those who sympathise with him : " The key of our position is the Training College. While we have religious teachers, it is really of secondary importance under what regulations they carry on their work. Such as the teacher is, such will be the school "—a statement in which, by the way, we cordially agree, and it is one not borne in mind by those who think the Conscience Clause a perfect guarantee for unsectarian teaching in the hours of secular instruction. "The responsibility thrown upon Training Colleges can hardly be overrated," continues Canon Norris. . . . . . "The contrast between their papers as candidates in 1871, and these same young people's papers in 1872, proves most satisfactorily what an advance in religious thoughtfulness a single year in a Training College may effect." Of course, the teachers are perfecting themselves in religious thoughtfulness at the cost of arithmetical, grammatical, and geographical thoughtfulness.

Nor does the inferiority of the teacher arise merely from the wretched kind of intellectual cultivation he receives. His whole position under the denominational system is the most unfavourable that can be imagined to anything like manly vigour and self-respect. He is the mere creature of the clergyman, and he knows it, and so also do both the clergyman and the children in the school know it. Some brawl took place this year between a vicar and the master of his schools. In the course of it, the vicar presumed to write a public letter in which he says, with more truth and boldness than discretion :—"I, not he [the master], am vicar of Dudley ; I, not he, am chairman of the managers ; and I will not allow him to insult me openly *without letting him know that our relative positions are those of master and servant."* There is perhaps rather more Christian energy than Christian moderation here, but the vicar of Dudley has very fairly emphasised the situation. It is true that the state grant is won by the exertions of the teacher, and that the state contributes largely to the school in other ways. This does not in the least diminish the clerical manager's sense of proprietorship. The relation between him and his teacher does really figure itself, as their too candid representative says, as the relation of master to servant. How can we expect to find " learning and zeal " in a teacher, who is only an upper dependent of the rectory ?

This is not a figure of speech. If any one will take the trouble to turn over the advertisements for schoolmasters and schoolmistresses he will get a useful glimpse into the working of the denominational system, and understand, first, why dissenters object to pay money for its support and extension, and, secondly, why the educational results are so lamentable. Sound churchmanship is one constant requirement, though the definition of sound churchmanship must be elastic. One teacher is required to be " Church, earnest, but moderate;" another "Church, sound and active." One must be free from rationalism and ritualism. Another must have "thorough evangelical principles." A third, wanted for some Protestant schools near the London Docks, must be "an earnest Catholic, and might live with the clergy if desired." To act as choirmaster, as organist, as parish clerk, " to train a surpliced choir in services mostly Gregorian in a beautiful church," " to attend

Sunday-school and take charge of the children at church, and to and from church," "to live in a parsonage, and take charge of and teach a little boy," to be a communicant—such are conditions prescribed again and again. In one case a "preference would be given to one who would do a little secretary's work, and give an hour's private instruction daily to a little boy of seven." In another, the teacher is "to act as clerk and *sexton;* harmonium, singing, and sewing required. House and £50, and two-thirds of government grant." Can you expect "learning and zeal" in the department of secular instruction from a class whose members are first and above all things required to fill minor church and domestic offices, down to superintending choir linen and digging the graves of the parish?

Let us here pause for a moment to meet an objection. We have been arguing that one of the reasons why the secular instruction of denominational schools is so inferior, lies in the fact that they are denominational schools. So, it will be said, are the Prussian schools. This is quite true. But mark two important points of difference. First, in Prussia the minister of the parish is personally charged with the religious instruction of the school. That is not added to the proper duties of the schoolmaster, nor, I believe, is the function of digging graves. The teacher is left to his own business. Secondly, in Prussia, denominationalism is not militant as it is here. There is the great chasm between Protestant and

Catholic, but you will not find, as in England, those
violently opposed sects within the body of the state
church, and outside of it sects enough to need a little
dictionary for their enumeration, all animated by that
spirit of "watchful jealousy" which Mr. Winterbotham used to admire so much before he joined the
government. It is the angry feud between Evangelical, Sacramentalist, and Latitudinarian—between
the state church and that dissent which an eminent
prelate classed with overcrowded cottages and beer-
shops, as one of the three great hindrances to the
progress of morality—it is this active passion which
gives to denominationalism in England a complexion
and significance which belong to it in no other
country. The denominational distinctions in Prussia
do not represent a violent social combat, and the
moment denominationalism was supposed to mean a
combat of this kind in the case of the priests, we
know what became of it. In England the sects are
at open war, and the schools represent one of the most
important battle-fields. "We want church teachers,"
says the organ of the strongest sect, "as the true
protection of society against modern dissent, which
does not believe enough, against Romanism which
believes too much, and against infidelity that believes
nothing at all." Again: "We have elevated the people
to the franchise, and by their use of it they can now
practically rule the course of legislation. Here then
is the Church's opportunity. She has two-thirds of
the voters of England under her direct teaching!

It will be her own fault if she do not imbue them with her principles, and secure their allegiance to her cause." " If the Church has made proper use of her schools, her grown-up children will know how to make a proper use of what they have learnt, and will manfully defend her." [1] We may be quite sure that if the German schools became inspired by designs so alien as this from a loyal and hearty devotion to the chief cause for which they exist, they too would soon have to lower their standards of secular attainment until they reached our own miserable level.

Let us not omit one more reason of the inefficiency of the denominational schools—their want of funds. Previously to the recent agitation the clergy who now boast of the extraordinary sacrifices of their party, were loud in their complaints of the meanness of wealthy churchmen, and the straits to which they were put, especially in country districts. Hence a low class of teachers and inefficient educational appliances. Now no augmentation in the subscriptions from private sources is to be expected, and every attempt will be, and is being, made to keep the cost down to the level of the barest necessity—just sufficient to earn the full grant from the state.

v.

By the consolidation and extension of the policy of leaving the clergy to administer the educational funds

[1] National Society's *Monthly Paper* for June (p. 122), and for July (p. 145).

of the country, we threw away one of the rarest and
most convenient opportunities, first of inculcating and
diffusing a new sense of the value of instruction, and
of national responsibility in undertaking its provision
and control; secondly, of deepening those habits of
local self-government which, as the contemporary
history of other countries is every day proving to us,
are at the very root of our superior political advancement. And we threw away this opportunity especially in the rural districts, where it was most
desirable to seize it and make the most of it. It
is a passing fashion at present to disparage self-
government, as cumbrous, tardy, unscientific, and
inefficient. People are ready to laugh at the vulgarity, the personalities, the tediousness of vestries,
town-councils, and boards; and undoubtedly there is
only too much room for improvement in all these
respects. Yet on the whole, when the vulgarity and
personality has filled its share of the time spent in
discussion, it is the opinion of those who have had
most experience of these bodies that they usually
come to the right practical conclusion. They do what
their most competent advisers would have wished
them to do. They occasionally bungle, and they
occasionally job, but all this amounts to an extremely
small fraction by the side of the bungling, the job-
bery, and the wasteful outlay, of the most minutely
centralized systems. From the Byzantine empire
down to the last Napoleonic empire, all history tells
the same story in this respect.

The services of local self-government in preserving good political habits in those who take part in it are too familiar a theme among English publicists to need further commemoration. Now all the objections in the mouths of the clergy and others against establishing School-boards in country parishes are simply objections to self-government, and a denial of its services exactly in those conditions where they are most needed. It is precisely in the rural districts that the consciousness of national life is feeblest, the sense of public responsibility most confused, the habits of collective action for public objects least formed and least on the alert. It is precisely in these districts that our present educational policy takes an important department of the local affairs out of the hands of all but the clergy (for as a rule the lay managers are dummies), and so there is a double loss. Not only does the administration of an enterprise largely conducted by means of government grants lose the wholesome supervision of a miscellaneously composed body of laymen. The laymen themselves lose one of the very few fields of public co-operation open to them. With that they lose the chance of improving in all the habits which such public co-operation implies, and they fail to acquire what it is so vastly important that they should acquire, the sense that the school represents a national duty and not a clerical hobby. We do not expect any transcendental enthusiasm from small farmers and country shop-keepers, but there is among them, as among other

people, a certain amount, if not a very large amount,
of the capacity of public spirit.   To make them take a
part in controlling the school would be doing all that is
possible, whether that all be much or little, towards
evoking and stimulating this public spirit in that very
department where its absence is most mischievous.
It may be urged that rural School-boards would never
avail themselves of the permission to make compulsory bye-laws.   Even then the rural districts would
be in this respect no worse off than they are now.
But of course no statesmanlike settlement of the question will leave so important a general principle as
compulsion to be applied at the will of the Boards.

Though tenderness for denominational schools did
not lead the government away from our admirable tradition of local administration in the towns, yet even
in them this tenderness has had most evil effects.   The
effect of the Act has been first, as every one knows,
that the election of members of the Boards is the cause
of the most bitter kind of sectarian struggle on every
occasion.   Secondly, in consequence of the action of the
cumulative vote, the Boards are often filled with eager
sectarian representatives, who attend to push or guard
the interests of this or that religious faction, rather
than to co-operate in the largest and most free spirit
in one of the greatest of public works.   Hence, while
in the country districts the opportunity of stirring
lay interest and securing active lay participation has
been thrown away, in the towns it has been used, but
used in the worst manner possible.

A final point deserves notice. One of the prime advantages which local self-government is believed to confer upon us lies in its guarantees for thrifty administration. The ratepayers themselves elect the men to whom the expenditure of rates is entrusted; the discussion as to the disposal of funds raised by rates is more or less public; the accounts of outlay are accessible to any ratepayer who cares to know how his money is going. None of these conditions is complied with under the Act of 1870, or the Amendment Act of 1873. School-boards and boards of guardians are empowered to pay the fees of children of indigent parents in denominational schools, and a steadily increasing sum will be paid in this way. Now, what does this come to? Why that, for the first time in our history, a sum of money raised by rates is to be handed over to irresponsible bodies, over whom the ratepayers have not the smallest control, who may spend the money so procured as extravagantly and with as little effective return as they like, whose proceedings are private, and who often publish no statement of accounts. A more flagrant violation of an organic principle of our constitution has never been committed.

VI.

An eminent leader of the agitation against the Act of 1870, a Christian minister of unimpeachable orthodoxy according to the Independent standard, which is no lax one, has been pronounced extravagant for comparing our battle against clerical control of the

national schools with Prince Bismarck's battle against
Ultramontanes and Jesuits.   Yet the comparison is
perfectly sound.   Of course he did not mean that the
English clergy are Jesuits, but that the expediency of
entrusting the clergy and the Catholic priests with
the control of national instruction turns upon the
same set of general considerations with reference to
progress, enlightenment, and the common weal, as
those which determine the expediency of allowing
Jesuits and others to corrupt public spirit and weaken
national life in Germany.   This is really a true account of the matter, and it brings us to the root of
the present dispute.

We have seen that the secular instruction furnished
in the denominational schools is thoroughly bad and
inefficient, when tested either by the educational
achievements of other countries, or by the practical
requirements of life.   This is so, first, because the
teachers are bad ; secondly, because the managers are
only moderately desirous that either teachers or teaching should be really good ; thirdly, because the
voluntary part of the funds is not adequate; fourthly,
because the schools are constantly found to be too
small to support an efficient system.   These hostile
conditions, especially the two first, we have seen to
be bound up with the continued association between
the schoolhouse and the parsonage.   We have seen,
moreover, that so long as parliament neglects to compel the formation of School-boards in rural parishes,
we are losing the only means of breaking this most

narrowing and crippling association, and we are at the same time losing one of the very few means open to us of stirring public activity and public spirit in the parts of the country where these virtues are naturally rarest. Our present educational policy means a continuance of bad instruction on the one hand, and an extension of ecclesiastical and sectarian influences on the other. Instead of an energetic effort to raise the quality of instruction, we are content with multiplying the recipients of an education that is in the vast majority of cases barely worth receiving. Instead of giving to the schools the mark of an independent province of the national government, we leave them in the dark, close, depressing, hollows of sectarianism. Instead of consistently adhering to the progressive principle of religious equality, we have gone back several steps to give new life to the principle of Anglican supremacy. In short, as if the state church were too poor or too weak before, we have provided it with new revenues, armed it with fresh instruments of social influence, and finally confirmed it in the possession of an authority and an office which it has proved itself wholly incapable of discharging efficiently in the past, and which its leaders and spokesmen now openly declare their intention of using for their own sinister purposes in the future.

These are no mere phrases. I have already quoted passages from the organ of the National Society and other sources, in which the deliberate intention of

E

indirectly making the schools active sectarian agencies is avowed openly and without shame. More than this, we may test the disinterestedness of that educational zeal for which the clergy have taken such grossly excessive credit to themselves, by a single fact—their energetic opposition to the formation of School-boards. I never met a country clergyman who did not acknowledge the necessity of compulsion, direct or indirect, as the only means of rescuing the children from the eagerness of parents for their earnings, and the eagerness of the farmers for their labour. Some were for direct parliamentary compulsion, others for enforced labour certificates with progressive standards according to age, and penalties on the employer in case of breach. In either case, compulsion was uniformly admitted to be indispensable, the first essential of improved instruction. A law is passed, conferring this power of compulsion for which the clergy professed to be hungering and thirsting. And what happens? Why, the clergy instantly unite with one consent and with all their might to withstand the introduction of the machinery appointed by law for the introduction of compulsion, simply because that machinery would involve lay participation in school management, and the disuse of denominational formularies, though not the abandonment of denominational teaching. In other words, they are on their own showing wilfully sacrificing the instruction of the young to their own jealousy of lay co-operation, and their resolution not to part with the Church Catechism. In some cases, they even condescend to the device of frightening their parishioners by strange statements of the cost of board schools, into paying a so-called voluntary rate that amounts to exactly the same sum as a legitimately levied rate. They thus relieve themselves and the previous subscribers, and make the parish pay for the school, while they keep from the parish any share in the control of the school which it pays for, and reject that power of obtaining compulsory attendance which before the Act they habitually pronounced to be the one change which is more indispensable and important than all others put together. With such an exhibition as this before our eyes, it is no breach of charity to regard the clerical professions of disinterested zeal for the instruction of the rural poor as too often a mere piece of self-deception in some, and of pure hypocrisy in others.

Nor again is the term of re-endowment a mere phrase. The church schools do, as a matter of fact, receive half a million a year from the public taxes, and this sum is likely very rapidly to rise to three quarters of a million, besides what they receive from rates, what they have received from building grants, and what is paid to the church training schools.[1] This glaring fact of sectarian endowment is met by the

[1] The grant for year ending August 31, 1872, £561,655 11s. 1d. The Church of England schools, before the Act, had received about a million and a quarter for buildings. The Church of England Training Schools receive some £60,000 a year from Government, as against slightly more than half that sum given to the training schools of all the other denominations together.

assertion that such payments are only made for the secular part of the teaching, and do not therefore constitute an appropriation for sectarian purposes. Such an assertion is a mere verbal proposition, without the slightest correspondence to the real conditions of the case. In the first place, large and well-managed schools may be, and actually are, paid for by fees and grants; the parents and the government pay for the whole outlay, and that voluntary aid which is theoretically supposed to provide the sectarian instruction, neither does nor is required to do any such thing.

I extract the following instances of what are meant by voluntary schools, from a parliamentary return of income and expenditure for Manchester and Salford, for 1870 and 1871, now before me :—

St. Saviour's, Chorlton, total income in 1870, £610, to which the voluntary contribution was £16.

Ancoats (Presbyterian), in 1871, total income, £717, to which the voluntary contribution was £66.

St. Barnabas, £356, of which the voluntary contribution was £5.

St. Jude's, total, £330 ; voluntary, £35.

St. Philip's, total, £505 ; voluntary, £45.

St. Wilfrid's (Catholic), total income, £891 ; voluntary part of it, £56 (not much more than the amount paid by the Board under the Twenty Fifth Clause).

St. George's, Hulme, in 1870, total, £458, of which the voluntary portion was exactly *one pound;* in 1871, total £483, voluntary £11.

Thus a school may be pointed to as a triumph of

the voluntary system when one four-hundred-and-fifty-eighth part of its income is derived from subscriptions! People ordinarily suppose that there is some obligatory proportion between voluntary subscriptions and government grants, as there used to be in respect of building grants. The minister has been vainly pressed to establish some such proportion. In the Debates of 1870, it was pointed out very clearly that "if denominational schools could be carried on by government grants and school pence, the principle laid down by the Prime Minister would be completely broken through—the principle, namely, that the government did not pay for the religious teaching of children in denominational schools. The government, therefore, should require that a certain proportion of the money for these schools should be raised by means of voluntary contributions. The amount might be fixed at one-sixth of the total expense, or at an amount equal to one-third of the grant." [1] No such amount has been fixed, and there is nothing to hinder a denominational school from subsisting wholly on the pence and the grants. The operation of the Twenty Fifth Clause, especially if the clause were applied as it would be but for the incessant vigilance of secularists and nonconformists, would obviously tend to make this proceeding still easier and more common.

In the second place, it is a palpable fallacy to say that the state aid does nothing for the sectarian part of the instruction. A payment without which an

---

[1] Mr. Hibbert in the House of Commons, June 23, 1870.

institution could not subsist, though it may be nominally made for special purposes, is and must be a payment for the institution as a whole. If I subscribe to a trade union, that subscription supports the strike fund no less than the benefit fund, however decisive may be the limitation of my intention to one of them. If a rich man subscribes to a newspaper that advocates the politics which he approves, while it also advocates the theology which he disapproves, though it may for this or that reason be worth his while to overlook the points of disagreement, yet he would certainly never pretend that he was not in fact helping to pay for the theological, as well as the political advocacy.

It is not merely that the state chooses to buy certain wares, of which it is in need, from a number of people who happen to keep in their shops a stock of wares of another kind as well as these. The state is something very different from a mere customer, unless we extend the idea of a customer so as to make it describe the person who has found the larger part of the capital, and assists in the organization of the business, and virtually confers a partial monopoly on the dealer. The state may disclaim all concern in the sectarian teaching, but as the school in which it is given could only be kept open on condition of state aid, it is the shallowest quibble to say that this state aid does not go to the maintenance of the sectarian teaching which would not be so given without it. We are told, for instance, that no subject has been taught in the training schools with greater care than the Book of Common Prayer, nor any subject in which the students have made so much improvement. Next let us remember that these schools receive from the State about six times as much per annum as they receive from voluntary sources.[1] Is it not childish to ask us to believe that not a penny of these six-sevenths of the expenditure helps to pay for that part of the instruction for which the managers are most careful, and in which the students have most improved?

No sensible man will be imposed on for a moment by an artificial division of the purposes of the grants. In subsidising the denominational system you are subsidising all the incidents of the system. Every grant to a sectarian school is a direct grant to the sect. These payments constitute a policy of concurrent endowment in thin disguise. And they are made on the evil principle that to him that hath shall be given; the sect which is the strongest is made yet stronger. It has been constantly said that as the other sects may all establish schools equally entitled to state aid with those of the state church, the latter has no advantage and the former have no grievance. This is to forget that those who are not members of

[1] In the year 1870 for instance, the voluntary subscriptions to the Church of England training schools were £10,064 9s. 2d., and the Government grants to the same schools, £59,016 5s. 2d. From the same Report, the following important fact is also to be drawn. There are three British or unsectarian training schools, and forty-two undenominational schools. Of the students from the three undenominational schools, 30 per cent. passed in the first division. Of the students from the forty-two denominational schools, 17 per cent. passed in the first division. Even making all allowance for the circumstance, so unlucky for the credit of human nature, that with every increase of the area we must expect an increase in the ratio of blockheads, this is still a striking comment on the relative efficiency of the two systems.

the state church and belong to the less wealthy classes of the community have to pay for their own places of worship, and their own ministers. Churchmen have not had to provide their own religious service and ministration. Besides this they are by far the richest of the sects. It is not wonderful, then, that they should have built more schools and done more than the other sects for the cause of sectarian education, little as all that they have done really comes to.

Mr. Dale has put the state of the case very clearly: —" The Church of England, notwithstanding its internal divisions, has a very compact organization. All the churchmen in a parish can unite without difficulty to erect a school and to contribute to its maintenance. The school buildings can be used for church purposes—for Sunday-schools, for evening Bible-classes, for mothers' meetings, and for all the religious organizations which the church sustains. The Nonconformists in the parish may be more numerous than the churchmen, and may be equally zealous for education. But the Wesleyans may not be strong enough to support a Wesleyan school, nor the Congregationalists to support a Congregational school, nor the Unitarians to support a Unitarian school. If they suppress their religious differences and agree to establish a school in which there shall be no religious teaching to which Wesleyans, Congregationalists, or Unitarians can object, the obvious result is that the buildings cannot be used by any of them for religious purposes, and that while, from the conditions under

which the state makes its grants for educational purposes, the Church of England has a school in which
Church of England doctrine is taught, the various
Nonconformist churches are precluded, even if they
desire it, from teaching their own faith in the school
which they assist to maintain. Except in large towns,
where individual congregations are large and wealthy,
and can maintain schools of their own, all that the
Nonconformist churches can do is to secure a school
with no theological colour at all, while all over the
country the Church of England can have schools in
which its catechisms and formularies are taught with
all the fulness that its most zealous adherents can
desire."

Yet because it is the richest sect and is already an
endowed church, this is the body which is to receive
a further endowment of seventy-three per cent. out of
the annual grant for elementary education. " If it be
said," Mr. Gladstone urged, " that there is a recognition of the church in the liberal terms we propose for
the voluntary schools, such an assertion would only
mean that the palm is given to those who win."[1] A
poorer sophism was never coined even in that busy
mint of logical counterfeits. The palm given to those
who win! As if, when the barrier was dropped, the
competitors started fair ; as if the one had not had
every advantage which the public wealth could confer
and private wealth utilize and augment, while the
other was gleaning for bare subsistence among the

[1] Speech in the House of Commons, June 24, 1870.

lean fields of voluntaryism. The church had gone
through a long course of diligent preliminary training
in the race for public money, while Dissent had stood
with austere self-respect aloof from what she deemed
an ignoble chase. Why, the dissenters have in an
immense proportion of the parishes in England been
forcibly prevented by the landowners from so much as
acquiring a bit of land on which to rear chapel or
school, and on more than one great estate there has
been a sort of private Conventicle Act positively for-
bidding, under penalty of ejection, so much as a
prayer-meeting in a cottage kitchen. A strange
handicap, indeed, in which you clap the heaviest
weight on to the youngest competitor, and give the
longest start to the stoutest and strongest, and then
magnanimously hail the winner with an unctuous cry
of *The palm to him who wins !*

This is not the place for a general discussion of the
policy of religious endowment, concurrent or otherwise. The difference between concurrent and single
endowment is not important, because after all the
funds of the Anglican Church are really devoted to
concurrent endowment. The Anglican body, for all
its sacerdotal pretensions, is only a loose bundle of
discordant sects, who are constituted into one Catholic
and Apostolic Church by the Erastian bonds of an
act of parliament. We shall only make two remarks.
One is that this was not the policy which the Liberal
voters intended to support in 1868. The other is
that if we are to have the sects endowed with public

money, that policy ought to be carried out directly, and not by impeding so momentous a national function as the provision of instruction for the people. And the present system does impede this function. It hands over the difficult and important task of controlling secular instruction to persons who are thinking not of knowledge, but of " bulwarks of the Church," "nurseries of Church principles," institutions for " rescuing souls from Dissent," and the other sinister uses to which men put the schools that are called national, when they are in truth sectarian, and voluntary, when they are in truth largely paid for out of taxes, rates, and fees.

VII.

The re-endowment of the group of sects calling themselves the Church of England is not more important nor more mischievous in its effect on national instruction than the indirect influence of various kinds which has been placed, and according to present appearances permanently placed, in the hands of the clergy. To give them the schools is to give them a new platform, a new instrument, a new organ of power—paid for by public money, and instituted by the law of the land. To do this is to augment their social authority and to strengthen their sectarian power. Do the English constituencies in their hearts desire either of these results ? The resolution of five years ago to pull down the Protestant establishment in Ireland is the answer to such a question as this.

Our people have an instinctive distrust of clerical influence—a distrust which often takes vulgar and even unjust forms, but which is at bottom one of the soundest and shrewdest of all our national impulses. What respect can we have in a time of active scientific inquiry for men who at the age of three-and-twenty bind themselves in heavy penalties never again to use their minds freely so long as they live? We may look upon the victims of these emasculating vows with more or less of friendly tolerance and personal sympathy, but it is impossible to forget that as an order they move through the world of light and knowledge, of discovery and criticism and new truth,. with bandaged eyes and muffled ears. They are in their non-official relations as amiable, kindly, well-meaning as other bodies of men, if you will only excuse them from using their minds out of the prescribed bounds, or from coming to other than the prescribed conclusions. They are ever warning the world against science falsely so called, by which they mean the principal triumphs of genius and industry; and you can hardly go into a church without hearing a sermon against that abuse of intellect, that pride of reason, which is the awful and desolating mark of these latter days. Laymen cannot discuss with figures in masks, fearful of gainsaying an article, or infringing a rubric, or slipping beyond a judgment of the Privy Council. "There appears to me in all the English divines," said Dr. Arnold, "a want of believing or disbelieving anything because it is true or false. It is a question which does not seem to occur to them." This is really the case. It is as true of the most obscure, as of the most illustrious of these divines ; of the village rector as of the primate ; and if the valorous man who made this most just remark had lived, he would have found it especially true of some distinguished laymen and divines who were inspired at Rugby.

It has been contended that dissenting ministers are as narrow, as hostile to science, as ungenerously cultivated, as little imbued with faith and hope in progress, as the clergy of the established church. I question the fact, but what if they are ? However narrow they may be, at least they do not impudently ask the state to give them my money for teaching their opinions. They attend to their own doctrines and leave me to mine. I am in no way concerned with the religious notions of dissenting ministers, because dissenters claim neither money nor position nor official recognition in virtue of these notions. I am concerned with the notions of the state clergy, because the clergy aspire to control the instruction of the people, and to make the tax-gatherers and rate-collectors provide them with funds.

A little shiver of intellectual liberalism in some of the more courageous of the Anglican clergy should not blind us to the intensely obscurantist character of the rank and file. It is of no avail to point to the tiny handful of clergymen who accept liberal and modern ideas, from Dr. Thirlwall downwards. Such

men, like Mr. Jowett and other academic liberals of
his stamp, as well as the head masters of some of the
public schools, are only clergymen by accident. They
do not belong to the clerical profession. If any one
wants to understand the real composition of the great
clerical army, he should read the proceedings of the
two houses of Convocation. It is here that we perceive the clerical mind in its nakedness—here, or in
petitions for the recognition of the practice of auricular confession, or in remonstrances against the
appointment of Dr. Temple, or in applications for a
faculty to set up a baldacchino, or in such papers as
the *Church Times*, which curses " the miserable Protestants," and the *Rock* and the *Record*, which curse
" the miserable Ritualists," or in such protestations
as that of so comparatively modern and enlightened a
person as Mr. Kingsley, that life will be worth very
very little to him if there is to be any tampering with
that priceless monument of wisdom and charity, the
Athanasian Creed.

And we have to remember that all the movement is
in this direction ; is towards what the Primate the
other day called " strong opinions." These widening
extremes of repulsion are in the nature of things. As
the speculation of the age drifts further and further
away from the too narrow contents of the ancient formularies, those who cling to these formularies cling
to them all the more tightly, and interpret them all
the more superstitiously. Twenty years ago you could
not have found five hundred men in English orders

to petition for auricular confession. To-day we have an eminent dignitary thanking the Almighty that "priests by thousands are teaching and practising private confession." The old-fashioned moderation of doctrine is changed into enthusiasm and excess, and our age of science is also the age of deepening superstition and reviving sacerdotalism. The same tendency is at work in that older church which emulates the zeal of the Church of England for sectarian teaching. There, too, the spread of liberal ideas has engendered a vehement reaction, and the catholic piety of an older time has been transformed into the black and anti-social aggression of the Syllabus and the Encyclical.

Yet these are the bodies, standing thus markedly in hostility to all the progressive tendencies of the time, which it has been thought statesmanlike and liberal to invest with a new kind of social authority, and formally to re-entrust with a most important social function. While the statesmen of every other country in Europe, from Austria downwards, are fully aware that the priests had too much power, it was left for liberal leaders in England to find out that priests had too little power, and straightway to hasten to make it greater. This is no wrangle about the drawing of a clause, no dispute as to the payment of a few hundred pounds a year. It is the very gravest question of public policy that could have been raised, and can only be understood by those who take the very widest measure of political expediency.

It is no answer to our contention of the retrograde direction of the course that the Liberal leaders have pursued, to repeat the worn assertions that the English clergy are not as other clergy, that they have never been a caste apart from the rest of men, that they are connected with the public life of the country in many ways, that they are English gentlemen before they are clergymen, and so forth. The English clergy are not ultramontane, if you mean that, and they are not celibate nor childless, nor have they by any means taken vows of poverty or obedience. But they represent a strong and resolute corporate spirit in spite of these humanizing conditions, and in spite of the deep mutual hatred of the rival factions of which they are composed. They may fill the air with remonstrances and petitions and gravamina against one another, but they always close their ranks against the common enemy. A Broad churchman will resent the formation of a School-board in his parish as energetically as the sacerdotalist. Individually often mild and candid, collectively they are always as narrow, intolerant, and angry as circumstances permit. For individual clergymen one often has, and cannot but have, the warmest respect and affection; like other men, they are often full of that milk of human kindness which is dearer to us than light and dearer than new ideas. But they are seldom strong enough to resist the overwhelming pressure of the organization to which they belong, and few persons reflect how closely and in how many forms this organization

comes to the life of the ordinary working clergyman. He has his company drill, his regimental
drill, his brigade drill, his battalion drill; he is
banded with his fellows as a unit in the ruridecanal
system, in the archidiaconal system, in the diocesan
system. The habit of acting together in bodies which
broadens and strengthens other citizens by forcing
them to sacrifice personal prejudices for the sake of a
public cause, narrows and weakens the priest by
forcing him to sacrifice his civic impulse for the sake
of mere ecclesiastical ends. They all alike come to
distrust the lay mind. Above all, they are secretly
big with the consciousness that they represent a great
dominant organization, which some of them believe to
be the mystic creation of saints and apostles, and
others more prosaically believe to come from the Act
of Uniformity, but which on either theory confers on
its ministers the blessed rights of classifying dissent
with beerhouses, and of despising and denouncing all
who use their minds independently as schismatical,
heretical, and anti-social.

We have no wish to carry rationalistic criticism,
either of the clergy or any other existing corporation,
too far. Many an institution that cannot stand purely
rationalistic tests is yet not in any way worth attack-
ing, and may in many circumstances be well worth
defending. We are not now concerned with the
question of church government, nor with the inter-
necine feuds of church parties, nor with the scandals
of neo-Catholicism, nor the scandals of neo-Chris-

tianity. The question is not theological but political, not doctrinal but social. The state church stands for a decaying order of ideas, and for ideas that grow narrower and more intense in proportion as they fall more out of harmony with the intellectual life of the time. What statesmanship is that which, at a time like this and with such an outlook, invests its priests with a new function, and entrusts afresh a holy army of misologists with the control of national instruction ? Is it expedient in constituting and defining a great department of the state organization, which must depend for its vitality and efficiency on the amount of interest, sympathy, and active co-operation that may gradually be provoked in the body of the people, to attach it to the retrogressive or stationary elements in our civil life rather than to its progressive elements ; to place its springs in the emulation of sects rather than in the disinterested energies of the nation ?

Champions of sectarianism and bureaucrats from the Education Department may tell us that the nation cannot be trusted with the provision of instruction ; that there is in England very little real love of instruction, very little real faith in it, very little confidence that we shall be really any the better for it. To this I reply by two remarks. First, even if it be true that laymen are thus distrustful of the worth of secular instruction, thus indifferent to its efficient provision, the clergy have not shown themselves any less so. The lowness of the standards, the fewness of the children who pass even in the higher of these, the

avowedly sectarian purposes of the schools as shown
in the prolonged resistance to a Conscience Clause and
other ways—these are the proofs that the clergy care
as little for good elementary instruction as the laity
are alleged to care.[1] Secondly, it is the fundamental assumption of a popular as distinguished
from a paternal system of government, that a nation
which is not too backward to be capable of managing
its own affairs, may be awakened to its responsibilities, and that boldly to throw these responsibilities
upon its citizens is the best way of making sure that
they will be fulfilled. There is a profound saying
that if you would improve a man, it is well to let
him suppose that you already believe him such as
you would have him to be. This is even more true
of a nation than it is of an individual. To insist that
the clergy are the only body who can be trusted with
the control of education, even if it be not a calumny

---

[1] Consider this one fact. Nowhere are the clergy stronger than in the
county of Lancaster, the new fastness of Conservatism. In this county no
less than 40 per cent. of the women married in 1870 could not sign their own
names, and had to make their mark in the register! We shall see whether
the prudence, zeal, benevolence, and proved capacity of Bishop Fraser will
make any impression on his retrograde clergy. At present, if anything
specially atrocious or silly is said on public matters, we may be sure that its
author is a clergyman from Lancashire; for instance, the charitable gentleman who cried out not long ago, at a public meeting at Darwen, that " he
thanked God he was not a dissenter."

At Keighley, in Yorkshire, the ratepayers were polled for or against a
School-board. The voting papers showed that 37 per cent. of the supporters
of the Denominational system signed their names with a mark. Of the
opponents of the Denominational system, who were in a decisive minority,
only 7 per cent. were compelled to resort to this device. In one district, out
of 194 opponents of a board, 120 signed with a mark; in other words those
who are most sorely in need of a new system are the easiest and most
numerous dupes of the partisans of the old.

on English patriotism, as I for one am convinced that
it is, still implies a deep misapprehension of the way
in which new public interests may be excited, and of
the degree in which a people accustomed to self-
government is capable of responding to a new demand. Unhappily this misapprehension seized the
very ministers who had come into power on a tide
of national enthusiasm, of which the main force was
derived from hopes of a great measure of national
education. Instead of preparing the way for the
ecclesiastical changes which they must know sooner
or later to be inevitable, they could think of nothing
more hopeful than a law for re-invigorating the state
church in functions which are not proper to it, and
discouraging to a corresponding degree the willingness of the better part of the laity to undertake functions which can never be justly and efficiently discharged on any other terms.

It is not merely a decaying order of ideas that the
ministers of the state church exist to advocate. They
represent the forces of social, no less than of intellectual, reaction. There would be no great harm in
this, perhaps, were it not that their assumption of the
civilizing offices is taken to discharge laymen from the
active performance of social duty. This is no discredit to the clergy. On the contrary, it is to their
credit, though it is to the discredit of the laity and
the great detriment of the community that this care
for the poor in country districts, alike in education
and in other matters, is thus delegated to the priestly

order. But mark the sympathies of the priestly order.
It has often been said that the Church of England is
a democratic institution—apparently for no better
reason than that plebeian curates sometimes marry into
the best families. We have now an opportunity of
seeing how much the priestly order cares for the poor
common people. The first current of a strange social
agitation is passing over the land. At last, after
generations of profound torpor, our eyes discern slow
stirrings among the serfs of the field. The uncouth
Atlantes who have for generations upborne the
immense structure of civilization in which they have
no lot, have at length made a sign. The huge dumb
figure has tried to shift a little from a position of
insufferable woe. Little may come of it. The current may soon spend itself; the monstrous burden
soon settle pitilessly down again on the heavy un-
conquerable shoulders. The many are so weak, the
few are so strong; the conditions of social organization shut effort so fast within an iron circle. However this may be, the attempt is being made by a
company of poor men to win a few pence more for
the week's toil, to raise the mere material conditions
of life for their wives and their children a little further away from the level of the lives of brute beasts.
What sympathy, or counsel, or help, or word of God-
speed, or word of compassionate warning, have they
had from the men who pretend to be spiritually
descended in line of apostolic succession from the
chosen companions and followers of the divine in-

carnation of human pity? What comment have we had in this singular crisis on the sacred text that the peacemakers are blessed? Such men as Bishop Ellicott and the two magistrates of Chipping Norton may tell us, and they are presumably not any more brutal than other Anglican feeders of Christ's sheep. And the labourers themselves tell us every week, how keenly they are alive to the angry enmity of the clergy, and how eternally they will resent it.[1] Their phrases are harsh, rough, inelegant; they have at least the eloquence of a bitter sincerity; there is much excuse for men brutalised by adversity, ignorance, and hard usage, there is none for men brutalised by prosperity and comfortable living. In short, the national church has once more shown itself not the church of the nation, but the church of a class; not the benign counsellor and helpful protectress of the poor, but the mean serving-maid of the rich. She is as inveterate a foe to a new social hope as we know her to be to a new scientific truth.

To sum up this part of the subject. First, the pretensions of the state church in the face of dissent are the bane of spiritual and intellectual life in England. How can religion be a truly civilizing force in a society, while one half of its preachers are incessantly struggling for social mastery over the other half, and, like the late Dr. Wilberforce, denouncing dissent as a co-equal cause with beerhouses in producing rural immorality? These pretensions are ratified and con-

[1] The *Labourers' Union Chronicle,* almost any week.

firmed by the working of the Education Act. Secondly, some of the strongest tendencies of the age are stimulating ecclesiasticism, and inflaming its ardour, and drawing it further apart from the really vital elements of national life. Thus, in fine, the present educational policy divorces machinery from force. The nation can only be efficiently instructed through the agency of men who have faith in intelligence, and ample hope of social improvement. The Anglican clergy have as a body shown themselves to be without either one or the other. Like every other corporation representing great privileged sects, they identify all their aspiration and all their effort with the extension and confirmation of sectarian supremacy. All that they understand by higher national life is a more undisputed ecclesiastical authority. If liberalism means anything at all beyond a budget of sounding phrases, such ideas are thoroughly retrograde, and any policy that countenances them is a policy of retrogression, or in other words is the very climax of impolicy. True statesmanship lies in right discernment of the progressive forces of a given society, in strenuous development of them, and in courageous reliance upon them. Even a sensible bishop might smile in his lawn sleeves, if he heard of the clergy of the Church of England being the depositaries of the progressive forces of the nation.

VIII.

So much for the general expediency of present
policy in view of future national growth. We may
pass on to consider what is called the religious difficulty in a more special sense. "The nation," it is
contended, "has shown in a hundred different ways its
invincible hostility to anything like the exclusion of
religious instruction from the schools. It is wholly
alien from all our established traditions of government
to attempt to force any system upon the country
which the country itself does not willingly accept.
Any departure from these traditions would be exceptionally impolitic in a matter so delicate as the education of the children of the poor. If you are going to
interfere with all the weight of state authority to
compel the parent to send his child to school, in most
cases at a certain immediate sacrifice to himself, you
will at least do well not to add to the enormous difficulties of your undertaking by provoking the religious
conscience of the parent into the bargain. To set
up a secular school system would be doing the
utmost violence to this religious conscience, and
you would never be able to work it, even if it were
proved expedient on theoretical grounds to give
the young an education from which religion should
be omitted."

Let us notice in passing that this forcible plea
for the relief of the parental conscience, this tender
anxiety for religious rights, is most vehemently urged

by the party that has for a whole generation opposed
a Conscience Clause with might and main, and the
trust-deeds of whose schools in nearly every case contained a fundamental rule that all the children should
be compelled to attend the Anglican church and the
Anglican Sunday-school. This solemn warning to
us to revere the parent's religious scruple is pro-
digiously touching on the lips of the men who for half
a century forced the children of dissenters to come
to services and Sunday-school instruction which the
parents abhorred, or else refused to admit them to the
only secular instruction that was within their reach.
"What, you wish to rob the parent of the right to
choose his child's religious teaching !"—this from the
men who for fifty years, in conformity with the trust-
deeds of their schools and the rules of the great
National Society, systematically robbed the dissenting
parent of the right of taking his child to his own place
of worship or his own Sunday-school !

The plea, however, may be worth something, though
urged in a false spirit by men whose whole tradition
is an arrogant repudiation of it. The answer to it is
so simple, so obvious, and has been so constantly kept
before the public, that one is half ashamed of again
reproducing such trite matter. Only in the struggle
with a huge vested interest, strong by its privileges and inveterate in its prejudices, a politician is
forced, in spite of literary fastidiousness, to keep
stating and restating with indefatigable iteration an
elementary principle of justice and a mere rudiment

of political prudence. Parents have an inalienable right to choose the kind of religious instruction which their children shall receive. No one disputes that. Our simple contention is that along with this right of choosing their religious instruction, goes the duty of paying for it. If I say to the parent, "Your child shall not be allowed to receive instruction in Catholic doctrine, or in Baptist doctrine," I am a tyrant. If the parent should say to me, "I insist that you shall pay for instructing my child in doctrines which you do not accept," then it is he who is the tyrant. Yet nothing less than this is involved in the present educational system. We are teaching the religion of some with money raised by the taxation of all. Every man, as has been said, pays for the religion of everybody else—the bad principle which we all supposed to have been permanently abandoned by English statesmen when church-rates disappeared, until Mr. Gladstone and Mr. Forster revived it.

Writers for the newspapers, who have not always time to think about the terms they use, have the face to insist that we are for depriving the majority of the community of the right of giving their children a religious education. What we really seek is to deprive the majority of the right of making the minority pay for giving this religious education to other people's children. No one now has a word to say in favour of church-rates, yet the principle of church-rates and the principle of grants and local rates to denominational schools are identical. The only difference is that justice and reason have been brought to bear on one application of this principle and not on the other. "Few are the partisans of departed tyranny," said Burke, "and to be a Whig on the business of a hundred years ago is very consistent with every advantage of present servility. Retrospective wisdom and historical patriotism are things of wonderful convenience."

Then we are told by the easy people who think any slipshod reasoning good enough for politics, that as the dissenters have their religious instruction paid for out of the taxes and rates of churchmen, they cannot seriously complain of having to pay taxes and rates for Anglican instruction. To which slovenly argument we reply, first, that it is no consolation to people who suffer an injustice in more than three-fourths of the schools, that they have a chance of retaliating in the remaining fourth.

Secondly, that the dissenters do not desire to have sectarian teaching in their day-schools, but only the reading of the Bible, and therefore they do not desire to have the chance of making churchmen pay for the dissemination of the principles of dissent.

Thirdly, that owing to the way in which the dissenting population is distributed, any one of its sects is not only in a minority in the whole as against the Church of England, but is always in a minority in the several parts (except in Wales), and therefore the Church of England is always strong enough to secure the establishment of its own sectarian school, even if obliged to assent to the establishment of an unsectarian one by the side of it.

Fourthly, there is a not wholly inconsiderable body of taxpayers and ratepayers who do not desire to have any religious instruction for their children whatever, and who therefore are absolutely cut off from that singular and most sweet compensation for having to pay for what you hate, that you can make other people in turn pay in the same proportion for what they hate. On all these grounds the notion that wrong becomes right if you only complete the circle, is seen to be as gross a fallacy in public as in private transactions, and those who resort to it only venture to do so in the just confidence that bad logic goes as far as good in persuading those who have got what they want that they ought to be allowed to keep it.

We are next told that the ratepayers, when asked to speak for themselves, reply all over the kingdom by overwhelming majorities that their consciences revolt against any system of education of which religion is not a part. As if *in religious affairs* it were not a settled principle of our government that the majority, however great it may be, and however strenuous its convictions, shall still not force the conscience of the minority. We force Quakers to pay for war, and Peculiar People to call in doctors. But the protection of the realm and the protection of life are secular ends, not religious ends, like teaching the catechism. I know nothing grosser, nothing which shows more strongly how sectarian supremacy coarsens and corrupts the sense of justice, nothing which illustrates more decisively how little people even now either comprehend or accept our vaunted axioms of religious liberty, unless they happen to be on the losing side, than this habitual assumption that because the members of the Church of England are in the majority in most parishes, therefore they have a right to make the minority pay for their schools and for the teaching of church doctrine. And the assumption is particularly flagitious in the members of a church that only a few years ago wrung the tithe on which its ministers subsisted from the Catholic cottiers of Ireland, and extorted church-cess for maintaining the fabric of the minority from ratepayers who were in a majority against it of seven or eight to one. In Ireland the conscience of the majority counted for nothing, in England it is the conscience of the minority that counts for nothing. Really Jesuit casuistry is a system of rigid moral inflexibility compared with our state church, which never knows how to be true to a single principle, nor how to respect a single general maxim, except the mean principle and the unchristian maxim that her own poor prerogatives are all, and the free consciences of men are naught. Some writers in the public press who ought to know better have borrowed the ecclesiastical vein, and made merry over the ratepayer's scruple. Judging from their own readiness to comply with the formalities of a creed which they no more believe than Voltaire did, they impute to others their own indifference; and because they are willing

without ado to burn a pinch of incense in the temple
of the gods, they can see nothing but besotted fanaticism or odious hypocrisy, or at best unspeakable child-
ishness, in those who still think that one creed is more
true than another, and still show some earnestness in
their preference. Surely there is not so much conscience to spare in modern society that we can afford
to sneer at any manifestation of it which may happen
to inconvenience ourselves, as a piece of puerile scru-
pulosity and ridiculous niceness.

The last sophism of the advocates of the system of
making the whole country pay for the religion of the
richer part is that public money does not pay for the
religious teaching, but only for the secular. So far
as the parliamentary grants are concerned I have
already considered this position, and already shown
that in subsidising the denominational system the
government subsidises all the incidents of the system,
denominational teaching included. In the case of
rate-supported schools—and Mr. Forster professed to
expect this kind of school to increase in number—the
sophism is still more barefaced. These schools live
on rates and grants, that is, from rates and taxes.
Therefore if the ratepayer and the taxpayer do not pay
for the religious teaching, who does pay for it? The
children with their pence? At the Manchester schools
of which we have already spoken, did the five pounds
which were voluntarily subscribed in one case, and
the single pound which was subscribed in the other,
exactly suffice to pay for the religious instruction?

Our heedless opponents will hardly say this, and they may be left to find a way out of their position as they best can.

Let us look this question of the parent's conscience boldly in the face, not like fanatics, but like politicians in face of a practical task. Now what is the limit and intention of state interference in any part of education? With education in the largest and most complete sense the state has nothing to do. It only professes to deal with that narrow portion of education which is described as secular instruction, and it is a great pity that we are obliged to give the wider name to the question, because unscrupulous or inconsiderate persons have been enabled to say that we want to force a godless education on the poor, and the like falsehoods. The state is only concerned with the supply and regulation of secular instruction. As Mr. Gladstone himself expressed it, "The duty of the state is to make use of the voluntary schools for the purposes of the secular instruction which they give, but *to hold itself entirely and absolutely detached from all responsibility with regard to their religious teaching.*" [1]

You may say that this is to degrade the state. Possibly. But whether or no, this is the principle already accepted and already acted upon, and distinctly formulated. Religious inspection is now given up. Payments from the public funds are in theory strictly confined to proficiency in secular knowledge. Public money will be given just as readily and on precisely the

[1] Speech in the House of Commons, June 24, 1870.

same terms to purely secular schools. Above all,
every school manager who accepts the Conscience
Clause accepts this principle, and agrees that, excepting
for a certain time at the beginning or end, or the
beginning and end, of the work of the school, the instruction given in the school shall be as purely secular,
irreligious, godless, as in any school in the land. It
is not we who begin to make the schools secular. That
is already done in principle in every public elementary school, denominational or otherwise, by the first
and second sub-sections of the seventh clause of the
Elementary Education Act of 1870.[1] When the clergy
surrendered the Conscience Clause, they instantly became parties to the very system of education which
they choose to call godless. How—asks the vivacious
editor of a well-known religious newspaper—how can a
man teach geography without Genesis ? The illustration does not strike me as happy, for in truth I see no
more connection between geography and Genesis than
between Macedon and Monmouth. But, at any rate,
if anybody teaches religion out of the time set in the
table, he is violating the contract he has made with
the government, and either forfeiting his grant or else
procuring it fraudulently. And hence the absurd

---

[1] "It shall not be required, as a condition of any child being admitted into
or continuing in the school, that he shall . . . . . . attend any religious observance, or any instruction in religious subjects in the school or elsewhere. . . . .

"The time or times during which any religious observance is practised, or
instruction in religious subjects is given at any meeting of the school, shall
be either at the beginning or at the end, or at the beginning and the end, of
each meeting. . . . . ."—33 & 34 Vict., c. 75, § 7.

folly of the Bishop of Peterborough—we humbly borrow for once the Bishop of Peterborough's own particular phrase for describing what he does not agree with—in his memorable assertion that all instruction that excludes religious teaching is atheistic. As if religious teaching were not excluded from every State-aided school both in the diocese of Peterborough and every other diocese in England during some five-sixths of the school-time. So that if his description be correct, the Church schools are atheistic institutions for nearly the whole of the solid day. The clergy and the clerically-minded journalists do not see that the Conscience Clause makes every public elementary school in the land a secular school pure and simple, except for a short and specified time daily. Some of the clergy do see this, and act consistently and honourably by withdrawing their schools from government inspection and participation in parliamentary grants; Archdeacon Denison, for instance. Prebendary Kemble at the meeting of the Bath and Wells Diocesan Conference in August (1873), said that "what he felt very strongly with regard to this Act and government intervention was the godless and irreligious character of the Conscience Clause. A school he maintained in a neighbouring diocese which used to receive a considerable government grant, he had withdrawn altogether from government supervision, rather than hang up the Conscience Clause." These are clearly the words of a man of integrity and accurate judgment. The Conscience Clause *is* godless and irreligious, if we choose to import this particular kind of language. When the religious journalist insists that history and geography should be penetrated with religious significance, when the organ of the National Society demands that " the whole school-time of a child " should lead up to making the child a communicant of the Church of England, these devout persons are simply inciting the teachers and school managers clandestinely to break their bargain with the state, and to obtain the state money on false pretences. This is the plain truth. They are preaching a fraud.

That in practice the Conscience Clause is often contravened in spirit if not in letter is tolerably well known. No legal enactment can prevent the clerical manager from refusing to allow any children who are withdrawn from religious instruction or from attendance at church or Sunday school, to compete for prizes, or to share the school treat, and cases have been brought forward of double fees being charged to the children of dissenters. Mr. Forster has repeatedly asked those who deny the effectiveness of the Conscience Clause why they do not bring cases of its infraction before the Department. To this we may reply first that such cases have been brought before the Department;[1] second, that there is obviously great difficulty in finding them out, as the places

---

[1] One of the Inspectors in the last Blue Book reports that as a result of his visits of surprise he found " the time-table violated, and *in one or two cases the Conscience Clause infringed.*" (Mr. Bowstead's Report for 1872, p. 47.) Now were the schools in these one or two cases punished or not? And if not, why not?

where they are likely to happen are usually the
furthest removed from the public eye and ear; and
thirdly, that it is by indirect rather than direct means
that the supposed protection of the Clause is nullified.
We are naturally ready to give to clergymen the
same credit for honour and law-abidingness as we give
to other men. But then clergymen somehow are not
exactly like other men. They are very apt to look
at laws as those people do, who never can be taught
that it is wrong to smuggle or to cheat a railway
company. None but clergymen would think it honest
to draw pay for forcing what they call Catholic practices and Catholic truth into a Protestant establishment. Indeed one can hardly imagine a more admirable training for a low-class attorney than a short
apprenticeship to one of these heroic Anglicans, whose
whole lives seem spent in finding out by how many
little devices of costume, lights, banners, processions,
practices, postures, they can strain and evade the law
without being convicted and punished. The organ of
the rising party in the Church has actually enjoined
upon the clergy to hear confessions in spite of the
mandate of the Ordinary to whom he has sworn
obedience; for "who is to know when a priest is
hearing a confession, or when he is arguing in the
vestry with a Congregationalist enquirer upon, let us
say, the divine institution of episcopacy?"[1] Tartufe
was a man of honour, a creature of a fine moral sense,
compared with this sly priest, solacing or chastening

[1] Leading article in the *Church Times* for July 4.

the penitent soul, tongue in cheek. If he will cheat his bishop, are we to blame if we suspect him of willingness to cheat the law? Liberal clergymen used to evade the clauses in the trust-deeds making attendance at church compulsory on the children. Why should not illiberal clergymen now show equal ingenuity for ends which they think equally laudable? It is not our fault if we are suspicious of clerical loyalty in administering the Conscience Clause, when we are confronted on every side by open declarations that a teacher should not attempt to teach geography without Genesis; that the whole school-time of a child should lead up to making him an Anglican communicant; that so long as you have sectarian teachers, it is of secondary importance under what regulations they carry on their work, for " such as the teacher is, such will be the school." "The time has come," says the National Society, " when probably the whole fate of the Church of England will turn upon the hold she may have upon the rising generation. Political changes are giving more and more power to the people. If the church have the people with her, she will be beyond all power of adverse legislation. Let her, then, educate the children of the people in her principles. Let her, as we said above, *not only teach them to be good Christians; let her teach them to be good churchmen. The National schools of England are the training ground of English churchmen.* Let not the opportunity be lost; let EVERY child who leaves a National school be fortified with a sound training in

the distinctive theology of the church, as well as in
secular elements, and in due time the results will be
seen in the loyalty of the people to their spiritual
mother, and their ready championship of her cause in
any hour of danger that may arrive in the course of
political events."[1]

Whatever practical evasions of the law may take
place, and whether they be few or many, the principle laid down by the law, and accepted by the
manager of every State-aided school in the country, is
clearly this—that secular instruction is the only part
of education for which the state pays or with which
it is in any way concerned, and that secular instruction is capable of being imparted, and must by law be
imparted in all such schools without any admixture of
religious instruction.   The separation between secular
and religious teaching which the clergy now denounce
as atheistic, was actually petitioned for by the archbishop of Dublin and many of the Irish bishops and
clergy in a memorial to the Privy Council in 1866.
What was orthodox in Ireland is atheistic in England.
This is only another instance of the flagitious want of
principle which marks the course of the clerical party.
At any rate, here is the principle of the law as it
stands.   We others have so far no conversion to make,
though we have a gigantic task to perform in persuading people to recognise the principle they have
formally conceded, and to act on the recognition.

From one of the *Monthly Papers*, published in 1871.

For the worst of a concession made by Conservatives or ecclesiastics is that you must never hurt their feelings by acting upon it. Thus they introduced household suffrage, transferring power to the common people, whenever they choose to unite in the use of it. The moment you appeal to the common people as the depositaries of power, you are denounced as a revolutionist and an ochlocrat. And so with the Conscience Clause. In accepting this, they distinctly excluded religion from the hours of secular instruction. The moment you take them at their word, and assume that they have really separated religious from secular teaching, they break out against you as heathens and godless. A Conservative would seem to be so-called from his tenacity in keeping what he has long given away.

The state, then, imposes on the parent the duty of submitting his children to a certain amount of drill in secular instruction, just as in some other countries the state insists on universal submission to a course of military drill. The attendance on this instruction is as purely a secular duty as the payment of taxes. A parent who comes forward and declines to let his children attend school unless they receive religious instruction, might as well decline to pay his taxes unless the State would guarantee a mass for his soul or provide him with a chaplain. Secular instruction is one thing, and religious instruction is something quite different. No one who accepts government aid on condition of a Conscience Clause can deny this absolute separation.   The state has no more to do with the provision of religious instruction, than it has to do with the provision of a band of music for each parish.   That is the affair of those who want music or who want religious instruction.   There is no prohibition, nor wish to prohibit.   There is only absolute neutrality and indifference.

Now it is perfectly well known by all who have taken the pains to inquire into the subject that this supposed eagerness of the parent to send his child to a school of a special denomination is a mere invention of the clergy and the priests.   It does not exist. What a parent wants is a school that is convenient. Let us take from actual experience an important illustration how artificial this cry is.   The London School-board remits to divisional tribunals the cases of parents who are summoned for neglecting to send their children to school, and who plead poverty.   These are the cases coming under the Seventeenth and Twenty Fifth clauses.   The divisional tribunal has the power of recommending the Board to remit or pay the fees. In either case, whether of remission or payment, the parent is of course absolutely free to select the school to which he will have the child sent.   In the Greenwich division the four divisional members constitute the tribunal, and take its duties each a month in turn. Their district embraces a population of 200,000, of all classes, from the gentility of Sydenham down to the most miserable parts of Deptford.   What happens? "Eighteen months' experience on this tribunal,"

writes the Rev. Mr. Waugh, to whose courtesy I am
indebted for this information, "leave this fact: that
not in one single case where a parent has chosen a
denominational school, has he done so because it was
a denominational school. In every case the 'choice'
was made because there was no choice. In the
immediate locality of the chooser's home, there were
no schools for girls but denominational schools, or else
there were no schools for boys but denominational
schools, or no schools for infants but denominational
schools. Where the family consisted of boys and
girls, and the locality provided schools for boys under
the Board, and for girls under the Church, or *vice
versa,* one half of the family attended Board schools,
and the other half Church schools. In not *one single
case has a denominational school been preferred for any
other than physical or geographical reasons.*" The
scruple of the indigent parent is thus seen, in this
immense district at any rate, to be a figment.
Another member of the London School-board writes
to me:—" My experience quite coincides with Mr.
Waugh's, that the parents who come before the
divisional committee, of which I am a member, are
quite indifferent to the religious question, and the
main points are convenience of locality or lowness of
fee charged to the scholars." A clergyman in the
east end of London tells a story of a good widow
whose children were in the habit of attending the
church school. One day he noticed that two of these
children were absent, and on inquiry learned that

they had ceased to attend, and were now going to a British school. He went to the mother and asked her pleasantly why she had withdrawn two of her children from his school? "Why, sir," she answered, "the truth is, that between this and your school there are two very dangerous crossings, and I was afraid of the youngest being run over, so I thought I might as well send it to the Dissenting school; and then the other one has to go to take care of it." That is the common-sense account of parental scruple in this matter. The clergy and the priests have done their best to stimulate the parents to feign this eager conscientiousness. They have failed. But the device was too good to be thrown away, so, hollow invention as it is, they have given it the main place on their banner.

Still as we have to work the system, we must meet as well as we can the prejudices excited by this artificial and spurious cry. Now what objection can the clergy make to the scheme which meets the conscientious objections of the dissenting or secularist ratepayer by taking the function of imparting religious instruction from the secular teacher, and then meets the conscientious objection of the scrupulous parent by empowering the clergyman or the priest or some one deputed by him, other than the schoolmaster or schoolmistress, to give religious instruction at a distinct time, just as it is now given at a distinct time? If the parent really wants his child to have religious instruction in the week-day, his child has it. If the clergyman is really anxious that the young of his flock should be instructed in the word and the doctrine, who can teach with such fulness of knowledge or exhort with such amplitude of authority as himself?[1] If the state aid really supports only the secular instruction, what heavier call will there be upon voluntary aid than there is now? The parent's conscience is satisfied. The ratepayer's conscience is not forced.

It may be said that this is only adding still more directly to clerical power, and augmenting the clerical element in education. Such an objection is unreal. The schoolmaster, as it is, teaches what the clergyman, who is his master, tells him to teach, and he dare not do otherwise. And therefore a parish with an unpopular clergyman would be no worse off in the tenour of the religious instruction imparted to its children, than it is now. The great advantage gained would be that the lay teacher would come fresh to the secular instruction, would look to that as other men

[1] The Bishop of Manchester, formerly an Inspector of Schools, has declared this solution to be compatible with adequate religious instruction. " He did not think that it was a fair description of the work of the Birmingham League to say that they went in for secularism pure and simple. So far as schools come down upon the rates or upon the taxes of the country for support, so far they said, in view of the present difficulties and divisions, instruction should be secular; but every religious body might retain the full use and possession of that school outside the time for secular instruction, providing their own teachers at their own cost. He was not saying that this was the programme that he individually would most desire to see; but if they were only faithful to their own convictions, if all they had been talking about religious education in their different parishes had any meaning at all, and was not merely talk, they certainly had still, as managers and teachers of such schools, ample scope and opportunity for indoctrinating their children with that sound religious teaching they thought most conducive to their welfare."—Extract from a speech delivered in Convocation at York, February, 1872.

look to their professions, would not be distracted by
alien subjects. This is the point which seems to the
present writer by far the most important—to improve
the aims and heighten the self-respect of the teacher,
by showing him that the state puts him in a definite,
an independent, an honourable post with specified
functions. The separation of religious from secular
instruction in the person of the teacher, no less than
in the time of giving it, is as indispensable a condition
of this, though by no means the only condition, as it
is an indispensable condition of putting an end to the
wrangling among the parish sects. What we want,
is to erect secular teaching among the class who go
to these elementary schools, into a distinct and recognised department of national activity and public duty.
Until this is done, you will never have good teaching,
and you will never have in your people any hearty
recognition of the value of knowledge.

IX.

But, it will be said, religious instruction will suffer.
As one of the most prominent defenders of Mr.
Forster's policy writes to me:—" Religion can only
be taught to boys effectually by the lay master. It
[*i.e.* teaching by the clergyman] would only be regarded
as an insufferable bore." This is a pleasant compliment to his spiritual friends, but let us see what the
effectual teaching of religion by the lay master really
comes to, when put into plain English. The answer
shall come from an authority whose friendliness to our

adversaries is beyond suspicion. Canon Norris is reporting the results of the examination of candidates for admission into the Training Colleges. Four-fifths of the candidates were pupil-teachers. "I have the papers," he says, "of the 217 who failed last Christmas before me: there is not one of them that would not be considered disgraceful by a panel of a dozen teachers or clergymen. . . . Two-thirds of the pupil-teachers failed to obtain half-marks." And this is admittedly a religious examination of the most elementary kind. "In 1871 I inquired of 500 students in Training Colleges how many had received assistance in their religious studies from their clergy during their apprenticeship, and ascertained that only 42 out of the 500 (or 12 per cent.) had been instructed or even examined by their clergy in this part of their work." "And if the pupil-teachers be thus ignorant," says the organ of the National Society with plaintive groan, "what must be the condition of the children who have not had the same advantages?"[1] This is no Birmingham invention, no Nonconformist calumny. Every Diocesan Inspector's report tells the same tale of poor and unsatisfactory answers, "showing unmistakably that the whole preparation for them consists in a few days' hasty cramming." The pupils know a few bare facts, but they do not know their connection with one another, while even "the Catechism itself is neither accurately learnt nor intelligently understood."[2]

[1] National Society's *Monthly Paper* for May, 1873, p. 99.
[2] National Society's *Monthly Paper* for June, 1873.

Let the reader calmly weigh the significance of this. Consider the light it throws on all this dire contention. The children no more learn religion than they learn anything else. It is on their own authority that we thus know, what every sensible man suspected before, that if the results of the secular teaching of the sectarian schools are unworthy and despicable beyond all estimation, the results of their religious teaching are more unworthy and despicable still. Yet it is for this poor ragged tatter and pretence of serious religious instruction, this scanty covering of spiritual nakedness with a few catechismal thrums, that the parent's conscience is said to yearn with a yearning that will not be gainsaid! The same parent, be it observed, who is commonly described as "neither earnest nor religious, but apathetic and slothful," and whose apathy and sloth are the reasons alleged why religion, if it is to be learnt at all, must be learnt at school.[1] What clearer evidence is needed than the fact of this ignorance and apathy on the part of previous generations of school-goers, combined with the fact of the utter and avowed badness of the religious instruction which is given to the school-goers of the present generation, to persuade us that this noisy cry on the parent's behalf for a religious education is entirely hollow and artificial, merely invented to serve a turn in the contest for the maintenance of an external sectarian supremacy? They impose on the world with the sounding phrase of religious

[1] National Society's *Monthly Paper* for May, 1873, p. 96.

education. Yet it seems after all that the thing itself has no effectual existence in the schools. This good and effective religious education for which there is such strife is a myth. "Long before the passing of the Act of 1870," says the Principal of the Battersea Training College, "it was notorious that after years of instruction in the Bible and Catechism large numbers of children lapsed into Dissent or utter godliness." It is hardly honourable in the face of a mass of statements of this kind to charge us with wishing to found heathen schools, when we only desire to take the religious instruction out of the hands of lay teachers who have, to such a degree as this, demonstrated their unfitness to impart it.

The fear of the proselytising effect of the religious hour is a secondary thing, and there is a fine contemptuousness in the common indifference among Dissenting parents about withdrawing their children from it. The Welsh poor are nearly all Dissenters, yet they suffer their children to learn the Catechism, and gravely to declare that they have been made children of grace through baptism, though they have never been baptized, and that their godfathers and godmothers have vowed divers fine things in their names, though they have never known the blessing of godfathers and godmothers at all. Surely we are the religious party, who seek to put a stop to ghastly mummery like this. What moves the indignation of sensible and patriotic observers is that these men who provide a slovenly and wretched religious instruction

and a slovenly and wretched secular instruction, and
who are fully aware from their own reports how ill
they are doing the work they have undertaken, yet
obstinately cling to a function which they are found
incompetent to perform, and stubbornly refuse to
stand aside to give a chance to fresh principles and
new forces and untried agencies, which may perhaps
perform the work as ill, but which at least cannot
possibly perform it worse. And mark that these are
the men, this great Church-party, who uniformly bid
us rely upon improved education as the one panacea
for the backwardness of our humbler population.
When we ask them how to deal with the drunkenness
that is the arch-curse of the land, they cry, Educate
the people. We point to our million of paupers,
breeding a devouring pauper race to come after them :
education is declared the one cure, the single assured
remedy. We pray them to consider the problem of a
wage-earning class acquiring a new measure of material prosperity which they know no more how to use
in a wise, sober, and civilized way than their suddenly
enriched betters know how to use it so. They reply,
We have considered your problem, we solve it by
education. We inquire of them whether it is not
pitiable to think of the brutalising lives that are led
by the rural and urban poor in their crowded hovels,
with no hope nor interest nor outlook for themselves
or their descendants. They answer, Yes, it is pitiable;
you must educate. Can you believe, we ask, that
any nation is great and stable or will hold a foremost

place in the civilized system, with huge classes of its members sunk in the degradation of the lower English labourers ? Ah, they say, you must open the mind and heart, you must discipline the intelligence and train the affections. And then they press on with a headlong enthusiasm to employ badly-taught teachers to discipline the intelligence up to the superb attainments of the Third Standard, and to train the affections by a few bits of the Church Catechism "neither accurately learned nor intelligently understood"!

It is barely credible that men who thus obstruct all other social reforms by a parrot's repetition about the necessity of education, are most persistent in obstructing all reforms in education itself. They substitute education for every other kind of improvement, and then for education they substitute those paltry scraps of instruction, whether secular or religious, of which low standards and inspectors' rebukes tell the sorry tale, and which no more deserve the name of education than a savage scratching a little patch of ground with a stick or the shoulder-blade of a beast deserves to be called a scientific agriculturist.

X.

In the preceding pages we have seen how Mr. Forster's Act and his administration of its provisions give a direct subsidy from the public purse to the clergy of the Church of England and the priests of the Church of Rome. We have seen that the sectarian system of education means new power and more public money for the two great hierarchies of obscurantism. We have seen the religious difficulty to be exaggerated and factitious, and that the same separation in the person of the instructor which is already conceded in the time of the instruction, furnishes the only just and tolerant solution. Let the school be the property of a board of public representatives; let the teacher be confined to secular instruction, just as he now is most rigidly so confined for five-sixths of the working day; then let the clergyman, the priest, or anyone else, where the ratepayers wish it, come in and give the religious instruction in the time which is already set apart for it in the time-table.

If the religious difficulty arose from sincere religious conviction, it would be completely met by this simple change in school administration. Candidates for parliament tell us they are against any scheme that will separate religious from secular instruction. They really talk nonsense. The separation has already been definitely settled by the Conscience Clause, which insists on the religious instruction being strictly confined to a certain time at the beginning or end of the day's work, and punishes any attempt to evade this separation by withdrawal of the grant. All we ask is that for the sake of avoiding everlasting feud, in the first place, and for the sake of leaving the teacher free for his own proper business in the second, this separation should be extended from the time at which it is given, to the person who gives it. Whoever after this accuses us of driving the Bible out of the schools,

H

of hindering religion, of forcing godless knowledge on the people, must either be too stupid to understand the meaning of the existing Conscience Clause, or else he is a deliberate calumniator, willing to use any word that serves his turn. And whoever declines to accept this compromise must do so, because he is thinking of other ends than the religious nurture and admonition of the children.

We saw from the words of denominational inspectors that what is called religious instruction is avowedly a miserable failure, so that the sectarian schools do ill even the kind of work for which they are especially cherished. It is not merely because the system is sectarian and involves dogmatic instruction that the present writer, at any rate, would gladly see it extinguished as rapidly as may be, and replaced by a system which will certainly be more costly, but which would at least have the merit of giving us a substantial return on our outlay. Our contention is that at present we are paying increasingly large sums of money to sectarian schools, and that these schools do not and cannot, so long as they remain under the control of sectarian authorities, perform the work for which they are paid, and for which their managers and champions take most extravagant credit.

Here, then, is the true education question, not merely in the honourable struggle of the dissenters for justice, nor in the base struggle of the Anglican sects for supremacy. To what abject proportions do these sectarian pretensions shrink as we realise the depths of the abyss of ignorance in which the masses of our people lie sunken. If the church schools or the catholic schools could pass two hundred thousand children a year in the Sixth Standard, then one might be willing to shut his eyes to the injustice of paying for them out of the pockets of those who are neither churchmen nor catholics. We might be willing to run the risk of strengthening ecclesiasticism and spreading superstition, being well assured that an instructed people will know better than any other how to deal with these and all other pestilent social growths. But the denominational system not only cannot pass two hundred thousand children in the Sixth Standard, it cannot even *present* sixteen thousand, and cannot pass nine thousand! We have a policy of injustice unredeemed and of retrogression without recompense. You give new props to the established sects at the cost of the whole nation, you exclude the public from the administration of their own funds, you discourage lay participation in school management, you fill the country with strife and dissension, and yet after all this violation alike of principle and policy you cannot justify yourselves by educational success, or give us a single new guarantee that the children shall be turned out of the schools less ignorant than the majority of them are turned out now.

In 1867 we learnt on the authority of one of the ablest men who have ever filled the office of inspector, that nearly 90 per cent. of the scholars were leaving the primary schools destitute of that rudimentary knowledge without which all teaching of science, even if it were offered to them, would be unintelligible. This is the state of things which the vaunted denominational system has left us, and it is a state of things which that system is essentially incompetent to reform. What is there to make the schools give any better instruction now than they did in 1867? The gratuitous and unexpected increase in the grants by fifty per cent. is a most substantial encouragement to the managers not to take too much trouble in reaching the highest standards. It is a direct weakening of the incentives to earn more money by procuring a greater number of pupils and a greater number of good passes. What was there in the Education Act to give managers a motive for paying more attention to those extra subjects which are in truth the part of instruction that gives most life and significance to the rest? Half of the inspectors complain that these subjects are indifferently regarded, and one or two of them distinctly assert the reason of this to be that the managers have seldom or ever any pecuniary interest in their result.[1]

Again, even the very cessation of religious inspection is not unlikely in many cases to have the effect of injuring the secular instruction, and in this way. The Government inspector has now been replaced so far as religious examination is concerned by a Diocesan Inspector, whose salary is provided by voluntary contributions, and the acceptance or refusal

[1] Mr. Kennedy's Report, p. 101.

of whose services is, of course, at the choice of the school managers. What happens ? We find advertisements for masters, informing them that they will receive additions to their salary if the Diocesan Inspector's report is satisfactory. What is this but to bribe the master to postpone useful secular instruction to instruction in the Catechism? A certificated mistress who is a good witness because she would apparently on no account wish to see religious instruction taken out of her hands, writes thus : " Since the Education Act became law, it has been a most difficult matter to keep strict faith with the Government, and at the same time in Church schools to satisfy the requirements of the Diocesan Inspector."[1] With a competition of this sort going on, we may be quite sure that, whatever else may happen, at least there will be no rise in the secular standards reached by this correspondent's pupils. The teachers are no doubt delighted in their hearts by the Time-table Conscience Clause. That at any rate makes some four solid hours a day secure against the hymn-singing and other interruptions to serious business, in which clerical managers and manageresses used to rejoice. But, this gain notwithstanding, so long as the school " belongs to " the clergyman—though the parents and the tax-payers may pay four-fifths or five-sixths, or even four hundred and fifty-eight four hundred and fifty-ninths of its cost[1]—for so long the

---

[1] Letter to the *Times*, September 5, 1873.
[2] See above, p. 52.

dependent teacher will inevitably be tempted to give his best mind to what pleases his employer best.

What again has the Act done in the all-important matter of improving the capacity and position of the teacher ? Absolutely nothing. The increased grants might be supposed to go to increase the teacher's salary, and so by-and-by be the means of introducing a more highly educated class of men and women into the profession. It is notorious that nothing of the kind happens. The increase can only serve to relieve the private subscribers, and thus render the schools even less worthy of the name of voluntary than they were before. One of the inspectors distinctly remarks "the increasing tendency among managers of schools to free themselves from pecuniary responsibility by allowing teachers to take the whole of the pence and a consider-able portion of the capitation grant as part of their salaries ; in some instances they practically farm their schools."[1]

And how has the Act lessened the burden of those irrelevant drudgeries which are inseparable from a system that makes the schools an appendage to the church and the parsonage, and which rob the master at once of his needful leisure and his lawful independence ? The same correspondent from whom I have already quoted says : "It is untrue that the majority of teachers have no Sunday duties : in nearly all country schools the Sunday-school rests almost entirely on the teachers. They are also often required to play an organ or a

[1] Mr. Blandford's Report for 1872, p. 35.

harmonium, and to train the choir."[1] So long as the
Church remains in possession of the schools, this fatal
drawback to the character of the teaching profession
is certain to remain. Again, it is perfectly assured
in the opinion of the most competent judges and those
who see the working of the schools most closely, that
compulsory provisions, probably in various forms
direct and indirect, reaching parent and employer, are
indispensable to check, even if they prove unable to
put an end to, that irregularity of attendance, that
frequent absence from school on frivolous pretexts,
which is one of the chief secrets of the low standards.
Well, for this the statesmen who claim so loudly to
have reared a national system of education, have done
the least possible, with their ricketty framework of
permissive boards and permissive compulsion. Preston, for example, with a population of some 90,000,
and where the average school attendance falls short of
what it ought to be by 4,000, has no board and no
compulsion, though its neighbour Blackburn has both,
with excellent results. Birkenhead, a still larger
borough, has no board. Of the whole population of
England and Wales, only 39 per cent. are under the
rule of compulsory attendance.

Finally, next to irregularity of attendance as a
cause of the inefficiency of our system, comes the
insufficiency of the school age. In most parts of Germany the limits of school age are from 6 or 7 to 14,
in Switzerland from 6 to 14 or 15, while in Saxony a

[1] See Mr. J. Storr's letter to the same effect, *Times*, September 11.

child at work is a half-timer up to 16. With us a half-timer is a child between 8 and 13, and 13 is the limit prescribed for compulsion by the Education Act. More time is an indispensable condition of anything like a solid education, and children must be made to stay later as well as come in earlier, for in this more than anything else it is the ending that crowns the work. Here, then, we are left, and seem likely to be left, just where we were.

XI.

People console themselves for the failure of the Act of 1870, and for the indifference shown by many of the constituencies to the momentous national interests which that Act has for the time sacrificed, by the comfortable reflection that England was great and strong before primary instruction was ever thought of, and that therefore she may well continue to be great and strong even though primary instruction should remain the poor and inadequate thing which it now is. Decidedly there are circumstances in which a rude and elemental vigour may stand a people in a thousand times better stead than the most widespread culture. But are these circumstances ours? Will rude vigour, undisciplined by intellectual training, undirected by intellectual skill, uninformed by knowledge, suffice for England in the conditions of modern society? Let two considerations dispel this fallacy of indolent complacency for ever. First, have we not to compete now, with a degree of intensity not dreamed of fifty years ago and only half realised even at this very day, with Germany and the United States, whose systems may abound in imperfections of detail, but are at least not so absolutely illusory as to turn out the majority of their workers in the numb ignorance of an English boy to whom the Third Standard is an impassable bridge? We have to compete with these populations, too, under conditions which place the uninstructed workman at a growing disadvantage. It is true that some of our greatest mechanical inventors have been illiterate, but to make this an argument against education is as childish as to bring forward the cases of men like Marlborough, Clive, Nelson, against scientific military training. A man with inventive genius will work miracles in spite of his literary ignorance, but the average workman does not work miracles: and a miracle it would be if a set of men who had passed through the effective school training of Prussia did not in the long-run outstrip in dexterity, quickness of apprehension, readiness of adaptation, a set of men who had tried to learn reading and writing and had failed, as is the case with the majority of the English labouring class.

Observe that this position is quite independent of any controversy as to the curative effects of teaching, and any question whether there is the least "connection between learning that certain clusters of marks on paper stand for certain words and the getting a higher sense of duty." This high matter does not now concern us, nor shall we exercise ourselves in it.

The clusters of marks on paper do at any rate constitute the chief instrument in many of the most important practical arts, and not to be able to read nor to work sums nor to draw lines is to miss the use of this instrument, and to be condemned to the lowest place in the least important practical arts. I am far from wishing to press the advantages of instruction over mother-wit further than they will bear, but these advantages will certainly bo more powerful in proportion as brute labour becomes less valuable, as machines grow more delicate and complex, as inventions multiply, as more and more has to be acquired from books, as new processes decide victory in this or that department of manufacture, and financial exactitude, foresight, and science, exert increasing influence over commerce. England has a long start in the competition. Is it not exasperating to see her losing the untold advantages which would come from an efficient training of her people, simply in order that the clergy may have a barely controlled mastery in the schools,—a fruitless mastery, moreover, which they do not use even so far as to give the children effective instruction in their own Bible and their own Catechism.

Our kinsmen in Australia might, one would suppose, be content to trust to rude elemental vigour if any set of men in the world ever could. Yet they find that they cannot. Experience of the disadvantages of brute ignorance in an age of cultivated skill has been too strong for fallacies of *à priori*. The people of Victoria had to fight the battle which we are fight-

ing. So long as education was no more than a name
for a quarrel among sects, they could get nothing
done. Therefore, as a sensible community was likely
to do, and as we shall be driven by the irresistible
pressure of circumstances before many more years to
do, they have taken the function of controlling primary
instruction into their own hands, thrown a handful
of dust over the raging insects, released the clergy
and the teachers each from the business that belongs
to the other, compelled every child between the ages
of six and fifteen to attend school until it is able
to pass a certain examination, and have fully
established that system of compulsory, free, and
secular instruction which they felt to be neither more
nor less than indispensable to the welfare of their
society.

Secondly, in our complacent trust in rude vigour as
a substitute for trained intelligence, we forget that
these ignorant multitudes are now what they never
were before, the political masters of the realm. So
far, the old social organization has neutralised the
new distribution of power. Household suffrage as
yet is only a thing on paper. We have still to feel
its reality. The new possessors of power are still
hardly aware that it is theirs. And who are the
new possessors of power? The skilled artisans, the
leaders of trade societies, and the like? Alas, no; it
is not they but those below them, those between the
artisan and the pauper, whenever they choose to
awake, or whenever they choose in their dreams to let

somebody else lead them, who hold the destinies of our society in their hands. "If I have twenty-one men in my bar on the day of polling," a respectable publican is reported to have said, "I can make sure of twenty votes by distributing twenty pints of fourpenny : I have done it and can do it at any time." You may say that this is an exception, an accident, an exaggeration. It may be so, but what is neither exception nor accident nor exaggeration is the bald fact that of "four-fifths of the scholars who leave school in a given year either no account at all or a very unsatisfactory one is given by an examination of the most strictly elementary kind." In plain English, a majority of those who come out of the schools cannot read a newspaper. This unfortunate class is our ruling class. Their votes can carry elections, change administrations, decide policies. As yet they have no initiative, and it may be some time before they cease to follow the initiative of others. When their time comes and a leader, they will make terribly short work with a good deal that you hold precious now. Journalists gird at three or four writers who press for public consideration, while there is yet time, some of the questions connected with the tenure of land, with taxation, with endowments, above all with education. The sophists of the newspaper press are so busily fighting momentous practical issues with the lath sword of some little abstract theory, that they have no eyes for the gulf which is ready to open at the feet of them and the institutions which they so absurdly suppose themselves to be defending. The prospect of a Beer parliament has no terrors for blind politicians of this stamp. They do not discern that the same classes who are now believed to be on the point of following the publicans and the clergy to the polls, to the strangely compounded cry of an open Bible and a flowing barrel, are one day very likely to invent cries of their own that will bring destruction where the abused reformer of to-day only seeks improvement, and, where we only seek to amend, will trample, efface, obliterate.

The Englishman is inclined to be law-abiding and fair, no doubt, within limits. But since the Reform Act of 1867 the power of making the laws by which all have to abide is going to the class that cannot read a newspaper, and that with our present educational system is not likely to be able to read a newspaper. Political infatuation seems to reach its climax when those who have most to gain by our having an intelligent and instructed people, decline to discuss the question how the people are to be made so, or whether the present system can ever lead to so indispensable a result; and instead of keeping the subject constantly before their eyes in all its magnitude and all the fulness of its importance to the national well-being, make no worthier contribution to the greatest of public interests than puny railing against the League and irrelevant gibing at dissenters. Let dissent be annihilated; will that prevent the majority of your children from coming out of your schools below the Fourth Standard ?   Let the League perish ; will that educate your masters ?

Yet, no ; this is not the climax of political infatuation.   Something remains that to those of another time will seem more incredible still.   The statesmen who decline to give us a national system of education are the very men who have just declared for household suffrage in the counties.   They are going to add to the constituencies many thousands of voters from the very class for whose instruction in the elements of knowledge they will not even enforce those compulsory provisions which are thought indispensable for the large towns.   They are supposed to be going to the country with the cry of more rural voters, but no rural School-boards and no rural compulsion. Could recklessness go further ?   Household franchise in the counties by all means, if it be accompanied by School-boards and the machinery of compulsory attendance ; but to go on in this headlong course of "leaps in the dark," of giving power without training intelligence, of multiplying electors without improving schools, of making men vote without making them learn how to read, is a policy from which the most desperate of the ministers who preceded the first Revolution in France might have shrunk, and which the most insensate anarchist of the International might welcome as the surest promise that he shall one day secure the chance for which he is waiting.   In France, it is true, the peasants are believed always to use their political power in favour of order and the

existing government, and their peasants are as ignorant as ours. But they have the education of property or the reasonable hopes of property. They
have something to lose by disorder. What has our
peasant to lose by disorder, and how can society do
less for him than it does now? Take the United
States again. The most vehement lovers of democracy in America still look with amazement at the
spectacle of statesmen hurrying us on to a régime
of universal suffrage without instructing the people
who are to exercise it. They tell us that their political system could not last half a century without
their schools. It is as much as ever they can do,
or perhaps more, to make headway against the floods
of ignorance which throw themselves every year on
to their shores from our side of the Atlantic. The
latest notion of policy in England is to entrust the
great ship of our state to the floods of ignorance that
are left behind; and new generations of rural voters
are to grow up without any really effective provision
that they shall any more know how to read than
their fathers did, lest such provisions should wound
the fine susceptibilities of an order of men who, under
the pretext that secular instruction without religious
is full of peril, are suffered to maintain a sham system
that gives the public illusory secular instruction and a
religious instruction more illusory still.

Nearly every Inspector agrees that without compulsion you can do nothing. Yet the machinery of
compulsion is systematically discouraged. Let us

look at the state of things in a typical rural district, the counties of Bedford and Huntingdon. Of 219 parishes, 82 were found supplied with efficient schools, 34 from their small size or neighbourhood to other schools requiring no supply, 39 imperfectly supplied, and 64, *though requiring it, with no supply at all;* "thus giving as a result an educational provision that falls short by nearly one half of what is required." That is the least part of the matter, because new schools 'can be built. But in the schools already at work, not even reading has been carefully taught. "The three elementary subjects appear to have been taught with the simple view of enabling the children to scrape through the examination, and not with the object of attaining any excellence. . . . A teacher cultivates the memory but not the intelligence of his children; if they can pronounce a word, it matters little whether they know its meaning. . . . Many parishes have been returned, as having sufficient education, though in reality the character of their education is of an exceedingly low kind."[1] This all really means that the bulk of the children cannot read even if they have been to the schools. Yet to these poor souls we are going to confide the destinies of an empire.

XII.

We must repeat again and again that in our struggle for national instruction there is not the least desire to exaggerate the value of even the best

[1] Mr. Johnstone's Report.

instruction which the bulk of a vast population like ours is ever likely to receive. No one now pretends that ability to read and write is any assurance of honesty or manual skill or sobriety. No one pretends that the provision of elementary instruction absolves the legislature from all further attention to evils which are within the reach of legislation, and are as hostile to the common weal as the prevailing ignorance. Skill in reading and counting will not protect its possessor against the mischief that is wrought by overcrowding, by exhausting labour in childhood and youth, by unbounded temptations to get drunk, by inveterate traditions and class habits of self-indulgence. But it will give the man a better chance. Reading furnishes him with the instrument by which he may know how the world fares outside his narrow penfold. Writing and counting enable him to manage his own small affairs with order and confidence. We make no transcendental claims for primary instruction and what it can do. The influence of its effective diffusion would always have to be expressed in very homely terms. But these homely terms cover large spaces in the art of more orderly living.

If an English peasant, for instance, knew how to read and count as a Scotch or an American peasant does, he would have a chance of finding out the monstrous percentage which the village shopkeeper makes him pay, and will continue to make him pay, until the victim has arithmetic enough, and can get

I

from the papers knowledge enough of wholesale prices, to let him see the cost in hardly-earned cash of his present ignorance of his letters. " The wages of the agricultural labourer are positively frittered away to almost nothing by the way in which he is well-nigh obliged to spend them," says one who knows well what he is speaking about. " Unable in consequence of his small earnings and unthrifty habits to have enough in hand to make his purchases on any day but pay day ; paid often too late on that day to leave him time to go to the distant market-town, or obliged by debt incurred during sickness or bad weather to deal at one village shop, often without even daring to question the fairness of the price or the quality of the article ; and having no duplicate of the book in which his purchases are entered, the poor fellow is constrained to spend his scanty earnings, bound hand and foot, so to speak, and of course suffers in proportion. Whenever a co-operative store has been set up on sound principles, and has been well managed by the labouring classes, it has not only enabled them to buy all they want, whether in food or clothing, at wholesale price and of the best quality, and so made every shilling worth a shilling, but—which is still more important—has generated in them habits of thrift, foresight, and independence ; taught them the real value of money, and rescued them from debt and the public-house." [1]

How is the man to be a co-operator, to watch

[1] Canon Girdlestone.

accounts, to supervise transactions, when he left school at the age of ten in the Second Standard, and at the age of five and twenty could no more cast up a money column or calculate a percentage than he could solve a cubic equation? Let the reader with an income from the funds imagine how much less it would be worth to him, if he could neither read nor compute, could neither check the weekly bills, nor compare their prices with those of the wholesale market, nor change the tradesmen; let him realise how much familiarity with the art of reckoning, and the practice of putting money into black and white have to do with thrift and good house-keeping; and then let him try to calculate the loss to the poor of never having acquired this familiarity and practice.

Again, we are always chiding the labourer for not saving, and reproaching him for the constant break-down of his clubs and benefit societies. What club or benefit society would not break down, when most of its members are incompetent to supervise their own club accounts or accurately watch the management of the club affairs? To have just scraped through in the Third Standard ten or eleven years back will do nothing to help a man here, and the result is that in most cases the village club is managed by the village publican, with break-down for a consequence. It is quite true that even if all the children in the village had passed in the Fourth Standard, a great many of them would possibly lose much of their habit and facility by the time of manhood. But some of them would not lose it; the stronger and more alert people would preserve it; and there would be enough of them in most villages to keep the club affairs in good order and to set a tolerably efficient example of management to their weaker mates, for are not the strong and alert always a minority, and is it not one of the main objects of social activity to give the strong and alert the best possible chance of using their strength for the common good?

While, therefore, wholly repudiating the extravagant expectations of large classes of people, that mere spread of knowledge will transform the whole face of society, we contend that such an improved capacity of taking care of their own affairs as I have just described would be a most substantial social gain. It would be a most substantial gain if our labouring class in England could all talk as articulately, as rationally, and as instructedly, and could take care of their interests as acutely, as you may trust the labouring class in Scotland to do.

It may be urged that the Scotch training is penetrated with theology, and is biblical and dogmatic in the highest degree. Very likely it is. That is no answer to those who think with me that though education without theology is better, yet education with theology is better than helpless and sodden ignorance. The Scotch denominationalists at least do their work well. The people in England who fatigue us by their artificial cry for an open Bible—which nobody wishes to shut—effectually hinder what they profess to desire,

for a considerable proportion of those who come out of
the schools find reading so hard that they never open
the Bible or any other book from year's end to year's
end, while a further considerable proportion of our
children do not even go to the schools at all, nor will
ever be legally compelled to go, if the clergy can help
it, and are therefore effectually robbed of any chance
of reading either the Bible or anything else.

It is not, then, I repeat, any educational fanaticism,
any mere superstition as to the worth of instruction,
which underlies our conviction of the supreme necessity for such measures as universal and compulsory
instruction. We do not say that improved primary
instruction will work miracles, that it will purify the
drains, or deodorize refuse, or extinguish thirst for
beer, or breed industry, or prevent overcrowding, or
prevent the moral depravation that comes from overcrowding. On the other hand it is just as unreasonable to disparage "the learning that certain clusters
of marks on paper stand for certain words," as it
would have been in duelling days to disparage the art
of fencing, and as it would be now to laugh at men
for working hard to obtain so many more gold and
silver counters for their year's labour. Gold and
silver counters do not feed you, nor make the body
warm; and sensible men covet them, not for themselves, but for the sake of that to which they give
access. And so the marks on paper happen to be the
instrument of some of the most serious transactions in
life. To have perfect mastery over the marks is an

indispensable condition of understanding these transactions, or taking a rational part in them, or simpli-
fying them; and to be in a modern society without
this mastery of them is like being in the market-place
without money. When a distinguished philosopher
lectures us for our struggle after " superficial intellec-
tualization," it is not disrespectful, I hope, to say that
he recalls one of those rich men who acquire a great
fortune, and then like to stand with their backs to the
fire, telling some poverty-stricken hearer how little it
is that money can do for a man, and what supreme
vanity is the laying up of much goods.

"Few, I suppose, will deliberately assert," Mr.
Spencer says, " that information is important and character unimportant." But surely this antithesis is as
unreal as Dr. Magee's opposition between freedom and
sobriety. The possession of information is an element
in character, and therefore shares the importance of
character. " What effect will be produced on character by artificial appliances for spreading knowledge is
not asked. Of the ends to be kept in view by the
legislator, all are unimportant compared with the end
of character-making, and yet character-making is an
end wholly unrecognised." There is a measure of
truth in this, no doubt, and as I pointed out in a previous passage, there has been a strong disposition in
many quarters to make improved education a panacea
for all the evils of our present stage of social development, which it is not nor ever can be. But we may
be very much in earnest for the spread of instruction,

without falling into any delusion of this kind. Knowledge is not character, and information is not a rightly fashioned will. Has any advocate of national instruction ever asserted the contrary? And to accuse us of not asking what effect will be produced on character by artificial appliances for spreading knowledge, is to overlook the most prominent motives of those who have tried to stir public feeling in this matter. The whole contention of this party has its root in a conviction that the faculty of using the instruments of knowledge is capable of producing a very marked and distinct effect upon character. The present writer at any rate lays very little stress on the probability of wider instruction being sufficient to lead to a large decrease of crime, and its effect upon the minor morals may very possibly prove extremely slight, indirect, and distant.[1] The nation will have to do a great many other things for itself, as well as provide good schools, before any great general advance is made in these respects.

Although, however, effective instruction does not cover nor touch the whole field of character and conduct, it does most manifestly touch some portions of

[1] It is, however, well worth noting that M. Duruy, late Minister of Instruction in France, reported that the effect of the national system of education in Switzerland had been to empty the gaols. In Baden, prisoners decreased from 1,426 in 1854, to 691 in 1861. In Germany crime decreased 30 per cent. in twenty-five years. But we must remember that other social changes co-operated in this reduction of crime. Of our own criminals ninety-six per cent. are illiterate; and one cannot help contrasting Switzerland, which spends seven times as much on education as on pauperism and crime, with England, which spends five times as much on pauperism and crime as upon education.

it. It adds, for instance, to the consciousness of power and faculty, and this increases the invaluable and far-reaching quality of self-respect. Hence even if a great effort to provide our people with the instruments of knowledge did not reduce the number of criminals, it would still improve the tone of those who are not criminals. In a rude age a man may respect himself perfectly, however illiterate he may be ; but in an age where so much of the business of the world is transacted by writing, and so much more of the business of the world is recorded by writing, and can only be understood, judged, and utilised by those who can read, then a man or a woman who is expected to take a part in this business, and yet is debarred by ignorance from taking an independent part, and is obliged to trust wholly to the representations of luckier people, like the blind or like one groping his way in darkness, such a one is constantly vexed by shame and humiliation ; not merely ought to feel shame, observe, but actually does feel it, as anybody knows who has ever seen adult pupils in a rural night-school or the evening classes in a town institute. Here, then, is one way in which instruction does directly affect character.

And indirectly what consequences to character follow from that power of participating in national or parochial or club affairs, which can never be more than nominal for one to whom the instruments of knowledge are either a mystery wholly unfathomable, or at best an art once distantly approached and now daily fading away from numbed memories. And mastery of these instruments can only be acquired in youth, before the necessity of bread-winning engrosses the day, and while the faculties are still fresh and moderately unclouded. Hence the obvious fallaciousness of a theory which insists on our being content with "keeping men subordinate to the requirements of orderly social life—letting them suffer the inevitable penalties of breaking these requirements." Letting *them* suffer! As if it were the parent only, and not the child, who suffers from the latter being left unprovided with instruction during the only years in which he has any real chance of acquiring it.

XIII.

There is no necessity to prolong this digression into the region of first principles. The social advantages of having an instructed people, a people equipped with the means of acquiring knowledge, are now so generally admitted in theory, as not to need serious defence against those who do most to retard them in practice. The clergy even nominally concede that it is better to know how to read and write than not, and Conservatives like Mr. Forster and Sir John Pakington tell us that they are in favour of compulsory attendance. The task which we have to achieve is to turn this nominal belief into a reality, to transform an illusory system into an effective force. Let any reader weigh the arguments for instruction which have been suggested in the preceding section, and which have been worked out with all their force in a hundred places since the education controversy first began ; let him consider that we are living under circumstances in which trained intelligence is growing every day a more indispensable condition of success, and in which our competitors are laying themselves out with a steady care to give this trained intelligence to their people ; let him remember that the great mass of ignorant householders in the towns now possess the franchise, and that in a short time it will certainly be possessed by the yet more ignorant householders in the country ; and then in fine let him observe that the English system of securing for the children of the poor the knowledge of which we are all saying such fine things is the wretched slovenly makeshift we see. We let any little self-selected knot of people who choose to take the business in hand set up a school at a small outlay; then we let them take the expenses of the school to the extent of four-fifths, or more, out of the pockets of the taxpayer, the ratepayer, and the parents, themselves only paying the remaining fraction. They make the school the stronghold of what theological system they choose. The state has really a comparatively small voice in its administration. The parent has no voice at all—the same parent, mark, for whose conscience, for whose rights, for whose feelings, for whose opinions, the clerical party are so unspeakably solicitous on paper. Public opinion is not invited as to the system of administration, and would not be listened to if it offered itself. The place, in short, has not a single quality of a national establishment about it. And yet the existence of such an institution as this, unless the instruction fall 'under a mark so low as hardly to be capable of being missed, prevents the establishment in that place of an effective system of municipal supervision and control, and prevents the power of compelling the attendance of the very children whom it is most desirable to bring in. In short, we permit the clergy and their patrons to bribe us with a fraction of voluntary subscription to allow them to prevent a certain number of children from being well instructed, and a certain other number from being instructed at all. We sell the chances of the young for the thirty or more pieces of silver of the system which is absurdly called voluntary.

There is no more unworthily saved money in our whole administration than the very moderate sum which voluntary subscriptions are the means of sparing to the ratepayer, because, in order to save ourselves from having to pay that fraction, we sacrifice the efficiency of the returns on the money which we do actually pay. Let us notice what the sacrifice of the voluntary contributions would really come to. In the year 1872 the total amount of the voluntary subscriptions to the maintenance of the public elementary schools under inspection was £570,975.

This may seem a considerable sum, but let us look at it in its true light. To measure its real weight, we may reflect that, if Mr. Goschen's Report on Local Taxation is to be relied on, *this sum amounts to about*

one penny in the pound on the rateable value of property subject to local taxation. The sum is in fact
a substitute for a rate. Nay, a small portion of it
actually is the product of a rate,—namely, that impu-
dent device called a voluntary rate, which is levied
by some private individual who tells people how
much cheaper this will be, though he does not tell
them that the result will be worthless; or else it is
levied by a rural vestry under the direction of a
clergyman, who has previously warned his flock how
onerous would be a school-rate levied by a board,
though it would not really exceed the voluntary
exaction which he himself proposes to them, and who,
moreover, after he has got his own voluntary rate
safely levied and collected, is perpetually assuring us
that the parish would never stand an education rate.

Well, this farce accounts for part of the money,
which though not a very important part, is likely to
increase. The whole is subscribed by 253,296 con-
tributories, who, therefore, on an average give something more than two pounds a-piece. Now, of this
quarter of a million of people some no doubt also pay
a school-rate, but we know that the larger part of the
sum comes from districts in which there is no school-
rate. The voluntary contribution in such cases is
paid instead of a rate. The amount of the voluntary
subscriptions, therefore, is not the measure of the
sacrifice of the subscribers, because if they did not
give the money, they would still have to pay it in
another shape. A great many country gentlemen are

at this moment taking credit for liberality, when they are in truth subscribing less money than a fair rate would take out of their pockets. Instead of welcoming this kind of substitution, it would be sounder policy to repulse it. An insufficient sum of money is raised, preventing resort to methods which would raise a sufficient sum. It is raised unequally, exonerating hundreds even of the subscribers from the duty of contributing as much to the provision of education as is paid by everybody in a school-rated district, and exonerating all those who are not subscribers from the necessity of contributing anything at all, beyond their share in the Queen's taxes, to this national duty. For instance, in one case cited in the last Blue-book. where a voluntary rate was introduced in order to avoid a board, we learn that "while some paid more than their rates, many escaped ; among these, the guardians of the poor, the directors of Parkhurst prison, the water, gas, and railway companies, the Priory of St. Dominic, a few of the small farmers, and six or eight gentlemen."[1] Why should the gas, water, and railway companies, and the six or eight gentlemen, evade this any more than other just local charges ?

We contend that if every man of this quarter of a million of subscribers could be by any means induced to keep his two pounds in his pocket, it would be the very best thing that could happen to us. We should then have without further ado to introduce School-

[1] Page 207.

boards all over the country, which would raise a far
more adequate sum without adding a farthing to the
charges of those who are now even moderately liberal,
and without placing any serious burden on those who
now contrive almost wholly to escape from what is
practically recognised by the legislature to be as
proper a local charge as police, poor, and high-
ways.

As for the alleged impracticability of any scheme
which depends on the good-will of farmers and people
like them, this is the kind of despondent cry which
greets the reform of every abuse. We are always
told that the improved system will never work, and
that every village in England will resist education,
the moment after it is taken from the clergyman's
hands. This again is a mere paper argument, invented by the country clergy and accepted without
investigation by journalists who live in London.
Take the Inspector's account of the feeling about
education in two of the most purely agricultural
counties in England. "There have been grumblings
at increased expense, and complaints that when the
buildings are erected children will not be found to fill
them, but out of the 219 parishes within my district
only two have made appeal against what is proposed
to be required of them. The necessity and even the
propriety of what has been asked has been generally
recognised, and this is saying a great deal for counties
in which the large predominance of the farmer class
might have argued obstinate hostility to the spread of

education."[1] It would be the same everywhere else. Let the legislature and the Education Department settle what Boards have to do, and then no one seriously doubts that an elective body of ratepayers appointed *ad hoc* will discharge their duties with a perfectly satisfactory amount of loyalty. If Boards have not yet fully answered the expectations of their friends in every case, one main cause has been in the ineptitude of the Act, which not only expressly threw down the bone of religious contention among them, but also hindered their efficiency by leaving to them the decision of a number of grave matters which ought to have been settled for them by the imperial legislature.

Ah, we are told, if ever the voluntaryist (so-called) friends of denominational education are discouraged and snubbed, it would be hopeless to "supply their place in philanthropic zeal and earnest effort." This is mere talking. First, philanthropic zeal and earnest effort, however much we may respect the men and women by whom they were exhibited, have been proved utterly and absolutely inadequate to the great work to which they were devoted. We have no choice about supplying their place. It must be supplied, and this is just what the whole agitation means.

Second, it is above all things desirable to remove the task of national instruction as far away as possible from the region of philanthropy, into the drier climate

[1] Mr. Johnstone's Report, p. 95.

of business and public duty.   Of philanthropy which
takes the form of sectarian supremacy for one thing,
and bad instruction for another, we have had more
than enough.   The managers of schools are the
administrators of a large sum of the public money,
and as one of the inspectors remarks, we have "a
right to expect that gentlemen who undertake the
responsible office of manager would take pains to
ascertain that all the conditions under which public
money is paid are fulfilled."[1]   Do they take such
pains?   On the contrary, there is hardly one single
Report for the last year which does not contain bitter
complaints of the carelessness with which the school
registers are habitually kept, though public money is
paid in reliance on their accurate marking of attendances.   A manager has no more obvious duty than
the supervision of these registers, and yet this is the
way in which it is performed.   "Sometimes," writes
another inspector, "I find by the log-book that not one
of the managers has visited the school from year's end
to year's end; their duties have begun and ended
with signing the papers at the time of inspection,
and there has probably been some difficulty in procuring from them the performance of even that duty."[2]

[1] Mr. Smith's Report, p. 127.
[2] Mr. Parez's Report, p. 115.   Here is one more extract from the Report
on the District of South Yorkshire: "In a few cases there has been positive
dishonesty in the teachers, deliberate tampering with the returns, alteration
of figures to a great extent, clever manipulation of imperfect entries, &c.   In
a great many cases there has been much carelessness in keeping the registers;
they have either been entrusted entirely to the apprentices without any
regular or careful supervision. . . . so that very many, some very important,

Once more, the provision and control of education are matters of business, not of philanthropy.

Third, if this philanthropic zeal and earnest effort are really and truly inspired by an honest desire to instruct the people, will it not be something of a prodigy if they are extinguished by a scheme that must assuredly extend this instruction to the most neglected classes, and improve the instruction of those who are not neglected?

And fourthly, will there be no room for zeal and effort on the part of the clergymen or the clerically minded laymen, when we have got Boards? In the United States, if I am not mistaken, no minister of any denomination can be a school trustee. No one proposes such exclusion in this country. The present writer, for one, would warmly oppose any such exclusion. If I were in the House of Commons I should vote against a bill for the exclusion of the clergy from the office of justice of the peace. Disqualification never made anybody better. The best thing that can happen to a clergyman is to have to transact plenty of civil business along with laymen, and the more important the business, the better. To sit on a Board with a Baptist or two, a Wesleyan or two, a man of the world or two belonging to Chesterfield's religion, which was that of every wise man but which no wise man ever told; to have to compromise, to conciliate, to struggle, to submit

mistakes have been found in them. In such cases there was, I believe, no dishonest purpose, but really culpable negligence, leading to grossly inaccurate returns, and involving unfair demands on the public purse."—Mr. Watkins's Report, p. 216.

to defeat, to face facts : why, no better process could be devised for softening clerical manners and hindering them from being fierce.   In educating the people we should thus be educating the clergy also, and exactly in those matters where their "educational destitution" is at present most insufferable.

The so-called zeal of the clergy for education may perhaps not unfairly be analysed in the following manner :—1. Many of them have fostered schools out of mere fussiness and petty self-consequence.   2. Many of them out of eagerness to rear "bulwarks of the church" and "nurseries of church principles."   3. Many of them from a love of orderliness and good government in a parish.   4. Many of them from a real zeal for the main object of a school, namely the good instruction of the children.   As for the first two classes, they will no doubt be discouraged; the more desperate their discouragement, the better for other people.   The second two classes are not likely to be at all discouraged by making the schools national; their activity will take a wider and more effective form, that is all.

The question whether there should be a Board for every parish, or a Board for every union, or a Board for united districts with a population of 2,000 or 3,000, is one of detail.[1]   A question of great importance, and one that will require very mature consideration on the part of parliament, but still a question of

---

[1] See on this question the last Report of the Committee of Council on Education, Part ii. of Appendix, pp. 43—4.

administrative detail. It is enough here to lay down the general principle of the expediency of their universal establishment under one scheme of arrangement or another. There is some probability that, in order to evade this necessity, proposals will be made for giving compulsory powers to justices or perhaps to Boards of Guardians. No proposal ought to be listened to which does not lead to the creation of bodies expressly elected for purposes of school management and for such purposes only, though it might be expedient to have ex-officio members also. The work to be done is special, and needs to be undertaken with a special sense of its high dignity and importance. What we gain by a School-board is shortly this. (1) We transfer the control of a large amount of national expenditure from a private and irresponsible body to a responsible body of representatives chosen by the persons concerned. (2) We gradually diffuse the notion of the school being an object of public care, and the provision of instruction a public duty. This will have in time the double effect of enlisting a constantly greater amount of interest in its success and efficiency on the part of the superintending bodies, and next of inducing the parents to associate the attendance of their children at school with what is right, proper, legally appointed, and usual. (3) Boards would drive out of existence many of the private adventure schools which are so unjustifiably counted among the educational equipments of the country. (4) Without Boards you cannot have the machinery of compulsion, and without

2

compulsion you cannot touch an immense mass of your people. If compulsory attendance, which of course ought to be settled by the imperial legislature, be supplemented, as will undoubtedly be found expedient, by provisions affecting employers of labour, it would naturally be the business of the Board to see that such provisions should not remain a dead letter.

It is a mistake to suppose that the last of these objects is the only real reason for anxiety to have the control of education given to Boards, properly directed by a central department. The others are equally important, for in them is involved first a great principle of our constitution, and next that unwritten moral influence of legislation to which we have to look in course of time for making all compulsory devices as superfluous in England as they have now become in Prussia. We have to build up a sense of the necessity and desirableness of instruction, until it grows to be an accepted tradition of our people. To take part in such a task may well be the highest aspiration of patriotism. If that timorous and disparaging estimate of public spirit which in some conspicuous politicians passes current for a profound sagacity, should prove to be the right estimate; if the influential and enlightened classes stand aloof from School-boards, and leave their management to the meaner and darker sort, as the clerical partisans are not ashamed to threaten, then will the penalties assuredly fall on the social defaulters, who having received most from the energy and service of the past are ignobly content to do least for the service of present or future. If the evil that is foretold should come to pass, be it so. Meanwhile, you will perhaps do no ill in borrowing the sentiment of old Rome, who paid most heed and most honour to those counsellors who insisted on not despairing concerning the commonwealth.

XIV.

I shall now pass to another branch of my subject, which only comes last in order because it is that on which public opinion is least informed; I mean the question of Free Schools. Is it expedient in our present state of national ignorance that admission to primary instruction should be gratuitous?

The question is raised to a place among urgent practical problems in consequence of the application of compulsion. When opinion has ripened sufficiently, and the requisite measures have been passed to compel every parent to send his children to some school, we shall then be inevitably confronted by a multitude of practical difficulties which can only be met by making primary instruction gratuitously accessible. Indeed, we have already been confronted by these difficulties, and have already met them by giving free schooling. For what was the Act of last session but a law making primary instruction free for some 200,000 children? What were the Seventeenth and Twenty Fifth clauses of the Act of 1870 but partial applications of a principle which will have to be more widely extended in

proportion as compulsion extends the area over which
the children are to be driven into the schools ?

Nor, so far as the principle of gratuitousness goes,
are we at issue with the clergy. They are as anxious
to extend free instruction as we are, if the country
will only let them extend it in their own way. The
Twenty Fifth clause is the road to free instruction
which finds favour in their eyes, and they are willing
to adopt its machinery almost to any extent, so far as
they can make sure that free instruction shall only be
given in their own denominational schools. In applying this clause, in Salford for instance, their definition
of indigence is of the roomiest ; no argument about
weakening   parental   responsibility,   or   impairing
parental self-respect, or lessening the value of instruction in parental eyes, or overburdening the rate-payer,
or making the provident pay for the improvident, has
a feather's weight, so long as they can appropriate the
rates for sectarian schools. It is only when the instruction is to be given in Board schools or secular
schools, that all these considerations become formidable in their eyes. However, let us take as much of
their alliance as they will concede, and be glad that
the clergy at least see no objections to gratuitous
instruction in principle, any more than the legislature
which passed the Twenty Fifth clause and the Education Act Amendment Act can consistently be supposed
to see any.

Mr. Mill stated the case many years ago very
clearly. " It is an allowable exercise of the powers of

government," he wrote, "to impose on parents the legal obligation of giving elementary instruction to their children. This, however, cannot fairly be done without taking measures to ensure that such instruction shall be always accessible to them either gratuitously or at a trifling expense." "It may indeed," he continued, "be objected that the education of children is one of those expenses which parents, even of the labouring class, ought to defray; that it is desirable that they should feel it incumbent on them to provide by their own means for the fulfilment of their duties, and that by giving education at the cost of others, just as much as by giving subsistence, the standard of necessary wages is proportionately lowered, and the spring of exertion and self-restraint is so much relaxed. This argument could at best be only valid if the question were that of substituting a public provision for what individuals would otherwise do for themselves; if all parents in the labouring class recognised and practised the duty of giving instruction to their children at their own expense. But inasmuch as parents do not practise this duty, and do not include education among those necessary expenses which their wages must provide for, therefore the general rate of wages is not high enough to bear those expenses, and they must be borne from some other source. And this is not one of the cases in which the tender of help perpetuates the state of things which renders help necessary. Instruction, when it is really such, does not enervate, but strengthens as well as enlarges the active faculties: in whatever manner acquired, its effect on the mind is favourable to the spirit of independence ; and when, unless had gratuitously, it would not be had at all, help in this form has the opposite tendency to that which in so many other cases makes it objectionable ; it is help towards doing without help."[1]

Mr. Mill was a thoroughly scientific economist, and therefore he knew the limits of his science. He constantly corrected and qualified the deductions of mere verbal logic by reference to the facts to which they related. Writers who fancy that it must be scientific to push premisses that are strictly conditional to their furthest logical and most unconditional conclusions, actually declare with rigorous gravity that a parent who has his child's fees remitted, "ought" to be publicly declared a pauper. They define pauper to suit their own ridiculous, unsocial, and inhuman notions of the growth and maintenance of a community, and then if the facts do not coincide with the definition, so much the worse for the facts. Let us in the face of these dreary fallacies adhere to Mr. Mill's wiser opinion, that " help in this form is help towards doing without help."

It is absurd to treat relegation to the pauper class, as a just and proper punishment for a parent who had brought more children into the world than he can educate. As Mr. Chamberlain—to whose courage and tenacity the cause of national education owes so much—points out, there are two answers to this :—

[1] *Political Economy*, Book V., ch. xi. § 8.

(*a.*) Our object is not to punish the parent but to educate the child, and the latter is sacrificed to the former by our present arrangement. (*b.*) Even if punishment be due, it is desirable that it should take some more remedial form than the infliction of the stigma of pauperism. Society is punishing itself when it goes out of its way to turn an imprudent parent into a pauper. He never gets over the taint, and remains for the rest of his life a permanent charge on the rates.

This points to the very conclusive answer which is to be given to those writers and politicians who insist that it is no more a primary duty of the state to provide a child with the elements of instruction than it is to supply it with bread. " Parents cannot justly be forced to give their children a certain amount of education," says Mr. Fawcett, " unless it is assumed that this education is as necessary for the mind as food and clothing are for the body." [1] The expediency of compulsion does not rest upon any such assumption. If it were to do so, it would fall to the ground, for the assumption is obviously untrue. Literary education is not in the least degree necessary to the mind in the same sense in which food and clothing are necessary to the body. Without food and clothing the body comes to an end. Nobody can pretend that the mental faculties come to an end if they are not subjected to a certain amount of literary discipline. Food is a physical necessity. Literary instruction is not a necessity at all. It is, no doubt, an

---

[1] *Pauperism and its Remedies*, p. 62.

indispensable condition of a man being able to do the best with his mind, but his mental faculties can subsist in a very real though very limited state of efficiency without it. His body cannot subsist either efficiently or otherwise without food.

If any one objects that I prove too much, and that as food is indispensable to life, while education is only the perfection of intelligence, it must be more the duty of the state to provide the necessity than the superfluity, the reply is simply this : Food being necessary, people will naturally make the most strenuous efforts to procure it for themselves ; the motive of self-preservation is so strong that you may trust to it. Education being a superfluity, there is here no motive universally strong enough for us to rely on its spontaneous operation, and its provision becomes a collective interest.

As the alleged assumption is manifestly false, we must seek for some other justification for interfering with parental authority, when the parent neglects to provide instruction for his child. That justification rests on no assumption at all, but on some such propositions as the following, which are, whether rightly or wrongly, believed to be drawn from positive experience :—

(*a.*) It is not in the least necessary, but it is highly expedient, in a country situated as ours is at the present time, that every child born in it should be equipped with a certain amount of elementary instruction.

(*b.*) It is the duty of every parent, therefore, in view alike of the interests of his child and of the interests of the community, to provide this instruction for his children.

(*c.*) The child is unable to protect itself against the neglect of this duty on the part of its parent, and can never in after life wholly repair the consequences of that neglect.

(*d.*) This duty is systematically neglected by immense numbers of parents, with most mischievous consequences to the rest of society.

(*e.*) These consequences, negative and positive, are so serious, that the common interest in this case, as in the case of respect for property, demands the erection of a moral duty into a legal obligation.

(*f.*) The disadvantages and inconveniences of legal interference with parental freedom are more than counterbalanced by the disadvantages and inconveniences arising from a parent's abuse of this freedom to the detriment of other people.

These, or some such propositions, seem to be the ground on which compulsion is to be defended. The argument is in a general way analogous to that of a country whose geographical position and the menaces of whose neighbours make it expedient for every man in it to be legally compelled to undergo a certain amount of military training. It is exactly the same argument as that which warrants the imposition of a legal obligation on a parent to have his child vaccinated.

If we view compulsion in this way, and consider the attendance of a child at school as something which we exact from the parent for the general good, no less than for the good of the individual child, the question of providing elementary instruction at the public charge becomes very simple. This was felt in the case of vaccination, and provision for free vaccination was rightly deemed an indispensable condition of making it obligatory. So if a government insists that every man shall perform military duties, the cost of arms, uniform, and drilling is invariably defrayed from the public purse.

" It should not be forgotten," Mr. Fawcett warns us, " that free education is the first plank in the programme of the International, which is pervaded throughout by the same principle. The state is to provide land for the people at a low price ; the state is to provide houses for them at a cheap rate ; the state is to lend capital to co-operative associations ; and if this demand for free education is not resisted, encouragement will be given to socialism in its most baneful form." [1] This is a very successful and time-honoured way of frightening people, but it is hardly worthy of a man who uses his mind so seriously and independently as Mr. Fawcett usually does. As if it followed from our acceptance of a principle in one set of circumstances, that therefore we are bound to accept it in every other set that any body of men may choose to

[1] *Times*, March 6, 1872.

think equally proper for its application. The question of the propriety of the state providing cheap houses and low-rented land must be decided on its own merits. So must the question of lending capital to co-operative associations be decided on its own merits. It might be desirable to lend capital to co-operative associations, and yet be most highly undesirable for the state to become the universal landowner. And again, both these forms of public intervention might be extremely pernicious—as the present writer believes them to be —and yet it might be extremely desirable to pay for the elementary schools out of rates and taxes. Surely the scale on which a principle is to be applied has something to do with the prudence of applying it. The replacing of the school-pence by rates or taxes would involve a very moderate sum of money, and would be one of the simplest and most practicable tasks ever laid on a Chancellor of the Exchequer. Nobody will say the same of a process which would convert the government into an owner of houses and lands for all the workmen in the country. It is both unfair and illogical, therefore, to try to direct upon one scheme a sidewind of odium and ridicule from other schemes which do not in the least form any part of it. If we happen to agree with the members of the International in the article of free schools, that is no reason why we should accept every or any other article in its programme. "If I and several men," said Horne Took, "are in the Windsor stage-coach, we travel together as long as it may suit us. When I find

myself at Hounslow I get out. They who want to go
further may go to Windsor or where they like. But
when I get to Hounslow, there I get out ; no further
will I go, by G——."

In truth, all objections based upon the abstract principle that a parent should provide for the instruction
of his children apply to the existing system. This
system, we should never forget, does already provide
about two-thirds of the cost of instruction for all
parents ; and in the case of parents coming within the
Seventeenth and Twenty Fifth clauses of the Act of
1870, and within the amending Act of last session, it
provides the whole cost. The opponents of gratuitous
instruction who ask us why we do not insist on the
state providing gratuitous bread and milk, might
therefore just as well ask the administrators of the
present system why they do not provide two-thirds of
the food required for the children of the poor. We
have admitted the principle that the whole community
has such a special kind of interest in getting the children instructed, as to make it worth while to pay from
the public purse the greater part of the cost. As
soon as you have admitted this, the question whether
certain parents shall or shall not pay the fraction that
remains unpaid, is only a question of detail.

Then we are told that to be the recipient of instruction provided by the government lowers a parent in
his own just self-esteem. Everybody who knows the
parents whose children go to the primary schools, is
perfectly aware that this is mere moonshine. There

are plenty of parents who would not choose to allow you or me to hand them their children's school-pence out of charity or in a spirit of patronage. But if the school were open, and belonged to that mysterious agency known as government, the parent would no more be humiliated or demoralised by sending his child there, than he is humiliated by going into a free library. Why should a free school humiliate, while a free library delights and elevates? The parent is heartily glad that the government relieves him of two-thirds of the cost of schooling, and he would have no other feeling but entire satisfaction if he were relieved of the other third also. Again, why should a workman be more degraded by free instruction being provided for his children, than the shopkeeper or the professional man, whose son is educated free of cost at a grammar school or at an Oxford college?

Finally, in considering the relative merits of the two systems, is it not evident that the present plan is eleemosynary in principle, and that a workman suffers greater loss of self-respect in accepting education for his children partly at the hands of private managers, who dictate the character of the school and hold its keys in their own hands, than in sharing the advantages of a public institution, to which he is sensible that he has already contributed his fair share of its cost, and which is managed by his representatives?

Apart from theory, are the Americans, Swedes, Swiss, Danes, or Australian colonists wanting in independence or self-respect? Yet they all have free schools.

But the parents, it is contended, would cease to value a commodity for which they paid nothing. To this we make four answers. First, if he were a sensible man he would know perfectly well that the commodity does cost him something ; namely his share, direct or indirect, of rates and taxes. Second, those who send their children to school from a deliberate and rational appreciation of the advantages of schooling, would naturally perceive that those advantages remain the same, whether the child carries its pence in its hand or not. Third, those who only send their children out of respect for custom or fear of the law, attach too small a value to instruction now and as it is, for the fact of their being freed from payment to make any difference. They do not esteem schooling now, and they will not then, but they will, at any rate, have less aversion for it, because it will cost them less. Fourth, the objection is wholly unfounded in fact, like so many others with which the educational controversy is encumbered by writers and speakers who evolve arguments out of their own heads instead of looking at the actual matter of the controversy. On this subject I shall quote the testimony of M. Laveleye, because English writers usually pay a respect to the authority of foreigners which they do not pay to their countrymen, except when they happen to take the same side. " In France," he says, " M. Duruy's report of 1867, discloses to us the fact, that the children who pay follow the course less regularly than the others. The same fact has been established in Belgium. On an average the number of attendances was 181 for scholars who paid, and 184 for the gratuitous scholars ; and yet the latter, belonging as they do to poor families, have far more reasons for absenting themselves than the others. In some Belgian provinces, in Limburg, and Luxemburg, they raised the school fees : at once a certain number of parents ceased to send their children to school. . . . . . . In America, in some of the States, New York, Connecticut, Michigan, and New Jersey, fees used to be exacted : they were afterwards suppressed, and immediately the number of pupils was considerably increased. . . . . . The various courses for adults recently opened in France are gratuitous. Are they deserted, or is it not rather their gratuitousness which causes them to be thronged ? In 1863, 5,000 communal schools out of 52,000 were gratuitous. Were they less followed than the others ? No, they were more followed." [1]

The last Connecticut Report says :—" The proof now before the public that over 10,000 children were barred from school by the Rate Bill [*i. e.*, school fees], buries it beyond the possibility of a resurrection. . . . Michigan quoted our arguments and followed our example in 1869, and during the last month New Jersey adopted a most liberal Free School law ; and thus the only vestige of the Rate Bill left in this broad land was abolished."

[1] *L'Instruction du Peuple.* Par Emile de Laveleye, p. 40. A specially good authority in the United States writes to me :—" The opinion in America as to free instruction is practically unanimous—not only that it works well, but that everything else would work ill without it."

It is urged that it is unfair to make the man who abstains from marriage, and the production of children contribute by his share of the rates and taxes towards the instruction of the children of his less prudent and self-controlling neighbour. To this the following are the answers :—

(*a.*) The amount of the school-pence is comparatively so small an item—in relation to rent, price of food, clothing, and the substantials of house-keeping—that practically it does not influence a man's calculations whether he can afford to marry or not.

(*b.*) Already the bachelor, with the rest of the community, contributes the most considerable part of the cost of the instruction of other people's children. To be consistent you ought to put a stop to capitation grants and all other state aid to education.

(*c.*) Is not the education rate as real a check as the fee ? As Sir Charles Dilke has well put it, " The rate falls upon the unmarried lodger the moment that he marries. The fee does not begin to touch him for six years, when his first child is five years old."

(*d.*) Everybody, unmarried or single, has an equal interest in his neighbour's child having a chance of receiving instruction. It is a matter of public concern and obligation that the population should be instructed, and a man can no more legitimately excuse himself from forwarding this object, than he can excuse himself from paying for a new road in his parish on the ground that he will never use it, or from paying his lighting rate on the ground that he never goes out at night, or from paying for judges on the ground that nothing would induce him to go to law.

(*e.*) In the case of the unmarried, who do marry sooner or later, the rate may be regarded as an insurance spread over many years. Under the free school system, the cost of instruction is spread over a lifetime; whereas, on our present system, a man has to find the whole expense just when he is least able to bear it, having also to provide for the subsistence of his family.

It is contended, as a kind of *reductio ad absurdum*, that if you have free education for one class you must have free education for all. This objection has been stated in its most excessive shape by Dr. Rigg. " It is impossible to draw the line between class and class. The skilled workman in England is in proportion far richer, as a rule, than the professional man ; the factory operative with his children at work, than the clergyman with his children to send to school ; the foundryman than the striving physician. If schools and free education are provided for the operatives, they must assuredly be provided for the professional classes; if for the mechanic, for the retail tradesman ; if for the small tradesman, for the large ; if for the shopkeeper, also for the merchant and manufacturer. There must be national provision of elementary schools, and grammar schools, and high schools." [1]

[1] *National Education*, p. 230.

This bubble of an argument barely needs puncturing. Here, however, are the answers.

(*a.*) The ground of state interference in education is the expediency, not of having citizens who know Latin and history and drawing, but of making sure that every child shall have a chance of acquiring mastery over the essential instruments of knowledge. On no defensible principle, regard being had to all the conditions of what is practicable, can we ask more than this. The public purse, as we hold, ought on grounds of social expediency to ensure the gratuitous provision of this amount of instruction and no more. In Australia, for example, that limitation has been accepted. No school fees are allowed to be paid for learning reading, writing, grammar, and geography: all higher branches have to be paid for. Why should not this line be drawn? Yet even Mr. Forster, whose strong point, we must admit, whatever else it may be, is not a keen discernment of principles, assured the House of Commons that if primary education be provided free, "secondary education must also be provided free." [1] Pray, why? The only 'must' in the matter is the principle that whatever instruction is provided freely for one citizen ought to be provided freely for every other citizen. If the striving physician and the clergyman want their children to know more than the foundryman's child knows, and more than the state chooses either to insist upon or to provide gratuitously, then let the clergyman and the striving

[1] July 1, 1870.

physician pay for the superfluity. What does the state know of classes ? It would undertake to provide a certain amount of instruction gratuitously for everybody. How does this bind it to provide more than that amount for somebody ?

To borrow an excellent illustration, a man may think the services of the police insufficient protection for his property, and may employ a private watchman as well. But he has no claim to more than the ordinary services of the police, afforded alike to all classes, and he must pay his watchman from his own pocket.

(*b.*) There is real effrontery in this contention that to pay the remaining fraction of the school money of the workmen's children would be a wrong to the professional classes, when we reflect on the enormous mass of educational endowments from which the workmen's children are debarred, and to which the children of the professional classes or those above them have exclusive access. Count up, if you can, the multitude of scholarships, exhibitions, and fellowships, connected with the universities and with the secondary schools all over England ; measure the chance which the son of the foundryman has of acquiring the instruction needed for gaining a share in this enormous fund ; and then estimate, if you can, the gravity of the complaint that if you provide free primary instruction for the workman you are placing the clergyman, the physician, the tradesman, the manufacturer, at a disadvantage ! Why, one of the very strongest arguments for free primary instruction is the desirableness of ending the monopoly of educational endowments by a very small fraction of the community.

"At present," says Dr. Rigg, "our Endowed Schools Commission is spreading far and wide the benefits of old endowments. By means of a more economical and stimulating application of endowments, it will diffuse the benefits of education over wide sections of society, in such a way as to reach and help the most really needy and deserving cases."[1] Well, this is seriously questioned by very competent authorities. Many persons believe that the action of the Commission tends to make merit a more essential condition of participation in endowments—which is no doubt a most excellent alteration—but that at the same time it tends to bestow those endowments on a kind and degree of merit to which the children of the very poor cannot possibly attain, just because they are very poor. However that may be,—and I do not venture to pronounce an opinion either way,—a share in endowments can only be attained by immense numbers of our population, on condition that somebody or other has provided them with means of acquiring mastery over the primary elements of knowledge free of cost to themselves.

Let us now notice some of the practical considera-

_____
[1] *National Education*, p. 238.

tions which commend the abolition of the school-pence in cases where they are not already abolished by the operation of powers conferred on Boards.

Every School-board has now to lay down some rule defining indigence, and fixing the exact degree of poverty which shall entitle a parent to have his children's school-pence remitted, or else paid by the Board on his behalf. This is in itself an extremely difficult task to perform—to say that with such and such earnings a parent is to be classed as indigent, and cannot fairly be called on to provide instruction for his children. The line must be something like a hard and fast one ; and no one who has not sat down to the task can know how difficult it is to make up your mind what income in any given locality marks the exact point at which the addition of school-pence can be fairly borne and reasonably imposed.

Then, when you have fixed it, a new set of difficulties make their appearance. How are you to find out, where a multitude of cases are pressed on before you, whether the applicants for remission of payment of school-pence are stating their resources truly ? How are you to verify every statement as to the amount of the wages which come to a family ? Everybody knows the fraudulent under-statements of income of which the middle classes are guilty when making returns for the income-tax. Can we expect the semi-indigent classes to be more accurate and scrupulous in the statements they make to the School-board ?

Again, supposing that the Board has drawn its line

wisely, and that the applicants state their wages truly, there still remain the class whose wages are just above the line.   If the Board resolves to pay or remit fees for a parent whose total incoming per week is 17s. 6d., do you think there is no sense of injustice and uneven usage in the mind of the man whose total incoming is 18s., 19s., or £1, and who is forced to pay an extra rate in the shape of the school-pence, from which his neighbour who is earning almost as much is wholly exempt ?   I do not say there is any injustice in this, but only that the people who earn small wages, to whom every fourpence and sixpence counts for something worth considering, whose minds are fretful with hardship and sore with struggling, are very apt to feel an injustice in it, and so to find one more odious association connected with the school and its surroundings.   This is no mere logical objection to the present system.   It is derived from experience, and describes an actual state of things.   A. withdraws his children from school.   The Board wants to know why. He says he only earns 17s. a week.   Then, says the Board, send your children back, and we will not ask you for their pence.   B. watches the process, and sees that A. by taking his children from school has put eightpence or a shilling a week into his pocket. Surely that is a very good argument with B. why he should go and do likewise.

Another point.   When bad times come, and wages fall, and a man or woman has a hard struggle, what expense are they so sure to cut off as the superfluity of schooling for their children ? Indeed they have not much choice. The consequence is that unless instruction is gratuitous, every occasion of bad times, whether local or general, is the signal for the interruption of instruction, and the child misses six months or a year—a loss which can never be replaced. Then, you say, the Board will provide the instruction gratuitously during this time. Good, that is the free schooling we ask for. But it is free schooling in its most inefficient and troublesome shape. For it would be generally some weeks before the child's non-attendance at any school would be observed, and when it was discovered, the whole machinery of inquiry and investigation, which takes time and probably costs money, would have to be put into motion—still with a very good chance of many of the missing children escaping notice. If primary instruction were free, bad times would make no alteration. The child's attendance would continue as regular as before. Our great principle should be to overlook nothing that helps to interrupt facility and regularity ; we should make the regular attendance of children at school as easy, as inviting, as free from liability to interruption from outer circumstances, as the conditions of the matter will by any possibility allow.

But the school-pence are so small an amount. Well, they are to a workman something like the amount of income-tax to ourselves. Now observe what the attitude of the state comes to in this matter of instruction. It says to the labouring man this :—" Though you think reading and writing of no value, we insist for the common good that you shall send your child to school. Though he could bring two or three or more shillings a week to the earnings of the family, we insist that you shall surrender this addition. Not only that. You shall further be compelled to pay a weekly sum out of your pocket for this commodity which you don't want. In short, we insist that you shall not only give up a certain amount of money which he might have earned, but also that you shall give up a further amount of money which you have yourself earned." Is it any wonder that the education cry is so little popular in the new constituencies, or that education itself is so little attractive to the poor?

And if the poor could read the Inspectors' Reports, compulsory education and compulsory fees would be less attractive still. For they would learn from them that this sacrifice of possible earnings and actual earnings is mostly waste. "I don't wonder," says one Report already quoted, "that even the most intelligent parents take away their children from the elementary schools after 10 or 11 years of age; perhaps it is their very intelligence that makes them do so." [1] For my own part, I must frankly say that if I were an industrious workman, and were forced to choose between spending eighteenpence a week on ale and tobacco for my bodily refreshment and a social homely supper at the end of the day, and on the other hand spending that sum on a school that would turn

---

[1] Cited above, p. 23.

out my children at the end of their time in the Third Standard, I should deliberately look upon the outlay in ale and tobacco as much the more rational and profitable of the two.

One more consideration is worth urging. The present system gives free instruction to many thousands of children, and the number of children receiving instruction on these terms is sure to be increased by such measures as the Act of last session. But every child who now goes into a school without paying his fees does so, as has been said, "ticketted with the badge of poverty." He does not carry his weekly pence like the other children, and is therefore marked.

An instance of this occurred at Salford, where one of the denominational school houses was disfigured by a board with the words, "Entrance for assisted children *at the back*." How far this, and the annoyances which such a mark will assuredly entail, are likely to promote self-respect in the scholar, we may know from the experience in our own class of sizars and servitors at Oxford and Cambridge.

Finally we may be asked how we should propose to deal with the educational resources already existing in the country, to which voluntary efforts have made a more or less valuable contribution. The establishment of free Board schools, it may be said, would speedily close the sectarian schools. The sectarian schools, in spite of their being called voluntary, cannot

subsist unless the parents help to pay for them; and
no parent would pay for bad instruction in a sectarian
school, when he could procure good instruction for
nothing in a Board school. Well, I cannot see that
any wrong would be done to the sectarian managers
by such a proceeding. I cannot admit that the owners
of the sectarian schools have the shadow of a vested
interest, though they have a claim not to be dealt
with in an injuriously hasty manner. It is simply
monstrous to urge that these volunteers are for ever
to stop the way to the formation of a national force.
The owners of schools only provided half the original
cost of the buildings, and they have always provided
a great deal less than half of the cost of the maintenance
of the school. On what principle does this constitute
an eternal right to the everlasting control of our educational system, and an inexpugnable claim to exclude
all other schools from their parishes ?

This amazing pretension was forcibly exposed in 1870
by Mr. Winterbotham :—" They say the public faith
is pledged to them, that they have been induced to
build schools, and partially maintain them, by the
expectation of public aid, and that therefore it would
be a breach of public faith now to withdraw or withhold it. Now I think this is a most dangerous doctrine, and one which the government would hesitate
to apply in any other case. If the present system of
voluntary schools aided by the state be a wise one,
then let it be defended on its merits. But if it be not,
and if it cannot be shown that it is for the public

interest that the system should be continued, I deny
altogether that any existing school has any, the
smallest, claim upon the public purse. When and
by whom was this pledge given? Who had power
to give it? You offered help to build schools.
Schools were built, and you paid what you offered.
You offered aid to qualified teachers. Teachers
qualified and you paid them. You changed your
plan, you offered payment for each child educated.
Children were educated, and you paid what you
offered. But where in all this is there any pledge for
the continuance of these payments? You have altered
from time to time the conditions and modes of your
aid, and this without the consent and against the protest of those who received it. . . . . Yet if you are
bound at all you are bound altogether, and you have
no more right to alter the terms of the contract than
to abolish it altogether. This theory of the faith of
the country being pledged to the maintenance of the
existing system will not bear a moment's investigation. How does it differ from the case of Maynooth
College, or indeed of the Irish Church? The Church
had not received only annual aid dependent on the
annual vote of parliament, but held and had held for
centuries, the capital of the public property they
enjoyed. And in expectation of its continued enjoyment much more had been done and paid and risked
than the managers of aided schools have done or paid.
Yet that did not prevent your resuming public property when you thought fit, and is it to be said that

all schools you have aided have a right to continued
support from the state for ever ?"[1]

Nothing can be added to this. If it be expedient
to establish free Board schools, there is no lawful
obstacle to such a step in the vested rights of the
sectarian schools. The managers of these schools are
perfectly at liberty to keep them open, if they can
support them wholly out of their own pockets, or if
they can persuade the parents to go on paying for a
worse instruction than they can procure gratuitously
elsewhere. In some cases, no doubt, they would
avail themselves of this right, and insist on competing
with the Board school. In the majority of cases,
however, they would no doubt lose no time in transferring their buildings to the Board, reserving to
themselves the privilege of sending the clergyman or
some other person at times agreed upon with the
Board to give religious instruction of the kind which
they happened to prefer.

It is therefore not true that the scheme of
gratuitous secular instruction would involve a vast
waste and sacrifice of all that voluntary effort has
done for the country. There would be no waste or
sacrifice at all. Voluntary effort has done two things.
It has helped to provide instruction for certain hundreds of thousands of children during the last thirty
years; and it has helped to build certain hundreds of
school-houses. You cannot possibly sacrifice the first
of these results of voluntary effort. The instruction

[1] Speech in the House of Commons, March 15, 1870.

has been acquired, such as it is, and there is an end of that. The school-houses certainly are capable of being sacrificed, if the managers insist on not transferring them to the Boards. But what respectable motive will they have for keeping them shut up and empty? And this will be the only alternative to transferring them. Managers of schools are like other people, and if they find that the country is bent on having free instruction and abandoning the so-called voluntary system, they will very soon make their account with the new state of things. That is, they will hand their school-houses over to the Boards. In ninety cases out of a hundred this will be equivalent to handing them over to themselves, for it will mostly be their own fault if the managers of the existing schools do not form part of the bodies which have to administer the same schools when reconstituted. If their zeal for popular education is as disinterested as they pretend, they will have the same reasons for taking a part in it as they have now. If their zeal is not for popular education, but for sectarian influence, then the sooner they are dispossessed of the means of gratifying this zeal at the expense of other people, the better it will be for the cause which they profess to have so deeply at heart.

Once more, then, the only possibility of wasting what voluntaryism has done for us in education lies in the disuse of the school-houses. That disuse would not practically ever take place. The managers are rate-payers; they are as sensible as their neighbours;

they are influenced as much as their neighbours by
public opinion; they have everything to lose, and
nothing to gain by insisting on keeping a fabric which
the parish would want, and for which they would
have no use. Let no amount of sulky menace persuade us that they would not transfer, when they
found their scholars' fees about to be withdrawn.
They would be guided by their interests, and all their
interests would point in one way.

XV.

Let us turn to the question of cost. To begin with,
the cost of a free school would not be a penny more
than the cost of the same school partially supported by
the children's pence. Everything would go on just as
it does now, except that either rates or taxes would
make up the whole instead of the greater part of the
expense, which they have to make up now. The controversy as to the relative cheapness of voluntary and
rate-supported schools does not touch this question.
The management of the school would be just as economical or just as extravagant whether the final fraction
is provided by private or public pence. The people
therefore whose contribution to the question of
national education consists first in warning us that
School-boards will spoil the instruction by niggardli-
ness and parcimony, and then in assuring our opponents that School-boards will not care how lavishly
they spend the public money—these eminently consistent reasoners have nothing to say on the question

whether it is well to extend the principle of free primary instruction from a part to the whole of the community.

Under the present system, taking the figures for 1872,—

	£	s.	d.
The average grant per scholar in average attendance was	0	11	9¾
The total cost per scholar	1	7	8½

Now we contend that if you establish School-boards, and so stop the excessive multiplication of schools on a very small scale, as well as amalgamate existing schools so as to secure larger aggregates with a corresponding improvement both in efficiency and economy, the cost would not exceed £1 5s. per head at the most. Supposing this to be correct, the total cost of educating 3,000,000 children up to a very high standard would be £3,750,000.

Now it would be eminently presumptuous in any private individual or non-official body to insist on this sum being raised in any particular way. Grant that the nation has to provide this sum; the precise mode of providing it is a detail which belongs to the Chancellor of the Exchequer. Still, it is well in order to give a certain precision and reality to our ideas on the subject, to make definite suggestions on this part of it. The candid disputant will take them in good faith for what they are, as tentative suggestions which may be varied and improved to any extent, as financial authorities may deem best.

M

It is suggested then, that two-thirds of the amount should come from the Consolidated Fund. The government now pay 11*s.* 9¾*d.* per head. Supposing the cost to be 25*s.*, then on this plan the government would have to raise their average payment from 11*s.* 9¾*d.* to 16*s.* 8*d.* Thus towards the £3,750,000 the Consolidated Fund would contribute £2,500,000. The remaining third, that is £1,250,000, would have to be raised out of the local rates.

Assuming the rateable value of property throughout the country to be £100,000,000, this sum would be exactly covered by a 3*d.* rate.

Of course it would be easier, and would avoid a good deal of popular outcry, if you took the whole sum required out of the Consolidated Fund. One unanswerable objection to this is that we should lose the only guarantees we have for thrifty administration. We must boldly face whatever outcry the clergy and others may succeed in raising. And we face it by two arguments :—First, that the total cost to the community would be not a penny more, but something less. If the system of local taxation is a bad and unjust one, let it be amended. That is a financier's question. If the incidence of the rates is unequal or unfair, let it be re-adjusted. If there are burdens imposed on localities which it is expedient to shift to the national exchequer, shift them. No one can seriously think that a three-penny rate—liberating the voluntary subscriber from the necessity of contributing, and *liberating the parent from the necessity of providing school-pence* — would be found an excessive burden. Let us take a practical case, the details of which are furnished to me by Mr. Collings, who has done so much to press the question of free schools on public attention. According to a very high calculation there should be in the primary schools of Birmingham 60,000 children. Let us allow them 25*s.* per head per annum. The government grants would cover two-thirds of this. A 5*d.* rate would more than cover the balance. Thus :—

Grants	£51,240
A 5*d.* rate	25,620
	76,860
Amount required	75,000
	1,860

Or let us put it more simply and intelligibly still. A workman living in a ten pound house would pay 4*s.* 2*d.* per annum, and would receive in return instruction for his children. And he would know that all his neighbours were doing the same.[1]

The second reply to the popular outcry about rates

---

[1] The following budget for the Birmingham day-schools in 1869 may be useful to the reader who does not know the present way of raising the school money. Of course, the proportion among the several items is not the same everywhere, but this is probably a fair example of the educational budget of a large town :—

	£	*s.*	*d.*
Government grants	7,673	18	0
Voluntary subscriptions . . .	3,455	7	8
Congregational collections	894	2	6
Endowments, and other sources . . .	1,749	2	9
School pence	10,252	5	2
	£24,024	16	1

is this. If we have to pay more money, we should get so much more for it, that the new system will still be the cheaper of the two. The cost of the present system properly considered is enormous. Its advocates divide the total expenditure by the total number of children at school. This is unreasonable and absurd. The greater number of these children get no instruction of the smallest value, and might nearly, if not quite, as well be amusing themselves in the streets. What would be thought of a manufacturer who should in reckoning the cost of production count the ' wasters ' for as much as the perfected article ? As Mr. Fitch has said, "the true measure of success are those who pass, and not those who float in and out, and whose instruction is purely nominal."

In the year ending August 31, 1871, the total expenditure was £1,643,669 2*s*. 8*d*.

The total number of children making full passes in the three highest standards was 122,905.

The total number in Sixth Standard, 19,735.

Reckoning cost on the former it is £13 7*s*. 5*d*. per head ; on the latter, £83 5*s*. 9*d*.

Would it not be the truest economy to spend a million a year more, at the same time increasing the number of really educated children to something like the Prussian standard, thus reducing the cost per head ten or twenty fold ?

Those who find it difficult to answer the arguments advanced in the preceding pages, appear, if one may judge from the criticisms which have been passed upon them in the press, to find comfort in the assertion that public opinion rejects the proposals to which these arguments are intended to lead. This assertion usually means no more than that a measure could not be got through the House of Commons. Perhaps on the whole it is well that out of the many scores of writers on public affairs, there should be one or two who hesitate to accept the feasibility of immediately carrying a measure as the final test of its wisdom and fitness. It may be very well for a writer of leading articles in the *Times* to insist on limiting his outlook to to-morrow morning, but surely there is no harm in occasionally considering a subject with a slightly wider horizon. The evils of a narrow and inadequate preparatory discussion were never more vividly exemplified than in that unfortunate piece of legislation which was so ridiculously believed by its authors to have settled the question of public instruction.

The question of free schools, for instance, can hardly be said to have received any discussion at all in this country, though no article in the modern programme has been more vigorously sustained by the best continental reformers, from Condorcet downwards. Perhaps one reason for this is the just suspicion on the part of many influential persons, who take a sort of interest in popular education, and yet are still more deeply interested in certain abuses, that if we are to impose a heavier burden on the country for the sake of pro-

viding gratuitous instruction, people may begin to
look around them and ask, whether after all the whole
of the endowments of the National Church are at present put to the most wise, just, and useful purposes
that the electors can think of.

APPENDIX.

(A.)

The Elementary Education Act of 1870.

I have thought it might be useful to print here some of the principal portions of this Act.

Regulations for Conduct of Public Elementary Schools.

7. Every elementary school which is conducted in accordance with the following regulations shall be a public elementary school within the meaning of this Act; and every public elementary school shall be conducted in accordance with the following regulations (a copy of which regulations shall be conspicuously put up in every such school); namely,

(1.) It shall not be required, as a condition of any child being admitted into or continuing in the school, that he shall attend or abstain from attending any Sunday school, or any place of religious worship, or that he shall attend any religious observance or any instruction in religious subjects in the school or elsewhere, from which observance or instruction he may be withdrawn by his parent, or that he shall, if withdrawn by his parent, attend the school on any day exclusively set apart for religious observance by the religious body to which his parent belongs :

(2.) The time or times during which any religious observance is practised or instruction in religious subjects is given at any meeting of the school shall be either at the beginning or at the end or at the beginning and the end of such meeting, and shall be inserted in a time-table to be approved by the Education Department, and to be kept permanently and conspicuously affixed in every school-room; and any scholar may be withdrawn by his parent from such observance or instruction without forfeiting any of the other benefits of the school:

(3.) The school shall be open at all times to the inspection of any of Her Majesty's inspectors, so, however, that it shall be no part of the duties of such inspector to inquire into any instruction in religious subjects given at such school, or to examine any scholar therein in religious knowledge or in any religious subject or book:

(4.) The school shall be conducted in accordance with the conditions required to be fulfilled by an elementary school in order to obtain an annual parliamentary grant.

Management and Maintenance of Schools by School Board.

14. Every school provided by a school board shall be conducted under the control and management of such board in accordance with the following regulations:

(1.) The school shall be a public elementary school within the meaning of this Act:

(2.) No religious catechism or religious formulary which is distinctive of any particular denomination shall be taught in the school.

15. The school board may, if they think fit, from time to time delegate any of their powers under this Act except the power of raising money, and in particular may delegate the control and management of any school provided by them, with or without any conditions or restrictions, to a body of managers appointed by them, consisting of not less than three persons.

17. Every child attending a school provided by any school board shall pay such weekly fee as may be prescribed by the school board, with the consent of the Education Department, but the school board may from time to time, for a renewable period not exceeding six months, remit the whole or any part of such fee in the case of any child when they are of opinion that the parent of such child is unable from poverty to pay the same, but such remission shall not be deemed to be parochial relief given to such parent.

Transfer of Private Schools to Boards.

23. The managers of any elementary school in the district of a school board may, in manner provided by this Act, make an arrangement with the school board for transferring their school to

such school board, and the school board may assent to such arrangement.

An arrangement under this section may þe made by the managers by a resolution or other act as follows ; (that is to say,)

(1.) Where there is any instrument declaring the trusts of the school, and such instrument provides any manner in which or any assent with which a resolution or act binding the managers is to be passed or done, then in accordance with the provisions of such instrument :

(2.) Where there is no such instrument, or such instrument contains no such provisions, then in the manner and with the assent, if any, in and with which it may be shown to the Education Department to have been usual for a resolution or act binding such managers to be passed or done :

(3.) If no manner or assent can be shown to have been usual, then by a resolution passed by a majority of not less than two-thirds of those members of their body who are present at a meeting of the body summoned for the purpose, and vote on the question, and with the assent of any other person whose assent under the circumstances appears to the Education Department to be requisite.

And in every case such arrangement shall be made only—

(1.) With the consent of the Education Department; and,

(2.) If there are annual subscribers to such school, with the consent of a majority, not being less than two-thirds in number, of those of the annual subscribers who are present at a meeting duly summoned for the purpose, and vote on the question.

Boards may Pay Fees.

25. The school board may, if they think fit, from time to time, for a renewable period not exceeding six months, pay the whole or any part of the school fees payable at any public elementary school by any child resident in their district whose parent is in their opinion unable from poverty to pay the same ; but no such payment shall be made or refused on condition of the child attending any public elementary school other than such as may be selected by the parent ; and such payment shall not be deemed to be parochial relief given to such parent.

Boards may establish Free Schools.

26. If a school board satisfy the Education Department that, on the ground of the poverty of the inhabitants of any place in their district, it is expedient for the interests of education to provide a school at which no fees shall be required from the scholars, the board may, subject to such rules and conditions as the Education Department may prescribe, provide such school and may admit scholars to such school without requiring any fee.

And Industrial Schools.

27. A school board shall have the same powers of contributing money in the case of an industrial school as is given to a prison authority by section twelve of "The Industrial Schools Act, 1866;" and upon the election of a school board in a borough the council of that borough shall cease to have power to contribute under that section.

28. A school board may, with the consent of the Education Department, establish, build, and maintain a certified industrial school within the meaning of the Industrial Schools Act, 1866, and shall for that purpose have the same powers as they have for the purpose of providing sufficient school accommodation for their district : Provided that the school board, so far as regards any such industrial school, shall be subject to the jurisdiction of one of Her Majesty's Principal Secretaries of State in the same manner as the managers of any other industrial school are subject, and such school shall be subject to the provisions of the said Act, and not of this Act.

Constitution of Boards.

29. The school board shall be elected in manner provided by this Act,—in a borough by the persons whose names are on the burgess roll of such borough for the time being in force, and in a parish not situate in the metropolis by the ratepayers.

Cumulative Vote.

At every such election every voter shall be entitled to a number of votes equal to the number of the members of the school board to be elected, and may give all such votes to one candidate, or may distribute them among the candidates, as he thinks fit.

The school board in the metropolis shall be elected in manner hereinafter provided by this Act.

United School Districts.

40. Where the Education Department are of opinion that it would be expedient to form a school district larger than a borough or a parish or any school district formed under this Act, they may, except in the metropolis, by order made after such inquiry and notice as hereinafter mentioned, form a united school district by uniting any two or more adjoining school districts, and upon such union cause a school board to be formed for such united school district.

Contributory Districts.

49. The Education Department may by order direct that one school district shall contribute towards the provision or maintenance of public elementary schools in another school district or districts, and in such case the former (or contributing district) shall pay to the latter (or school owning district or districts) such proportion of the expenses of such provision or maintenance or a sum calculated in such manner as the Education Department may from time to time prescribe.

Permissive Compulsion.

74. Every school board may from time to time, with the approval of the Education Department, make bye-laws for all or any of the following purposes :—

(1.) Requiring the parents of children of such age, not less than five years nor more than thirteen years, as may be fixed by the bye-laws, to cause such children (unless there is some reasonable excuse) to attend school :

(2.) Determining the time during which children are so to attend school ; provided that no such bye-law shall prevent the withdrawal of any child from any religious observance or instruction in religious subjects, or shall require any child to attend school on any day exclusively set apart for religious observance by the religious body to which his parent belongs, or shall be contrary to anything contained in any Act for regulating the education of children employed in labour :

(3.) Providing for the remission or payment of the whole or any part of the fees of any child where the parent satisfies the school board that he is unable from poverty to pay the same :

(4.) Imposing penalties for the breach of any bye-laws :

(5.) Revoking or altering any bye-law previously made.

Provided that any bye-law under this section requiring a child between ten and thirteen years of age to attend school shall provide for the total or partial exemption of such child from the obligation to attend school if one of Her Majesty's inspectors certifies that such child has reached a standard of education specified in such bye-law.

Any of the following reasons shall be a reasonable excuse; namely,

(1.) That the child is under efficient instruction in some other manner:

(2.) That the child has been prevented from attending school by sickness or any unavoidable cause:

(3.) That there is no public elementary school open which the child can attend within such distance, not exceeding three miles, measured according to the nearest road from the residence of such child, as the bye-laws may prescribe.

Parliamentary Grant.

96. After the thirty-first day of March one thousand eight hundred and seventy-one no parliamentary grant shall be made to any elementary school which is not a public elementary school within the meaning of this Act.

No parliamentary grant shall be made in aid of building, enlarging, improving, or fitting up any elementary school, except in pursuance of a memorial duly signed, and containing the information required by the Education Department for enabling them to decide on the application, and sent to the Education Department on or before the thirty-first day of December one thousand eight hundred and seventy.

97. The conditions required to be fulfilled by an elementary school in order to obtain an annual parliamentary grant shall be those contained in the minutes of the Education Department in force for the time being, and shall amongst other matters provide that the thirty-first day of March one thousand eight hundred and seventy-one—

(1.) Such grants shall not be made in respect of any instruction in religious subjects:

(2.) Such grant shall not for any year exceed the income of the school for that year which was derived from voluntary contributions, and from school fees, and from any sources other than the parliamentary grant;

but such conditions shall not require that the school shall be in connection with a religious denomination, or that religious instruction shall be given in the school, and shall not give any preference or advantage to any school on the ground that it is or is not provided by a school board :

Provided that where the school board satisfy the Education Department that in any year ending the twenty-ninth of September the sum required for the purpose of the annual expenses of the school board of any school district, and actually paid to the treasurer of such board by the rating authority, amounted to a sum which would have been raised by a rate of threepence in the pound on the rateable value of such district, and any such rate would have produced less than twenty pounds, or less than seven shillings and sixpence per child of the number of children in the average attendance at the public elementary schools provided by such school board, such school board shall be entitled, in addition to the annual parliamentary grant in aid of the public elementary schools provided by them, to such further sum out of moneys provided by Parliament as, when added to the sum actually so paid by the rating authority, would, as the case may be, make up the sum of twenty pounds, or the sum of seven shillings and sixpence for each child, but no attendance shall be reckoned for the purpose of calculating such average attendance unless it is an attendance as defined in the said minutes :

Provided that no such minute of the Education Department not in force at the time of the passing of this Act shall be deemed to be in force until it has lain for not less than one month on the table of both Houses of Parliament.

98. If the managers of any school which is situate in the district of a school board acting under this Act, and is not previously in receipt of an annual parliamentary grant, whether such managers are a school board or not, apply to the Education Department for a parliamentary grant, the Education Department may, if they think that such school is unnecessary, refuse such application.

99. The managers of every elementary school shall have power to fulfil the conditions required in pursuance of this Act to be fulfilled in order to obtain a parliamentary grant, notwithstanding any provision contained in any instrument regulating the trusts or management of their school, and to apply such grant accordingly.

(B.)

Extracts from the Privy Council Rules.

Grants to Day Schools.

19. The managers of a school which has met not less than 400 times, in the morning and afternoon, in the course of a year, as defined by Article 13, may claim at the end of such year—

A. The sum of 6*s.* per scholar, according to the average number in attendance throughout the year (Article 26).
B. For every scholar present on the day of examination, who has attended not less than 250 morning or afternoon meetings of the school :—
   1. If above four, and under seven years of age at the end of the year (Article 13),—

      (*a.*) 8*s.*, or
      (*b.*) 10*s.* if the infants are taught as a separate department, by a certificated teacher of their own, in a room properly constructed and furnished for their instruction.

   2. If more than seven years of age, 12*s.*, subject to examination (Article 28), viz.—

      4*s.* for passing in reading ;
      4*s.* for passing in writing ;
      4*s.* for passing in arithmetic.

20. 150 attendances (Article 23) qualify for examination—

      (*a.*) Scholars attending school under any half-time Act.
      (*b.*) Boys above 10 attending school in a rural district.

21. If the time-table of the school, in use throughout the year, has provided for one or more specific subjects of secular instruction beyond Article 28,—

A grant of 3*s.* per subject may be made for every day scholar, presented in Standards IV.—VI. (Article 28) who passes a satisfactory examination in not more than two of such subjects (Schedule IV.)
No grant may be claimed under this Article on account of any scholar who has been examined, in the same subject, within the preceding year, by the Department of Science and Art.

Grants to Evening Schools.

22. The managers of a school which has met not less than 60 times in the evening, in the course of a year, as defined by Article 107, may claim (Article 108 and 109),—

(*a.*) The sum of 4*s.* per scholar, according to the average number in attendance throughout the year (Article 26).

(*b.*) For every scholar who has attended not less than 40 evening meetings of the school 7*s.* 6*d.*, subject to examination (Article 28), viz., 2*s.* 6*d.* for passing in reading, 2*s.* 6*d.* for passing in writing, and 2*s.* 6*d.* for passing in arithmetic.

Calculation of Attendance.

23. Attendance at a morning or afternoon meeting may not be reckoned for any scholar who has been under instruction in secular subjects less than two hours, nor attendance at an evening meeting for any scholar who has been under similar instruction less than one hour and a half.

24. Attendance of boys at drill, under a competent instructor, for not more than two hours a week, and 40 hours in the year, may, in a day school be counted as school attendance.

25. Attendances may not be reckoned for any scholar above 18, or in a day school under 3, or, in an evening school, under 12 years of age.

26. The average number of scholars in attendance for any period is found by adding together the attendances of all the scholars for the same period, and dividing the sum by the number of times the school has met within the same period; the quotient is the average number in attendance.

27. In calculating the average number in attendance, the attendances of half-time scholars reckon for no more than those of other scholars.

Standards of Examination.

(These have been given at p. 20 of the text.)

29. No scholar may be presented a second time for examination.

(*a.*) Under a lower standard; or,
(*b.*) Under the same standard.

30. *After Dec.* 31, 1874, no day scholar above 9 years of age, and no evening scholar above 13, will be examined in Standard I.

31. *After Dec.* 31, 1875, no day scholar above 9 years of age, and no evening scholar above 13, will be examined in Standard II.

Pupil-teachers.

70. Pupil-teachers are boys or girls employed to serve in a school on the following conditions, namely :

(*a.*) *That the school* is reported by the inspector to be—
1. Under a duly certificated teacher (Articles 43 and 57).
2. Held in suitable premises.
3. Well furnished and well supplied with books and apparatus.
4. Properly organized and skilfully instructed.
5. Under good discipline.
6. Likely to be maintained during the period of engagement.

(*b.*) *That the pupil-teachers* be not less than 13 years (completed) of age at the date of their engagement.

(*c.*) Be of the same sex as the certificated teacher under whom they serve ; but in a mixed school female pupil-teachers may serve under a master, and may receive instruction from him out of school hours, on condition that some respectable woman, approved by the managers, be invariably present during the whole time that such instruction is being given.

(*d.*) Be presented to the inspector for examination at the time and place fixed by his notice (Article 11).

(*e.*) Pass the examinations and produce the certificates specified in Schedule I.

(*f.*) *That the managers* enter into an agreement in the terms of the memorandum in the Second Schedule to this Code, a copy of which memorandum is sent to the managers for every candidate approved by the Department.

(*g.*) That not more than *four* pupil-teachers are engaged in the school for every certificated teacher serving in it. (*This Article will take effect from the* 1*st of April* 1874.)

71. The Education Department is not a party to the engagement, and confines itself to ascertaining, on the admission of the pupil-teacher and at the end of each year of the service—

(*a.*) Whether the prescribed examination is passed before the inspector.

(*b.*) Whether the prescribed certificates are produced from the managers and teachers.

TRAINING SCHOOLS.

Section I.

83. A training school includes—

(*a*) A college, for boarding, lodging, and instructing candidates for the office of teachers in elementary schools ; and

(*b*.) A practising department, in which such candidates may learn the exercise of their profession.

84. No grant is made to a training school unless the Education Department is satisfied with the premises, management, and staff.

Section II.

Grants to Training Schools.

35. Annual grants are made to the practising departments on the same condition as to other public elementary schools.

86. Grants are placed to the credit of each college of £100 for every master, and of £70 for every mistress who, having been trained in such college during two years, has, since December 1862,—

(*a*.) completed the prescribed period of probation (Article 51), and become qualified to receive a certificate as a teacher in a public elementary school, or in a training college ;

(*b*.) been reported by the proper department in each case to have completed a like period of good service as an elementary teacher in the Army or Royal Navy, or (within Great Britain) in Poor Law Schools, Certified Industrial Schools, or Certified Reformatories.

87. Teachers who have been trained for one year only may obtain certificates after probation (Article 51), or may be reported by the proper department, upon the same terms as others ; and grants, of half the amounts specified in Article 86, may be placed to the credit of the colleges in which they were trained, provided—

(*a*.) they completed their training before 1st January, 1864 ; *or*

(*b*) are teachers of infants, having—

1, received a complete and special course of training for that service in their colleges, which must have been previously recognised by the Education Department as providing such a course; and

2, undergone their probation in infant schools.

88. (*Lapsed Article.*)

N

89. The annual grant to each college is paid out of the sums placed to its credit (Articles 86, 87), and must not exceed—

(*a.*) 75 per cent. of the expenditure of the college for the year, certified in such manner as their Lordships may require.

(*b.*) £50 for each male, and £35 for each female, Queen's scholar (Article 96), in residence for continuous training throughout the year for which it is being paid.

90. The annual grant to each college is paid as follows :—

(*a.*) An instalment of £12 (males), or £8 (females) is paid on 1st March, 1st June, and 1st September, in respect of every Queen's scholar (Article 96) in residence for continuous training throughout the year.

(*b.*) The balance is adjusted as soon as the college accounts for the year have been closed, audited, and approved by the Education Department.

Section III.
Admission into Training Schools.

91. An examination of candidates for admission into training schools is annually held at each college in December, during the week following the examination for certificates (Article 100).

92. The examination extends to the subjects required in the course of a pupil-teacher's engagement (Schedule I.)

93. The candidates are selected, and admitted to the examination, by the authorities of each training school on their own responsibility, subject to no other conditions, on the part of the Education Department, than the candidates—

(*a.*) intend *bonâ fide* to adopt and follow the profession of teacher in schools fulfilling the conditions of Article 86 (*a*) or

(*b.*) having been pupil-teachers, have successfully completed their engagement.

(*c.*) not having been pupil-teachers, will be more than 18 years of age on the 1st of January next following the date of the examination. This article will apply to pupil-teachers whose engagement may have been determined under section 5 of the memorandum agreement (Article 70 *f*), (1) without discredit to themselves, and (2) for reasons approved by the Education Department.

94. The successful candidates are arranged in two classes in order of merit.

95. The authorities of each training school may propose to the Education Department for admission any candidate declared to be admissible pursuant to Article 94.

REGULATIONS OF THE SCHOOL BOARD FOR LONDON,
FOR THE MANAGEMENT OF ITS SCHOOLS.

I.—*General Regulations.*

1. Infant schools shall be mixed.
2. Senior schools shall be separate.
3. Large schools shall be provided wherever it is practicable to do so.
4. As a general rule, female teachers only shall be employed in infant and girls' schools.
5. The period during which the children are under actual instruction in school shall be five hours daily for five days in the week.
6. During the time of religious teaching or religious observance, any children withdrawn from such teaching or observance shall receive separate instruction in secular subjects.
7. Every occurrence of corporal punishment shall be formally recorded in a book kept for the purpose. Pupil-teachers are abso-lutely prohibited from inflicting such punishment. The head teacher shall be held directly responsible for every punishment of the kind.
8. Music and drill shall be taught in every school during part of the time devoted to actual instruction.
9. In all day schools provision shall be made for giving effect to the following resolution of the board passed on the 8th March, 1871:—

"That in the schools provided by the board the Bible shall be read, and there shall be given such explanations and such instruction therefrom in the principles of morality and religion, as are suited to the capacities of children: provided always—

1. That in such explanations and instruction the provisions of the Act in Sections VII. and XIV. be strictly observed, both in letter and spirit, and that no attempt be made in any such schools to attach children to any particular denomination.
2. That in regard of any particular school, the board shall consider and determine upon any application by mana-gers, parents, or ratepayers of the district, who may show special cause for exception of the school from the opera-tion of this resolution, in whole or in part."

10. In all schools provision may be made for giving effect to the following resolution of the board passed on July 26th, 1871:—

"1. That in accordance with the general practice of existing elementary schools, provision may be made for offering

prayer and using hymns in schools provided by the board
at the 'time or times' when, according to Section VII.,
Sub-Section II., of the Elementary Education Act,
'religious observances' may be 'practised.'

" 2. That the arrangements for such 'religious observances'
be left to the discretion of the teachers and managers of
each school, with the right of appeal to the board, by
teacher, managers, parents, or ratepayers of the district:

Provided always—

" That in the offering of any prayers, and in the use of any
hymns, the provisions of the Act in Sections VII. and
XIV. be strictly observed, both in letter and spirit, and
that no attempt be made to attach children to any particular denomination."

11. All the children in any one infant, junior, or senior school,
shall pay the same weekly fees.

12. The minimum weekly fee in infant, junior, and senior schools,
shall be one penny, and the maximum fee ninepence.

13. The half-timers attending any school shall pay half the
weekly fees chargeable in that school, provided that such half-fees
be not less than one penny.

14. The fees payable in evening schools shall be left to the discretion of the managers, subject to the approval of the board.

15. If exceptional circumstances should appear to render the
establishment of a free school, in any locality, expedient, the facts
shall be brought before the board, and its decision taken upon the
special case.

II.—*Regulations for Infant Schools.*

16. In infant schools instruction shall be given in the following
subjects :—

(*a.*) The Bible, and the principles of religion and morality, in
accordance with the terms of the resolution of the board
passed on the 8th March, 1871.

(*b.*) Reading, writing, and arithmetic.

(*c.*) Object lessons of a simple character, with some such
exercise of the hands and eyes as is given in the " Kinder-
Garten " system.

(*d.*) Music and drill.

III.—*Regulations for Junior and Senior Schools.*

17. In junior and senior schools, certain kinds of instruction
shall form an essential part of the teaching of every school; but

others may or may not be added to them, at the discretion of the managers of individual schools, or by the special direction of the board. The instruction in discretionary subjects shall not interfere with the efficiency of the teaching of the essential subjects.

18. The following subjects shall be essential.

(a.) The Bible, and the principles of religion and morality, in accordance with the terms of the resolution of the board, passed on the 8th March, 1871.

(b.) Reading, writing, arithmetic; English grammar and composition, and the principles of book-keeping in senior schools; with mensuration in senior boys' schools.

(c.) Systematized object-lessons, embracing in the six school years a course of elementary instruction in physical science, and serving as an introduction to the science examinations which are conducted by the Science and Art Department.

(d.) The History of England.

(e.) Elementary geography.

(f.) Elementary social economy.

(g.) Elementary drawing.

(h.) Music and drill.

(i.) In girls' schools, plain needlework and cutting out.

19. The following subjects shall be discretionary:—

(a.) Domestic economy.

(b.) Algebra.

(c.) Geometry.

20. Subject to the approbation of the board, any extra subjects recognised by the New Code (1871) shall be considered to be discretionary subjects.

(C.)

Outlay on Education in Chicago.

To understand clearly the figures in the following statement of the cost of education in the public schools of this city, the following things must be borne in mind :—

1. The High School, in which are educated over 500 scholars, ages from 15 to 20, is no part of the common school system. The course of study is an advanced one, and the cost is greatly in excess of the cost of the ordinary schools. The same remarks apply to the normal school. Both schools are supported out of the taxes and funds raised for the public schools.

2. The land, and school buildings, have been bought and paid for out of the public funds. In computing the interest on the money thus invested, the values given are not the cost, but the present values, including, of course, the great rise in the value of the land which has taken place since the same was bought for the schools. The actual outlay for the land and schools does not probably exceed one half the amount at which they are now valued, and on which interest is computed. With this explanation, the enclosed statement compiled from the official records of the Board of Education will be better understood. Here is the actual cost for the years 1871-2 and 1872-3.

	1871-2	1872-3
No. of Teachers	477	560
Average number of Pupils for the Year	24,539	28,833
Paid for Tuition	$378,671	$430,643
Average cost of Tuition per Pupil .	15.43	14.93
Paid for Fuel	25,980	30,351
Paid for Janitors	27,956	31,442
Cost per Pupil for Fuel and Janitors	2.20	2.11
Cost of Repairs, Supplies, and General Expenses . . .	46,837	32,441
Total for *support* of Schools . .	$479,444	$524,202
Average cost per Pupil . . .	19.54	18.20
Six per cent. interest on present value of Land and Buildings .	117,158	134,834
Grand total of cost of Schools, including six per cent. on value of Lands and Buildings . .	596,602	659,536
Average cost per Pupil on grand total of cost	24.31	22.87

The average cost of pupils in the High and Normal Schools, included in the above general table, was as follows :—

	High School.		Normal.	
	1871-2	1872-3	1871-2	1872-3
Cost per Pupil for Tuition .	$56.19		$60.06	
Cost per Pupil for Janitors and Fuel . . .	1.96		5.10	
Cost per Pupil for support of Schools	60.06		67.07	
Average cost per Pupil on grand total of cost . .	70.76		79.04	

The whole number of pupils in the High and Normal schools in 1872-3 was 667. Deducting the cost of those two schools for the year 1872-3, the average cost of pupils in the common schools proper, and excluding the charge for interest, was $18 56c. 7m. (eighteen dollars, fifty-six cents, and seven mills.)

In the cost of janitors is included the wages of

engineers, firemen, and all the expense of care of buildings. This cost does not include books, though it does that of ink, pencils, and chalk.

Note.—The foregoing expenses are of course given in United States currency. The average value of the currency dollar during the period named has been 88 cents in coin, 5 dollars coin supposed to be equal to the pound sterling.

THE END.

PRINTED BY VIRTUE AND CO., CITY ROAD, LONDON.